AMERICAN HISTORIANS

American Historians

A SELECTION

EDITED BY
HARVEY WISH

New York · Oxford University Press · 1962

Copyright © 1962 by Oxford University Press, Inc.
Library of Congress Catalogue Card Number: 62-16580
This reprint, 1967
Printed in the United States of America

To Carl F. Wittke,
Inspiring Scholar and Teacher

PREFACE

This anthology of historians is intended to acquaint the reader with some of the richness of the best of American historical writing. For the student of American history it should provide some interesting perspective and added dimension to his reading, which is necessarily centered on present-day scholarship. The student of historiography will find examples in these pages of the approaches and methods of the leading chroniclers of American history. Since it is hoped that many readers will be tempted to read further in the field, we have provided a selective bibliography listing significant works, many of which are now available in inexpensive editions.

Historians, like everyone else, are subject to fashion, and professional writers of history often have been under the influence of dominant contemporary viewpoints. Thus, as an example of Ranke's "scientific history," we read Henry Adams's brilliantly detailed attack on John Smith's trustworthiness in telling the Pocahantas story. Charles Beard later attacks this approach in his noted essay, "That Noble Dream"; and, more recently, S. E. Morison in his "Faith of a Historian" rejects Beard's historical relativism. Similarly the writings of Turner, a scientific historian, may be contrasted with the "romantics," Parkman and Bancroft. And Arthur Schlesinger, Jr., in criticizing the Civil War "revisionists" like Randall and Craven, urges the kind of critical moralistic approach that was offered years earlier in a far less sophisticated form by James Ford Rhodes.

Other fruitful contrasts and comparisons may be made. In so doing, it is hoped that the student will develop a deeper understanding of American history as it is interpreted and written by our leading historical scholars.

Western Reserve University   Harvey Wish
May 1962

Contents

AMERICAN HISTORIANS

INTRODUCTION

The writing of American history reflects clear-cut patterns of thought at various periods. The Puritans had their Christian (Augustinian) interpretation of history. The historians of the eighteenth-century Enlightenment stressed the idea that reason would guide men along the path of progress. The literary historians of the next century, reacting perhaps to the threat of a dehumanized machine culture, turned to romantic beliefs in hero worship and adventure. Thereafter, many historians came under the spell of natural science and urged a positivist or "scientific" formula for writing of the past. And, during the Great Depression of the 1930's, practically no study wholly escaped an economic interpretation. Historiography is not static but represents a creative branch of scholarship always sensitive to the spirit of the times.

Calvinist historians of New England like William Bradford and John Winthrop found the Christian interpretation of history an indispensable framework for their narratives. While Bradford sought to tell the truth in the rational spirit of the ancient Greek historians, he was above all anxious to demonstrate the special concern of God to direct his newly chosen people to a destination in an American Canaan. This story, told partly in the traditional form of annals, was part of the larger Christian epic in which man progressed from the Creation to the Ultimate Redemption, combating the constant efforts of Satan to seduce him from his path. Thus history moved along a single upward line, except for such Satanic interruptions as "men's inventions" in religion, Roman Catholicism, and schisms. Such was the purposeful theory of history that the Puritans built upon St. Augustine's *City of God*.

This Christian theory of history contained many ingredients that made the modern writing of history possible. Out of ancient Egypt had come experiences of basic ideas of time such as the solar year. The Babylonians contributed annalistic compilations, and the Hebrews, who stressed history as the chief clue to their divine mission, offered the basic ideas of genesis and development as opposed to static notions of the past. The Bible is filled with a teleology that transforms successive events into an understandable pattern. Thus the Judaeo-Christian historians escaped the anti-historical bias of so many ancient writers who were concerned with genealogy, military prestige, literary interest, the teaching of ethical lessons, and ideas that clung to the status quo rather than to any concept of mission or unbroken development. The Greeks saw permanence in science and mathematics, but history seemed to them merely fortuitous change. The New England Calvinists like Bradford, Winthrop, and Cotton Mather borrowed from the ancient Hebrews the dynamic idea of a Chosen People, a "saving remnant" of the regenerate to fulfill God's purpose.

In the eighteenth century, with Voltaire and Gibbon, certain basic classical ideas entered American and European historiography. The Christian interpretation of history with its supernaturalism was replaced by a secular notion of human progress and rationalism. While the Greeks rejected the concept of progress in favor of a theory of endless cycles such as the rise and decline of civilizations, the eighteenth-century historian came to believe that man, by becoming thinking man, could ensure material and intellectual progress. The Greek rationalistic spirit is reflected in many Americans who wrote or thought about history, including Jefferson, who reacted against supernatural ideas of causation in favor of making historical experience serve social reform; Thomas Hutchinson, who looked at his Puritan ancestors through the spectacles of the Enlightenment; Benjamin Franklin, who stressed the idea of man's self-interest as a rational guide to historical causation; and William Smith of New York, who showed the tolerance and rationalism of this new era. But most of the able historians then were Tories in sympathy, conservative in economic attitudes, and hostile to American nationalism.

The Revolution eliminated the Tories, but the new generation of native patriotic historians generally lacked craftsmanship and often surrendered to the uncritical nationalistic bias of Federalist-Whig writers. In writing about the Revolution, quite a few yielded to the provincial temptation to plagiarize from Edmund Burke's *Annual Register* when they told how the mistakes of George III caused the Revolution. Some even went to absurd lengths, as did Parson Weems, who concocted the cherry tree story as part of an ultranationalistic image of Washington and the Revolution. Provincialism also showed itself in the lax editorial standards of Jared Sparks, but his enormous labors in publishing the papers of Washington and other patriots inspired men like Washington Irving to improve the level of biography.

Most successful in reaching a large reading public were the great literary historians of the nineteenth century—George Bancroft, Francis Parkman, Washington Irving, William H. Prescott, John L. Motley, and, to a lesser extent, at the end of the century, Theodore Roosevelt. While these men thought of history primarily as literature governed by aesthetics rather than scientific method alone, they were usually industrious researchers who carefully examined a great number of manuscript sources. As romantics, they dwelt upon the interplay of personality (Bancroft probably excepted), stirring adventure, and engrossing narrative. Francis Parkman, one of the most readable of the literary historians, is best remembered for his skillful portrayal of Montcalm and Wolfe, of Pontiac and the British, and for his account of the adventures of the heroic Jesuits.

Bancroft was a romantic idealist who thought of history as the unfolding of divine intention—a rationalistic version of the Christian theory of history. To him the American was the inevitable heir and missionary of modern individualistic and democratic movements. Irving was a delightful narrator, but a superficial research man. All these nineteenth-century historians, except Bancroft, subscribed to a conservative Whig philosophy: distrustful of the masses but definitely nationalistic. Their heroes were usually the Protestant Anglo-Saxon peoples who were destined to triumph over the Catholic French and the Indians.

Eventually, the literary historians were displaced, particularly in the academic world, by various kinds of "scientific" historians. One major source of scientific history was the philosophy of positivism, which thrived on the prestige of new discoveries in natural science. These positivists excluded everything from consideration but natural phenomena and knowable things. They rejected the vague or mystical philosophical generalities uttered by the disciples of Hegel. Too many of these philosophers of history had tried to substitute general philosophical formulas for actual trends and facts. Positivists, therefore, sought scientific detachment by collecting isolated facts and expected that some scholar with sociological tastes would then mold these facts into "laws" of historical development. As a result many historians buried themselves in detailed studies, writing highly specialized monographs on limited themes and problems. The monotony of these drove away the many thousands of readers who had taken delight in the writings of the great literary historians.

Few positivists could claim that they actually discovered any laws of history. Many admiring American historians of the nineteenth century thought that the English historian Henry T. Buckle, who looked to the physical environment as holding the clue to human behavior and history, had uncovered valuable historical laws, such as the so-called "laws of intellectual progress" derived from studying large masses of men. The loose methods of the positivists encouraged the rising generation of historians and other social scientists to ignore philosophy altogether and to emphasize political or diplomatic history at the expense of cultural developments because they lacked the techniques for handling social and cultural history. Their search for mechanical objectivity led them to avoid moral judgments and evaluative criticisms.

Quite unfairly, this barren school of positivist historiography claimed the German historian Leopold von Ranke as theirs, the patron saint of scientific history. They took his injunction to "stick to the facts" and to relate the past "as it actually happened" literally. Some self-styled disciples assumed that Ranke wished a wholly neutral, "value-free," kind of historiography in which complete objectivity existed. To these writers history was a precious collection of detached facts which required no philosophical integration. Actually, Ranke was not so philosophically naïve regarding subjective influences upon the historian as to encourage mere fact collecting independent of any larger context or theory. To attain the largest practicable measure of objectivity he introduced the German historical seminar, which focused upon original sources, rules of evidence, tests for authenticity by internal and external examination, and other techniques. This has remained a vital part—though only a part—of present-day graduate training in history.

Two eminent scientific historians, Frederick Jackson Turner and Henry Adams, who admired Buckle's dream of a science of history, hoped to transfer the processes of Darwinian biology and the new physics with its Second Law of Thermodynamics to historical narration. Turner leaned heavily upon the idea of evolutionary stages of development to explain the American frontier as an inevitable growth that was repeated at the outer edge of population settlements as settlers moved westward. Therefore, he thought that American characteristics came into existence as part of the process of adaptation to a frontier environment—equalitarianism, self-reliance, indifference to the fine arts, and toughness.

One of the chief results of this evolutionary historical process, as Turner saw it, was the "section" or region which crystallized the frontier experience. Thus America was a federation of geographical and cultural "sections" each with its own characteristics. Turner also made historians more keenly aware of the recurrent debtor-creditor conflicts which influenced so much of the history of each section. One of his controversial ideas was that the frontier supplied a safety valve for Eastern labor discontent and an outlet for class explosions. However, critics have argued that workers without capital or without farming experience were not likely to become farmers in large numbers, but were much more apt to seek better jobs in other places. Despite continuing criticism of various parts of the Turner thesis, few teachers nowadays neglect to discuss his interpretation of the role of the West in determining American development, although increasing attention is being given to the influence of European changes upon this country.

Another original frontier historian, Walter P. Webb of the University of Texas, reflects positivist assumptions. Independently of Turner, he has tried to demonstrate (as Buckle might have done) that each physical region brings forth its own cultural adaptation to circumstances. While early America produced an everyday culture dominated by woodcraft, the later Trans-Mississippi West with its Great Plains developed "plainscraft" instead. Only this adjustment made it possible to build towns in a semi-arid area and to cope with swift Indians on horseback. Both Turner (posthumously) and Webb contributed greatly to the enthusiasm for the study of frontier history that swept the United States during the 1930's. Scholars turned to the economic problems of the West, the influence of barbed wire on settlement, land speculation, railroad colonization of public lands, conservation, agrarian discontent, the sod-house frontier, Indian trade, transportation studies, the impact of frontier sectionalism, and the influence of the frontier on diplomacy. In the Far West, Herbert Bolton of Stanford went beyond the Anglo-American frontier of Turner to treat the Anglo-French and Anglo-Spanish frontiers in his study of Spanish and French archives. The thesis that the frontier in America has disappeared caused considerable pessimistic conjecture for a time.

While the principles of Darwinism had enthusiastic historical exponents in Turner, Webb, John Fiske, and Edward Channing, among many others, only two eminent historians (Henry Adams and his brother Brooks) tried to use physical concepts, specifically the Second Law of Thermodynamics, as a guide for historical analysis. At various times Henry Adams sought guidance in Darwinism, Marxism, and other philosophies, but his actual histories reveal a sophisticated and restrained use of positivist ideas. His classical account of the Jefferson and Madison administrations is a well-written yet critical diplomatic, cultural, and military history. In his final chapters he speculates upon the possibility of history as a natural science.

Just as evolutionism almost dominated social studies, including history, until the 1920's, a formidable rival appeared in the renewed emphasis on "diffusionism" urged by Franz Boas and other leading anthropologists. They looked upon cultural development not as an inevitable evolutionary process but as a product of borrowing. Since, as folk wisdom holds, necessity is the mother of invention, they postulated that men preferred to imitate before they tried the more painful path of experimentation. However, diffusion did not work mechanically but depended upon the psychological and material preparation for the borrowing of civilizations. This line of thinking challenged the logic of Turner's frontier theory, which minimized European influences in favor of indigenous factors. But, by the 1950's, the conservative nationalistic historians reverted to an emphasis upon the uniqueness of the American experience.

Few themes have absorbed historians as fully as the Old South, the Civil War, and Reconstruction. From Czarist Russia and Germany came Professor Hermann von Holst, whose admiration for Prussian centralization led him to concentrate on state rights as a leading cause of the Civil War; and his resentment at Czarist abuses may have encouraged him to analyze slavery, the planters, and the war from a moralistic viewpoint. James Ford Rhodes, who retired early from his Cleveland factory to become a historian, also used a predominant moralistic approach. But as he and other historians studied Reconstruction—particularly as presented by the influential Dunning-Burgess school of Columbia—they dropped their humanitarian antislavery sympathies in favor of a racist interpretation. They convinced textbook writers that Radical Reconstruction was a basic error because the Stevens-Sumner ruling group assumed that Negroes were capable of self-government. As for the lasting image of the Old South, no historian eclipsed the Georgia-born U. B. Phillips, a Dunning-Burgess disciple, in picturing the Cotton Kingdom as a land of kindly planters and contented slaves. Phillips believed that Northern abolitionist fanatics raised the specter of race war and that they inadvertently convinced white Southerners that they must resist Northern pressures, even at the cost of civil war.

During the Great Depression, when economic interpretations were popular, Charles Beard, Louis Hacker, and others interpreted the

Civil War as a conflict between rival capitalisms—the Northern industrialist versus the Southern planter. The secession of the agrarian South permitted Congress to subsidize Northern transcontinental railways, give away homesteads to aspiring small farmers, and benefit the businessman generally—all of which seemed premeditated to the economic determinist.

In the late 1930's and afterwards, as the economic emphasis declined, "revisionist" historians like James G. Randall and Avery Craven turned toward psychological factors. Randall blamed the war on emotional influences that led a "blundering generation" to create a needless conflict. They minimized the depth of the antislavery crusade and rejected the idea of the inevitability of the war. Political leadership had failed to solve the slavery problem. A decade later, Arthur M. Schlesinger, Jr. made a vigorous onslaught upon revisionism and again emphasized the duty of moral judgments by historians.

Meanwhile the Dunning-Burgess-Phillips school with its racist bias against Negroes in Reconstruction times met vehement criticism from professional Negro historians like William E. B. DuBois, Carter Woodson, and Charles Wesley, all with doctorates from first-rate universities. As active historians interested in abolitionism and freedom, not merely passive individuals directed by whites, they were eager to examine the role of the Negro in American history (and, to some extent, African history). DuBois, particularly, influenced others in reinterpreting Black Reconstruction, although few were in sympathy with his Marxist overtones. More historians became convinced that the so-called Carpetbag legislators made constructive contributions toward schools, orphanages, and welfare agencies for both races; the planters had been too laissez-faire and hostile to substantial taxation to achieve much along these lines. A large part of the heavy expenditures of these legislators went for postwar rebuilding rather than wholesale graft, as usually charged. The founding of *The Journal of Negro History* in 1915 by Dr. Carter G. Woodson of Washington, D. C., marks the real professionalization of Negro studies with excellent research contributions from both white and Negro scholars. Later, in 1935, Southern white scholars joined with their Northern brethren and with interested Negro historians to establish *The Journal of Southern History* as the organ of the Southern Historical Association.

The economic interpretation of history had flourished during the Progressive era, but it achieved dominance during the Great Depression years. During the mid-nineteenth century Richard Hildreth went further than most historians in using economic analysis by drawing upon the Utilitarian philosophy of Jeremy Bentham. Among these ideas was the principle that society is ruled by interests and classes and that man, by pursuing his self-interest in an enlightened way, was thereby serving all society. This emphasis on pressure groups as a key to history was taken up by the Marxist Algie Simons, by Charles Beard, and by Edwin R. A. Seligman—the last two from Columbia. F. J. Turner had elaborated upon the fundamental nature of the creditor-debtor struggle in American history and this was emphasized by Beard in his explanation of the Constitution as a product of creditor interests. Beard believed that the Constitution's strength rested upon the fact that it drew from the solid source of self-interest. He wrote of the Civil War as the fruit of planter-industrialist rivalry. Reconstruction appeared partly as the result of corporate business pressures; and America's entrance into the First World War was due to munitions makers, bankers, and kindred interest groups. Beard pointed out that he owed little to Marx, but a great deal to James Madison and Hildreth. During the 1930's, such economic interpretations affected many major historical topics. Those who studied the causes of the American Revolution, for example, emphasized the role of the colonial merchants or the oppressive mercantilistic policies as seen by the American business classes. But, by the 1950's, with prosperity, historians became more interested in psychological motivations, the role of personality, laws, and political theories.

This social-cultural history had deep European roots, but it was particularly congenial to democrats who wished to know more about ordinary people, not merely the elite. Voltaire had been among the first to urge and practice the writing of social-cultural history with particular emphasis upon arts and sciences, men and manners. One of the significant pioneers of social history, Edward Eggleston, better remembered for his novel, *The Hoosier Schoolmaster,* was also a distinguished president of the American Historical Association, who gave an address on "The New History" which called for a "real history of men and women." Inspiration for such an ideal came from nineteenth-century England where John Richard Green had told the story of England, devoting more space to Chaucer than to the Battle of Crécy. Here, too, was Thomas B. Macaulay, who wrote a masterly chapter on the social condition of England in 1685. These men undoubtedly countered the powerful influence of another English "scientific historian," Edward A. Freeman, who stated, "history is past politics and politics is present history." Germany contributed its *Kulturgeschichte* (cultural history), which had an unusual amount of social theory in it, and this had its effect on many visiting American scholars.

At the University of Pennsylvania, John Bach McMaster wrote a genuine social history of great length in *A History of the People from the Revolution to the Civil War.* Although he told about the everyday affairs of ordinary people (as well as those of the leaders), he did not glorify them as Bancroft had done, but kept to a conservative middle-class nationalistic position. Arthur M. Schlesinger, Sr. of Harvard, was very influential; he admired Edward Eggleston and chose to use a title suggested by the latter's correspondence, *A History of American Life,* for his novel series of social histories beginning with colonial times. There evolved entire schools of historians specializing in the history of cities, the contributions of immigrants, religious history in all its ramifications, and many other social themes. Most American social historians, unlike the outstanding European masters in this field, suffered from the difficulty of having to integrate a myriad of details about everyday life; and this required much theory along the lines followed by successful writers in sociology. Too often the results were brief listings of social facts arranged chronologically and topically.

The New History is usually thought of in connection with James Harvey Robinson rather than with Eggleston. Robinson had been impressed by Karl Lamprecht's emphasis on cultural anthropology which transcended mere national lines. To him the New History was a science which guided men toward social reform. Facts and extraordinary events were not enough for the pragmatic historian who revolted against formal treatment and wished to discover a usable past to solve current problems and prejudices. The New Historians believed in studying more modern history and in utilizing the latest discoveries of the anthropologists, psychologists, political scientists, and sociologists. These social studies would make possible an understanding of man's total experience—social, economic, political, diplomatic, etc. Hostile critics called this the "past everything" because it seemed too comprehensive for most people to master. But by the 1960's, historians like Allan Nevins were greatly widening the subject matter of history, even if they did not endorse the idea of stressing a "usable past" or reformist concepts.

Closely related to the New Historians were those who looked to intellectual history for the best understanding of our society. The intellectual historian, particularly in the United States, was interested not only in philosophical, literary, and aesthetic concepts but in "wild ideas" as well—whether from folklore, dime novels, or irrational attitudes. The study of ideas encouraged a strong vogue for "cross-fertilization," interdisciplinary studies, and intellectual integration. Social scientists shared this hope of escaping the confusion over the growing diversity of facts and interpretations by integrating knowledge wherever possible.

For some thoughtful historians, like Richard Hofstadter of Columbia, practically all history became intellectual history because historical motivation appeared to consist of ideas and attitudes. Arthur O. Lovejoy, the noted philosopher of history, and the new *Journal of the History of Ideas* added depth to historical knowledge by encouraging the co-operation of all social scientists. A decade later, another interdisciplinary journal, this time of American studies alone, was issued as the *American Quarterly*.

Ten professional societies in the 1930's sponsored the monumental *Encyclopaedia of the Social Sciences,* edited by Edwin R. A. Seligman and Alvin Johnson, which enabled students to read about the various intellectual trends in all the social disciplines. The elder Schlesinger's *History of American Life* series, as already noted, gave a useful descriptive survey of intellectual as well as social and aesthetic developments. More books and dissertations appeared on the history of such ideas as progress, liberalism, conservatism, Calvinism, capitalism, romanticism, loyalty, philanthropy, and historiographical concepts.

Merle Curti added depth to an undeveloped area of intellectual history with his book *The Social Ideas of American Educators,* which showed how formal theories of learning and school administration reflected basic social and philosophical assumptions that often escaped the professional educator. By the 1960's there seemed to be considerable interest among intellectual historians in the writing of American educational history. When historiography became a discipline of intellectual history rather than mere bibliography it also revealed the unspoken assumptions that controlled the historian's writings.

Intellectual history had its allies in related social studies and literature. Vernon Parrington's *Main Currents in American Thought* directed the attention of men in American literature to the social analysis of *belles-lettres.* Harvard's historians and teachers of literature such as S. E. Morison, Perry Miller, and Kenneth Murdock were especially influential in elaborating—most favorably—upon the rational assumptions underlying New England Puritanism. At Harvard also, Oscar Handlin examined the intellectual and psychological roots of immigration, while Arthur M. Schlesinger, Jr., penetrated into the mental atmosphere of Jacksonianism and the New Deal. Thus the line between intellectual and political history became tenuous as more historians utilized a broad view of historical developments.

Biography has special problems and so is more difficult to classify in terms of patterns. During the 1920's, when Lytton Strachey of England had many admirers and even imitators here, general biographers sought to apply modern psychological principles to their subjects. For a time a loosely conceived Freudian fad dominated considerable popular biography. Academicians usually held aloof from this trend. By the 1950's, however, writers with professional training in psychology attempted to reconstruct the major historical figures like Martin Luther in psychoanalytical and general psychological terms. But this tendency did not make great headway in American biography.

More enthusiastically received among American biographers were Douglas Freeman, noted for his narratives of Lee and Washington, and Allan Nevins. These men preferred to rely upon common-sense psychological insights rather than clinical observations; and they were extraordinarily industrious in examining vast bodies of original sources. In the flourishing field of business history and biography, Nevins dealt sympathetically yet objectively with the life and attitudes of John D. Rockefeller and Henry Ford. For the most part, his judgments were thoughtfully traditionalist, with an emphasis on moral characteristics in subjects like Grover Cleveland, "a study in courage."

On the whole, American historians of today are much more sophisticated in method and outlook than those of 1900 when the racist Dunning-Burgess school was in flower; or of 1850 when the absence of modern social knowledge led to confusing explanations of motivational and environmental determinants. Critics have lamented the fact that too few historians have the literary talent of Francis Parkman, but the mid-twentieth century saw the rise of a remarkable number of fine writers who escaped the arid presentation of the old positivist historians. Increasingly, historians have become interested in philosophical analysis, as the controversy over historical relativism revealed. They are concerned now with the task of attaining self-critical procedures and verifiable methods in order to escape the dilemma of relativism, which looks upon historical objectivity as a myth.

It is still true that American historians generally are pragmatic in outlook, but this is not a loose eclecticism without guiding principles. They remain suspicious of doctrinaire Marxism and mystical repetitive cycles of history after the fashion of Oswald Spengler. Most admire Arnold Toynbee's masterful studies of civilizations, but are not tempted to emulate his methods or seek his goal. While the slogan of the New History is not the banner of this generation, its comprehensive methods and ideals seem to influence most sensitive historians.

William Bradford (1589/90–1657) and the Christian Interpretation of History

William Bradford is not only our main source writer for Pilgrim history but he also exemplifies historical craftsmanship in his efforts to emulate the honesty of Herodotus and Thucydides in the telling of contemporary history. He looked at the world as a devout Separatist would: one who believed that the "Pilgrims" as he called them were the chosen people destined to establish a New Jerusalem across the Atlantic and who believed that the eyes of the world were upon them. Hence his *History,* even though it remained in manuscript form for two centuries, enabled historians to confirm the Puritan notion of the Calvinist mission.

Raised in Austerfield, Yorkshire, by middle-class parents, he gave up Anglicanism for the radical Protestant and Calvinist congregation of Scrooby, where William Brewster's friends endured religious persecution for conscience's sake. These Calvinists, or Puritans, were influenced by the earlier teachings of Robert Browne that called for complete separation from the Anglican Church because of its surviving Roman Catholic practices. Bradford tells the fascinating story of the escape to Calvinist Amsterdam and Leyden and of the *Mayflower* voyage as well as the Plymouth colony's struggles. After a short rule under Governor John Carver, the colony selected Bradford as his successor in 1622, re-electing him, except for brief interims, until 1656. Under Bradford's vigorous leadership, Plymouth thrived under a modified theocracy, but its Congregationalism had large democratic elements for laymen, permitting common consultation, even if limited to occasions "when we thinke good," as the Governor put it.

Bradford had no university training, unlike William Brewster, a Cambridge graduate, and so many members of the rival Massachusetts Bay Colony. He was, however, an unusually acute person, possessing excellent judgment as well as rich aptitudes. He dealt successfully with complex economic, political, social, and religious questions. His *History of Plymouth Plantation* (to use one of its various titles) abounds in historical and scriptural references. He knew ancient history, philosophy, and sufficient theology to cope with the church controversies of his day, controversies that had split other Puritan congregations. His aptitude for foreign languages served him well in Holland, and in his final years he set himself to mastering Hebrew because, he said of himself, "he would see with his own eyes the ancient oracles of God in their native beauty." He professed to write in a "plaine stile," free of aristocratic embellishments and allegedly indifferent to learned classical allusions. Like many writers of his day, he used an inconsistent spelling and grammar, reflecting the haste of a busy executive even in little Plymouth with its population that remained under one thousand. Although he used the historical organization of the annalist, he enriched it by citing profusely from contemporary letters and documents and by drawing from his notes and once-extant Letter Books. As a strict Calvinist he inclined to an introspective and self-critical manner of a man who believed that his people were ever on trial before an inscrutable God.

Of Plymouth Plantation circulated in manuscript until 1856, when the Massachusetts Historical Society managed to have it copied from the original which was then in England. Nathaniel Morton (Bradford's nephew), Cotton Mather, Thomas Prince, William Hubbard, and Thomas Hutchinson drew freely from the manuscript. During the American Revolution it was somehow taken to England and lodged in the library of the Bishop of London. But the actual transfer of the Bradford manuscript occurred only in 1897. The famous Maypole story as told by the critical Bradford should be contrasted with another version given in *The New English Canaan of Thomas Morton* (Boston, 1883), edited by Charles Francis Adams, Jr.

Of Plymouth Plantation

Of their setling in Holand, & their maner of living, & entertainmente ther.   Being now come into the Low Countries, they saw many goodly & fortified cities, strongly walled and garded with troopes of armed men. Also they heard a strange & uncouth language, and beheld the differente manners & customes of the people, with their strange fashons and attires; all so farre differing from that of their plaine countrie villages (wherin they were bred, & had so longe lived) as it seemed they were come into a new world. But these were not the things they much looked on, or long tooke up their thoughts; for they had other work in hand, & an other kind of warr to wage & maintaine. For though they saw faire & bewtifull cities, flowing with abundance of all sorts of welth & riches, yet it was not longe before they saw the grimme & grisly face of povertie coming upon them like an armed man, with whom they must bukle & incounter, and from whom they could not flye; but they were armed with faith & patience against him, and all his encounters; and though they were sometimes foyled, yet by Gods assistance they prevailed and got the victorie.

Now when Mr. Robinson, Mr. Brewster, & other principall members were come over, (for they were of the last, & stayed to help the weakest over before them,) such things were thought on as were necessarie for their setling and best ordering of the church affairs. And when they had lived at Amsterdam aboute a year, Mr. Robinson, their pastor, and some others of best discerning, seeing how Mr. John Smith and his companie was allready fallen in to contention with the church that was ther before them, & no means they could use would doe any good to cure the same, and also that the flames of contention were like to breake out in that anciente church it selfe (as afftwerwards lamentably came to pass); which things they

From the original manuscript (Boston: Wright and Potter, 1901), Commonwealth of Massachusetts Edition, pages 22–9, 111–16, 135–7, 162–4, 283–92. (Text has been modernized to some extent.)

prudently foreseeing, thought it was best to remove, before they were any way engaged with the same; though they well knew it would be much to the prejudice of their outward estats, both at presente & in licklyhood in the future; as indeed it proved to be.

Their remoovall to Leyden. For these & some other reasons they removed to Leyden, a fair & bewtifull citie, and of a sweete situation, but made more famous by the universitie wherwith it is adorned, in which of late had been so many learned men. But wanting that traffike by sea which Amsterdam injoyes, it was not so beneficiall for their outward means of living & estats. But being now hear pitchet they fell to such trads & imployments as they best could; valewing peace & their spirituall comforte above any other riches whatsoever. And at lenght they came to raise a competente & comforteable living, but with hard and continuall labor.

Being thus setled (after many difficulties) they continued many years in a comfortable condition, injoying much sweete & delightefull societie & spirituall comforte togeather in the wayes of God, under the able ministrie, and prudente governement of Mr. John Robinson, & Mr. William Brewster, who was an assistante unto him in the place of an Elder, unto which he was now called & chosen by the church. So as they grew in knowledge & other gifts & graces of the spirite of God, & lived togeather in peace, & love, and holines; and many came unto them from diverse parts of England, so as they grew a great congregation. And if at any time any differences arose, or offences broak out (as it cannot be, but some time ther will, even amongst the best of men) they were ever so mete with, and nipt in the head betims, or otherwise so well composed, as still love, peace, and communion was continued; or els the church purged of those that were incurable & incorrigible, when, after much patience used, no other means would serve, which seldom came to pass. Yea such was the mutuall love, & reciprocall respecte that this worthy man had to his flocke, and his flocke to him, that it might be said of them as it once was of that famous Emperour Marcus Aurelious, and the people of Rome, that it was hard to judge wheather he delighted more in haveing shuch a people, or they in haveing such a pastor. His love was greate towards them, and his care was all ways bente for their best good, both for soule and body; for besids his singuler abilities in devine things (wherin he excelled), he was also very able to give directions in civill affaires, and to foresee dangers & inconveniences; by which means he was very helpfull to their outward estats, & so was every way as a commone father unto them. And none did more offend him then those that were close and cleaving to them selves, and retired from the commone good; as also such as would be stiffe & riged in matters of outward order, and invey against the evills of others, and yet be remisse in them selves, and not so carefull to express a vertuous conversation. They in like maner had ever a reverente regard unto him, & had him in precious estimation, as his worth & wisdom did deserve; and though they esteemed him highly whilst he lived & laboured amongst them, yet much more after his death, when they came to feele the wante of his help, and saw (by woefull experience) what a treasure they had lost, to the greefe of their harts, and wounding of their sowls; yea such a loss as they saw could not be repaired; for it was as hard for them to find such another leader and feeder in all respects, as for the Taborits to find another Ziska. And though they did not call themselves orphans, as the other did, after his death, yet they had cause as much to lamente, in another regard, their present condition, and after usage. But to returne; I know not but it may be spoken to the honour of God, & without prejudice to any, that such was the true pietie, the humble zeale, & fervent love, of this people (whilst they thus lived together) towards God and his waies, and the single hartednes & sinceir affection one towards another, that they came as near the primative patterne of the first churches, as any other church of these later times have done, according to their ranke & qualitie.

But seeing it is not my purpose to treat of the severall passages that befell this people whilst they thus lived in the Low Countries, (which might worthily require a large treatise of it selfe,) but to make way to shew the begining of this plantation, which is that I aime at; yet because some of their adversaries did, upon the rumore of their removall, cast out slanders against them, as if that state had been wearie of them, & had rather driven them out (as the heathen historians did faine of Moyses & the Isralits when they went out of Egipte), then that it was their owne free choyse & motion, I will therfore mention a perticuler or too to shew the contrary, and the good acceptation they had in the place wher they lived. And first though many of them weer poore, yet ther was none so poore, but if they were known to be of that congregation, the *Dutch* (either bakers or others) would trust them in any reasonable matter when they wanted money. Because they had found by experience how carfull they were to keep their word, and saw them so painfull & dilligente in their callings; yea, they would strive to gett their custome, and to imploy them above others, in their worke, for their honestie & diligence.

Againe; the magistrats of the citie, aboute the time of their coming away, or a litle before, in the publick place of justice, gave this comendable testemoney of them, in the reproofe of the Walloons, who were of the French church in that citie. These English, said they, have lived amongst us now this 12. years, and yet we never had any sute or accusation came against any of them; but your strifs & quarels are continuall, &c. In these times allso were the great troubls raised by the Arminians, who, as they greatly mollested the whole state, so this citie in particuler, in which was the cheefe universitie; so as ther were dayly & hote disputs in the schooles ther aboute; and as the students & other lerned were devided in their oppinions hearin, so were the 2. proffessors or devinitie readers them selves; the one daly teaching for it, the other against it. Which grew to that pass, that few of the disciples of the one would hear the other teach. But Mr. Robinson, though he taught thrise a weeke him selfe, & write sundrie books, besids his manyfould pains otherwise, yet he went constantly to hear ther readings, and heard the one as well as the other; by which means he was so well grounded in the controversie, and saw the force of all their arguments, and knew the shifts of the adversarie, and being him selfe very able, none was fitter to buckle with them then him selfe, as appered by sundrie disputs; so as he begane to be terrible to the Arminians; which made Episcopius (the Arminian professor) to put forth his best strength, and set forth sundrie Theses, which by publick dispute he would defend against all men. Now Poliander the other proffessor, and the cheefe preachers of the citie, desired Mr. Robinson to dispute against him; but he was loath, being a stranger; yet the other did importune him, and tould him that such was the abilitie and nimblnes of the adversarie, that the truth would suffer if he did not help them. So as he condescended, & prepared him selfe against the time; and when the day came, the Lord did so help him to defend the truth & foyle this adversarie, as he put him to an apparent non-plus, in this great & publike audience. And the like he did a 2. or 3. time, upon such like occasions. The which as it caused many to praise God that the trueth had so famous victory, so it procured him much honour & respecte from those lerned men & others which loved the trueth. Yea, so farr were they from being weary of him & his people, or desiring their absence, as it was said by some, of no mean note, that were it not for giveing offence to the state of England, they would have preferd him otherwise if he would, and alowd them some pub-like favour. Yea when ther was speech of their remoovall into these parts, sundrie of note & eminencie of that nation would have had them come under them, and for that end made them large offers. Now though I might aledg many other perticulers & examples of the like kinde, to shew the untruth & unlicklyhode of this slander, yet these shall suffice, seeing it was beleeved of few, being only raised by the malice of some, who laboured their disgrace.

[ANNO 1620]

In these hard & difficulte beginings they found some discontents & murmurings arise amongst some, and mutinous speeches & carriags in other; but they were soone quelled & overcome by the wisdome, patience, and just & equall carrage of things by the Govr. and better part, which clave faithfully togeather in the maine. But that which was most sadd & lamentable was, that in 2. or 3. moneths time halfe of their company dyed, espetialy in Jan: & February, being the depth of winter, and wanting houses & other comforts; being infected with the scurvie & other diseases, which this long vioage & their inacomodate condition had brought upon them; so as ther dyed some times 2. or 3. of a day, in the foresaid time; that of 100. & odd persons, scarce 50. remained. And of these in the time of most distres, ther was but 6. or 7. sound persons, who, to their great comendations be it spoken, spared no pains, night nor day, but with abundance of toyle and hazard of their owne health, fetched them woode, made them fires, drest them meat, made their beads, washed their lothsome cloaths, cloathed & uncloathed them; in a word, did all the homly & necessarie offices for them which dainty & quesie stomacks cannot endure to hear named; and all this willingly & cherfully, without any grudging in the least, shewing herein their true love unto their freinds & bretheren. A rare example & worthy to be remembred. Tow of these 7. were Mr. William Brewster, ther reverend Elder, & Myles Standish, ther Captein & military comander, unto whom my selfe, & many others, were much beholden in our low & sicke condition. And yet the Lord so upheld these persons, as in this generall calamity they were not at all infected either with sicknes, or lamnes. And what I have said of these, I may say of many others who dyed in this generall vissitation, & others yet living, that whilst they had health, yea, or any strength continuing, they were not wanting to any that had need of them. And I doute not but their recompence is with the Lord.

But I may not hear pass by an other remarkable passage not to be forgotten. As this calamitie fell among the passengers that were to be left here to plant, and were hasted a shore and made to drinke water, that the sea-men might have the more bear, and one * in his sicknes desiring but a small cann of beere, it was answered, that if he were their owne father he should have none; the disease begane to fall amongst them also, so as allmost halfe of their company dyed before they went away, and many of their officers and lustyest men, as the boatson, gunner, 3. quarter-maisters, the cooke, & others. At which the master was something strucken and sent to the sick a shore and tould the Govr. he should send for beer for them that had need of it, though he drunke water homward bound. But now amongst his company ther was farr another kind of carriage in this miserie then

* Which was this author him selfe.

amongst the passengers; for they that before had been boone companions in drinking & joyllity in the time of their health & wellfare,
begane now to deserte one another in this calamitie, saing they would
not hasard ther lives for them, they should be infected by coming to
help them in their cabins, and so, after they came to dye by it, would
doe litle or nothing for them, but if they dyed let them dye. But
shuch of the passengers as were yet abord shewed them what mercy
they could, which made some of their harts relente, as the boatson (&
some others), who was a prowd yonge man, and would often curse
& scofe at the passengers; but when he grew weak, they had compassion on him and helped him; then he confessed he did not deserve it
at their hands, he had abused them in word & deed. O! saith he,
you, I now see, shew your love like Christians indeed one to another,
but we let one another lye & dye like doggs. Another lay cursing his
wife, saing if it had not ben for her he had never come this unlucky
viage, and anone cursing his felows, saing he had done this & that,
for some of them, he had spente so much, & so much, amongst them,
and they were now weary of him, and did not help him, having need.
Another gave his companion all he had, if he died, to help him in
his weaknes; he went and got a litle spise & made him a mess of
meat once or twise, and because he dyed not so soone as he expected,
he went amongst his fellows, & swore the rogue would cousen him,
he would see him choaked before he made him any more meate; and
yet the pore fellow dyed before morning.

All this while the Indians came skulking about them, and would
sometimes show them selves aloofe of, but when any aproached near
them, they would rune away. And once they stoale away their tools
wher they had been at worke, & were gone to diner. But about the
16. *of March* a certaine Indian came bouldly amongst them, and spoke
to them in broken English, which they could well understand, but
marvelled at it. At length they understood by discourse with him, that
he was not of these parts, but belonged to the eastrene parts, wher
some English-ships came to fhish, with whom he was acquainted, &
could name sundrie of them by their names, amongst whom he had
gott his language. He became proftable to them in acquainting them

with many things concerning the state of the cuntry in the east-parts wher he lived, which was afterwards profitable unto them; as also of the people hear, of their names, number, & strength; of their situation & distance from this place, and who was cheefe amongst them. His name was *Samaset;* he tould them also of another Indian whos name was *Squanto,* a native of this place, who had been in England & could speake better English then him selfe. Being, after some time of entertainmente & gifts, dismist, a while after he came againe, & 5. more with him, & they brought againe all the tooles that were stolen away before, and made way for the coming of their great Sachem, called *Massasoyt;* who, about 4. or 5. *days after,* came with the cheefe of his freinds & other attendance, with the aforesaid *Squanto.* With whom, after frendly entertainment, & some gifts given him; they made a peace with him (which hath now continued this 24. years) in these terms.

1. That neither he nor any of his, should injurie or doe hurte to any of their peopl.

2. That if any of his did any hurte to any of theirs, he should send the offender, that they might punish him.

3. That if any thing were taken away from any of theirs, he should cause it to be restored; and they should doe the like to his.

4. If any did unjustly warr against him, they would aide him; if any did warr against them, he should aide them.

5. He should send to his neighbours confederats, to certifie them of this, that they might not wrong them, but might be likewise comprised in the conditions of peace.

6. That when ther men came to them, they should leave their bows & arrows behind them.

After these things he returned to his place caled *Sowams,* some 40. mile from this place, but *Squanto* continued with them, and was their interpreter, and was a spetiall instrument sent of God for their good beyond their expectation. He directed them how to set their corne, wher to take fish, and to procure other comodities, and was also their pilott to bring them to unknowne places for their profitt, and never left them till he dyed. He was a *native of this place,* & scarce any left

alive besids him selfe. He was caried away with diverce others by one
Hunt, a master of a ship, who thought to sell them for slaves in
Spaine; but he got away for England, and was entertained by a
marchante in London, & imployed to New-found-land & other parts,
& lastly brought hither into these parts by one Mr. *Dermer,* a gentleman imployed by Sir Ferdinando Gorges & others, for discovery, &
other designes in these parts. Of whom I shall say some thing, because
it is mentioned in a booke set forth Anno: 1622. by the Presidente &
Counsell for New-England, that he made the peace betweene the
salvages of these parts & the English; of which this plantation, as it is
intimated, had the benefite. But what a peace it was, may apeare by
what befell him & his men. . . .

[1621: THE NEW ARRIVALS]

On the day called Chrismasday, the Governor caled them out to
worke, (as was used,) but the most of this new company excused
themselves and said it wente against their consciences to work on that
day. So the Govr. tould them that if they made it mater of conscience,
he would spare them till they were better informed. So he led-away
the rest and left them; but when they came home at noone from their
worke, he found them in the streete at play, openly; some pitching
the barr, & some at stoole-ball, and shuch like sports. So he went to
them, and tooke away their implements, and tould them that was
against his conscience, that they should play & others worke. If they
made the keeping of it mater of devotion, let them kepe their houses,
but ther should be no gameing or revelling in the streets. Since which
time nothing hath been atempted that way, at least openly.

ANNO 1622.

At the spring of the year they had apointed the Massachusets to come
againe and trade with them, and begane now to prepare for that
vioag about the later end of March. But upon some rumors heard,
Hobamak, their Indean, tould them upon some jealocies he had, he
feared they were joyned with the Narighansets and might betray
them if they were not carefull. He intimated also some jealocie of

Squanto, by what he gathered from some private whisperings betweene him and other Indeans. But they resolved to proseede, and
sente out their shalop with 10. of their cheefe men aboute the begining of Aprill, and both Squanto & Hobamake with them, in regarde
of the jelocie betweene them. But they had not bene gone longe, but
an Indean belonging to Squantos family came runing in seeming
great fear, and tould them that many of the Narighansets, with
Corbytant, and he thought also Massasoyte, were coming against
them; and he gott away to tell them, not without danger. And being
examined by the Govr., he made as if they were at hand, and would
still be looking back, as if they were at his heels. At which the Govr.
caused them to take armes & stand on their garde, and supposing the
boat to be still within hearing (by reason it was calme) caused a
warning peece or 2. to be shote of, the which they heard and came in.
But no Indeans apeared; watch was kepte all night, but nothing was
seene. Hobamak was confidente for Massasoyt, and thought all was
false; yet the Govr. caused him to send his wife privatly, to see what
she could observe (pretening other occasions), but ther was nothing
found, but all was quiet. After this they proseeded on their vioge to
the Massachusets, and had good trade, and returned in saftie, blessed
be God.

But by the former passages, and other things of like nature, they
begane to see that Squanto sought his owne ends, and plaid his owne
game, by putting the Indeans in fear, and drawing gifts from them to
enrich him selfe; making them beleeve he could stur up warr against
whom he would, & make peece for whom he would. Yea, he made
them beleeve they kept the plague buried in the ground, and could
send it amongs whom they would, which did much terrifie the
Indeans, and made them depend more on him, and seeke more to
him then to Massasoyte, which proucured him envie, and had like to
have cost him his life. For after the discovery of his practises, Massasoyt sought it both privatly and openly; which caused him to stick
close to the English, & never durst goe from them till he dyed. They
also made good use of the emulation that grue betweene Hobamack
and him, which made them cary more squarely. And the Govr.

seemed to countenance the one, and the Captaine the other, by which
they had better intelligence, and made them both more diligente.

Now in a maner their provissions were wholy spent, and they
looked hard for supply, but none came. But about the *latter end of
May,* they spied *a boat* at sea, which at first they thought had beene
some Frenchman; but it proved a shalop which came from a ship
which Mr. Weston & an other had set out a fishing, at a place called
Damarins-cove, 40. leagues to the eastward of them, wher were that
year many more ships come a fishing. This boat brought 7. passengers
and some letters, but no vitails, nor any hope of any. . . .

[ANNO 1623]

All this whille no supply was heard of, neither knew they when they
might expecte any. So they begane to thinke how they might raise as
much corne as they could, and obtaine a beter crope then they had
done, that they might not still thus languish in miserie. At length,
after much debate of things, the Govr. (with the advise of the cheefest
amongest them) gave way that they should set corne every man for
his owne perticuler, and in that regard trust to them selves; in all
other things to goe on in the generall way as before. And so assigned
to every family a parcell of land, according to the proportion of their
number for that end, only for present use (but made no devission for
inheritance), and ranged all boys & youth under some familie. This
had very good success; for it made all hands very industrious, so as
much more corne was planted then other waise would have bene by
any means the Govr. or any other could use, and saved him a great
deall of trouble, and gave farr better contente. The women now wente
willingly into the feild, and tooke their litle-ons with them to set
corne, which before would aledg weaknes, and inabilitie; whom to
have compelled would have bene thought great tiranie and oppression.

The experience that was had in this commone course and condition, tried sundrie years, and that amongst godly and sober men, may
well evince the vanitie of that conceite of Platos & other ancients,
applauded by some of later times;—that the taking away of propertie,
and bringing in communitie into a comone wealth, would make them

happy and florishing; as if they were wiser then God. For this comunitie (so farr as it was) was found to breed much confusion & discontent, and retard much imployment that would have been to their benefite and comforte. For the yong-men that were most able and fitte for labour & service did repine that they should spend their time & streingth to worke for other mens wives and children, with out any recompence. The strong, or man of parts, had no more in devission of victails & cloaths, then he that was weake and not able to doe a quarter the other could; this was thought injuestice. The aged and graver men to be ranked and equalised in labours, and victails, cloaths, &c., with the meaner & yonger sorte, thought it some indignite & disrespect unto them. And for mens wives to be commanded to doe servise for other men, as dresing their meate, washing their cloaths, &c., they deemd it a kind of slaverie, neither could many husbands well brooke it. Upon the poynte all being to have alike, and all to doe alike, they thought them selves in the like condition, and one as good as another; and so, if it did not cut of those relations that God hath set amongest men, yet it did at least much diminish and take of the mutuall respects that should be preserved amongst them. And would have bene worse if they had been men of another condition. Let none objecte this is men's corruption, and nothing to the course it selfe. I answer, seeing all men have this corruption in them, God in his wisdome saw another course fiter for them.

But to returne. After this course setled, and by that their corne was planted, all ther victails were spente, and they were only to rest on Gods providence; at night not many times knowing wher to have a bitt of any thing the next day. And so, as one well observed, had need to pray that God would give them their dayly brade, above all people in the world. Yet they bore these wants with great patience & allacritie of spirite, and that for so long a time as for the most parte of 2. years. . . .

[ANNO 1628]

In the mean time it maks the Indeans of these parts rich & power full and also prowd therby; and fills them with peeces, powder, and shote.

which no laws can restraine, by reasone of the bassnes of sundry unworthy persons, both English, Dutch, & French, which may turne to the ruine of many. Hithertoo the Indeans of these parts had no peeces nor other armes but their bowes & arrowes, nor of many years after; nether durst they scarce handle a gune, so much were they affraid of them; and the very sight of one (though out of kilter) was a terrour unto them. But those Indeans to the east parts, which had commerce with the French, got peces of them, and they in the end made a commone trade of it; and in time our English fisher-men, led with the like covetoussnes, followed their example, for their owne gaine; but upon complainte against them, it pleased the kings majestie to prohibite the same by a stricte proclaimation, commanding that no sorte of armes, or munition, should by any of his subjects be traded with them.

Aboute some 3. or 4. years before this time, ther came over one Captaine Wolastone, (a man of pretie parts,) and with him 3. or 4. more of some eminencie, who brought with them a great many servants, with provissions & other implments for to begine a plantation; and pitched them selves in a place within the Massachusets, which they called, after their Captains name, Mount-Wollaston. Amongst whom was one Mr. Morton, who, it should seeme, had some small adventure (of his owne or other mens) amongst them; but had litle respecte amongst them, and was sleghted by the meanest servants. Haveing continued ther some time, and not finding things to answer their expectations, nor profite to arise as they looked for, Captaine Wollaston takes a great part of the sarvants, and transports them to Virginia, wher he puts them of at good rates, selling their time to other men; and writs back to one Mr. Rassdall, one of his cheefe partners, and accounted their marchant, to bring another parte of them to Verginia likewise, intending to put them of ther as he had done the rest. And he, with the consente of the said Rasdall, appoynted one Fitcher to be his Livetenante, and governe the remaines of the plantation, till he or Rasdall returned to take further order theraboute. But this Morton abovesaid, haveing more craft then honestie, (who had been a kind of petiefogger, of Furnefells Inne,) in the others absence, watches an oppertunitie, (commons being but hard amongst them,) and gott some strong drinck & other junkats, & made them a feast; and after they were merie, he begane to tell them, he would give them good counsell. You see (saith he) that many of your fellows are carried to Virginia; and if you stay till this Rasdall returne, you will also be carried away and sould for slaves with the rest. Therfore I would advise you to thruste out this Levetenant Fitcher; and I, having a parte in the plantation, will receive you as my partners and consociats; so may you be free from service, and we will converse, trad, plante, & live togeather as equalls, & supporte & protecte one another, or to like effecte. This counsell was easily received; so they tooke oppertunitie, and thrust Levetenante Fitcher out a dores, and would suffer him to come no more amongst them, but forct him to seeke bread to eate, and other releefe from his neighbours, till he could gett passages for England. After this they fell to great licenciousnes, and led a dissolute life, powering out them selves into all profanenes. And Morton became lord of misrule, and maintained (as it were) a schoole of Athisme. And after they had gott some good into their hands, and gott much by trading with the Indeans, they spent it as vainly, in quaffing & drinking both wine & strong waters in great exsess, and, as some reported, 10 pounds worth in a morning. They allso set up a May-pole, drinking and dancing aboute it many days togeather, inviting the Indean women, for their consorts, dancing and frisking togither, (like so many fairies, or furies rather,) and worse practises. As if they had anew revived & celebrated the feasts of the Roman Goddes Flora, or the beasly practieses of the madd Bacchinalians. Morton likwise (to shew his poetrie) composed sundry rimes & verses, some tending to lasciviousnes, and others to the detraction & scandall of some persons, which he affixed to this idle or idoll May-polle. They chainged allso the name of their place, and in stead of calling it Mounte Wollaston, they call it Meriemounte, as if this joylity would have lasted ever. But this continued not long, for after Morton was sent for England, (as follows to be declared,) shortly after came over that worthy gentlman, Mr. John Indecott, who brought over a patent under the broad seall, for the govermente of the Massachusets, who visiting those parts caused that May-polle to be cutt downe, and rebuked them for their profannes, and admonished them to looke ther should be better walking; so they now, or others, changed the name of their place againe, and called it Mounte-Dagon.

Now to maintaine this riotous prodigallitie and profuse excess, Morton, thinking him selfe lawless, and hearing what gaine the French & fisher-men made by trading of peeces, powder, & shotte to the Indeans, he, as the head of this consortship, begane the practise of the same in these parts; and first he taught them how to use them, to charge, & discharg, and what proportion of powder to give the peece, according to the sise or bignes of the same; and what shotte to use for foule, and what for deare. And having thus instructed them, he imployed some of them to hunte & fowle for him, so as they became farr more active in that imploymente then any of the English, by reason of ther swiftnes of foote, & nimblnes of body, being also quick-sighted, and by continuall exercise well knowing the hants of all sorts of game. So as when they saw the execution that a peece would doe, and the benefite that might come by the same, they became madd, as it were, after them, and would not stick to give any prise they could attaine too for them; accounting their bowes & arrowes but bables in comparison of them.

And here I may take occasion to bewaile the mischefe that this wicked man began in these parts, and which since base covetousnes prevailing in men that should know better, has now at length gott the upper hand, and made this thing commone, notwithstanding any laws to the contrary; so as the Indeans are full of peeces all over, both fouling peeces, muskets, pistols, &c. They have also their moulds to make shotte, of all sorts, as muskett bulletts, pistoll bullets, swane & gose shote, & of smaler sorts; yea, some have seen them have their scruplats to make scrupins them selves, when they wante them, with sundery other implements, wherwith they are ordinarily better fited & furnished then the English them selves. Yea, it is well knowne that they will have powder & shot, when the English want it, nor cannot gett it; and that in a time of warr or danger, as experience hath manifested, that when lead hath been scarce, and men for their owne defence would gladly have given a groat a pound, which is dear enoughe, yet hath it bene bought up & sent to other places, and sould to shuch as trade it with the Indeans, at 12. pence the pound; and it is like they give 3. or 4. shilling the pound, for they will have it at any rate. And these things have been done in the same times, when some of their neigbours & freinds are daly killed by the Indeans, or are in deanger therof, and live but at the Indeans mercie. Yea, some (as they have aquainted them with all other things) have tould them how gunpowder is made, and all the materialls in it, and that they are to be had in their owne land; and I am confidente, could they attaine to make saltpeter, they would teach them to make powder. O the horiblnes of this vilanie! how many both Dutch & English have been latly slaine by those Indeans, thus furnished; and no remedie provided, nay, the evill more increased, and the blood of their brethren sould for gaine, as is to be feared; and in what danger all these colonies are in is too well known. Oh! that princes & parlements would take some timly order to prevente this mischeefe, and at length to suppress it, by some exemplerie punishmente upon some of these gaine thirstie murderers, (for they deserve no better title,) before their collonies in these parts be over throwne by these barbarous savages, thus armed with their owne weapons, by these evill instruments, and traytors to their neigbors and cuntrie. But I have forgott my selfe, and have been to longe in this digression; but now to returne. This Morton having thus taught them the use of peeces, he sould them all he could spare; and he and his consorts detirmined to send for many out of England, and had by some of the ships sente for above a score. The which being knowne, and his neigbours meeting the Indeans in the woods armed with guns in this sorte, it was a terrour unto them, who lived straglingly, and were of no strenght in any place. And other places (though more remote) saw this mischeefe would quietly spread over all, if not prevented. Besides, they saw they should keep no servants, for Morton would entertaine any, how vile soever, and all the scume of the countrie, or any discontents, would flock to him from all places, if this nest was not broken; and they should stand in more fear of their lives & goods (in short time) from this wicked & deboste crue, then from the salvages them selves.

So sundrie of the cheefe of the stragling plantations, meeting togither, agreed by mutuall consente to sollissite those of Plimoth (who were then of more strength then them all) to joyne with them, to prevente the further grouth of this mischeefe, and suppress Morton & his consortes before they grewe to further head and strength. Those that joyned in this acction (and after contributed to the charge of sending him for England) were from Pascataway, Namkeake, Winisimett, Weesagascusett, Natasco, and other places wher any English were seated. Those of Plimoth being thus sought too by their messengers & letters, and waying both their reasons, and the commone danger, were willing to afford them their help; though them selves had least cause of fear or hurte. So, to be short, they first resolved joyntly to write to him, and in a freindly & neigborly way to admonish him to forbear these courses, & sent a messenger with their letters to bring his answer. But he was so highe as he scorned all advise, and asked who had to doe with him; he had and would trade peeces with the Indeans in dispite of all, with many other scurillous termes full of disdaine. They sente to him a second time, and bad him be better advised, and more temperate in his termes, for the countrie could not beare the injure he did; it was against their comone saftie, and against the king's proclamation. He answerd in high terms as before, and that the kings proclaimation was no law; demanding what penaltie was upon it. It was answered, more then he could bear, his majesties displeasure. But insolently he persisted, and said the king was dead and his displeasure with him, & many the like things; and threatened withall that if any came to molest him, let them looke to them selves, for he would prepare for them. Upon which they saw ther was no way but to take him by force; and having so farr proceeded, now to give over would make him farr more hautie & insolente. So they mutually resolved to proceed, and obtained of the Govr. of Plimoth to send Captaine Standish, & some other aide with him, to take Morton by force. The which accordingly was done; but they found him to stand stifly in his defence, having made fast his dors, armed his consorts, set diverse dishes of powder & bullets ready on the table; and if they had not been over armed with drinke, more hurt might have been done. They sommaned him to yeeld, but he kept his house, and they could gett nothing but scofes & scorns from him; but at length, fearing they would doe some violence to the house, he and some of his crue came out, but not to yeeld, but to shoote; but they were so steeld with drinke as their peeces were to heavie for them; him selfe with a carbine (over charged & allmost halfe fild with powder & shote, as was after found) had thought to have shot Captaine Standish; but he stept to him, & put by his peece, & tooke him. Neither was ther any hurte done to any of either side, save that one was so drunke that he rane his owne nose upon the pointe of a sword that one held before him as he entred the house; but he lost but a litle of his hott blood. Morton they brought away to Plimoth, wher he was kepte, till a ship went from the Ile of Shols for England, with which he was sente to the Counsell of New-England; and letters writen to give them information of his course & cariage; and also one was sent at their commone charge to informe their Honours more perticulerly, & to prosecute against him. But he foold of the messenger, after he was gone from hence, and though he wente for England, yet nothing was done to him, not so much as rebukte, for ought was heard; but returned the nexte year. Some of the worst of the company were disperst, and some of the more modest kepte the house till he should be heard from. But I have been too long aboute so unworthy a person, and bad a cause.

This year Mr. Allerton brought over a yonge man for a minister to the people hear, wheather upon his owne head, or at the motion of some freinds ther, I well know not, but it was without the churches sending; for they had bene so bitten by Mr. Lyford, as they desired to know the person well whom they should invite amongst them. His name was Mr. Rogers; but they perceived, upon some triall, that he was crased in his braine; so they were faine to be at further charge to send him back againe the nexte year, and loose all the charge that was expended in his hither bringing, which was not smalle by Mr. Allerton's accounte, in provissions, aparell, bedding, &c. After his returne he grue quite distracted, and Mr. Allerton was much blamed that he would bring such a man over, they having charge enough otherwise.

Thomas Hutchinson (1711–1780) and the Tory Influence

The outstanding American historians of the eighteenth century were Tories, who blended their upper-class bias with a persistent loyalty to the Empire—William Smith, Cadwallader Colden, George Chalmers, and Thomas Hutchinson, the Royal Governor of the Massachusetts Bay Colony. Hutchinson, like his fellow Tories, reflected the intellectuality and religious tolerance of the Enlightenment as well as the narrow class interests of many colonial ruling families. As a well-to-do descendant of the Puritans, he felt a definite stake in both New England and old England. When these loyalties became conflicting, he attempted to find a compromise by minimizing abstract arguments in favor of practical ones. When he failed to close the breach, he and other wealthy, educated historians fled to the land of their ancestors.

His classical education came from a Boston grammar school and Harvard College from which he was graduated in 1727, and it included wide reading in literature and history as well as Latin and French. At the same time he learned modern business practices in his father's commercial house and profited from shrewd personal speculations and shipping investments. At home he was influenced by the mercantile and political atmosphere which blended with the cultural life of the Hutchinsons. His father and grandfather were also influential local officials. It was, therefore, not surprising that Thomas Hutchinson became a Boston selectman, a member of the colony's House of Representatives, a Council member, the Lieutenant Governor, the Chief Justice, and finally, in 1771, the Governor of Massachusetts. On basic economic issues such as currency inflation he was conservative and took a "hard-money" position in his *History* as well as in everyday public policy. As an importer as well as an old American he disliked the British practice of issuing general warrants to check smuggling. But as a firm believer in Parliamentary supremacy as the prop of a sound social order he broke with the followers of James Otis, who denied the right of Parliament to overturn the rights that Otis insisted were inherent in the British constitution. Inevitably these beliefs colored Hutchinson's historical writing.

Even more evident in its influence upon his interpretation of history, particularly in his final volume of *The History of the Colony of Massachusetts Bay,* was the mob attack of 1765. Led by a shoemaker, local patriots invaded his mansion, destroyed much of it, and threw out his furnishings and books, including his historical manuscripts. Escaping to England, where he finished his third volume, he remained an embittered Tory.

Yet the first volume of the *History,* covering the years 1730 to 1750 (1764), showed considerable objectivity from the patriot's viewpoint. It was not crudely filiopietistic, for it made careful use of available manuscripts and was even critical of his own ancestor—when her views seemed to threaten the stability of the Puritan social order. But as a true son of the Enlightenment he condemned early colonial bigotry and mistreatment of the Indians, and even displayed a modern liberal attitude toward race. His growing hostility to the rising spirit of political independence was clear in the second as well as the third volume.

The following selections from the *History of Massachusetts Bay* (1765-1828), taken from the original edition, reflect Hutchinson's Tory interpretation of the Boston Massacre and the Stamp Act and his unusual facility in acquiring official information. It also tells of the mob attack on his home.

The History of Massachusetts Bay

[THE STAMP ACT–1765]

The distributor of stamps for the colony of Connecticut [1] arrived in Boston from London; and, having been agent for that colony, and in other respects of a very reputable character, received from many gentlemen of the town such civilities as were due to him. When he set out for Connecticut, Mr. Oliver, the distributor for Massachusetts Bay, accompanied him out of town. This occasioned murmuring among the people, and an inflammatory piece in the next Boston Gazette. A few days after, early in the morning, a stuffed image was hung upon a tree, called the great tree of the south part of Boston. Labels affixed denoted it to be designed for the distributor of stamps. People, who were passing by, stopped to view it, and the report caused others to gather from all quarters of the town, and many from the towns adjacent. The governor caused the council to be convened. Before they came to any determination, the sheriff, with his deputies, had been to the place, but, by advice of some of the graver persons present, forbore any attempt to remove the image. The majority of the council, but not the whole, advised not to meddle with it; and urged as a reason, that the people were orderly, and, if left alone, would take down the image, and bury it without any disturbance; but an attempt to remove it would bring on a riot, the mischief designed to be prevented.

The governor, however, thought fit to meet the council again in the afternoon. Before night, the image was taken down, and carried through the townhouse, in the chamber whereof the governor and council were sitting. Forty or fifty tradesmen, decently dressed, preceded; and some thousands of the mob followed down King street to Oliver's dock, near which Mr. Oliver had lately erected a building, which, it was conjectured, he designed for a stamp office. This was laid flat to the ground in a few minutes. From thence the mob pro-

Volume III, pages 120–28, 270–78 (London, 1828).

ceeded for Fort Hill, but Mr. Oliver's house being in the way, they endeavoured to force themselves into it, and being opposed, broke the windows, beat down the doors, entered, and destroyed part of his furniture, and continued in riot until midnight, before they separated.

The next day, the governor, by advice of council, issued a proclamation, offering a reward for discovering offenders, &c. Many of the offenders were known, and the proclamation was considered as a mere matter of form. Some of the council advised to a military watch in the town the next night, but a majority were against it, and thought it enough to recommend to the select men and justices, to increase the number of the ordinary town watch; but even this was not done. Several of the council gave it as their opinion, Mr. Oliver being present, that the people, not only of the town of Boston, but of the country in general, would never submit to the execution of the stamp act, let the consequence of an opposition to it be what it would. It was also reported, that the people of Connecticut had threatened to hang their distributor on the first tree after he entered the colony; and that, to avoid it, he had turned aside to Rhode Island.

Despairing of protection, and finding his family in terror and great distress, Mr. Oliver came to a sudden resolution to resign his office before another night, and immediately signified, by a writing under his hand, to one of his friends, that he would send letters, by a ship then ready to sail for London, which should contain such resignation; and he desired that the town might be made acquainted with it, and with the strong assurances he had given, that he would never act in that capacity.

This victory was matter of triumph. The mob assembled in the evening; not to insult the distributor, but to give him thanks, and to make a bonfire upon the hill near his house.

It was hoped that the people, having obtained all that they desired, would return to order, but, having repeatedly assembled with impunity, a very small pretence served to induce them to re-assemble.

The next evening, the mob surrounded the house of the lieutenant-governor and chief justice. He was at Mr. Oliver's house when it was assaulted, and had excited the sheriff, and the colonel of the regiment, to attempt to suppress the mob. A report was soon spread, that he was a favourer of the stamp act, and had encouraged it by letters to the ministry. Upon notice of the approach of the people, he caused the doors and windows to be barred; and remained in the house. After attempting to enter, they called upon him to come into the balcony, and to declare that he had not written in favour of the act, and they would retire quite satisfied. This was an indignity to which he would not submit; and, therefore, he made no answer. An ancient reputable tradesman obtained their attention, and endeavoured to persuade them, not only of the unwarrantableness of their proceedings, but of the groundlessness of their suspicions of the lieutenant-governor, who might well enough wish the act of parliament had not passed, though he disapproved of the violent opposition to its execution. Some were for withdrawing, and others for continuing; when one of the neighbours called to them from his window and affirmed, that he saw the lieutenant-governor in his carriage, just before night, and that he was gone to lodge at his house in the country. Upon this, they dispersed, with only breaking some of the glass.

These attacks upon two of the principal officers of the crown struck terror into people of inferior rank; and though they saw the danger from this assumed power in the populace, yet they would give no aid in discountenancing it, lest they should become obnoxious themselves; for there were whisperings of danger from further acts of violence. On Sunday the 25th of August, a sermon was preached, in what was called the West meeting-house, from these words, "I would they were even cut off which trouble you." [2] The text alone, without a comment,[3] delivered from the pulpit at that time, might be construed by some of the auditory into an approbation of the prevailing irregularities. One, who had a chief hand in the outrages which soon followed, declared, when he was in prison, that he was excited to them by this sermon,[4] and that he thought he was doing God service.

Certain depositions had been taken, many months before these transactions, by order of the governor, concerning the illicit trade carrying on; and one of them, made by the judge of the admiralty, had, at the special desire of the governor, been sworn to before the lieutenant-governor, as chief justice. They had been shewn, at one of the offices in England, to a person who arrived in Boston just at this time, and he had acquainted several merchants, whose names were in some of the depositions as smugglers, with the contents. This brought, though without reason, the resentment of the merchants against the persons who, by their office, were obliged to administer the oaths, as well as against the officers of the customs and admiralty, who had made the depositions; and the leaders of the mob contrived a riot, which, after some small efforts against such officers, was to spend its principal force upon the lieutenant-governor.

And, in the evening of the 26th of August, such a mob was collected in King street, drawn there by a bonfire, and well supplied with strong drink. After some annoyance to the house of the registrar of the admiralty, and somewhat greater to that of the comptroller of the customs, whose cellars they plundered of the wine and spirits in them, they came, with intoxicated rage, upon the house of the lieutenant-governor. The doors were immediately split to pieces with broad axes, and a way made there, and at the windows, for the entry of the mob; which poured in, and filled, in an instant, every room in the house.

The lieutenant-governor had very short notice of the approach of the mob. He directed his children, and the rest of his family, to leave the house immediately, determining to keep possession himself. His eldest daughter, after going a little way from the house, returned, and refused to quit it, unless her father would do the like.

This caused him to depart from his resolution, a few minutes before the mob entered. They continued their possession until daylight; destroyed, carried away, or cast into the street, every thing that was in the house; demolished every part of it, except the walls, as far as lay in their power; and had begun to break away the brick-work.

The damage was estimated at about twenty-five hundred pounds sterling, without any regard to a great collection of publick as well as private papers, in the possession and custody of the lieutenant-governor.

The town was, the whole night, under the awe of this mob; many of the magistrates, with the field officers of the militia, standing by as spectators; and no body daring to oppose, or contradict.[5]

The governor was at the castle, and knew nothing of what had happened until the next morning. He then went to town, and caused a council to be summoned. Before they could meet, the inhabitants of Boston assembled in Faneuil Hall; and in as full a meeting as had been known, by an unanimous vote, declared an utter detestation of the extraordinary and violent proceedings of a number of persons unknown, against some of the inhabitants of the town, the preceding night; and desired the select men, and magistrates of the town, to use their utmost endeavours to suppress the like disorders for the future; the freeholders, and other inhabitants, being ready to do every thing in their power to assist them. It could not be doubted, that many of those who were immediate actors in, as well as of those who had been abettors of, those violent proceedings, were present at this unanimous vote.

The council advised to a proclamation, with promise of 300*l.* reward for discovering the leader or leaders, and 100*l.* for every other person. Information had been before given to the justices of peace in the town, and warrants had been issued and delivered to the sheriff for apprehending several persons. One of them, a tradesman of the town, whose name was Mackintosh, was soon taken in King street; but the sheriff was immediately surrounded by a number of merchants, and other persons of property and character, who assured him, that, if he apprehended Mackintosh, not a man would appear in arms, as had been proposed, for the security of the town the next night. The sheriff released him, and made return of his doings to the governor, then in council. Some of the council gave their opinion, that the sheriff was inexcusable; but it passed over without any act of council to shew a disapprobation. To this feeble state were the powers of government reduced.[6]

Six or eight other persons were apprehended, and, upon examination, committed to prison in order to trial, and were generally considered as capital offenders. Before the time of trial, a considerable number of people entered the house of the prison-keeper late in the evening, compelled him, by threats, to deliver to them the keys of the prison, which they opened, and then set the prisoners at liberty; and all this without any tumult. The prisoners thought fit to disappear for some months; but there was no authority, which thought it advisable to make any inquiry after them.

The next day after the riot, happened to be the first day of the superior court for the county of Suffolk. The four judges attended in their robes; the lieutenant-governor as chief-justice, in an ordinary undress, in which he was sitting in the evening when the alarm was given him; his robes and every other garment being taken out of his house, or destroyed in it. Instead of a charge to the grand jury, the chief-justice, in a long speech to the people, endeavoured to convince them of the fatal effects to the province of the violent opposition to government which was beginning to take place; and the court shewed their resentment by refusing to do any business while the town was in that disorderly state, and adjourned for six weeks.[7]

Many of the most ruffian part of the mob, who left the town the next day after the riot, returned in the evening, and attempted again to collect the people together, in order to further rapine: but a military watch having been ordered, and the governor's company of cadets appearing in arms, and shewing great spirit, the mob was dispersed. People came in from many parts of the country, to view the ruins of the lieutenant-governor's house, outhouses, garden, &c., and, from the shocking appearance, could not help expressing a disapprobation of such acts of violence. Their prejudices, however, were not abated against the stamp act. The execution of it must be hindered in some other way.

The officer appointed to receive the stamped paper, which was daily expected, having resigned his office, the governor determined to receive the paper into his own charge at the castle; and, by advice of council, he ordered the enlistment of a number of men to strengthen the garrison. This caused great murmur among the people. To pacify them, he made a declaration in council, that he had no authority to open any of the packages, or to appoint a distributor of stamps; that his views, in depositing the stamped paper in the castle, and in strengthening the garrison there, were to prevent imprudent people from offering an insult to the king; and to save the town, or province, as it might happen, from being held to answer for the value of the stamps, as they certainly would be, if the papers should be taken away. This declaration the council desired him to publish; but it did not stop the clamour. He was forced to stop the enlistment, and to discharge such men as had been enlisted.

The news of the change of ministry in England, which arrived about this time,[8] tended more to peace and quiet, at least for a time, than any thing in the power of the governor, or of any authority within the province, could have done. Hopes were immediately conceived that the stamp act would be repealed the next session. It certainly was more likely that a new ministry should be in favour of repealing acts brought forward by the old, than that the old should be inclined to the repeal of their own acts.

The hopes of this repeal were increased by the news, day after day, of the same spirit of opposition to the act in many other colonies, as had shewn itself in Massachusetts Bay. The distributors were compelled to resign in every colony. Mobs became frequent in Connecticut, Rhode Island, and New York. Nothing more was judged necessary, at present, to affect it: but if it should not be repealed the next session, further measures must be then devised.

It was necessary, however, to determine how to proceed, after the 1st of November, until the repeal. It was the general voice, that, at all events, the act must not be executed. . . .

[THE BOSTON MASSACRE–1770]

A more tragical affair, and which had very important consequences, happened soon after. The two regiments in the town of Boston were a continual eyesore to the inhabitants. During the winter, there had been frequent frays, in the streets, between the soldiers and the town's people. The pains taken by the officers, to keep their men from shewing their resentment at hissings and insults, were conspicuous; but it was not possible to prevent a return, and there appeared a rooted enmity on each side. The journal of occurrences, sent to New York to be published, seems to have had its first effect there,[9] which tended to encourage the people in Boston, where discontent was evidently increasing all the month of February.

On Saturday, the 3rd of March, lieutenant-colonel Carr, the commanding officer of the 29th regiment, made complaint in a letter to the lieutenant-governor, of the frequent abuses offered to his men, and of very insolent, provoking language given to some of them on that day, by certain journeymen ropemakers, which had brought on a fray, in which one of the soldiers was very dangerously wounded. On Monday, the 5th, the lieutenant-governor laid this letter before the council, for their advice and assistance. Several of the council signified their opinions, that the people would never be satisfied with any thing short of the removal of the troops. One gentleman said, that he knew that some of the principal inhabitants had several times met together, to consult upon the proper means for effecting their removal. The council, however, could not agree in any advice; though it was apprehended that the smaller frays would be followed by one more general.

Early in the evening, clusters of the inhabitants were observed in different quarters of the town. Parties of soldiers were also driving about the streets, as if the one and the other, had something more than ordinary upon their minds. About eight o'clock, one of the bells of the town was rung in such manner as is usual in case of fire. This called people into the streets. A large number assembled in the marketplace, not far from King street, armed with bludgeons, or clubs. A small fray between some of the inhabitants and the soldiers, at or near the barracks at the west part of the town, was of little importance, and soon over. A sentinel, who was posted at the custom-house, not far from the main guard, was next insulted, and pelted with pieces of ice, &c., which caused him to call to the main guard to protect him. Notice was soon given to captain Preston, whose company was then on guard. A serjeant, with six men, was sent to protect the sentinel; but the captain, to prevent any rash, precipitate action, followed them himself. There seem to have been but few people collected, when the assault was first made on the sentinel; but the serjeant's guard drew a greater number together, and the guards were more insulted than the sentinel had been, and received frequent strokes from snowballs, lumps of ice, &c. Captain Preston, thereupon, ordered them to charge; but this was no discouragement to the assailants, who continued to pelt the guard, daring them to fire. Some of the people who were behind the soldiers, and observed the abuse, called on them to fire. At length, one of them received a blow with a club, which brought him to the ground; but, rising again, he immediately fired, and all the rest, one excepted, followed the example. This seems, from the evidence at the trials, and the observation of persons present, to have been the course of the material facts. Three men were killed outright, two mortally wounded, who died soon after, and several slightly wounded. Gray, one of the killed, was one of the ropemakers who had been in quarrels with the soldiers, and he, with Attucks, a mulatto, another of the killed, were among the most active in this attack. Carr, one of the mortally wounded, acknowledged, upon his death bed, that he had seen mobs in Ireland, but never knew troops bear so much without firing, as these had done. The soldiers, immediately after the action, withdrew to the main guard, which was strengthened by additional companies.

Two or three of the persons who had seen the action ran to the lieutenant-governor's house, which was about half a mile distant, and begged, for God's sake, he would go to King street, where, they feared, a general action would come on, between the troops and the inhabitants. He went immediately, and, to satisfy the people, called for captain Preston, and inquired why he fired upon the inhabitants without the direction of a civil magistrate. The noise was so great, that his answer could not be understood, and some, who were apprehensive of the lieutenant-governor's danger from the general confusion, called out, "the town house, the town house," and, with irresistible violence, he was forced up by the crowd into the council chamber. There, demand was immediately made of him, to order the troops to withdraw from the town house to their barracks. He refused to comply; and calling from the balcony to the great body of people which remained in the street, he expressed his great concern at the unhappy event, assured them he would do every thing in his power in order to a full and impartial inquiry, that the law might have its course, and advised them to go peaceably to their several homes. Upon this there was a cry—"home,—home," and a great part separated, and went home. He then signified his opinion to lieutenant-colonel Carr, that, if the companies in arms were ordered to their barracks, the streets would be cleared and the town in quiet for that night. Upon their retiring, the rest of the inhabitants, except those of the council chamber, retired also.

Lieutenant-colonel Dalrymple, at the desire of the lieutenant-governor, came to the council chamber, while several justices were examining persons who were present at the transactions of the evening. From the evidence of several, it was apparent that the justices would commit captain Preston, if taken. Several hours passed before he could be found, and the people suspected that he would not run the hazard of a trial; but, at length, he surrendered himself to a warrant for apprehending him, and, having been examined, was committed to prison. The next morning, the soldiers who were upon guard surrendered also, and were committed. This was not sufficient to satisfy the people; and early in the forenoon they were in motion again. The lieutenant-governor caused his council to be summoned, and desired the two lieutenant-colonels of the regiments to be present. The select men of Boston were waiting the lieutenant-governor's coming to council, and, being admitted, made their representation, that, from the contentions arising from the troops quartered in Boston, and, above all, from the tragedy of the last night, the minds of the inhabitants were exceedingly disturbed; that they would presently be assembled in a town meeting; and that, unless the troops should be removed, the most terrible consequences were to be expected. The justices, also, of Boston and several of the neighbouring towns, had assembled, and desired to signify their opinion, that it would not be possible to keep the people under restraint, if the troops remained in town. The lieutenant-governor acquainted both the select men and the justices, that he had no authority to alter the place of destination of the king's troops; that he expected the commanding officers of the two regiments, and would let them know the applications which had been made. Presently after their coming, a large committee from the town meeting presented an address, or message, to the lieutenant-governor, declaring it to be the unanimous opinion of the meeting that nothing can rationally be expected to restore the peace of the town, "and prevent blood and carnage," but the immediate removal of the troops. The committee withdrew into another room to wait for an answer. Some of the council urged the necessity of complying with the people's demand. The lieutenant-governor, thereupon, declared that he would upon no consideration whatever give orders for their removal. Lieutenant-colonel Dalrymple then signified, that, as the 29th regiment had originally been designed to be placed at the castle, and was now peculiarly obnoxious to the town, he was content that it should be removed to the castle, until the general's pleasure should be known. The committee was informed of this offer, and the lieutenant-governor rose from council, intending to receive no further application upon the subject; but the council prayed that he would meet them again in the afternoon, and, colonel Dalrymple desiring it also, he complied. Before the council met again, it had been intimated to them that the "desire" of the governor and council to the commanding officer to remove the troops, would cause him to do it, though he should receive no authoritative "order." As soon as they met, a committee from the town meeting attended, with a second message, to acquaint the lieutenant-governor, that it was the unanimous voice of the people assembled, consisting, as they said, of near three thousand persons, that nothing less than a total and immediate removal of the troops would satisfy them.[10]

The council, who were divided in the forenoon, were now unanimous, and each of them, separately, declared his opinion, and gave his reason for it; and one or more of them observed to the lieutenant-governor, that he would not be able to justify a refusal to comply with the unanimous advice of the council, and that all the consequences would be chargeable upon him alone. The secretary of the province, who thought differently in the morning, the two lieutenant-colonels, and the commander of one of his majesty's ships then upon the station, who were all present in council, concurred in the necessity of his complying. He had signified his own opinion, that, at all events, the governor and council should avoid interfering in the destination of the troops, and leave it to the commanding officer; but when he considered that, by the charter, the council was constituted for advice and assistance to him, that he had called them together for that purpose, that his standing out alone would probably bring on a general convulsion, which the unanimity of the king's servants might have prevented, he consented to signify his desire, founded upon the unanimous opinion and advice of the council, that the troops might be removed to the barracks in the castle; at the same time disclaiming all authority to order their removal.

Some of the officers of the regiments appeared, the next day, to be greatly dissatisfied with being compelled by the people to leave the town so disgracefully. Expresses were sent away immediately to the general. The jealousy, that the general would forbid the removal, caused further measures to force the troops from the town before there could be sufficient time for his answer. Roxbury, the next town to Boston, assembled and sent a committee of their principal inhabitants with an address to the lieutenant-governor, praying him to interpose, and to order the immediate removal of the troops; but he refused to concern himself any further in the affair. As the time approached when a return might be expected from New York, it was thought fit to have another meeting of the town of Boston, and a committee was appointed further to apply to the lieutenant-governor to order the troops out of town; Mr. Adams, their prolocutor, pressing the matter with great vehemence, and intimating, that, in case of refusal, the rage of the people would vent itself against the lieutenant-governor in particular. He gave a peremptory refusal, and expressed his resentment at the menace. The committee then applied to the commanding officer, and, the same day,[11] the 29th regiment, and, the next morning, the 14th, were removed to the castle.

This success gave greater assurances than ever, that, by firmness, the great object, exemption from all exterior power, civil or military, would finally be obtained. Checks, and temporary interruptions, might happen; but they would be surmounted, and the progress of liberty would recommence.

A committee of the town of Boston then proceeded to the examination of witnesses, "in order to shew to the world, and especially to the friends of the colonies in England, that there were just grounds for insisting upon the removal of the troops." The variance of their account of facts from the statement of the whole evidence, as it afterwards appeared on the trials, is a strong instance of the small dependence which can be placed upon *ex-parte* witnesses, examined by men engaged in political contests.

To secure the first impressions, a letter was prepared by the committee, and despatched in a few days after the fact, exemplifications whereof were sent to a great number of persons of publick character in England; in which the sending and stationing troops in the town is charged "to the intrigues of wicked men, with design to enslave it"; complaint is made of "their landing with appearance of hostility, and marching with ensigns of triumph," of "continuing their enormities, by rescuing prisoners out of the hands of justice, and firing upon the inhabitants when in the peace of God, and of the king," of "overawing the magistrates and courts of justice; [12] who had shewn such mean submission, as gave disgust to the coolest and most judicious persons in the community." A narrative is then given of the unhappy action in King street; that a party of seven or eight soldiers, under the command of captain Preston, "and by his order," fired upon the inhabitants promiscuously in the street, "without the least warning," and killed three on the spot, and wounded others; that, "as witnesses swear, when the soldiers fired, several muskets were discharged from the house where the commissioners of the customs held their board"; that "a boy, servant to one Mainwaring, a petty officer, had, upon oath, accused his master of firing upon the people from a window of that house, a number of persons being in the room with him."

This short intimation, it was added, was sent, by order of the town, to prevent, for the present, any ill impression being made upon his majesty's ministers, and others, by the account from the commissioners of the customs, and other enemies, until a more full representation could be made.

This representation, with the depositions of a great number of witnesses to facts preceding, accompanying, and following what was pronounced a bloody -massacre, was printed a few days after, and many copies of it sent to England by a vessel hired by the town for that purpose. A certificate accompanied it, under the seal of the province, that the persons before whom the deponents were sworn had authority to administer oaths, and that credit ought to be given to their attestations.[13] A letter also, signed by Mr. Bowdoin, went with each copy, signifying his own belief of the truth of the depositions.

NOTES

[1] Jared Ingersoll, esq.

[2] Gal. chap. v. ver. 12.

[3] The verse which follows, "For, brethren, ye have been called unto liberty only; use not liberty for an occasion to the flesh," if properly enforced, would have been sufficient to have kept the people within bounds.

[4] Dr. Mayhew, the preacher, in a letter to the lieutenant-governor, a few days after, expressed the greatest concern, nothing being further from his thoughts than such an effect; and declared, that, if the loss of his whole estate could recall the sermon, he would willingly part with it.

[5] The lieutenant-colonel of the regiment, observing two men disguised, with long staves in their hands, who seemed to be directors, expressed his concern at the damage other people, besides the lieutenant-governor, might sustain by the destruction of so many papers. Answer was made, that it had been resolved to destroy every thing in the house; and such resolve should be carried to effect.

[6] The justices of peace being ordered to attend the governor and council, one, who had been most active in town meetings, &c., complained that his own life had been threatened, and wept. The governor observed to him, that he had raised the devil, and could not lay him again.

[7] In the counties distant from the town of Boston, this violence was at first generally condemned. The superior court was held a few weeks after in Worcester, and then in Hampshire. In each county, the grand jury addressed the chief justice, and declared, not as their own minds only, but

what they knew to be the minds of the people in general, a detestation of the proceedings in Boston.

[8] September 9th.

[9] Liberty pole, which had been erected at New York, was cut down (January 21), and some of the troops were charged with the fact. The next day, two or three thousand people assembled about the place where the pole had stood, and passed, and caused to be printed, a resolve in form; never to employ a soldier on any terms whatever; but to treat them with abhorrence and contempt, as the enemies of the constitution; and if any, except sentinels and orderly serjeants, should be found, in the night, with arms, or, after the roll is called, without arms, and behaving in an insulting manner, to treat them as enemies to the constitution. Quarrels ensued, in one of which a seaman was said to be killed. Other persons were badly wounded.

[10] The chairman of the committee, in conversation with lieutenant-colonel Dalrymple, said to him, that if he could remove the 29th regiment, he could remove the 14th also, and it was at his peril to refuse it. This was a strong expression of that determined spirit which animated all future measures.

[11] March 10th.

[12] This was an injurious reflection upon the judges of the superior court, who were men of great integrity; and, if they had any awe upon their spirits, it was the awe of the people.

[13] This certificate was drawn, and presented to the lieutenant-governor, in such form as included, not only the credit due to the attestation of the justice, but to the facts contained in the depositions; and he refused to suffer the seal to be affixed. This raised a clamour, until some of the town's committee, convinced of the propriety of the exception, were content with an alteration. The controversial writers in England, notwithstanding the alteration, laid great stress on the seal of the province, towards establishing the truth of the facts.

Francis Parkman (1823-1893) and the Pageant of Western History

Despite so many decades of revision by more recent scholars, few nineteenth-century historical reputations have suffered so little as that of Francis Parkman. His Boston-Brahmin background and his Harvard training resemble those of Bancroft and Hildreth, but he went beyond them to visualize the past by emulating the out-of-door experiences of the frontiersmen and meeting the Indians of his day. He disciplined himself to endure many hundreds of miles of hiking and horseback riding, and he embarked upon the famous western trip of the 1840's in order to know the Sioux, the hunters, the trappers, and the emigrant trains. These were the adventures told in his autobiographical book, *The Oregon Trail* (1846). On his European Grand Tour, he had observed something of the paternalistic influence of the Roman Catholic Church in Italy and he took this as a clue to understanding the power of the Church in old Canada. Here was his preparation for the magnificent historical narrative that he wished to make his life's work.

Even the mysterious nervous ailment which greatly weakened his eyesight—it forced him to invent a special wire frame to guide his writing in the dark—did not halt his brilliant career or diminish his incessant drive for action. In compensation, he even became a distinguished horticulturist as well as a historian. Fortunately he could afford assistance and had many manuscripts and books read to him. His early history, *The Conspiracy of Pontiac* (1851), showed his skill in portrayal of Indian life and the primitive forest environment; here he pointed out the provocations by the white men against the Indians. However, a recent historian, Howard H. Peckham, thinks that Parkman exaggerated the role of Pontiac as an Indian leader.

His histories of the colonial struggle between England and France began to appear at the end of the Civil War, the first in 1865, the last in 1892. Like Bancroft and others, he used the theme of a democratic Protestant Anglo-Saxon people overcoming the authoritarian, paternalistic, Roman Catholic French. Despite his social prejudices, which included a low opinion of Indian potentialities, Parkman drew much more realistic descriptions of men and background than did Bancroft or Hildreth. His anticlericalism did not prevent him from portraying the Jesuits as heroic martyrs and idealists in *The Jesuits in North America* (1867). Theodore Roosevelt, who made Parkman his idol and dedicated his own *Winning of the West* to him, praised his ability to see virtues in the opponents of the English, his love of the strenuous life, and his mastery of a graphic style. Parkman (like Roosevelt) prized masculinity and action; these traits appear in his descriptions of La Salle, Montcalm, Wolfe, and other leaders. But, loyal to the English dream of empire, he was ready to defend the tragic evacuation of the Acadians from their homes to scattered settlements thousands of miles away.

As a conservative Whig, he clung to the ideal of an educated and talented elite, just as he dwelt upon the great leaders of Old France and England, with all too little space given to the life of the plain people. In the America of his day, he deplored the spread of universal suffrage and the debasement of scholarship through mass education. He has escaped obsolescence despite a certain aristocratic bias, for he constructed a history of the past with such permanent materials, accuracy, general balance, and fascinating narrative, and without the extreme rhetorical flourishes of so many of his fellow historians. Allan Nevins, among other skillful mid-twentieth-century writers, has pointed to the necessity of historians like Parkman if a contemporary appreciation for history similar to that held by nineteenth-century readers is to be established.

La Salle and the Discovery of the Great West

1643–1669

Among the burghers of Rouen was the old and rich family of the Caveliers. Though citizens and not nobles, some of their connections held high diplomatic posts and honorable employments at Court. They were destined to find a better claim to distinction. In 1643 was born at Rouen Robert Cavelier, better known by the designation of La Salle.[1] His father Jean and his uncle Henri were wealthy merchants, living more like nobles than like burghers; and the boy received an education answering to the marked traits of intellect and character which he soon began to display. He showed an inclination for the exact sciences, and especially for the mathematics, in which he made great proficiency. At an early age, it is said, he became connected with the Jesuits; and, though doubt has been expressed of the statement, it is probably true.[2]

La Salle was always an earnest Catholic; and yet, judging by the qualities which his after life evinced, he was not very liable to religious enthusiasm. It is nevertheless clear that the Society of Jesus may have had a powerful attraction for his youthful imagination. This great organization, so complicated yet so harmonious, a mighty machine moved from the centre by a single hand, was an image of regulated power, full of fascination for a mind like his. But, if it was likely that he would be drawn into it, it was no less likely that he would soon wish to escape. To find himself not at the centre of power, but at the circumference; not the mover, but the moved; the passive instrument of another's will, taught to walk in prescribed paths, to renounce his individuality and become a component atom of a vast whole,—would have been intolerable to him. Nature had shaped him for other uses than to teach a class of boys on the benches of a Jesuit school. Nor, on his part, was he likely to please his directors; for, self-controlled and self-contained as he was, he was far too intractable

Pages 1–11, 28–38 (Little, Brown, 1879).

a subject to serve their turn. A youth whose calm exterior hid an
inexhaustible fund of pride; whose inflexible purposes, nursed in
secret, the confessional and the "manifestation of conscience" could
hardly drag to the light; whose strong personality would not yield to
the shaping hand; and who, by a necessity of his nature, could obey
no initiative but his own,—was not after the model that Loyola had
commended to his followers.

La Salle left the Jesuits, parting with them, it is said, on good
terms, and with a reputation of excellent acquirements and unim-
peachable morals. This last is very credible. The cravings of a deep
ambition, the hunger of an insatiable intellect, the intense longing for
action and achievement, subdued in him all other passions; and in his
faults the love of pleasure had no part. He had an elder brother in
Canada, the Abbé Jean Cavelier, a priest of St. Sulpice. Apparently,
it was this that shaped his destinies. His connection with the Jesuits
had deprived him, under the French law, of the inheritance of his
father, who had died not long before. An allowance was made to him
of three or, as is elsewhere stated, four hundred livres a year, the
capital of which was paid over to him; and with this pittance he sailed
for Canada, to seek his fortune, in the spring of 1666.[3]

Next, we find him at Montreal. In another volume, we have seen
how an association of enthusiastic devotees had made a settlement at
this place.[4] Having in some measure accomplished its work, it was
now dissolved; and the corporation of priests, styled the Seminary of
St. Sulpice, which had taken a prominent part in the enterprise, and,
indeed, had been created with a view to it, was now the proprietor
and the feudal lord of Montreal. It was destined to retain its sei-
gniorial rights until the abolition of the feudal tenures of Canada in
our own day, and it still holds vast possessions in the city and island.
These worthy ecclesiastics, models of a discreet and sober conservatism, were holding a post with which a band of veteran soldiers or
war-like frontiersmen would have been better matched. Montreal was
perhaps the most dangerous place in Canada. In time of war, which
might have been called the normal condition of the colony, it was
exposed by its position to incessant inroads of the Iroquois, or Five

Nations, of New York; and no man could venture into the forests or the fields without bearing his life in his hand. The savage confederates had just received a sharp chastisement at the hands of Courcelle, the governor; and the result was a treaty of peace, which might at any moment be broken, but which was an inexpressible relief while it lasted.

The priests of St. Sulpice were granting out their lands, on very easy terms, to settlers. They wished to extend a thin line of settlements along the front of their island, to form a sort of outpost, from which an alarm could be given on any descent of the Iroquois. La Salle was the man for such a purpose. Had the priests understood him,—which they evidently did not, for some of them suspected him of levity, the last foible with which he could be charged,—had they understood him, they would have seen in him a young man in whom the fire of youth glowed not the less ardently for the veil of reserve that covered it; who would shrink from no danger, but would not court it in bravado; and who would cling with an invincible tenacity of gripe to any purpose which he might espouse. There is good reason to think that he had come to Canada with purposes already conceived, and that he was ready to avail himself of any stepping-stone which might help to realize them. Queylus, Superior of the Seminary, made him a generous offer; and he accepted it. This was the gratuitous grant of a large tract of land at the place now called La Chine, above the great rapids of the same name, and eight or nine miles from Montreal. On one hand, the place was greatly exposed to attack; and, on the other, it was favorably situated for the fur-trade. La Salle and his successors became its feudal proprietors, on the sole condition of delivering to the Seminary, on every change of ownership, a medal of fine silver, weighing one mark.[5] He entered on the improvement of his new domain with what means he could command, and began to grant out his land to such settlers as would join him.

Approaching the shore where the city of Montreal now stands, one would have seen a row of small compact dwellings, extending along a narrow street, parallel to the river, and then, as now, called St. Paul Street. On a hill at the right stood the windmill of the seigniors, built of stone, and pierced with loopholes to serve, in time of need, as a place of defence. On the left, in an angle formed by the junction of a rivulet with the St. Lawrence, was a square bastioned fort of stone. Here lived the military governor, appointed by the Seminary, and commanding a few soldiers of the regiment of Carignan. In front, on the line of the street, were the enclosure and buildings of the Seminary, and, nearly adjoining them, those of the Hôtel-Dieu, or Hospital, both provided for defence in case of an Indian attack. In the hospital enclosure was a small church, opening on the street, and, in the absence of any other, serving for the whole settlement.[6]

Landing, passing the fort, and walking southward along the shore, one would soon have left the rough clearings, and entered the primeval forest. Here, mile after mile, he would have journeyed on in solitude, when the hoarse roar of the rapids, foaming in fury on his left, would have reached his listening ear; and at length, after a walk of some three hours, he would have found the rude beginnings of a settlement. It was where the St. Lawrence widens into the broad expanse called the Lake of St. Louis. Here, La Salle had traced out the circuit of a palisaded village, and assigned to each settler half an arpent, or about the third of an acre, within the enclosure, for which he was to render to the young seignior a yearly acknowledgment of three capons, besides six deniers—that is, half a sou—in money. To each was assigned, moreover, sixty arpents of land beyond the limits of the village, with the perpetual rent of half a sou for each arpent. He also set apart a common, two hundred arpents in extent, for the use of the settlers, on condition of the payment by each of five sous a year. He reserved four hundred and twenty arpents for his own personal domain, and on this he began to clear the ground and erect buildings. Similar to this were the beginnings of all the Canadian seigniories formed at this troubled period.[7]

That La Salle came to Canada with objects distinctly in view, is probable from the fact that he at once began to study the Indian languages, and with such success that he is said, within two or three years, to have mastered the Iroquois and seven or eight other languages and dialects.[8] From the shore of his seigniory, he could gaze westward over the broad breast of the Lake of St. Louis, bounded by the dim forests of Chateauguay and Beauharnois; but his thoughts flew far beyond, across the wild and lonely world that stretched towards the sunset. Like Champlain, and all the early explorers, he dreamed of a passage to the South Sea, and a new road for commerce to the riches of China and Japan. Indians often came to his secluded settlement; and, on one occasion, he was visited by a band of the Seneca Iroquois, not long before the scourge of the colony, but now, in virtue of the treaty, wearing the semblance of friendship. The visitors spent the winter with him, and told him of a river called the Ohio, rising in their country, and flowing into the sea, but at such a distance that its mouth could only be reached after a journey of eight or nine months. Evidently, the Ohio and the Mississippi are here merged into one.[9] In accordance with geographical views then prevalent, he conceived that this great river must needs flow into the "Vermilion Sea"; that is, the Gulf of California. If so, it would give him what he sought, a western passage to China; while, in any case, the populous Indian tribes said to inhabit its banks might be made a source of great commercial profit.

La Salle's imagination took fire. His resolution was soon formed; and he descended the St. Lawrence to Quebec, to gain the countenance of the governor for his intended exploration. Few men were more skilled than he in the art of clear and plausible statement. Both the governor, Courcelle, and the intendant, Talon, were readily won over to his plan; for which, however, they seem to have given him no more substantial aid than that of the governor's letters patent authorizing the enterprise.[10] The cost was to be his own; and he had no money, having spent it all on his seigniory. He therefore proposed that the Seminary, which had given it to him, should buy it back again, with such improvements as he had made. Queylus, the Superior, being favorably disposed towards him, consented, and bought of him the greater part; while La Salle sold the remainder, including the clearings, to one Jean Milot, an ironmonger, for twenty-eight hundred livres.[11] With this he bought four canoes, with the necessary supplies, and hired fourteen men.

Meanwhile, the Seminary itself was preparing a similar enterprise. The Jesuits at this time not only held an ascendency over the other ecclesiastics in Canada, but exercised an inordinate influence on the civil government. The Seminary priests of Montreal were jealous of these powerful rivals, and eager to emulate their zeal in the saving of souls, and the conquering of new domains for the Faith. Under this impulse, they had, three years before, established a mission at Quinté, on the north shore of Lake Ontario, in charge of two of their number, one of whom was the Abbé Fénelon, elder brother of the celebrated Archbishop of Cambray. Another of them, Dollier de Casson, had spent the winter in a hunting-camp of the Nipissings, where an Indian prisoner, captured in the North-west, told him of populous tribes of that quarter, living in heathenish darkness. On this, the Seminary priests resolved to essay their conversion; and an expedition, to be directed by Dollier, was fitted out to this end.

He was not ill suited to the purpose. He had been a soldier in his youth, and had fought valiantly as an officer of cavalry under Turenne. He was a man of great courage; of a tall, commanding person; and of uncommon bodily strength, which he had notably proved in the campaign of Courcelle against the Iroquois, three years before.[12] On going to Quebec to procure the necessary outfit, he was urged by Courcelle to modify his plans so far as to act in concert with La Salle in exploring the mystery of the great unknown river of the West. Dollier and his brother priests consented. One of them, Galinée, was joined with him as a colleague, because he was skilled in surveying, and could make a map of their route. Three canoes were procured, and seven hired men completed the party. It was determined that La Salle's expedition and that of the Seminary should be combined in one; an arrangement ill suited to the character of the young explorer, who was unfit for any enterprise of which he was not the undisputed chief.

Midsummer was near, and there was no time to lose. Yet the moment was most unpropitious, for a Seneca chief had lately been murdered by three scoundrel soldiers of the fort of Montreal; and, while they were undergoing their trial, it became known that three other Frenchmen had treacherously put to death several Iroquois of the Oneida tribe, in order to get possession of their furs. The whole colony trembled in expectation of a new outbreak of the war. Happily, the event proved otherwise. The authors of the last murder escaped; but the three soldiers were shot at Montreal, in presence of a considerable number of the Iroquois, who declared themselves satisfied with the atonement; and on this same day, the sixth of July, the adventurers began their voyage.

THE JESUITS ON THE LAKES
1670–1672

What were the Jesuits doing? Since the ruin of their great mission of the Hurons, a perceptible change had taken place in them. They had put forth exertions almost superhuman, set at naught famine, disease, and death, lived with the self-abnegation of saints and died with the devotion of martyrs; and the result of all had been a disastrous failure. From no short-coming on their part, but from the force of events beyond the sphere of their influence, a very demon of havoc had crushed their incipient churches, slaughtered their converts, uprooted the populous communities on which their hopes had rested, and scattered them in bands of wretched fugitives far and wide through the wilderness.[13] They had devoted themselves in the fulness of faith to the building up of a Christian and Jesuit empire on the conversion of the great stationary tribes of the lakes; and of these none remained but the Iroquois, the destroyers of the rest, among whom, indeed, was a field which might stimulate their zeal by an abundant promise of sufferings and martyrdoms, but which, from its geographical position, was too much exposed to Dutch and English influence to promise great and decisive results. Their best hopes were now in the North and the West; and thither, in great part, they had turned their energies.

We find them on Lake Huron, Lake Superior, and Lake Michigan, laboring vigorously as of old, but in a spirit not quite the same. Now, as before, two objects inspired their zeal, the "greater glory of God," and the influence and credit of the Order of Jesus. If the one motive

had somewhat lost in power, the other had gained. The epoch of the
saints and martyrs was passing away; and henceforth we find the
Canadian Jesuit less and less an apostle, more and more an explorer,
a man of science, and a politician. The yearly reports of the missions
are still, for the edification of the pious reader, filled with intolerably
tedious stories of baptisms, conversions, and the exemplary deport-
ment of neophytes; for these have become a part of the formula; but
they are relieved abundantly by more mundane topics. One finds observations on the winds, currents, and tides of the Great Lakes;
speculations on a subterranean outlet of Lake Superior; accounts of
its copper-mines, and how we, the Jesuit fathers, are laboring to
explore them for the profit of the colony; surmises touching the North
Sea, the South Sea, the Sea of China, which we hope ere long to discover; and reports of that great mysterious river of which the Indians
tell us,—flowing southward, perhaps to the Gulf of Mexico, perhaps
to the Vermilion Sea,—and the secrets whereof, with the help of the
Virgin, we will soon reveal to the world.

   The Jesuit was as often a fanatic for his Order as for his faith;
and oftener yet the two fanaticisms mingled in him inextricably.
Ardently as he burned for the saving of souls, he would have none
saved on the Upper Lakes except by his brethren and himself. He
claimed a monopoly of conversion, with its attendant monopoly of
toil, hardship, and martyrdom. Often disinterested for himself, he
was inordinately ambitious for the great corporate power in which
he had merged his own personality; and here lies one cause, among
many, of the seeming contradictions which abound in the annals of
the Order.

   Prefixed to the *Relation* of 1671 is that monument of Jesuit hardi-
hood and enterprise, the map of Lake Superior; a work of which,
however, the exactness has been exaggerated, as compared with other
Canadian maps of the day. While making surveys, the priests were
diligently looking for copper. Father Dablon reports that they had
found it in greatest abundance on Isle Minong, now Isle Royale. "A
day's journey from the head of the lake, on the south side, there is,"
he says, "a rock of copper weighing from six hundred to eight hun-

dred pounds, lying on the shore where any who pass may see it"; and he farther speaks of great copper boulders in the bed of the river Ontonagan.[14]

There were two principal missions on the Upper Lakes, which were, in a certain sense, the parents of the rest. One of these was Ste. Marie du Saut,—the same visited by Dollier and Galinée,—at the outlet of Lake Superior. This was a noted fishing-place; for the rapids were full of whitefish, and Indians came thither in crowds. The permanent residents were an Ojibwa band, whom the French called Sauteurs, and whose bark lodges were clustered at the foot of the rapids, near the fort of the Jesuits. Besides these, a host of Algonquins, of various tribes, resorted thither in the spring and summer; living in abundance on the fishery, and dispersing in winter to wander and starve in scattered hunting-parties far and wide through the forests.

The other chief mission was that of St. Esprit, at La Pointe, near the western extremity of Lake Superior. Here were the Hurons, fugitives twenty years before from the slaughter of their countrymen; and the Ottawas, who, like them, had sought an asylum from the rage of the Iroquois. Many other tribes—Illinois, Pottawattamies, Foxes, Menomonies, Sioux, Assiniboins, Knisteneaux, and a multitude besides—came hither yearly to trade with the French. Here was a young Jesuit, Jacques Marquette, lately arrived from the Saut Ste. Marie. His savage flock disheartened him by its backslidings; and the best that he could report of the Hurons, after all the toil and all the blood lavished in their conversion, was, that they "still retain a little Christianity"; while the Ottawas are "far removed from the kingdom of God, and addicted beyond all other tribes to foulness, incantations, and sacrifices to evil spirits." [15]

Marquette heard from the Illinois—yearly visitors at La Pointe—of the great river which they had crossed on their way,[16] and which, as he conjectured, flowed into the Gulf of California. He heard marvels of it also from the Sioux, who lived on its banks; and a strong desire possessed him to explore the mystery of its course. A sudden calamity dashed his hopes. The Sioux—the Iroquois of the West, as the Jesuits call them—had hitherto kept the peace with the expatriated

tribes of La Pointe; but now, from some cause not worth inquiry,
they broke into open war, and so terrified the Hurons and Ottawas
that they abandoned their settlements and fled. Marquette followed
his panic-stricken flock, who, passing the Saut Ste. Marie, and de-
scending to Lake Huron, stopped at length, the Hurons at Michillimackinac, and the Ottawas at the Great Manatoulin Island. Two
missions were now necessary to minister to the divided bands. That
of Michillimackinac was assigned to Marquette, and that of the Manatoulin Island to Louis André. The former took post at Point St.
Ignace, on the north shore of the Straits of Michillimackinac, while
the latter began the mission of St. Simon at the new abode of the
Ottawas. When winter came, scattering his flock to their hunting-
grounds, André made a missionary tour among the Nipissings and
other neighboring tribes. The shores of Lake Huron had long been
an utter solitude, swept of their denizens by the terror of the all-
conquering Iroquois; but now that these tigers had felt the power of
the French, and learned for a time to leave their Indian allies in peace,
the fugitive hordes were returning to their ancient abodes. André's
experience among them was of the roughest. The staple of his diet
was acorns and *tripe de roche,* a species of lichen, which, being boiled,
resolved itself into a black glue, nauseous, but not void of nourish-
ment. At times, he was reduced to moss, the bark of trees, or moccasins and old moose-skins cut into strips and boiled. His hosts treated
him very ill, and the worst of their fare was always his portion.
When spring came to his relief, he returned to his post of St. Simon,
with impaired digestion and unabated zeal.

Besides the Saut Ste. Marie and Michillimackinac, both noted
fishing-places, there was another spot, no less famous for game and
fish, and therefore a favorite resort of Indians. This was the head of
the Green Bay of Lake Michigan.[17] Here and in adjacent districts
several distinct tribes had made their abode. The Menomonies were
on the river which bears their name; the Pottawattamies and Winne-
bagoes were near the borders of the bay; the Sacs, on Fox River; the
Mascoutins, Miamis, and Kickapoos, on the same river, above Lake
Winnebago; and the Outagamies, or Foxes, on a tributary of it flow-

ing from the north. Green Bay was manifestly suited for a mission; and, as early as the autumn of 1669, Father Claude Allouez was sent thither to found one. After nearly perishing by the way, he set out to explore the destined field of his labors, and went as far as the town of the Mascoutins. Early in the autumn of 1670, having been joined by Dablon, Superior of the missions on the Upper Lakes, he made another journey, but not until the two fathers had held a council with the congregated tribes at St. François Xavier; for so they named their mission of Green Bay. Here, as they harangued their naked audience, their gravity was put to the proof; for a band of warriors, anxious to do them honor, walked incessantly up and down, aping the movements of the soldiers on guard before the governor's tent at Montreal. "We could hardly keep from laughing," writes Dablon, "though we were discoursing on very important subjects; namely, the mysteries of our religion, and the things necessary to escaping from eternal fire." [18]

The fathers were delighted with the country, which Dablon calls an earthly paradise; but he adds that the way to it is as hard as the path to heaven. He alludes especially to the rapids of Fox River, which gave the two travellers great trouble. Having safely passed them, they saw an Indian idol on the bank, similar to that which Dollier and Galinée found at Detroit; being merely a rock, bearing some resemblance to a man, and hideously painted. With the help of their attendants, they threw it into the river. Dablon expatiates on the buffalo, which he describes apparently on the report of others, as his description is not very accurate. Crossing Winnebago Lake, the two priests followed the river leading to the town of the Mascoutins and Miamis, which they reached on the fifteenth of September.[19] These two tribes lived together within the compass of the same enclosure of palisades; to the number, it is said, of more than three thousand souls. The missionaries, who had brought a highly-colored picture of the Last Judgment, called the Indians to council and displayed it before them; while Allouez, who spoke Algonquin, harangued them on hell, demons, and eternal flames. They listened with open ears, beset him night and day with questions, and invited him and his companion to unceasing feasts. They were welcomed in every lodge, and followed everywhere with eyes of curiosity, wonder, and awe. Dablon overflows with praises of the Miami chief, who was honored by his subjects like a king, and whose demeanor towards his guests had no savor of the savage.

Their hosts told them of the great river Mississippi, rising far in the north and flowing southward,—they knew not whither,—and of many tribes that dwelt along its banks. When at length they took their departure, they left behind them a reputation as medicine-men of transcendent power.

In the winter following, Allouez visited the Foxes, whom he found in extreme ill-humor. They were incensed against the French by the ill-usage which some of their tribe had lately met when on a trading visit to Montreal; and they received the Faith with shouts of derision. The priest was horror-stricken at what he saw. Their lodges, each containing from five to ten families, seemed in his eyes like seraglios; for some of the chiefs had eight wives. He armed himself with patience, and at length gained a hearing. Nay, he succeeded so well, that when he showed them his crucifix they would throw tobacco on it as an offering; and, on another visit which he made them soon after, he taught the whole village to make the sign of the cross. A war-party was going out against their enemies, and he bethought him of telling them the story of the Cross and the Emperor Constantine. This so wrought upon them that they all daubed the figure of a cross on their shields of bull-hide, set out for the war, and came back victorious, extolling the sacred symbol as a great war-medicine.

"Thus it is," writes Dablon, who chronicles the incident, "that our holy faith is established among these people; and we have good hope that we shall soon carry it to the famous river called the Mississippi, and perhaps even to the South Sea." [20] Most things human have their phases of the ludicrous; and the heroism of these untiring priests is no exception to the rule.

The various missionary stations were much alike. They consisted of a chapel (commonly of logs) and one or more houses, with perhaps a storehouse and a workshop; the whole fenced with palisades, and forming, in fact, a stockade fort, surrounded with clearings and cultivated fields. It is evident that the priests had need of other hands than their own and those of the few lay brothers attached to the mission. They required men inured to labor, accustomed to the forest life, able to guide canoes and handle tools and weapons. In the earlier epoch of the missions, when enthusiasm was at its height, they were served in great measure by volunteers, who joined them through devotion or penitence, and who were known as *donnés,* or "given men." Of late, the number of these had much diminished; and they now relied chiefly on hired men, or *engagés.* These were employed in building, hunting, fishing, clearing and tilling the ground, guiding canoes, and, if faith is to be placed in reports current throughout the colony, in trading with the Indians for the profit of the missions. This charge of trading—which, if the results were applied exclusively to the support of the missions, does not of necessity involve much censure—is vehemently reiterated in many quarters, including the official despatches of the governor of Canada; while, so far as I can discover, the Jesuits never distinctly denied it; and, on several occasions, they partially admitted its truth.[21]

NOTES

[1] The following is the *acte de naissance,* discovered by Margry in the *registres de l'état civil,* Paroisse St. Herbland, Rouen: "Le vingt-deuxième jour de novembre, 1643, a été baptisé Robert Cavelier, fils de honorable homme Jean Cavelier et de Catherine Geest; ses parrain et marraine honorables personnes Nicolas Geest et Marguerite Morice."

La Salle's name in full was Réné-Robert Cavelier, Sieur de la Salle. La Salle was the name of an estate near Rouen, belonging to the Caveliers. The wealthy French burghers often distinguished the various members of their families by designations borrowed from landed estates. Thus, François Marie Arouet, son of an ex-notary, received the name of Voltaire, which he made famous.

[2] Margry, after investigations at Rouen, is satisfied of its truth. *Journal Général de l'Instruction Publique,* xxxi. 571. Family papers of the Caveliers, examined by the Abbé Faillon, and copies of some of which he has sent to me, lead to the same conclusion. We shall find several allusions hereafter to La Salle's having in his youth taught in a school, which, in his position, could only have been in connection with some religious community. The

doubts alluded to have proceeded from the failure of Father Felix Martin, S.J., to find the name of *La.Salle* on the list of novices. If he had looked for the name of *Robert Cavelier,* he would probably have found it. The companion of La Salle, Hennepin, is very explicit with regard to this connection with the Jesuits, a point on which he had no motive for falsehood.
[3] It does not appear what vows La Salle had taken. By a recent ordinance, 1666, persons entering religious orders could not take the final vows before the age of twenty-five. By the family papers above mentioned, it appears, however, that he had brought himself under the operation of the law, which debarred those who, having entered religious orders, afterwards withdrew, from claiming the inheritance of relatives who had died after their entrance.

[4] The Jesuits in North America, c. xv.

[5] *Transport de la Seigneurie de St. Sulpice,* cited by Faillon. La Salle called his new domain as above. Two or three years later, it received the name of La Chine, for a reason which will appear.

[6] A detailed plan of Montreal at this time is preserved in the Archives de l'Empire, and has been reproduced by Faillon. There is another, a few years later, and still more minute, of which a fac-simile will be found in the Library of the Canadian Parliament.

[7] The above particulars have been unearthed by the indefatigable Abbé Faillon. Some of La Salle's grants are still preserved in the ancient records of Montreal.

[8] *Papiers de Famille.* He is said to have made several journeys into the forests, towards the North, in the years 1667 and 1668, and to have satisfied himself that little could be hoped from explorations in that direction.

[9] According to Dollier de Casson, who had good opportunities of knowing, the Iroquois always called the Mississippi the Ohio, while the Algonquins gave it its present name.

[10] *Patoulet à Colbert,* 11 *Nov.,* 1669.

[11] *Cession de la Seigneurie; Contrat de Vente* (Margry, I. 103, 104).

[12] He was the author of the very curious and valuable *Histoire de Montréal,* preserved in the Bibliothèque Mazarine, of which a copy is in my possession. The Historical Society of Montreal has recently resolved to print it.

[13] See The Jesuits in North America.

[14] He complains that the Indians were very averse to giving information on the subject, so that the Jesuits had not as yet discovered the metal *in situ,* though they hoped soon to do so. The Indians told him that the copper had first been found by four hunters, who had landed on a certain island, near the north shore of the lake. Wishing to boil their food in a vessel of

bark, they gathered stones on the shore, heated them red hot, and threw them in, but presently discovered them to be pure copper. Their repast over, they hastened to re-embark, being afraid of the lynxes and the hares, which, on this island, were as large as dogs, and which would have devoured their provisions, and perhaps their canoe. They took with them some of the wonderful stones; but scarcely had they left the island, when a deep voice, like thunder, sounded in their ears, "Who are these thieves who steal the toys of my children?" It was the God of the Waters, or some other powerful manito. The four adventurers retreated in great terror; but three of them soon died, and the fourth survived only long enough to reach his village, and tell the story. The island has no foundation, but floats with the movement of the wind; and no Indian dares land on its shores, dreading the wrath of the manito Dablon, *Relation*, 1670, 84.

[15] *Lettre du Père Jacques Marquette au R. P. Supérieur des Missions;* in *Relation*, 1670, 87.

[16] The Illinois lived at this time beyond the Mississippi, thirty days' journey from La Pointe; whither they had been driven by the Iroquois, from their former abode near Lake Michigan. Dablon (*Relation*, 1671, 24, 25) says that they lived seven days' journey beyond the Mississippi, in eight villages. A few years later, most of them returned to the east side and made their abode on the river Illinois.

[17] The Baye des Puans of the early writers; or, more correctly, La Baye des Eaux Puantes. The Winnebago Indians, living near it, were called Les Puans, apparently for no other reason than because some portion of the bay was said to have an odor like the sea.

Lake Michigan, the Lac des Illinois of the French, was, according to a letter of Father Allouez, called Machihiganing by the Indians. Dablon writes the name Mitchiganon.

[18] *Relation*, 1671, 43.

[19] This town was on the Neenah or Fox River, above Lake Winnebago. The Mascoutins, Fire Nation, or Nation of the Prairie, are extinct or merged in other tribes. See The Jesuits in North America. The Miamis soon removed to the banks of the river St. Joseph, near Lake Michigan.

[20] *Relation*, 1672, 42.

[21] This charge was made from the first establishment of the missions. For remarks on it, see The Jesuits in North America and The Old Régime in Canada.

The Conspiracy of Pontiac

To the credulity of mankind each great calamity has its dire prognostics. Signs and portents in the heavens, the vision of an Indian bow, and the figure of a scalp imprinted on the disk of the moon, warned the New England Puritans of impending war. The apparitions passed away, and Philip of Mount Hope burst from the forest with his Narragansett warriors. In October, 1762, thick clouds of inky blackness gathered above the fort and settlement of Detroit. The river darkened beneath the awful shadows, and the forest was wrapped in double gloom. Drops of rain began to fall, of strong, sulphurous odor, and so deeply colored that the people, it is said, collected them and used them for writing.[1] A literary and philosophical journal of the time seeks to explain this strange phenomenon on some principle of physical science; but the simple Canadians held a different faith. Throughout the winter, the shower of black rain was the foremost topic of their fireside talk; and forebodings of impending evil disturbed the breast of many a timorous matron.

La Motte-Cadillac was the founder of Detroit. In the year 1701, he planted the little military colony, which time has transformed into a thriving American city.[2] At an earlier date, some feeble efforts had been made to secure the possession of this important pass; and when La Hontan visited the lakes, a small post, called Fort St. Joseph, was standing near the present site of Fort Gratiot. The wandering Jesuits, too, made frequent sojourns upon the borders of the Detroit, and baptized the savage children whom they found there.

Fort St. Joseph was abandoned in the year 1688. The establishment of Cadillac was destined to a better fate, and soon rose to distinguished importance among the western outposts of Canada. Indeed, the site was formed by nature for prosperity; and a bad government and a thriftless people could not prevent the increase of the colony. At the

Pages 212–22 (Little, Brown, 1884).

close of the French war, as Major Rogers tells us, the place contained twenty-five hundred inhabitants.[3] The centre of the settlement was the fortified town, currently called the Fort, to distinguish it from the straggling dwellings along the river banks. It stood on the western margin of the river, covering a small part of the ground now occupied by the city of Detroit, and contained about a hundred houses, compactly pressed together, and surrounded by a palisade. Both above and below the fort, the banks of the stream were lined on both sides with small Canadian dwellings, extending at various intervals for nearly eight miles. Each had its garden and its orchard, and each was enclosed by a fence of rounded pickets. To the soldier or the trader fresh from the harsh scenery and ambushed perils of the surrounding wilds, the secluded settlement was welcome as an oasis in the desert.

The Canadian is usually a happy man. Life sits lightly upon him; he laughs at its hardships, and soon forgets its sorrows. A lover of roving and adventure, of the frolic and the dance, he is little troubled with thoughts of the past or the future, and little plagued with avarice or ambition. At Detroit, all his propensities found ample scope. Aloof from the world, the simple colonists shared none of its pleasures and excitements, and were free from many of its cares. Nor were luxuries wanting which civilization might have envied them. The forests teemed with game, the marshes with wild fowl, and the rivers with fish. The apples and pears of the old Canadian orchards are even to this day held in esteem. The poorer inhabitants made wine from the fruit of the wild grape, which grew profusely in the woods, while the wealthier class procured a better quality from Montreal, in exchange for the canoe loads of furs which they sent down with every year. Here, as elsewhere in Canada, the long winter was a season of social enjoyment; and when, in summer and autumn, the traders and voyageurs, the *coureurs de bois,* and half-breeds, gathered from the distant forests of the north-west, the whole settlement was alive with dancing and feasting, drinking, gaming, and carousing.

Within the limits of the settlement were three large Indian villages. On the western shore, a little below the fort, were the lodges of the Pottawattamies; nearly opposite, on the eastern side, was the village of the Wyandots; and on the same side, five miles higher up, Pontiac's band of Ottawas had fixed their abode. The settlers had always maintained the best terms with their savage neighbors. In truth, there was much congeniality between the red man and the Canadian. Their harmony was seldom broken; and among the woods and wilds of the northern lakes roamed many a lawless half-breed, the mongrel offspring of the colonists of Detroit and the Indian squaws.

We have already seen how, in an evil hour for the Canadians, a party of British troops took possession of Detroit, towards the close of the year 1760. The British garrison, consisting partly of regulars and partly of provincial rangers, was now quartered in a well-built range of barracks within the town or fort. The latter, as already mentioned, contained about a hundred small houses. Its form was nearly square, and the palisade which surrounded it was about twenty-five feet high. At each corner was a wooden bastion, and a blockhouse was erected over each gateway. The houses were small, chiefly built of wood, and roofed with bark or a thatch of straw. The streets also were extremely narrow, though a wide passage way, known as the *chemin du ronde,* surrounded the town, between the houses and the palisade. Besides the barracks, the only public buildings were a council-house and a rude little church.

The garrison consisted of a hundred and twenty soldiers, with about forty fur-traders and *engagés;* but the latter, as well as the Canadian inhabitants of the place, could little be trusted, in the event of an Indian outbreak. Two small, armed schooners, the Beaver and the Gladwyn, lay anchored in the stream, and several light pieces of artillery were mounted on the bastions.

Such was Detroit,—a place whose defences could have opposed no resistance to a civilized enemy; and yet, far removed as it was from the hope of speedy succor, it could only rely, in the terrible struggles that awaited it, upon its own slight strength and feeble resources.[4]

Standing on the water bastion of Detroit, a pleasant landscape spread before the eye. The river, about half a mile wide, almost washed the foot of the stockade; and either bank was lined with the white Canadian cottages. The joyous sparkling of the bright blue

water; the green luxuriance of the woods; the white dwellings, looking out from the foliage; and, in the distance, the Indian wigwams
curling their smoke against the sky,—all were mingled in one broad
scene of wild and rural beauty.

Pontiac, the Satan of this forest paradise, was accustomed to spend
the early part of the summer upon a small island at the opening of
the Lake St. Clair, hidden from view by the high woods that covered
the intervening Isle au Cochon.[5] "The king and lord of all this
country," as Rogers calls him, lived in no royal state. His cabin was a
small, oven-shaped structure of bark and rushes. Here he dwelt, with
his squaws and children; and here, doubtless, he might often have
been seen, lounging, half-naked, on a rush mat, or a bearskin, like
any ordinary warrior. We may fancy the current of his thoughts, the
turmoil of his uncurbed passions, as he revolved the treacheries which,
to his savage mind, seemed fair and honorable. At one moment, his
fierce heart would burn with the anticipation of vengeance on the
detested English; at another, he would meditate how he best might
turn the approaching tumults to the furtherance of his own ambitious
schemes. Yet we may believe that Pontiac was not a stranger to the
high emotion of the patriot hero, the champion not merely of his
nation's rights, but of the very existence of his race. He did not dream
how desperate a game he was about to play. He hourly flattered himself with the futile hope of aid from France, and thought in his ignorance that the British colonies must give way before the rush of his
savage warriors; when, in truth, all the combined tribes of the forest
might have chafed in vain rage against the rock-like strength of the
Anglo-Saxon.

Looking across an intervening arm of the river, Pontiac could see
on its eastern bank the numerous lodges of his Ottawa tribesmen,
half hidden among the ragged growth of trees and bushes. On the
afternoon of the fifth of May, a Canadian woman, the wife of St.
Aubin, one of the principal settlers, crossed over from the western
side, and visited the Ottawa village, to obtain from the Indians a
supply of maple sugar and venison. She was surprised at finding
several of the warriors engaged in filing off the muzzles of their guns,

so as to reduce them, stock and all, to the length of about a yard. Returning home in the evening, she mentioned what she had seen to several of her neighbors. Upon this, one of them, the blacksmith of the village, remarked that many of the Indians had lately visited his shop, and attempted to borrow files and saws for a purpose which they would not explain.[6] These circumstances excited the suspicion of the experienced Canadians. Doubtless there were many in the settlement who might, had they chosen, have revealed the plot; but it is no less certain that the more numerous and respectable class in the little community had too deep an interest in the preservation of peace, to countenance the designs of Pontiac. M. Gouin, an old and wealthy settler, went to the commandant, and conjured him to stand upon his guard; but Gladwyn, a man of fearless temper, gave no heed to the friendly advice.[7]

In the Pottawattamie village, if there be truth in tradition, lived an Ojibwa girl, who could boast a larger share of beauty than is common in the wigwam. She had attracted the eye of Gladwyn. He had formed a connection with her, and she had become much attached to him. On the afternoon of the sixth, Catharine—for so the officers called her —came to the fort, and repaired to Gladwyn's quarters, bringing with her a pair of elk-skin moccasins, ornamented with porcupine work, which he had requested her to make. There was something unusual in her look and manner. Her face was sad and downcast. She said little, and soon left the room; but the sentinel at the door saw her still lingering at the street corner, though the hour for closing the gates was nearly come. At length she attracted the notice of Gladwyn himself; and calling her to him, he pressed her to declare what was weighing upon her mind. Still she remained for a long time silent, and it was only after much urgency and many promises not to betray her, that she revealed her momentous secret.

To-morrow, she said, Pontiac will come to the fort with sixty of his chiefs. Each will be armed with a gun, cut short, and hidden under his blanket. Pontiac will demand to hold a council; and after he has delivered his speech, he will offer a peace belt of wampum, holding it in a reversed position. This will be the signal of attack.

The chiefs will spring up and fire upon the officers, and the Indians in the street will fall upon the garrison. Every Englishman will be killed, but not the scalp of a single Frenchman will be touched.[8]

Such is the story told in 1768 to the traveller Carver at Detroit, and preserved in local tradition, but not sustained by contemporary letters or diaries. What is certain is, that Gladwyn received secret information, on the night of the sixth of May, that an attempt would be made on the morrow to capture the fort by treachery. He called some of his officers, and told them what he had heard. The defences of the place were feeble and extensive, and the garrison by far too weak to repel a general assault. The force of the Indians at this time is variously estimated at from six hundred to two thousand; and the commandant greatly feared that some wild impulse might precipitate their plan, and that they would storm the fort before the morning. Every preparation was made to meet the sudden emergency. Half the garrison were ordered under arms, and all the officers prepared to spend the night upon the ramparts.

The day closed, and the hues of sunset faded. Only a dusky redness lingered in the west, and the darkening earth seemed her dull self again. Then night descended, heavy and black, on the fierce Indians and the sleepless English. From sunset till dawn, an anxious watch was kept from the slender palisades of Detroit. The soldiers were still ignorant of the danger; and the sentinels did not know why their numbers were doubled, or why, with such unwonted vigilance, their officers repeatedly visited their posts. Again and again Gladwyn mounted his wooden ramparts, and looked forth into the gloom. There seemed nothing but repose and peace in the soft, moist air of the warm spring evening, with the piping of frogs along the river bank, just roused from their torpor by the genial influence of May. But, at intervals, as the night wind swept across the bastion, it bore sounds of fearful portent to the ear, the sullen booming of the Indian drum and the wild chorus of quavering yells, as the warriors, around their distant camp-fires, danced the war-dance, in preparation for the morrow's work.[9]

[1] Carver, *Travels*, 153. *Gent. Mag.* XXXIV. 408.

[2] *Memorial of La Motte Cadillac.* See Schoolcraft, *Oneota*, 407.

[3] A high estimate. Compare Rameau, *Colonie de Detroit*, 28.

[4] Croghan, *Journal*. Rogers, *Account of North America*, 168. Various MS. Journals, Letters, and Plans have also been consulted. The most remarkable of these is the *Plan Topographique du Detroit*, made by or for General Collot, in 1796. It is accompanied by a drawing in water-colors of the town as it appeared in that year. A fac-simile of this drawing is in my possession. The regular fortification, which, within the recollection of many now living, covered the ground in the rear of the old town of Detroit, was erected at a date subsequent to the period of this history.

[5] Tradition, communicated to H. R. Schoolcraft, Esq., by Henry Conner, formerly Indian interpreter at Detroit.

[6] *St. Aubin's Account*, MS.

[7] *Gouin' Account*, MS.

[8] Letter to the writer from H. R. Schoolcraft, Esq., containing the traditional account from the lips of the interpreter, Henry Conner. See, also, Carver, *Travels*, 155 (Lond. 1778).

Carver's account of the conspiracy and the siege is in several points inexact, which throws a shade of doubt on this story. Tradition, however, as related by the interpreter Conner, sustains him; with the addition that Catharine was the mistress of Gladwyn, and a few other points, including a very unromantic end of the heroine, who is said to have perished, by falling, when drunk, into a kettle of boiling maple-sap. This was many years after (see Appendix). Maxwell agrees in the main with Carver. There is another tradition, that the plot was disclosed by an old squaw. A third, current among the Ottawas, and sent to me in 1858 by Mr. Hosmer, of Toledo, declares that a young squaw told the plot to the commanding officer, but that he would not believe her, as she had a bad name, being a "straggler among the private soldiers." An Indian chief, pursues the same story, afterwards warned the officer. The Pontiac MS says that Gladwyn was warned by an Ottawa warrior, though a woman was suspected by the Indians of having betrayed the secret. Peltier says that a woman named Catharine was accused of revealing the plot, and severely flogged by Pontiac in consequence. There is another story, that a soldier named Tucker, adopted by the Indians, was warned by his Indian sister. But the most distinct and satisfactory evidence is the following, from a letter written at Detroit on the twelfth of July, 1763, and signed James Macdonald. It is among the *Haldimand Papers* in the British Museum. There is also an imperfect copy, found among the papers of Colonel John Brodhead, in the library of the Historical Society of Pennsylvania: "About six o'clock that afternoon [May 7], six of their warriors returned and brought an old squaw prisoner, alleging that she had given us false information against them. The major declared she had never given us any kind of advice. They then insisted on naming the author of what he had heard with regard to the Indians, which he declined to do, but told them that it was one of themselves, whose name he promised never to reveal; whereupon they went off, and carried the old woman prisoner with them. When they arrived at their camp, Pontiac, their greatest chief, seized on the prisoner, and gave her three strokes with a stick on the head, which laid her flat on the ground, and the whole nation assembled round her, and called repeated times, 'Kill her! kill her!' "

Thus it is clear that the story told by Carver must be taken with many grains of allowance. The greater part of the evidence given above has been gathered since the first edition of this book was published. It has been thought best to retain the original passage, with the necessary qualifications. The story is not without interest, and those may believe it who will.

[9] *Maxwell's Account*, MS.

RICHARD HILDRETH, AMERICAN UTILITARIAN
(1807–1865)

Richard Hildreth was a unique "scientific" historian for his day. The son of a liberal Congregational minister who later taught mathematics at Phillips Exeter Academy, he was born on a farm in Deerfield, Massachusetts, attended his father's school and Harvard before embarking upon a law career; and he then gave up law for journalism. He edited several Boston Whig papers in which he urged the causes of temperance, hard money, and antislavery. His legal education made it possible for him to translate a French treatise on Jeremy Bentham's Utilitarian theory of legislation based on the reformer's ideal of "the greatest good of the greatest number." The philosophy of Utility as applied to the writing of history began with the assumption that society is ruled by personal interests and classes; therefore, man served all society by pursuing his "enlightened self-interest." Benthamism favored free competition, the right of labor to organize, an enlightened penology, universal secular education, and a gradualist political democracy rather than revolution. These ideas are clearly reflected in Hildreth's own histories, which also followed Bentham's injunction that historians use an utterly detached style.

Hildreth went beyond the average Whig in fighting slavery, writing one of the earliest antislavery novels, *The Slave; or Memoirs of Archy Moore* (1836), as well as newspaper editorials on the subject. He came to know slavery from having lived in British Guiana and arraigned the planter's society in *Despotism in America* (1840), an ironic reversal of Tocqueville's title, *Democracy in America*. His other books included *The History of Banks* (1837), which called for the elimination of federally favored banking monopolies such as that of Nicholas Biddle.

Two of his books, *Theory of Morals* (1844) and *Theory of Politics*

(1853), were very revealing of his radical social philosophy. Most important of course was his six-volume *History of the United States of America* (1849–52) which, unlike Bancroft's similar work, was based exclusively on published work instead of original source material. While it did not add many new facts to our history, it more than made up for this by its original and highly tenable syntheses. He thought of himself as a scientific Benthamite and eschewed the florid style and romanticism of Bancroft in favor of a direct narrative and strict analysis, frequently from an economic point of view which anticipated Charles Beard's economic interpretation of the Constitution. He sympathized with the Indians, rejected chauvinistic viewpoints, and—surprisingly for a radical—took a critical view of Thomas Jefferson for liberal Utilitarian reasons.

The selections, taken from the first edition, reveal his hard-money bias in discussing Shays's Rebellion, his antislavery interpretation of the Constitution, and his economic emphasis. His *Theory of Politics* contains the startling socialistic question: "Is there never to be an Age of the People—of the working classes?" Possibly he had read the Communist Manifesto of 1848.

Theory of Politics

HOPES AND HINTS AS TO THE FUTURE

In the cursory view taken in a preceding chapter of the history of Christendom for the last eight centuries, we have found that period divisible, without any very great forcing, into four ages of two centuries each, during which the Clergy, the Nobles, the Kings, and the Burghers successively enjoyed a certain headship and predomi-

Pages 267–74 (Harper, 1877).

nancy. But, besides these four ruling orders, we have also, during these centuries, caught some slight occasional glimpses of another order, to wit, the mass,—the delvers, agricultural and mechanical, those who work with their hands,—in numbers, at all times and every where, the great body of the people, but scarcely any where possessing political rights, and even where, by some fortunate chance, they have gained them, for the most part, speedily losing them again.

The clergy, the nobles, the kings, the burghers have all had their turn. Is there never to be an *Age of the People*—of the working classes?

Is the suggestion too extravagant, that the new period commencing with the middle of this current century is destined to be that age? Certain it is, that, within the last three quarters of a century, advocates have appeared for the mass of the people, the mere workers, and that movements, even during this age of the deification of money, and of reaction against the theory of human equality, have been made in their behalf such as were never known before.

We may enumerate first in the list of these movements the indignant protest against the African slave trade, and the combination for its suppression into which the governments of Christendom have been forced, by the efforts of a few humane individuals, appealing to the better feelings of their fellow-countrymen, and operating through them on the British and American governments. It has, indeed, become customary, among the advocates of money making, no matter by what means,—in which category we must place some London newspapers of great pretensions,—to sneer at the attempted suppression of the slave trade as a failure. It is true, that, by the connivance of the Portuguese, Brazilian, and Spanish authorities with scoundrel merchants, British and American, the trade still exists. But what is it compared with what it would be did it enjoy, as formerly, the patronage and favor of all the flags? and how much longer is it likely to flourish?

We may mention next among these movements on behalf of the laboring class the abolition of chattel slavery in so many of the ultramarine offshoots from Europe; not alone by the strong hand of the slaves themselves, as in Hayti; not alone in consequence of protracted civil war,—a consequence generally pretty certain to follow,—as in the Spanish-American republics; but also from a mere sense of shame and wrong, as in the now (so called) free states of the North American Union; and from an impulse of humanity and justice, even at a heavy outlay of money, as in the British tropical colonies.

We may mention further the subdivision which has been carried so far, in France, of the lands of that country among the actual cultivators; a subdivision objected to by certain British economists, as not so favorable to the production of wealth, a point, however, not to be hastily conceded—but which unquestionably does tend to give to the cultivators a certain social importance and political weight.

Let us add the system of savings banks, by which the English laborers for wages have been enabled to invest their savings in a comparatively safe and easy manner, and thus to share in that accumulation of wealth which forms so important an element of power.

Add further the constant advance and development of manufacturing industry, giving employment and high wages to a class of laborers vastly superior in intelligence to the stupid and thoughtless rustics by whom the fields of Europe are generally cultivated—a class among whom have arisen those Chartists and Socialists whom we have had occasion to notice, towards the close of our burgher age, as claimants for political rights; a class, in fact, from which the larger portion of the existing burgher class has itself derived its origin.

Such are some of the social changes which may be regarded as precursors and signs of the approaching Age of the People.

If the mass of the people are ever to be raised above the servile position in which they have been so long and so generally held, there would seem to be only one way in which it can be permanently and effectually done, viz., by imparting to them a vastly greater portion than they have ever yet possessed of those primary elements of power, sagacity, force of will, and knowledge, to be backed by the secondary elements of wealth and combination. Nor does the prospect of thus elevating them appear by any means one altogether so hopeless.

Whatever objections may be made to the existing distribution of riches, and to the artificial processes by which it is regulated,—subjects which will form important topics of the *Theory of Wealth,*—this at least must be conceded, that no mere redistribution of the existing mass of wealth could effectually answer the proposed purpose of elevating the people. Any such redistribution, even if means could be found—and they could not—to prevent this equalized wealth from running back again, more or less, into masses, would still leave every body poor, at the same time that it cut up by the roots a great mass of industrious occupations. What is vastly more important than the distribution of the actually accumulated wealth, is the distribution of the annual returns of human industry. But no redistribution even of that—though it might sweep away the existing comfortable class —would suffice, very materially, to elevate the condition of the great body of the people. Above and beyond any of these schemes of re-distribution, in order to redeem the mass of the people from poverty and its incidents, a great increase in the amount both of accumulated wealth and of annual products is absolutely essential.

Here, indeed, we discover one great reason of the state of social depression in which the mass of the people have been, and still are, so generally held. The good things which the combined efforts of any given community can as yet produce are not enough to give hardly a taste to every body; and the masses have of necessity been kept at hard labor, on bread and water, while luxuries and even comforts have been limited to a few. Labor—the sole resource of the mass of the people—has been of little value, because labor has been able to produce but little; and the proceeds of the labor of production being so small, hence the greater stimulus to substitute in place of it fraud and violence as means of acquisition. The same man who will re-morselessly cut your throat in the struggle for the scanty waters of a rivulet in the desert, not enough for the whole thirsty and gasping company, would readily share his cup with you did the stream only run a little fuller.

The first great necessity, then, of the human race is the increase of the productiveness of human labor. Science has done much in that respect within the last century, and in those to come is destined to do vastly more. Vast new fields are opening on our American continent, on which labor can be profitably employed. So far from labor being the sole source of wealth, all-sufficient in itself, as certain political economists teach, nothing is more certain than that Europe has long suffered, and still suffers, from a plethora of labor—from being obliged to feed and clothe many for whom it has had nothing remunerative to do. The United States of America have now attained to such a development, that they are able easily to absorb from half a million to a million annually of immigrants from Europe. What is more, the laborers of Europe have found it out, and are rapidly emigrating. In so doing, not only do they change a barren field of labor for a fertile one, and at the same time relieve the pressure at home, but, by becoming themselves consumers, far more so than ever they were able to be at home, of the more artificial products of the countries from which they emigrate, they contribute doubly to raise the wages of those whom they have left behind.

The development of productive industry seems then to be at this moment one of the greatest and most crying necessities of the human race. But what is more essential to this development than peace and social order? It is not pusillanimity, then, on the part of the people of Europe, but an instinct, more or less conscious, of what they need most, that prompts them to submit for the present, without further struggle, to the rulers who have shown themselves to possess, for the time being, the power to govern—a power, let it be noted, quite too unstable, however, not to require, even in the view of those who possess it, great circumspection and moderation in its exercise. War and civil commotions, though sometimes necessary to the preservation of popular liberties, have very seldom indeed been the means of their acquisition; conspiracies hatched abroad, never. When the fruit is ripe, it will fall almost without shaking the tree. What prompts to anticipate that period is much oftener individual or class suffering or ambition than the true interest of the mass of the people. The greatest obstacle at this moment to the comparative political freedom of Europe, is the vast aggregation of power in the shape of standing armies. But how are these armies possibly to be got rid of, except by a certain interval of uninterrupted quiet, dispensing with their use, and such a contemporaneous increase in the value of labor as to make the maintenance in idleness of so many hands, instead of being, as it now is, a sort of substitute for a poor law, and a relief to the over-stocked labor market, a useless sacrifice, and an expense too great for any community to submit to?

It surely is not from barricades and street insurrections, provoking the murder of quiet citizens in their own houses, by fusilades and grape shot, in the name of peace and order, but rather from a more careful, comprehensive, and profound study of social relations, joined to an interval of peaceful coöperation in the production of great eco-nomical results, that we are to hope for the dispersion and extinction of those unfortunate and unfounded antipathies, so rife at present between those who labor with their heads and those who labor with their hands; those who plan and those who execute—antipathies growing out of prevailing but mistaken theories of politics and polit-ical economy, which, by dividing the party of progress into two hostile sections, filled with jealousy, fear, and hatred of each other, have contributed so much more than any thing else to betray Samson, shorn, into the hands of the Philistines—jealousies, fears, and hatreds, not only the chief source of the discomfitures recently experienced by the popular cause, but which, so long as they shall continue, will render any further advancement of it hopeless.

This socialist question of the distribution of wealth once raised is not to be blinked out of sight. The claims set up by the socialists, based as they are upon philosophic theories of long standing, having, at least some of them, many ardent supporters even in the ranks of those who denounce the socialists the loudest, cannot be settled by declamations and denunciations, and mutual recriminations, any more than by bayonets and artillery. It is a question for philosophers; and until some solution of it can be reached which both sides shall admit to be conclusive, what the party of progress needs is not action —for which it is at present disqualified by internal dissensions—but deliberation and discussion. The engineers must first bridge this gulf of separation before all the drumming, and fifing, and shouting in the world can again unite the divided column, and put it into effectual motion.

The History of the United States

[SHAYS'S REBELLION]

. . . Nor were there wanting artful, restless, discontented individuals, deceivers rather than deceived, such as always step forth on such occasions for the gratification of their own uncomfortable feelings, or for the sake of a little notoriety, to inflame public discontent, and to flatter popular delusions. The example of the Revolution so lately accomplished naturally enough suggested an appeal to arms and the overthrow of the existing state government as appropriate means for the remedy of social evils. To that point matters in Massachusetts seemed to be fast tending.

The same ideas prevailed also in the neighboring states. Under the new Constitution of New Hampshire, Mesheck Weare had been chosen president in 1784, succeeded in 1785 by John Langdon, and the next year by General Sullivan. An armed mob surrounded the Legislature, in session at Exeter, demanding a remission of taxes and an immediate issue of paper money—a project which the Legislature had referred to the people, but upon which no vote had yet been taken. The energetic promptitude of Sullivan succeeded in dispersing this mob without bloodshed.

Alarmed at the aspect of affairs in Massachusetts, Governor Bowdoin called a special session of the General Court. The malcontents had no open advocates in that body; but they were not without strong

Volume III, pages 473–7, 484, 507–18, 533–7 (Harper, 1880).

sympathy there. An attempt was made to satisfy them by yielding to several of their demands. Acts were passed diminishing the legal costs of the collection of debts, and allowing the payment of back taxes and of private debts in certain articles of produce at specified prices. As the passage of these acts did not seem to allay the public agitation, Bowdoin called out the militia to protect the sessions of the courts in the southern counties. The Habeas Corpus Act was suspended, not, however, without an address from the General Court, in which pardon for past offenses was offered to all who would give over unlawful proceedings.

This condition of things in Massachusetts attracted the very serious attention of Congress. It was feared that the malcontents, who were very numerous in the western part of the state, might seize the arms in the federal arsenal at Springfield, and muster in sufficient force to overturn the government. Under pretense of raising troops to act against the northwestern Indians, Congress voted to enlist thirteen hundred men to sustain the government of Massachusetts. A special requisition of about half a million of dollars was made upon the states for the support of these troops, on the credit of which a loan was authorized, it being understood that some wealthy men of Boston would advance the money. But the insurrection had already broken out before these troops could be raised.

Daniel Shays, late a captain in the Continental army, at the head of a thousand armed men or more, took possession of Worcester, and effectually prevented the session of the Supreme Court in that town. At the head of another smaller body, he repeated the same operation at Springfield; but, beyond preventing the session of the courts, these insurgents do not seem to have had any plan. Bowdoin called out at once four thousand militia, to serve for thirty days, under the command of General Lincoln. The necessary means to sustain these troops in the field were obtained by loan in Boston. In the depth of one of the severest of winters, the quotas of the eastern counties assembled at Boston, whence they presently marched to Worcester, on their way to Springfield, to relieve General Shepherd, who was guarding the federal arsenal there, at the head of a small body of western militia.

The malcontents had appeared in that neighborhood to the number of near two thousand men, in three bodies, under three different leaders, of whom Shays was the principal. The others were Luke Day and Eli Parsons, from the district west of the river. Shays demanded possession of the arsenal, and approached from Wilbraham to take it. Shepherd pointed some pieces of cannon against the advancing column; and, when the insurgents persisted in approaching, he gave orders to fire. The first discharge was over their heads; when the pieces were leveled at their ranks, a cry of murder arose from Shays's men, who broke and fled in confusion, leaving three killed and one wounded.

Upon Lincoln's approach the next day, the insurgents retreated toward Amherst. They were followed, but made good their retreat to Pelham, where they took post on two high hills, almost inaccessible by reason of the snow. The weather was very severe, and Lincoln turned aside to Hadley to put his troops under cover. Negotiations ensued. The insurgents offered to disperse on condition of a general pardon; but Lincoln had no authority to make such a promise. While this negotiation was still pending, the insurgents, hard pressed for provisions, broke up their camp and retreated to Petersham, on the borders of Worcester county. As soon as Lincoln was informed of this movement, at six o'clock the same evening he started in pursuit. Pushing on all night through a driving northeast snow-storm, he accomplished a march of forty miles, one of the most remarkable on record, and entered Petersham early the next morning, to the utter astonishment of the insurgents, of whom one hundred and fifty were made prisoners. The rest, having had a few minutes' warning, fled hastily by the northern road. Most of the leaders escaped into New Hampshire. The insurgents east of the Connecticut being thus dispersed, Lincoln moved into Berkshire, the extreme western county, where the malcontents were still more numerous.

Meanwhile the General Court had been called together in a new special session. A declaration of rebellion was put forth, and money was voted, and men also, to supply the place of Lincoln's militia, whose term of service would soon expire. The neighboring states were called upon to assist in arresting and dispersing the insurgents, some of whom lurked in their borders, whence they made plundering incursions into Massachusetts, proceeding even so far as to kidnap and carry off some of their most obnoxious opponents. Some eighty of these plunderers from New York, after an attack on Stockbridge, were intercepted by as many militia, and an action ensued, in which two were killed and thirty wounded. New Hampshire, Connecticut, and New York promptly complied with the request of Massachusetts to assist in arresting these refugees. Rhode Island and Vermont were more backward. Some of the leaders fled to Canada, but they found no countenance there.

A free pardon, on laying down their arms and taking the oath of allegiance, was offered to all who had served among the insurgents as privates merely or as non-commissioned officers, with deprivation, however, for three years, of the right to vote, to serve as jurymen, or to be employed as schoolmasters, inn-keepers, or retailers of ardent spirits. A commission was instituted, authorized to confer pardon, on such terms as they might see fit, on those not included in this offer —active leaders, those taken in arms a second time, or such as had fired upon or wounded any loyal subject of the commonwealth. Of those taken in arms and tried by the courts, fourteen were found guilty of treason and sentenced to death. Many others were convicted of sedition. None, however, were executed; indeed, the punishments inflicted, and the terms imposed by the commission above mentioned, of which seven hundred and ninety persons took the benefit, were in general very moderate. Harsh measures would not have been safe. At least a third of the population were thought to sympathize more or less with the insurgents; and even the slight penalties imposed upon those who submitted did not pass without serious opposition. At the ensuing general election the prevalence of these sentiments became very apparent. The energetic Bowdoin was dropped, and the popular Hancock was reinstated as governor. Many of those, also, who had been most zealous against the insurgents, lost their seats in the General Court.

These events, during their progress, had excited the liveliest interest throughout the Union, and they tended to confirm the impression, for some time past every where gaining ground, that some extensive political change was absolutely necessary. That which struck every body as the first and most essential step was the reorganization of the federal government, with powers adequate to its important functions.

Hardly, indeed, had the Articles of Confederation been adopted, when the Assembly of New York unanimously recommended a convention to revise and amend them, by giving to Congress an increase of authority. The General Court of Massachusetts had subsequently passed similar resolutions; but, by the representation of their delegates in Congress, had lately been persuaded to repeal them. . . .

[THE FEDERAL CONVENTION]

The Convention, as a whole, represented, in a marked manner, the talent, intelligence, and especially the conservative sentiment of the country. The democracy had no representatives, except so far as the universal American sentiment was imbued, to a certain degree, with the democratic spirit. Jefferson, the ablest and most enthusiastic defender of the capacity of the people for self-government, was absent in Europe, and that theory, of late, had been thrown a little into the shade by the existing condition of affairs, both state and national. The public creditors, especially, demanded some authority able to make the people pay; and, among a certain class, even monarchy begun to be whispered of as a remedy for popular maladministration.

The Assembly of Rhode Island, under the lead of men without education or sound judgment, and some of them without principle, wholly intent upon wiping out public and private debts by the agency of paper money, refused to elect delegates to the Convention; but a letter was read from some of the wealthiest men and most respectable citizens of that little state, in which they sent their good wishes, and promised their adhesion. . . .

The draft [of the Constitution], notwithstanding the instructions to the committee, instead of reporting property qualifications for office holders, left that matter to be settled by Congress. C. Pinckney "was opposed to the establishment of an undue aristocratic influence; but he thought it essential that the members of the Legislature, the executive, and the judges should be possessed of competent property to make them independent and respectable. Were he to fix the quantum, he should not think of less than $100,000 for the President, half as much for each of the judges, and in like proportion for the members of the Legislature." A motion which he made for inserting property qualifications, leaving the sums blank, was seconded by Rutledge; but the whole project was opposed by Franklin, and abandoned on the ground stated by Ellsworth, on behalf of the committee, that no property qualifications could be fixed that would answer equally well in all the states.

The disqualification for office of members of Congress during the term for which they were elected was very warmly opposed by Wilson, C. Pinckney, and Gouverneur Morris. Mason, Randolph, Sherman, and Gerry were equally zealous the other way. After a great deal of discussion, at different stages, this disqualification was finally limited to offices created, or the salaries of which had been increased during the term of membership; but no person could hold any civil office under the authority of the United States, and be, at the same time, a member of Congress.

A power given to Congress, in the draft, to emit bills of credit, was struck out on the motion of Gouverneur Morris. "If the United States had credit, such bills would be unnecessary; if they had not, unjust and useless."

By a subsequent clause, the emission of bills of credit by the states was expressly prohibited, or the making any thing but gold and silver a tender for the payment of debts—a proposition supported by Ellsworth and Sherman, who thought this a favorable opportunity "for shutting and barring the door against paper money." Such was the general sentiment; but Virginia voted against it. The restriction upon paper money, originally enacted by the British Parliament, was thus incorporated, in a form still more stringent, into the Federal Constitution. Prohibitions were added against the enactment, by the states, of tender laws, *ex post facto* laws, attainders, or laws impairing the obligation of contracts, the imposition of duties on imports, the granting titles of nobility, the issue of letters of marque and reprisal, the maintenance of troops or armed vessels in time of peace, or the formation of treaties with foreign powers.

The question who should control the militia excited a very warm debate. That subject was referred to a grand committee of one from each state, and upon their report, the clauses, as they now stand in the Constitution, were agreed to, authorizing Congress to provide for organizing, arming, and disciplining the militia, and calling them out to execute the laws of the Union, suppress insurrections, and repel invasions, but reserving to the states respectively the appointment of officers, and authority to train the militia according to the discipline prescribed by Congress.

But the subjects which excited altogether the most feeling were taxes on exports, the regulation of commerce, and the migration or importation of such persons as any of the states might choose to admit —in plain terms, the importation of African slaves. The southern states, exporting largely, were decidedly opposed to duties on exports, to which the northern delegates, those particularly from Pennsylvania, looked as an equitable and necessary source of revenue—an important means of paying the public debt. The eastern ship-owning states, in hopes to secure a preference over foreign shipping, were very anxious to empower Congress to enact navigation laws—a point as to which the middle states were comparatively indifferent; while the southern exporting states dreaded any such laws as likely to enhance the cost of transportation. The sentiment was common to Virginia and all the states north of it—at least among the intelligent and educated—that slavery was cruel and unjust; in plain violation of those rights of man proclaimed as the foundation of the Revolution, and inconsistent with the doctrines assumed as the basis of the American constitutions. The delegates from Virginia and Maryland hostile to export duties and to navigation laws, were still more warmly opposed to the African slave trade. In this feeling the delegates from the eastern and middle states concurred; but those from Massachusetts thought more about navigation laws, and those from Pennsylvania about the taxation of exports; while those from Connecticut were willing to make almost any sacrifice for the sake of getting the others to agree.

The prohibition of the African slave trade was no new idea. The Continental Congress, while releasing the colonies from other provisions of the American Association, had expressly resolved "that no slave be imported into any of the United States." So long as the war lasted, the British cruisers had effectually secured the observance of this resolution. Delaware by her Constitution, Virginia and Maryland by special laws, had prohibited the importation of slaves. Similar prohibitions were in force in all the more northern states; but they did not prevent the merchants of those states from carrying on the slave trade elsewhere, and already some New England ships were engaged in an infamous traffic from the coast of Africa to Georgia and the Carolinas. Intoxicated by the immediate profits of slavery, deluded by false hopes of a vast influx of wealth and population, and forgetful of the pledges made in the face of the world by their concurrence in the Declaration of Independence, Georgia and South Carolina were fully determined to maintain, not the institution of slavery only, but the African slave trade also. The further importation of slaves into North Carolina was not yet prohibited; but that state had shown a disposition to conform to the policy of her northern sisters, by an act which denounced the further introduction of slaves into the state as "highly impolitic," and imposed a duty on future importations.

The report of the Committee of Detail had very much inflamed the zeal of the northern delegates against slavery. They considered it a grievance indeed, that, while any restriction on the importation of Africans was forbidden, the South should be indulged by requiring a vote of two thirds for the enactment of navigation laws, and by the absolute prohibition of the taxation of exports. This feeling of dissatisfaction found expression at the earliest opportunity. When the apportionment clause came before the Convention in the new draft, King denounced "the admission of slaves as a most grievous circumstance to his mind, and he believed it would be so to a great part of the people of America. He had not made a strenuous opposition to it heretofore, because he had hoped that this concession would have produced a readiness, which had not been manifested, to strengthen the general government. The report of the committee put an end to all those hopes. The importation of slaves could not be prohibited; exports could not be taxed. If slaves are to be imported, shall not the exports produced by their labor supply a revenue to help the government defend their masters? There was so much inequality and unreasonableness in all this, that the people of the northern states could never be reconciled to it. He had hoped that some accommodation would have taken place on this subject; that at least a time would have been limited for the importation of slaves. He never could agree to let them be imported without limitation, and then be represented in the national Legislature. Either slaves should not be represented, or exports should be taxable.

Gouverneur Morris, still more vexed and disappointed, broke out into an eloquent denunciation of slavery. "It was a nefarious institution. It was the curse of Heaven on the states where it prevailed. Compare the free regions of the middle states, where a rich and noble cultivation marks the prosperity and happiness of the people, with the misery and poverty which overspread the barren wastes of Virginia, Maryland, and the other states having slaves. Travel through the whole continent, and you behold the prospect continually varying with the appearance and disappearance of slavery. The moment you leave the eastern states and enter New York, the effects of the institution become visible. Passing through the Jerseys and entering Pennsylvania, every criterion of superior improvement testifies to the change. Proceed southwardly, and every step you take through the great region of slaves presents a desert, increasing with the increasing proportion of those wretched beings. Upon what principle is it that the slaves shall be computed in the representation? Are they men? Then make them citizens, and let them vote. Are they property? Why, then, is no other property included? The houses in this city"—Philadelphia—"are worth more than all the wretched slaves that cover the rice swamps of South Carolina. The admission of slaves into the representation, when fairly explained, comes to this, that the inhabitant of Georgia and South Carolina, who goes to the coast of Africa in defiance of the most sacred laws of humanity, tears away his fellow-creatures from their dearest connections, and damns them to the most cruel bondage, shall have more votes in a government instituted for protection of the rights of mankind than the citizen of Pennsylvania and New Jersey, who views with a laudable horror so nefarious a practice. He would add, that domestic slavery is the most prominent feature in the aristocratic countenance of the proposed Constitution. The vassalage of the poor has ever been the favorite offspring of aristocracy. And what is the proposed compensation to the northern states for a sacrifice of every principle of right, every impulse of humanity? They are to bind themselves to march their militia, for the defense of the southern states, against those very slaves of whom they complain. They must supply vessels and seamen in case of foreign attack. The Legislature will have indefinite power to tax them by excises and duties on imports, both of which will fall heavier on them than on the southern inhabitants; for the Bohea tea used by a northern freeman will pay more tax than the whole consumption of the miserable slave, which consists of nothing more than his physical subsistence and the rag which covers his nakedness. On the other side, the southern states are not to be restrained from importing fresh supplies of wretched Africans, at once to increase the danger of attack and the difficulty of defense; nay, they are to be encouraged to it by an assurance of having their votes in the national government increased in proportion, and, at the same time, are to have their slaves and their exports exempt from all contribution to the public service. Let it not be said that direct taxation is to be proportioned to representation. It is idle to suppose that the general government can stretch its hand directly into the pockets of the people, scattered over so vast a country. They can only do it through the medium of exports, imports, and excises. For what, then, are all these sacrifices to be made? He would sooner submit himself to a tax for paying for all the negroes in the United States than saddle posterity with such a Constitution." He moved to confine the representation to free inhabitants.

Sherman "did not regard the admission of the negroes as liable to such insuperable objections. It was the freemen of the southern states who were to be represented according to the taxes paid by them, and the negroes are only included in the estimate of the taxes. This was his idea of the matter."

C. Pinckney considered the fisheries and the western frontier more burdensome to the United States than the slaves, as he would demonstrate, if the occasion were a proper one.

After this ebullition of feeling, Morris's motion being sustained by the vote only of New Jersey, the matter subsided till the clause was reached authorizing Congress to levy and collect taxes, duties, imposts, and excises. In haste to secure the prohibition to tax exports, Mason moved its insertion here. He argued warmly in favor of the prohibition, and was earnestly supported by Rutledge, Williamson, Mercer of Virginia, and Carroll of Maryland, but as earnestly opposed by Gouverneur Morris and Wilson, with whom Madison, though he expressed himself very cautiously, seemed to concur. Sherman, Ellsworth, and Gerry were willing to concede the prohibition, but thought it best to wait till that part of the report was regularly reached. This was done, and the prohibition was then carried, seven states to four, New Hampshire, New Jersey, Pennsylvania, and Delaware in the negative.

The clause coming up forbidding restrictions on the migration or importation of any persons whom any of the states might choose to admit, Martin moved to amend by allowing such importations to be taxed. "As five slaves, in the apportionment of representatives, were reckoned as equal to three freemen, such a permission amounted to an encouragement of the slave trade. Slaves weaken the union which the other parts were bound to protect; the privilege of importing them was therefore unreasonable. Such a feature in the Constitution was inconsistent with the principles of the revolution, and dishonorable to the American character."

Rutledge "did not see how this section would encourage the importation of slaves. He was not apprehensive of insurrections, and would readily exempt the other states from every obligation to protect the south. Religion and humanity had nothing to do with this question. Interest alone is the governing principle with nations. The true question at present is whether the southern states shall or shall not be parties to the Union. If the northern states consult their interest, they will not oppose the increase of slaves, which will increase the commodities of which they will become the carriers."

Ellsworth was for leaving the clause as it stood. "Let every state import what it pleases. The morality or wisdom of slavery are considerations belonging to the states. What enriches a part enriches the whole, and the states are the best judges of their particular interests. The old Confederation had not meddled with this point; and he did not see any greater necessity for bringing it within the policy of the new one."

"South Carolina," said C. Pinckney, "can never receive the plan, if it prohibits the slave trade. In every proposed extension of the powers of Congress, that state has expressly and watchfully excepted the power of meddling with the importation of negroes. If the states be all left at liberty on this subject, South Carolina may perhaps, by degrees, do of herself what is wished, as Maryland and Virginia already have done."

Sherman was, like Ellsworth, for leaving the clause as it stood. He disapproved the slave trade; but, as the states now possessed the right, and the public good did not require it to be taken away, and as it was expedient to have as few objections as possible to the proposed scheme of government, he would leave the matter as he found it. The abolition of slavery seemed to be going on in the United States, and the good sense of the several states would probably, by degrees, complete it.

Denouncing the slave trade with great energy, Mason sought to lay the blame of it on "the avarice of British merchants." "The present question," he said, "concerns not the importing states alone, but the whole Union. The evil of having slaves was experienced during the late war. Had slaves been treated as they might have been by the enemy, they would have proved dangerous instruments in their hands. But their folly dealt by the slaves as it did by the Tories. Slavery discourages arts and manufactures. The poor despise labor when performed by slaves. They prevent the immigration of whites, who really enrich and strengthen a country. They produce the most pernicious effect on manners. Every master·of slaves is born a petty tyrant. They bring the judgment of Heaven on a country. By an inevitable chain of causes and effects, Providence punishes national sins by national calamities. He lamented that some of our eastern brethren, from a lust of gain, have embarked in this nefarious traffic. As to the states being in possession of the right to import, that was the case with many other rights now to be given up. He held it essential, in every point of view, that the general government should have power to prevent the increase of slavery."

Mason's fling at the New England slave traders did not pass without retort. "As I have never owned a slave," said Ellsworth, "I can not judge of the effects of slavery on character; but if slavery is to be considered in a moral light, the Convention ought to go further, and free those already in the country. As slaves multiply so fast in Virginia and Maryland, it is cheaper to raise them there than to import them, while in the sickly rice swamps foreign supplies are necessary. If we stop short with prohibiting their importation, we shall be unjust to South Carolina and Georgia. Let us not intermeddle. As population increases, poor laborers will be so plenty as to render slaves useless. Slavery, in time, will not be a speck in our country."

Rutledge and the two Pinckneys declared that, if the slave trade were prohibited, South Carolina would not come into the Union. "South Carolina and Georgia," said C. C. Pinckney, "can not do without slaves. As to Virginia, she will gain by stopping the importation. Her slaves will rise in value, and she has more than she wants. It would be unfair to ask Carolina and Georgia to confederate on such unequal terms. The importation of slaves would be for the benefit of the whole Union. The more slaves the more produce, the greater carrying trade, the more consumption, the more revenue." Baldwin made a similar declaration on behalf of Georgia. She would not confederate if not allowed to import slaves. Williamson expressed his conviction that the two southern states, if prohibited to import slaves, would not become members of the Union. Wilson suggested that, if negroes were the only imports not subject to a duty, such an exception would amount to a bounty. Gerry thought the Convention had nothing to do with the conduct of the states as to slavery; but they ought to be careful not to give any sanction to it. Dickinson and Langdon, of New Hampshire, maintained that neither honor, safety, nor good conscience would allow permission to the states to continue the slave trade. King thought the subject should be considered in a political light only. If two southern states would not consent to the prohibition, neither would other states to the allowance. "The exemption of slaves from duty while every other import was subject to it, was an inequality that could not fail to strike the commercial sagacity of the northern and middle states."

This hint about a tax was not thrown away. Charles Pinckney would consent to a tax equal to that imposed on other imports, and he moved a commitment with that view. Rutledge seconded the motion. Gouverneur Morris proposed that the whole article, including the clauses relating to navigation laws and taxes on exports, should be referred to the same committee. "These things," he remarked, "may form a bargain among the northern and southern states." Sherman suggested that a tax on slaves imported would make the matter worse, since it implied they were property. Randolph supported the commitment in hopes that some middle ground might be hit upon. He would rather risk the Constitution than support the clause as it stood. Ellsworth advocated the article as it was: "This widening of opinions had a threatening aspect. He was afraid we should lose two states, with such others as might be disposed to stand aloof, should fly into a variety of shapes and directions, and most probably into several confederations—not without bloodshed." The motion for reference prevailed, and the article was referred to a grand committee of one from each state. The report of this committee retained the prohibition of export duties, but struck out the restriction on the enactment of navigation laws. Until the year 1800 it allowed the unrestrained migration or importation of such persons as the states might see fit to receive, subject, however, to the imposition of a duty by Congress, the maximum of which was presently fixed at ten dollars.

Williamson declared himself, both in opinion and practice, against slavery; but he thought it more in favor of humanity, from a view of all circumstances, to let in South Carolina and Georgia on these terms, than to exclude them from the Union. Sherman again objected to the tax as acknowledging men to be property. Gorham replied that the duty ought to be considered, not as implying that men are property, but as a discouragement to their importation. Sherman said the duty was too small to bear that character. Madison thought it "wrong to admit, in the Constitution, the idea that there could be property in man"; indeed, several changes of phrase were made on purpose to avoid any such implication. Gouverneur Morris objected that the clause as it stood gave Congress power to tax freemen; to which Mason replied that such a power was necessary, to prevent the importation of convicts. A motion to extend the time from 1800 to 1808, made by C. C. Pinckney and seconded by Gorham, was carried. . . .

[THE FEDERAL CONSTITUTION]

North Carolina and Georgia being now loudly called upon for cessions of their western claims similar to those made by the other claimant states, Georgia presently offered to cede all the territory west of the Chattahoochee, and between the thirty-first and thirty-second parallels of north latitude—a territory to which Georgia had, in fact, no right, it having been formerly included in the British province of West Florida, and being now in the occupation of the Spaniards. She demanded, in return for this barren cession, a guarantee of the remaining territory north of the thirty-second parallel, which Congress refused to give, or to accept her cession, unless so extended as to include all the district west of the Chattahoochee—a cession not finally obtained till several years after, and then only by purchase and on conditions very onerous to the United States. The office of governor of Georgia had been filled in successive years by Lyman Hall, chosen in 1783, John Houston, Samuel Elbert, Edward Telfair, and George Matthews, presently succeeded by George Handley and George Walton.

It still remained very doubtful what would be the fate of the

Federal Constitution in the states. The debates in the Convention at Philadelphia, like those formerly in Congress on adopting the Articles of Confederation, had evinced a conflict of local interests, a jealousy of state sovereignty, and a distrust and dread of any superior or superintending authority, by no means favorable to the new system. Those debates had been secret, and still remained so; but similar ideas and feelings might be expected to influence the state conventions. The extensive powers which the new Constitution proposed to vest in the federal government might seem to bear too strong a resemblance to that controlling authority of the mother country so lately shaken off, and each state might entertain doubts whether her own small share in the national sovereignty would prove a sufficient protection against the rapacity of that great power and authority proposed to be vested in the federal government.

Besides these obstacles to the adoption of the Constitution which had been equally obstacles in framing it, there existed out of doors, widely diffused among the people, a sentiment, which, in the Convention, except once or twice from Franklin, had hardly found the slightest expression. The members of that Convention, belonging almost exclusively to what is called the conservative class, had seemed to look upon property not so much as one right, to be secured like the rest, but as the great and chief right, of more importance than all others. The great evils of the times, in their eyes, were the inability of the state governments to collect taxes enough to fulfill the public engagements, and the "leveling spirit of democracy," denounced by Gerry, in his closing speech, as "the worst of all political evils." This very spirit of democracy the new Constitution must now encounter —a spirit which pervaded the mass of the people, and made itself felt in the state Legislatures, disposing them rather to throw off old burdens than to submit to new ones, and filling them with apprehensions lest personal freedom should be sacrificed to the interests of property, and the welfare of the many to the convenience of the few. Hence that widespread outcry, so generally raised, the most popular objection to the new Constitution, that it had no Bill of Rights, and was deficient in guarantees for personal liberty—a cry very loudly echoed by Patrick Henry and others in Virginia, and along with it the somewhat inconsistent cry, that Congress, under the new Constitution, would have the power to abolish slavery.

As a counterbalance to this feeling of doubt and distrust on the part of the body of the people, a very large proportion of influential citizens at once declared themselves in favor of the plan. It was warmly supported by the public creditors, who saw in it their only prospect of payment, and by the merchants, who hoped much from the regulation of commerce. The depressed state of industry, the dangerous disturbances which had lately broken out, the general sentiment of the inefficiency of the existing system, and the hope of remedy from almost any change—these considerations were not without influence upon many who had no by-ends to serve, and whose interest was identical with the public welfare.

The small local politicians, especially the advocates and spokesmen of the feelings and wishes of the less educated and less wealthy portion of the community, were, for the most part, opposed to a system which, by diminishing the consequence of the state governments, might also diminish their own. The advocates of paper money, and of stop and tender laws, took the same side, as did all those whose ruined and desperate circumstances led them to prefer disturbance and revolution to the preservation of social order. Even a large number of worthy citizens, including several of great eminence and influence, thought it better to run the risk of anarchy than to adopt a frame of government which seemed to them a dangerous instrument of tyranny, certain to lead to great abuses, if not to the very overthrow of liberty.

On behalf of the friends of the new Constitution, or, as they soon began to call themselves, the Federal party, a series of articles, entitled the "Federalist," written by Hamilton and Madison, with a few numbers by Jay, made their appearance in a New York paper. These articles, which defended the new frame of government with uncommon ability, and answered the various objections against it, were generally republished throughout the Union, and every where produced a deep impression.

Delaware was the first state to accept the Constitution—an example speedily imitated by Pennsylvania. The Constitutionalists, as they called themselves, the partisans of the existing state Constitution, were inclined to go against it; but their opponents had now a majority in the Assembly, and in the Convention of that state the Constitution was very ably defended by Wilson, who had taken so active a part in framing it. Ratifications by New Jersey, Georgia, and Connecticut followed. Trumbull had been succeeded as governor of Connecticut in 1784 by Matthew Griswold, and in 1785 by Samuel Huntington, who held the office for the next nine years.

The Continental Congress at length organized itself by the election of Cyrus Griffin, of Virginia, as president; but attention was absorbed by the proceedings in the states respecting the proposed Constitution, and there was seldom a quorum to do business.

The Massachusetts Convention was looked to with great interest, both on account of the close division of opinion in that state, and of the effect which a decision either way would have in the neighboring doubtful states of New York and New Hampshire. The clergy, lawyers, and merchants of Massachusetts, and the late Continental officers, were almost unanimous in favor of ratification. The Constitution was opposed by the friends of paper money, by those concerned in the late insurrection, of whom some fifteen or twenty, in spite of the Disfranchising Act, had seats in the Convention, and by many of the delegates from Maine, who feared lest it might prove an obstacle to their favorite project of becoming an independent state. Momentous as the question was, it seems to have turned, like so many other great political questions, more upon the passions and interests of the moment than upon its own distinctive merits. Yet here, as elsewhere, a substratum of principle and great lines of demarkation were plainly visible. The aristocracy of talents, wealth, and intelligence supported the Constitution; the democratic masses opposed or hesitated. Nor did they lack distinguished leaders. Gerry, who had refused to sign the Constitution, was allowed a seat in the Convention, to give information and make explanations. Governor Hancock, the president of the Convention, and Samuel Adams, were reckoned among the doubtful.

Adams was a great stickler for state rights, and very much of a Republican. Hancock leaned always to the popular side; and such was the influence of these two men, that their opinion either way would go far to decide the result. Their support was finally secured by means of nine proposed amendments brought forward by Hancock, and which the Convention recommended for the approval of Congress and the consent of three fourths of the states, as provided for in the Constitution. Under cover of these proposed amendments the ratification was carried, one hundred and eighty-seven yeas to one hundred and sixty-eight nays. . . .

George Bancroft (1800–1891), German Romanticism and the Literary Historians

George Bancroft, another descendant of the early New England settlers, was born in Worcester, Massachusetts, the son of a liberal Congregational minister who became the first president of the American Unitarian Association. He took his doctor's degree in theology and philology at the eminent University of Göttingen in 1820 and attended lectures at the University of Berlin, where he must have been particularly impressed by Hegel's philosophy of history. After four years in Europe, Bancroft returned to Cambridge where he was an unenthusiastic tutor at Harvard and an ineffective preacher. Together with another German-trained Harvard man, Cogswell, he opened the experimental Round Hill School, introducing the latest German-Swiss methods of progressive education such as foreign-language tables and supervised play. But this proved too advanced for his time and he gave up the enterprise.

Much more scintillating was his career as a historian and as a powerful Democratic politician and statesman. He escaped the aristocratic Whig atmosphere of Brahmin Boston that captivated most of the "literary historians" and shocked his acquaintances by turning toward workingmen's causes and by running for local office—usually unsuccessfully. His party services earned for him the post of Customs Collector of the Port of Boston, an important source of political patronage, and his influential efforts to nominate Polk in 1844 were rewarded by cabinet appointments as the latter's Secretary of the Navy and acting Secretary of War. As a Manifest Destiny man, he was an ardent expansionist and a vigorous supporter of the movement to acquire California and to expel Mexico from all the disputed territory north of the Rio Grande.

By this time, George Bancroft had also won a national reputation as a popular historian that eclipsed his political career. In 1834, when he issued the first volume of his ten-volume work on the history of the United States, plaudits came from both the intellectual and the ordinary literate reader. His later volumes benefited from his archival contacts and diplomatic experiences during his three years as minister to England and later as minister to Prussia. He was close to the makers of history, especially the Democratic presidents, and in 1865 he served secretly as President Johnson's "ghost writer" in preparing the significant Annual Message. In 1876 he revised his great historical work in a six-volume centenary edition, managing to correct his earlier errors and to tone down the more chauvinistic passages and purple prose. Some of it remained, however, as the second selection given here shows.

Throughout the series, one may discern the large pattern of Hegelian and romantic interpretation. He leaned upon the germ theory of history that he acquired in Germany: out of ancient Teutonic practices or "germs" there had evolved superior Anglo-Saxon and Anglo-American peoples and their distinctive democratic institutions. Protestant individualism and civil liberty had triumphed over Roman Catholic authoritarianism in the New World as in the Old. Directly or indirectly he borrowed from Hegel the Idealistic view of history which saw the pattern of development in the direction of the inevitable triumph of civil liberty guided by divine purpose. Ideas and principles, more than materialistic determinants, were the hard core of history. Hence economic history was minimized.

As a good Jacksonian he held a romantic notion of the inherent potentialities and wisdom of the common man, almost a literal notion that the voice of the people was indeed the voice of God. Like Hegel, he pictured historical events as part of a teleological "universal history" in which certain incidents are the starting place for the next development. But despite his cosmic generalities Bancroft could write vigorous, convincing, and concrete narrative that has attracted readers at all times.

A History of the United States

The western territory, of which England believed itself to have come
into possession, was one massive forest, interrupted only by rocks or
prairies, or waters, or an Indian cleared field for maize. The English
came into the illimitable waste as conquerors, and here and there in
the solitudes, all the way from Niagara to the Falls of the St. Mary
and the banks of the St. Joseph's, a log fort with a picketed inclosure
was the emblem of their pretensions. In their presumptuous eagerness to supplant the French, they were blind to danger, and their
posts were often left dependent on the Indians for supplies. The
smaller garrisons consisted only of an ensign, a sergeant, and perhaps
fourteen men; and were stationed at points so widely remote from
one another, that, lost in the boundless woods, they could no more
be discerned than a little fleet of canoes scattered over the whole
Atlantic, too minute to be perceptible, and safe only during fair
weather. Yet, feeble as they were, their presence alarmed the red man,
for it implied the design to occupy the country which for ages had
been his own.[1] His canoe could no longer quiver on the bosom of the
St. Mary's, or pass into the clear waters of Lake Huron, or paddle
through the strait that connects Huron and Erie, or cross from the
waters of the St. Lawrence to those of the Ohio, without passing by
the British flag. By what right was that banner unfurled in the west?
What claim to the red man's forest could the English derive from
victories over the French?

The French had won the affections of the savages by their pliabil-
ity and their temperance, and retained it by religious influence; they
seemed no more to be masters, but rather companions and friends.
More formidable enemies now appeared, arrogant in their pretensions,

Volume V, pages 110–33 (ten-volume edition, Little, Brown, 1837–74). Second
selection: Volume IV, pages 3–18 (six-volume edition, Author's Last Revision,
D. Appleton, 1883–85).

scoffing insolently at those whom they superseded, driving away their Catholic priests, and introducing the traffic in rum, which till then had been effectually prohibited. Since the French must go, no other nation should take their place. Let the Red Men at once vindicate their right to what was their own heritage, or consent to their certain ruin.

The wide conspiracy began with the lower nations, who were the chief instigators of discontent.[2] The Iroquois, especially the Senecas,[3] who were very much enraged against the English,[4] joined with the Delawares and Shawnees, and for two years [5] they had been soliciting the north-western nations to take up arms. "The English mean to make slaves of us, by occupying so many posts in our country," said the lower nations to the upper.[6] "We had better attempt something now, to recover our liberty, than wait till they are better established." So spoke the Senecas to the Delawares, and they to the Shawnees, and the Shawnees to the Miamis [7] and Wyandots, whose chiefs, slain in battle by the English, were still unavenged,[8] until every where, from the falls of Niagara and the piny declivities of the Alleghanies to the whitewood forests of the Mississippi [9] and the borders of Lake Superior, all the nations concerted to rise and put the English to death.[10]

A prophetic spirit was introduced among the wigwams. A chief of the Abenakis persuaded first his own tribe, and then the red men of the west, that the Great Manitou had appeared to him in a vision, saying "I am the Lord of Life; it is I who made all men; I wake for their safety. Therefore, I give you warning, that if you suffer the Englishmen to dwell in your midst, their diseases and their poisons shall destroy you utterly, and you shall all die." [11] "The Master of Life himself," said the Potawatomies, "has stirred us up to this war."

The plot was discovered in March by the officer in command at Miami; [12] and the Bloody Belt, which was then in the village and was to be sent forward to the tribes on the Wabash,[13] was with great difficulty, "after a long and troublesome" interview, obtained from an assembly of the chiefs of the Miamis.[14]

On receiving the news, Amherst, who had not much alertness or
sagacity, while he prepared reinforcements, pleased himself with calling the acts of the Indians "unwarrantable"; hoped they would be
"too sensible of their own interest" to conspire against the English;
and declared that if they did, he wished them to know that, in his
eyes, they would make "a contemptible figure." Yes, he repeated, "a
contemptible figure." The mischief would recoil on themselves, and
end in their destruction.[15]

But Pontiac, the colossal chief of the North West, "the king and
lord of all that country"; [16] a Catawaba [17] prisoner, as is said, adopted
into the clan of the Ottawas, and elected their chief; [18] respected, and
in a manner adored, by all the nations around him; a man "of integrity and humanity," [19] according to the morals of the wilderness;
of a comprehensive mind, fertile in resources, and of an undaunted
nature, persevered in the design of recovering the land of the Senecas,
and all west of it, by a confederacy of insurgent nations. His name
still hovers over the north-west, as the hero who devised and conducted their great but unavailing struggle with destiny for the independence of their race.

Of all the inland settlements, Detroit was the largest and the most
esteemed. The deep, majestic river, more than a half mile broad,
carrying its vast flood calmly and noiselessly between the strait and
well-defined banks of its channel, imparted grandeur to a country
whose rising grounds and meadows, plains festooned with prolific
wild vines, woodlands, brooks and fountains, were so mingled together that nothing was left to desire.[20] The climate was mild, and
the air salubrious. Good land abounded, yielding maize, wheat, and
every vegetable. The forests were a natural park, stocked with buffaloes, deer, quails, partridges and wild turkeys. Water-fowl of delicious
flavor hovered along its streams, which yielded to the angler an
astonishing variety of fish, especially the white fish, the richest and
most luscious of them all. There every luxury of the table might be
enjoyed at the sole expense of labor.[21] The lovely and cheerful region

attracted settlers, alike white men and savages; and the French had so occupied the two banks of the river that their numbers were rated even so high as twenty-five hundred souls, of whom five hundred were men able to bear arms,[22] or as three or four hundred French families;[23] yet an enumeration, in 1764, proved them not numerous,[24] with only men enough to form three companies of militia;[25] and in 1768 the official census reported but five hundred and seventy-two souls,[26]—an account which is in harmony with the best traditions.[27] The French dwelt on farms, which were about three or four acres wide upon the river, and eighty acres deep; indolent in the midst of plenty, graziers as well as tillers of the soil, and enriched by Indian traffic.

The English fort, of which Gladwin was the commander, was a large stockade, about twenty-feet high and twelve hundred yards in circumference,[28] inclosing, perhaps, eighty houses.[29] It stood within the limits of the present city, on the river bank, commanding a wide prospect for nine miles above and below.[30] The garrison was composed of the shattered remains of the eightieth regiment,[31] reduced to about one hundred and twenty men and eight officers.[32] Two armed vessels lay in the river;[33] of artillery, there were but two six-pounders, one three-pounder, and three mortars, so badly mounted as to be of no use, except to inspire terror.[34]

The nation of the Pottawatamies dwelt at about a mile below the fort; the Wyandots a little lower down, on the eastern side of the strait; and five miles higher up, but on the same eastern side, the Ottawas.

On the first day of May, Pontiac entered the fort with about fifty[35] of his warriors, announcing his purpose in a few days to pay a more formal visit. He appeared on the seventh, with about three hundred warriors, armed with knives, tomahawks and guns, cut short and hid under their blankets.[36] He was to sit down in council, and when he should rise, was to speak with a belt white on one side and green on the other;[37] and turning the belt was to be the signal for beginning a general massacre. But luckily Gladwin, had the night before been informed of his coming,[38] and took such precautions that the interview passed off without results. Pontiac was allowed, perhaps unwisely, to escape.

On the morning of the same day, an English party who were sounding the entrance of Lake Huron were seized and murdered.[39] On the eighth, Pontiac appeared once more with a pipe of peace, proposing to come the next day, with the whole Ottawa nation to renew his friendship. But on the afternoon of the ninth, he struck his tent, began hostilities, and strictly beleaguered the garrison, which had not on hand provisions enough for three weeks. "The first man that shall bring them provisions, or any thing else, shall suffer death." Such was Pontiac's proclamation of the blockade of Detroit. On the tenth there was a parley, and the garrison was summoned to capitulate to the Red Men as the French had done to the English.[40] Not till after Gladwin had obtained the needed supplies did he break off the treaty, and bid the enemy defiance,[41] yet leaving in their hands the unhappy officer who had conducted the parley. The garrison was in high spirits, though consisting of no more than one hundred and twenty men,[42] against six or seven hundred besiegers.[43]

And now ensued an unheard of phenomenon. The rovers of the wilderness, though unused to enterprises requiring time and assiduity, blockaded the place closely. The French inhabitants were divided in their sympathies. Pontiac made one of them his secretary,[44] and supplied his wants by requisitions upon them all. Emissaries were sent even to Illinois to ask for an officer who should assume the conduct of the siege.[45] The savages of the west took part in the general hatred of the English, and would not be reconciled to their dominion. "Be of good cheer, my fathers"; such were the words of one tribe after another to the commander at Fort Chartres;—"do not desert thy children: the English shall never come here so long as a red man lives." "Our hearts," they repeated, "are with the French; we hate the English, and wish to kill them all. We are all united: the war is our war, and we will continue it for seven years. The English shall never come into the west." [46] But the French officers in Illinois, though their efforts were for a long time unavailing, sincerely desired to execute the treaty of Paris with loyalty.

On the sixteenth of May, a party of Indians appeared at the gate of the fort of Sandusky. Ensign Paulli, the commander, ordered seven of them—four Hurons and three Ottawas—to be admitted as old acquaintances and friends. They sat smoking, till one of them raised his head as a signal, on which the two that were next Paulli seized and tied him fast without uttering a word. As they carried him out of the room, he saw the dead body of his sentry. The rest of the garrison lay one here and one there; the sergeant in his garden, where he had been planting—all massacred. The traders, also, were killed, and their stores plundered. Paulli was taken as a trophy to Detroit.[47]

At the mouth of the St. Joseph's the Jesuit missionaries, for nearly sixty years, had toiled among the heathen, till, at the conquest of Canada, they made way for an English ensign, a garrison of fourteen soldiers, and English traders, stationed on a spot more than a thousand miles from the sea, and inaccessible except by canoes or boats round the promontory of Michigan. On the morning of the twenty-fifth of May, a party of Pottawatamies from Detroit appeared near the fort. "We are come," said they, "to see our relatives and wish the garrison a good morning." A cry was suddenly heard in the barracks; "in about two minutes," Schlosser, the commanding officer was seized, and all the garrison, excepting three men,[48] were massacred.[49]

Fort Pitt was the most important station west of the Alleghanies. Twenty boats [50] had already been launched upon the Ohio, to bear the English in triumph to the country of the Illinois. For three or four weeks bands of Mingoes and Delawares had been seen hovering round the place. On the twenty-seventh of May, these bitterest enemies of the English exchanged with English traders three hundred pounds worth of skins for powder and lead, and then suddenly went away, as if to intercept any attempt to descend the river. On the same day, an hour before midnight, the chiefs of the Delawares having received intelligence from the west, sent their message to Fort Pitt, recounting the attacks on the English posts. "We are sure," they added, giving their first summons, "a party is coming to cut you and your people off; make the best of your way to some place of safety, as we would not desire to see you killed in our town. What goods and other effects you have, we assure you we will take care of, and keep them safe." [51]

The next day Indians massacred and scalped a whole family,[52] sparing neither woman nor child, and left behind them a tomahawk,[53] as their declaration of war. Fort Ligonier was threatened, and the passes to the eastward were so watched, that it was very difficult to keep up any intercourse while the woods resounded with the wild death halloos,[54] which announced successive murders.

Near Fort Wayne, just where the great canal which unites the waters of Lake Erie and the Wabash leaves the waters of the Maumee, stood Fort Miami, garrisoned also by an ensign and a few soldiers. Those who were on the lakes saw at least the water course which would take them to Niagara. Fort Miami was deep in the forest, out of sight and hearing of civilized man. On the twenty-seventh of May, Holmes, its commander, was informed that the fort at Detroit had been attacked, and put his men on their guard; but an Indian woman came to him, saying that the squaw in a cabin, but three hundred yards off, was ill, and wished him to bleed her. He went on the errand of mercy, and two shots that were heard told how he fell. The sergeant following, was taken prisoner; and the soldiers, nine only in number, and left without a commander, capitulated.[55]

On the thirtieth of May the besieged garrison of Detroit caught a hope of relief, as they saw a fleet of boats sweeping round the point. They flocked to the bastions to welcome their friends; but the death-cry of the Indians announced that the English party, sent from Niagara to reinforce Detroit, had, two nights previously, just before midnight, been attacked in their camp, on the beach, near the mouth of Detroit River, and utterly defeated, a part turning back to Niagara, the larger part falling into the hands of the savages.[56]

At eight o'clock in the night of the last day of May, the war belt reached the Indian village near Fort Ouatanon, just below Lafayette, in Indiana; the next morning the commander was lured into an Indian cabin and bound, and his garrison surrendered. The French, moving the victors to clemency by gifts of wampum,[57] received the prisoners into their houses.

At Michilimackinac, a spot of two acres on the main land, west of the strait, was inclosed with pickets, and gave room for the cabins of a few traders, and a fort with a garrison of about forty [58] souls. Savages had arrived near it, as if to trade and beg for presents. From day to day, the Chippewas, who dwelt in a plain near the fort, assembled to play ball. On the second day of June,[59] they again engaged in the game, which is the most exciting sport of the red men. Each one has a bat curved like a crosier, and ending in a racket. Posts are planted apart on the open prairie. At the beginning of the game, the ball is placed midway between the goals. The eyes of the players flash; their cheeks glow; their whole nature kindles. A blow is struck; all crowd with violence and merry yells to renew it; the fleetest in advance now driving the ball home, now sending it sideways, with one unceasing passionate pursuit. On that day the squaws entered the fort, and remained there. Etherington, the commander, with one of his lieutenants, stood outside of the gate watching the game, fearing nothing. The Indians had played from morning till noon; when, throwing the ball close to the gate, they came behind the two officers, and seized and carried them into the woods; while the rest rushed into the fort, snatched their hatchets, which their squaws had kept hidden under their blankets, and in an instant killed an officer, a trader and fifteen men. The rest of the garrison, and all the English traders, were made prisoners, and robbed of every thing they had; but the French traders were left at liberty and unharmed. Thus fell the old post of Mackinaw on the main.

The fort at Presque Isle, now Erie, was the point of communication between Pittsburg and Niagara and Detroit. It was in itself one of the most tenable, and had a garrison of four and twenty men,[60] and could most easily be relieved. On the twenty-second of June, after a two days' defence, the commander, out of his senses [61] with terror, capitulated; [62] giving up the sole chance of saving his men from the scalping-knife.[63] He himself, with a few others, were carried in triumph by the Indians to Detroit.[64]

The capitulation at Erie left Le Bœuf without hope. Attacked on the eighteenth, its gallant officer kept off the enemy till midnight. The Indians then succeeded in setting the blockhouse on fire; but he escaped secretly, with his garrison, into the woods,[65] while the enemy believed them all buried in the flames.[66]

As the fugitives, on their way to Fort Pitt, passed Venango, they saw nothing but ruins. The fort at that place was consumed, never to be rebuilt; and not one of its garrison was left alive to tell the story of its destruction.[67]

Nor was it the garrisoned stockades only that encountered the fury of the savages. They roamed the wilderness, massacring all whom they met. The struck down more than a hundred [68] traders in the woods, scalping every one of them; quaffing their gushing life-blood, horribly mutilating their bodies. They prowled round the cabins of the husbandmen on the frontier; and their tomahawks struck alike the laborer in the field or the child in the cradle. They menaced Fort Ligonier, at the western foot of the Alleghanies, the outpost of Fort Pitt. They passed the mountains, and spread death even to Bedford. The unhappy emigrant knew not if to brave danger, or to leave his home and his planted fields, for wretchedness and poverty. Nearly five hundred families, from the frontiers of Maryland and Virginia, fled to Winchester, unable to find so much as a hovel to shelter them from the weather, bare of every comfort, and forced to lie scattered among the woods.[69]

To the horrors of Indian warfare were added new dangers to colonial liberty. In Virginia nearly a thousand volunteers, at the call of the Lieutenant Governor, hastened to Fort Cumberland and to the borders; and the Lieutenant Governor of Maryland was able to offer aid.[70] The undecided strife between the proprietaries and the assembly of Pennsylvania checked the activity of that province. Its legislature sanctioned the equipment of seven hundred men, but refused to place them under the orders of the British general. Its design was rather to arm and pay the farmers and reapers on the frontier as a resident force for the protection of the country. This policy, from which it would not swerve, excited the utmost anger in the officers of the army.[71] Their invectives [72] against Pennsylvania brought upon it once more the censure of the king [73] for its "supine and neglectful conduct"; but the censure was no longer addressed to its government; for the ministry was firm in the purpose of keeping up an army in America, and substituting taxes by parliament for requisitions by the crown.

So the general, with little aid from Pennsylvania, took measures for the relief of the West. The fortifications of Fort Pitt had never been finished, and the floods had opened it on three sides. But the brave Ecuyer, its commander, without any engineer, or any artificers but a few shipwrights, raised a rampart of logs round the fort, above the old one, palisaded the interior of the area, constructed a fire-engine, and in short took all precautions which art and judgment could suggest for the preservation of his post.[74] The garrison consisted of three hundred and thirty men,[75] officers and all included, and was in no immediate danger,[76] but it was weakened by being the asylum of more than two hundred women and children.[77]

On the twenty-first of June, a large party of Indians made a vigorous though fruitless assault on Fort Ligonier; [78] the next day, before the issue of this attempt could have been heard, other savages appeared on the clear ground before Fort Pitt, and attacked it on every side, killing one man and wounding another. The night of the twenty-third, they strolled round the fort to reconnoitre it, and after midnight sought a conference.[79]

"Brother, the commanding officer," said Turtle's Heart, a principal warrior of the Delawares, "all your posts and strong places, from this backwards, are burnt and cut off. Your fort, fifty miles down (meaning Ligonier), is likewise destroyed before now. This is the only one you have left in our country. We have prevailed with six different nations of Indians, that are ready to attack you, to forbear till we came and warned you to go home. They have further agreed to permit you and your people to pass safe to the inhabitants. Therefore, brother, we desire that you may set off to-morrow, as great numbers of Indians are coming here, and after two days we shall not be able to do any thing with them for you." [80]

The brave commander, in his reply to this second summons, warned the Indians of their danger from three English armies, on their march to the frontier of Virginia, to Fort Pitt and to the north-west.[81]

A schooner, with a reinforcement of sixty men, had reached the Detroit in June; at daybreak of the twenty-ninth of July the garrison was surprised [82] by the appearance of Dalyell, an aide-de-camp to Amherst, with a detachment of two hundred and sixty men.[83] They had entered the river in the evening, and came up under cover of the night, or so small a command would have been intercepted, for the enemy were numerous, brave, and full of confidence from success.

At once, after but one day's rest, Dalyell proposed a midnight sally against the besiegers. He was warned that they were on their guard; but the opinions and express instructions of Amherst were on his side. "The enemy," said he, "may be surprised in their camp and driven out of the settlement." Gladwin expressed a very different judgment. "You may do as you please," said Dalyell, "but there is no difficulty in giving the enemy an irrecoverable blow." [84] Gladwin reluctantly yielded, and, half an hour before three o'clock on the last morning of July, Dalyell marched out with two hundred and forty-seven chosen men, while two boats followed along shore to protect the party and bring off the wounded and dead. They proceeded in double file, along the great road by the river side, for a mile and a half, then forming into platoons, they advanced a half mile further, when they suddenly received, from the breastworks of the Indians, a very heavy and destructive fire, which staggered the main body and put the whole into confusion. As the savages outnumbered the English, the party which made the sally could escape being surrounded only by an inglorious retreat. Twenty of the English were killed, and forty-two wounded; leaving to a peaceful rivulet the name of The Bloody Run, in memory of that day. Dalyell himself fell while attempting to bring off the wounded; [85] his body remained to the victors; his scalp became one more ornament to the red man's wigwam.

The victory encouraged the confederates. The wavering began to fear no longer to be found on the side of Pontiac; two hundred recruits joined his forces, and the siege of Detroit was continued by bands exceeding a thousand men.[86]

The vigor and courage that pervaded the whole wilderness was without example. Once more the Delawares gathered around Fort Pitt, accompanied by the Shawnees. The chiefs, in the name of their tribes and of the north-western Indians, for a third time, summoned the garrison to retire. "You sent us word," said they, "that you were not to be removed. Brothers, you have towns and places of your own. You know this is our country, and that your having possession of it must be offensive to all nations. You yourselves are the people that have disturbed the chain of friendship. You have nobody to blame but yourselves for what has happened. All the nations over the lakes are soon to be on their way to the Forks of the Ohio. Here is the wampum. If you return quietly home to your wise men, this is the furthest they will go. If not, see what will be the consequence; so we desire that you do remove off." [87]

The next day Ecuyer gave his answer. "You suffered the French," said he, "to settle in the heart of your country; why would you turn us out of it now? I will not abandon this post; I have warriors, provisions, and ammunition in plenty to defend it three years against all the Indians in the woods. Go home to your towns, and take care of your women and children." [88]

No sooner was this answer received than the united forces of the Delawares, Shawnees, Wyandots, and Mingoes closely beset and attacked the fort. With incredible boldness they took post under the banks of both rivers, close to the fort, where, digging holes, they kept up an incessant discharge of musketry and threw fire arrows. They were good marksmen, and, though the English were under cover, they killed one and wounded seven. Ecuyer himself was struck on the leg by an arrow.[89] This continued through the last day of July, when they vanished from sight.

Bouquet was at that time making his way to relieve Fort Pitt and reinforce Detroit. His little army consisted chiefly of the remains of two regiments of Highlanders,[90] who, having been wasted by the enfeebling service of the West Indies, were now to brave the danger of mountain passes and a slow and painful journey through the wilderness. He moved onwards with but about five hundred men, driving a hundred beeves and twice that number of sheep, with powder, flour, and provisions on pack-horses and in wagons drawn by oxen. Between Carlisle and Bedford they passed the ruins of mills, deserted cabins, fields waving with the harvest, but without a reaper, and all the signs of a savage and ruthless enemy.

On the twenty-eighth of July the party left Bedford, to wind its way, under the parching suns of midsummer, over the Alleghanies, along the narrow road, which was walled in by the dense forest on either side.

On the second day of August the troops and convoy arrived at Ligonier, but the commander could give no intelligence of the enemy. All the expresses for the previous month had been killed or forced to return.

Leaving the wagons at Ligonier, Bouquet, on the fourth of August, proceeded with the troops and about three hundred and fifty pack-horses. At one o'clock on the fifth, the savages, who had been besieging Fort Pitt, suddenly attacked the advanced guard; but two companies of Highlanders drove them from their ambuscade. When the pursuit ceased, the savages returned. The Western Nations, as if at the crisis of their destiny, fought like men contending for their homes, and forests, and hunting grounds, and all that they loved most. Again the Highlanders charged with fixed bayonets; but as soon as the savages were driven from one post they appeared in another, and at last were in such numbers as to surround the English, who would have been utterly routed and cut to pieces but for the cool behavior of the troops and the excellent conduct of the officers.[91] Night intervened, during which the English remained on Edge Hill, a ridge a mile to the east of Bushy Run, commodious for a camp except for the total want of water.

All that night hope cheered the Red Men. Morning dawned only to show the English party that they were leaguered round on every side. They could not advance to give battle; for then their convoy and their wounded men would have fallen a prey to the enemy: if they remained quiet, they would be picked off one by one, and crumble away miserably and unavenged; yet the savages pressed upon them furiously, and grew more and more audacious. With happy sagacity, Bouquet took advantage of their resolute intrepidity, and feigned a retreat. The red men hurried to charge with the utmost daring, when two companies, that had been purposely concealed, fell upon their flank; others turned and met them in front; and the Indians, yielding to the irresistible shock, were utterly routed and put to flight.

But Bouquet in the two actions lost, in killed and wounded, about one-fourth of his men,[92] and almost all his horses; so that he was obliged to destroy his stores, and was hardly able to carry his wounded. That night the English encamped at Bushy Run, and in four days more they arrived at Pittsburg. From that hour the Ohio valley remained securely to the white man.

Before the news of the last disaster could reach New-York, the anger of Amherst against "the bloody villains" knew no bounds; and he became himself a man of blood. "As to accommodation with the savages, I will have none," said he, "until they have felt our just revenge. I would have every measure that can be fallen upon for their destruction taken." Pontiac he declared to be "the chief ringleader of mischief." "Whoever kills Pontiac," he continued, "shall receive from me a reward of one hundred pounds"; [93] and he bade the commander at Detroit make public proclamation for an assassin. He deemed the Indians not only unfit to be allies, and unworthy of being respected as enemies, "but as the vilest race of beings that ever infested the earth, and whose riddance from it must be esteemed a meritorious act, for the good of mankind. You will, therefore," such were his instructions to the officers engaged in the war, "take no prisoners, but put to death all that fall into your hands." [94]

Had this spirit prevailed, the war would have for ever continued in an endless series of alternate murders, in which the more experienced Indian excelled the white man. The Senecas, against whom Amherst had specially directed unsparing hostilities, lay in ambush for one of his convoys about three miles below Niagara Falls; and on its return down the carrying-place, fell upon it with such suddenness and vigor that but eight wounded men escaped with their lives, while seventy-two were victims to the scalping-knife.[95]

The first effective measures towards a general pacification proceeded from the French in Illinois. De Neyon, the French officer at Fort Chartres, sent belts and messages, and peace-pipes to all parts of the continent, exhorting the many nations of savages to bury the hatchet, and take the English by the hand, for they would never see him more.[96]

NOTES

[1] Hutchinson to Richard Jackson, August, 1763.

[2] Sir Jeffery Amherst to Major Gladwin, New-York, 29 May, 1763. "The nations below, who seem to be the chief instigators of this mischief. "

[3] Sir Jeffery Amherst to Sir William Johnson, New-York, 29 May, 1763. "The Senecas seem to have a principal hand. *** Other tribes enter into plots againt their benefactors," &c. &c.

[4] Speech of the Miami chief, 30 March, 1763.

[5] Speech of Pontiac. Harangue faite à la Nation Illinoise, et au chef Pondiak, &c. &c. 18 Avril, 1765. Aubry to the French minister, 16 May, 1765. Gayarre Histoire de la Louisiane, ii. 131. The work of Gayarre is one of great merit and authority, built firmly upon trustworthy documents.

[6] Major Gladwin, commanding officer at the Detroit, to Sir Jeffery Amherst, Detroit, 20 April, 1763. "They say we mean to make slaves of them," &c. &c.

[7] Speech made by the chief of the Miamis Indians at the delivery of the belt of wampum, sent to them from the Shawnee nation, at Fort Miamis, 30 March, 1763. "This belt we received from the Shawnees, and they received it from the Delawares, and they from the Senecas."

[8] Speech of Hudson, a Cayuga chief, to Captain Ourry, in June, 1763.

[9] Speech of Tamarois, chief of the Kaskaskias, to Fraser, in April, 1765.

[10] Speech of the Miamis Indians, of 30 March, 1763.

[11] M. de Neyon à M. de Kerlerec, au Fort de Chartres, le 1er Décembre, 1763.

[12] Ensign Holmes, commanding officer at Miamis, to Major Gladwin, dated Fort Miamis, 30 March, 1763.

[13] Speech of the Miamis Chief, 30 March, 1763.

[14] Holmes to Gladwin, 30 March, 1763.

[15] Letter of Amherst to Major Gladwin, May, 1763.

[16] Rogers: Account of North America.

[17] William Smith to H. Gates, 22 November, 1763. Gladwin speaks of the Ottawa Nation as Pontiac's Nation. A less authority than that of Smith might not deserve to be regarded; but Smith is one of the accurate.

[18] Gladwin to Amherst, 14 May, 1763.

[19] Fraser to Gen. Gage, 15 May, 1765.

[20] Charlevoix, iii. 256. 4th edit.

[21] Mante, 524, 525.

[22] Rogers: Account of North America, 168. "When I took possession of the country, soon after the surrender of Canada, they were about 2500 in number, there being near 500 that bore arms, and near 300 dwelling houses."

[23] Journal of George Croghan, 17 August, 1765: "The people here consist of three or four hundred French families." Craig's Olden Times, 414.

[24] Mante's History of the War in North America, 525.

[25] Ibid., 515.

[26] State of the Settlement of Detroit, in Gage to Hillsborough, No. 2, of 15 May, 1768: "Number of souls, 572; cultivated acres, 514½; corn produced yearly, 9789 French bushels; horned cattle, 600; hogs, 567."

[27] Mss. in my possession, containing the Recollections of Madame Catharine Thibeau; "About sixty French families in all, when the English took possession of the country; not more than eighty men at the time; very few farms, not more than seven or eight farms settled." Memory is here below the truth. It usually exceeds.

[28] Rogers: Concise Account, 168.

[29] Croghan's Jour. in Craig, i. 414.

[30] Croghan's Jour. in Craig, i. 414.

[31] Mante's History, 485.

[32] Cass: Discourse before the Michigan Historical Society, from an ancient Diary. Carver, 155, says, 300.

[33] Weyman's New-York Gazette, 11 July, 1763.

[34] Cass: Discourse, &c. &c.

[35] Major Gladwin to Sir J. Amherst, 14 May, 1763, enclosure No. 9 in Amherst to Egremont, 27 June, 1768.

[36] Same to same.

[37] Mante's History of the War, 486.

[38] The lover of the romantic may follow Carver, 155, 156, or the improvements upon his story, made by tradition, till the safety of the fort became a tale of love on the part of a Chippewa girl for Gladwin, the commander. Gladwin simply says, "I was luckily informed the night before that he was coming," &c.

[39] Amherst to Gladwin.

[40] Weyman's New-York Gazette, 11 July, 1763, No. 239, 3 1. Gladwin to Amherst.

[41] Gladwin to Amherst, 14 May, 1763. Letter from Detroit of 9 July, 1763, in Weyman's New-York Gazette of 15 August, 1763.

[42] Weyman's New-York Gazette of 15 August, 1763.

[43] Gladwin to Amherst: "I believe the enemy may amount to six or seven hundred." His own number he does not give.

[44] Mante: History, &c. 486.

[45] See the N. B. to the account of the loss of the post of Miamis.

[46] Neyon to Kerlerec, December 1, 1763.

[47] Particulars regarding the loss of Sandusky, as furnished by Ensign Paulli after his escape, in the abstract made by General Gage.

[48] The number of the garrison appears from Edward Jenkins to Major Gladwin, 1 June, 1763. "Eleven men killed and three taken prisoners with the officer."

[49] Particulars regarding the loss of St. Joseph's, &c. "They massacred all the garrison except three men, in about two minutes, and plundered the fort."

[50] Captain Ecuyer, Commanding Officer at Fort Pitt, to Colonel Bouquet, at Philadelphia. Fort Pitt, 29 May, 1763.

[51] Intelligence delivered, with a string of wampum, by King Beaver, with Shingas, Weindohela, &c. &c., Delaware chiefs, at Tuskarawa's, 27 May, 1763, 11 o'clock at night. Bouquet to Amherst, 10 June, 1763. Amherst to Secretary of State, 27 June, 1763.

[52] Ecuyer to Bouquet, 29 May, 1763. Letter from Fort Pitt, of 2 June, in Weyman's New-York Gazette, 20 June, 1763. Ecuyer's Message to the chiefs of the Delawares.

[53] Ecuyer to Bouquet, 30 May, 1763.

[54] Declaration of Daniel Collet, horse driver, 30 May, 1763.

[55] Account of the Loss of the Post of Miamis, by a soldier of the 60th Regiment, who was one of the garrison.

[56] Lieutenant Cuyler's Report of his being attacked and routed by a party of Indians on Lake Erie. Major Wilkins to Sir Jeffery Amherst, Niagara, 6 June, 1763.

[57] Lieutenant Jenkins to Major Gladwin, Ouatanon, 1 June, 1763.

[58] Captain Etherington to Major Gladwin, Michilimackinac, 12 June, 1763. Etherington's account, contemporary and official, reports but thirty-five privates.

[59] "Yet, on the second instant"— Capt. Etherington.—Henry's Travels and Adventures in Canada and the Indian Territories, between the years 1760 and 1776. The author in his old age prepared this interesting work for press, and gave it to the public in October 1809. He makes the garrison consist of ninety; he gives the game of ball as on the king's birth-day; and makes it a trial of skill between the Sacs and Chippewas. These incidents heighten the romance of the story; but I think it better "to stoop to truth," and follow the authentic contemporary account. The letter of Etherington, as published in Parkman's Pontiac War, 596, reads, "Yet, on the 4th instant."

[60] "I left Ensign Christy six men to strengthen his party, as he had but eighteen men." Lieut. Cuyler's Report, &c., 6 June, 1763.

[61] "I am surprised any officer in his senses would enter into terms with such barbarians." Amherst to Bouquet, 7 July, 1763.

[62] Particulars regarding the loss of the post at Presqu' Isle. See also the account of the soldier, Benjamin Grey, in Ecuyer to Bouquet, 26 June, 1763.

[63] Mante's History of the War, 483.

[64] Particulars regarding the loss of the post at Presqu' Isle.

[65] Ensign Price to Col. Bouquet, 26 June, 1763.

[66] Weyman's New-York Gazette, 11 July, 239, 3, 1.

[67] Captain Ecuyer to Colonel Bouquet, Fort Pitt, 26 June, 1763. Ensign Price to Bouquet, 26 June, 1763.

[68] Letter from Fort Pitt of 16 June, 1763, in Weyman's New-York Gazette of 4 July, 1763, No. 238, 3, 2.

[69] Letter from Winchester of 22 June, 1763, in Weyman, 238, 3, 2, of 4 July, 1763. Correspondence of Lieut. Governor Fauquier of Virginia with the Board of Trade.

[70] Amherst to Bouquet, 25 August, 1763.

[71] Lieut. Governor Hamilton of Pennsylvania to Gen. Amherst, 7 July, 1763. Amherst to Hamilton in reply, 9 July, 1763. Hamilton to Amherst, 11 July. Amherst to Hamilton, 16 July. Lieut. Colonel Robertson's Report on his return from Philadelphia.

[72] Amherst to Bouquet, 6 June, 1763: "I wish the Assembly would as

effectually lend their assistance; but as I have no sort of dependence on them," &c. &c. Compare Bouquet to Amherst, 11 August, 1763: "Had the Provinces assisted us, this would have been the favorable moment to have crushed the barbarians, a service we cannot effect with our forces alone."

[73] Secretary of State to Amherst, October, 1763.

[74] Col. Bouquet to Sir Jeffery Amherst, 11 August, 1763,.

[75] Capt. Ecuyer to Col. Bouquet, 26 June, 1763.

[76] Col. Bouquet to Gen. Amherst, 3 July, 1763.

[77] Ecuyer to Bouquet, 26 June, 1763.

[78] Lieutenant Blane to Col. Bouquet, Ligonier, 28 June, 1763.

[79] Ecuyer to Bouquet, 26 June, 1763.

[80] Speech of The Turtle's Heart, a principal warrior of the Delawares, to Capt. Ecuyer, 24 June, 1763, at nine in the morning.

[81] Answer of S. Ecuyer, captain commanding.

[82] Major Gladwin, to Sir J. Amherst, Detroit, 18 August, 1763.

[83] Dalyell to Amherst, 15 July, 1763, quoted in Amherst to Gladwin, 10 August, 1763.

[84] Detail of the action of the 31 July, 1763, commanded by Captain Dalyell, against the Indian nations, near Fort Detroit, inclosed in Gladwin to Amherst, 8 August, 1763.

[85] Amherst to Secretary of State, 3 Sept. 1753.

[86] Major Gladwin to Amherst, Detroit, 11 Aug. 1763.

[87] Speech of Shingas, with the principal warriors of the Delawares, and Big Wolf, with Shawnees, to Captain Ecuyer, 26 July, 1763.

[88] Captain Ecuyer's Answer, 27 July, 1763.

[89] Col. Bouquet to Amherst, 11 August, 1763. Weyman's New-York Gazette, 29 August, 1763, 246, 2, 3.

[90] "I have therefore ordered the remains of the 42d and 77th regiment, the first consisting of 214 men, including officers, and the latter of 133, officers included, which will march this evening." Amherst to Bouquet, 23 June, 1763.

[91] Col. Bouquet to Sir Jeffery Amherst: Camp at Edge Hill, 5 Aug. 1763.

[92] Return of killed and wounded in the two actions at Edge Hill, near Bushy Run, the 5th and 6th August, 1763: total killed, 50; wounded, 60; missing, 5. Total of the whole, 115.

[93] Sir J. Amherst to Major Gladwin, 10 August, 1763: "You will make known to the troops under your command, that whoever kills Pontiac, who seems to have been the chief ringleader of the mischief, shall receive from me a reward of one hundred pounds."

[94] Sir Jeffery Amherst's instructions to Captain Lieutenant Gardiner, to be shown to Major Gladwin, &c. New-York, 10 August, 1763: "The Senecas,

* * with all the other nations on the lakes, * * must be deemed our enemies, and, used as such; not as a generous enemy, but as the vilest race of beings that ever infested the earth, and whose riddance from it must be esteemed a meritorious act, for the good of mankind. You will, therefore, take no prisoners, but put to death all that fall into your hands of the nations who have so unjustly and cruelly committed depredations. * * I have thought proper to promise a reward of one hundred pounds to the man who shall kill Pontiac, the chief of the Ottawas—a cowardly villain," &c. &c. Signed Jeff. Amherst.

[95] Return of the killed, wounded and missing in the action on the carrying-place, at Niagara, 14 Sept. 1763.

[96] Neyon et Bobé à Kerlerec, Dec. 1763. Neyon à Kerlerec, 1 Dec. 1763.

AMERICA TAKES UP ARMS FOR SELF-DEFENCE AND ARRIVES AT INDEPENDENCE

The hour of the American revolution was come. The people of the continent obeyed one general impulse, as the earth in spring listens to the command of nature and without the appearance of effort bursts into life. The movement was quickened, even when it was most resisted; and its fiercest adversaries worked with the most effect for its fulfilment. Standing in manifold relations with the governments, the culture, and the experience of the past, the Americans seized as their peculiar inheritance the traditions of liberty. Beyond any other nation, they had made trial of the possible forms of popular representation, and respected individual conscience and thought. The resources of the country in agriculture and commerce, forests and fisheries, mines and materials for manufactures, were so diversified and complete that their development could neither be guided nor circumscribed by a government beyond the ocean. The numbers, purity, culture, industry, and daring of its inhabitants proclaimed the existence of a people rich in creative energy, and ripe for institutions of their own.

They refused to acknowledge even to themselves the hope that was swelling within them, and yet in their political aspirations they deduced from universal principles a bill of rights, as old as creation and as wide as humanity. The idea of freedom had always revealed itself at least to a few of the wise whose prophetic instincts were quickened by love of their kind, and its growth can be traced in the tendency of the ages. In America, it was the breath of life to the people. For the first time it found a region and a race where it could be professed with the earnestness of an indwelling conviction, and be defended with the enthusiasm that had marked no wars but those for religion. When all Europe slumbered over questions of liberty, a band of exiles, keeping watch by night, heard the glad tidings which promised the political regeneration of the world. A revolution, unexpected in the moment of its coming, but prepared by glorious forerunners, grew naturally and necessarily out of the series of past events by the formative principle of a living belief. And why should man organize resistance to the grand design of Providence? Why should not the consent of the ancestral land and the gratulations of every other call the young nation to its place among the powers of the earth? Britain was the mighty mother who bred men capable of laying the foundation of so noble an empire, and she alone could have trained them up. She had excelled all the world as the founder of colonies. The condition which entitled them to independence was now fulfilled. Their vigorous vitality refused conformity to foreign laws and external rule. They could take no other way to perfection than by the unconstrained development of that which was within them. They were not only able to govern themselves, they alone were able to do so; subordination visibly repressed their energies. Only by self-direction could they at all times employ their collective and individual faculties in the fullest extent of their ever-increasing intelligence. Could not the illustrious nation, which had gained no distinction in war, in literature, or in science, comparable to that of having wisely founded distant settlements on a system of liberty, willingly perfect its beneficent work, now when no more was required than the acknowledgment that its offspring was come of age? Why must the ripening of lineal virtue be struck at, as rebellion in the lawful sons? Why is their unwavering attachment to the essential principle of their existence to be persecuted as treason, rather than viewed with delight as the crowning glory of the country from which they sprung? If the institutions of Britain were so deeply fixed in its usages and opinions that their deviations from justice could not as yet be rectified; if the old continent was pining under systems of authority not fit to be borne, and not ripe for amendment, why should not a people be heartened to build a commonwealth in the wilderness, where alone it was offered a home?

So reasoned a few in Britain, who were jeered at "as visionary enthusiasts." Parliament had asserted an absolute lordship over the colonies in all cases whatsoever, and, fretting itself into a frenzy at the denial of its unlimited dominion, was destroying its recognised authority by its eagerness for more. The majority of the ministers, including the most active and resolute, were bent on the immediate employment of force. Lord North, recoiling from civil war, exercised no control over his colleagues, leaving the government to be conducted by the several departments. As a consequence, the king became the only point of administrative union. In him an approving conscience had no misgiving as to his duty. His heart knew no relenting; his will never wavered. Though America were to be drenched in blood and its towns reduced to ashes, though its people were to be driven to struggle for total independence, though he himself should find it necessary to bid high for hosts of mercenaries from the Scheldt to Moscow, and in quest of savage allies go tapping at every wigwam from Lake Huron to the Gulf of Mexico, he was resolved to coerce the thirteen colonies into submission.

On the tenth of May 1774, which was the day of the accession of Louis XVI, the act closing the port of Boston, transferring the board of customs to Marblehead, and the seat of government to Salem, reached the devoted town. The king was confident that the slow torture which was to be applied to its inhabitants would constrain them to cry out for mercy and promise unconditional obedience. Success in resistance could come only from an American union, which was not to be hoped for, unless Boston should offer herself as a willing sacrifice. The mechanics and merchants and laborers, altogether scarcely so many as thirty-five hundred able-bodied men, knew that they were acting not for a province of America, but for freedom itself. They were inspired by the thought that the Providence which rules the world demanded of them heroic self-denial as the champions of humanity, and they never doubted the fellow-feeling of the continent.

As soon as the act was received, the Boston committee of correspondence, by the hand of Joseph Warren, invited eight neighboring towns to a conference "on the critical state of public affairs." On the twelfth, at noon, Metcalf Bowler, the speaker of the assembly of Rhode Island, came before them with the cheering news that, in answer to a recent circular letter from the body over which he presided, all the thirteen governments had pledged themselves to union. Punctually, at the hour of three in the afternoon of that day, the committees of Dorchester, Roxbury, Brookline, Newton, Cambridge, Charlestown, Lynn, and Lexington, joined them in Faneuil Hall, the cradle of American liberty, where for ten years the freemen of the town had debated the question of justifiable resistance. The lowly men who now met there were most of them accustomed to feed their own cattle, to fold their own sheep, to guide their own ploughs; all were trained to public life in the little democracies of their towns; some of them were captains in the militia and officers of the church according to the discipline of Congregationalists; nearly all of them communicants, under a public covenant with God. They grew in greatness as their sphere enlarged. Their virtues burst the confines of village life. They felt themselves to be citizens not of little municipalities, but of the whole world of mankind. In the dark hour, light broke upon them from their own truth and courage. Placing Samuel Adams at their head, and guided by a report prepared by Joseph Warren of Boston, Thomas Gardner of Cambridge, and others, they agreed unanimously on the injustice and cruelty of the act, by which parliament, without competent jurisdiction and contrary as well to natural right as to the laws of all civilized states, had, without a hearing, set apart, accused, tried, and condemned the town of Boston. The delegates from the eight towns were reminded by those of Boston that that port could recover its trade by paying for the tea which had been thrown overboard; but they held it unworthy even to notice the offer, promising on their part to join "their suffering brethren in every measure of relief."

The meeting knew that a declaration of independence would have alienated their sister colonies, nor had they as yet found out that independence was the desire of their own hearts. To suggest nothing till a congress could be convened would have seemed to them like abandoning the town to bleed away its life. The king had expected to starve its people into submission; in their circular letter to the committees of the other colonies they proposed, as a counter action, a general cessation of trade with Britain. "Now," they added, "is the time when all should be united in opposition to this violation of the liberties of all. The single question is, whether you consider Boston as suffering in the common cause, and sensibly feel and resent the injury and affront offered to her? We cannot believe otherwise; assuring you that, not in the least intimidated by this inhuman treatment, we are still determined to maintain to the utmost of our abilities the rights of America."

The next day, while Gage was sailing into the harbor, Samuel Adams presided over a very numerous town-meeting, at which many were present who had hitherto kept aloof. The thought of republican Rome, in its purest age, animated their consultations. The port act was read, and in bold debate was pronounced repugnant to law, religion, and common sense. At the same time those, who from loss of employment were to be the first to encounter want, were remembered with tender compassion, and measures were put in train to comfort them. Then the inhabitants, by the hand of Samuel Adams, made their appeal "to all the sister colonies, inviting a universal suspension of exports and imports, promising to suffer for America with a becoming fortitude, confessing that singly they might find their trial too severe, and entreating not to be left to struggle alone, when the very being of every colony, considered as a free people, depended upon the event."

On the seventeenth, Gage, who had remained four days with Hutchinson at Castle William, landed at Long Wharf, amid salutes from ships and batteries. Received by the council and civil officers, he was escorted by the Boston cadets, whom Hancock commanded, to the state-house, where the council presented a loyal address, and his commission was proclaimed with three volleys of musketry and as many cheers. He then partook of a public dinner in Faneuil Hall, at which he proposed "the prosperity of the town of Boston." His toast in honor of Hutchinson "was received with a general hiss." Yet many favored a compromise, and put forward a subscription to pay for the tea. On the eighteenth, Jonathan Amory very strongly urged that measure in town-meeting, but it was rejected by the common voice. There still lingered a hope of relief through the intercession of Gage; but he was fit neither to reconcile nor to subdue. By his mild temper and love of society he gained the good-will of his boon companions and escaped personal enmities; but in earnest business he inspired neither confidence nor fear. He was so poor in spirit and so weak of will, so dull in his perceptions and so unsettled in his opinions, that he was sure to vacillate between words of concession and merciless severity. He had promised the king that with four regiments he would play the "lion," and troops beyond his requisition were hourly expected; but he stood too much in dread of the leading patriots of Boston to attempt their arrest.

The people of Massachusetts were almost exclusively of English origin; beyond any other colony, they loved the land of their ancestors; for that reason were they more sensitive to its tyranny. Taxing them without their consent was robbing them of their birthright; they scorned the British parliament as "a junto of the servants of the crown, rather than the representatives of England." Not disguising to themselves their danger, but confident of victory, they were resolved to stand together as brothers for a life of liberty.

The merchants of Newburyport were the first who agreed to suspend all commerce with Britain and Ireland. Salem, the place marked out as the new seat of government, in a very full town-meeting and after unimpassioned debates, decided almost unanimously to stop trade not with Britain only, but even with the West Indies. If in Boston a few still proposed to purchase a relaxation of the blockade by "a subscription to pay for the tea," the majority were beset by no temptation so strong as that of routing at once the insignificant number of troops who had come to overawe them. But Samuel Adams, while he compared their spirit to that of Sparta or Rome, inculcated "patience as the characteristic of a patriot"; and the people, having sent forth their cry to the continent, waited self-possessed for voices of consolation.

New York anticipated the prayer of Boston. Its people, who had received the port act directly from England, felt the wrong to that town as a wound to themselves, and even the lukewarm kindled with resentment. From the epoch of the stamp act, their Sons of Liberty, styled by the royalists "the Presbyterian junto," had kept up a committee of correspondence. Yet Sears, Macdougall, and Lamb, still its principal members, represented the mechanics of the city more than its merchants; and they never enjoyed the confidence of the great landed proprietors, who by the tenure of estates in New York formed a recognised aristocracy. To unite the province, a more comprehensive combination was required. The old committee, while they accepted the questionable policy of an immediate suspension of commerce with Britain, proposed, and they were the first to propose, "a general congress." These recommendations they forwarded through Connecticut to Boston, with entreaties to that town to stand firm; and, in full confidence of approval, they sent them to Philadelphia, and through Philadelphia to every colony at the south.

The inception of the continental congress of 1774 was the last achievement of the Sons of Liberty of New York. On the evening of the sixteenth of May they convoked the inhabitants of their city. A sense of the impending change tempered passionate rashness. Some who were in a secret understanding with officers of the crown sought to evade all decisive measures; the merchants were averse to headlong engagements for suspending trade; the gentry feared lest the men who on all former occasions had led the multitude should preserve the control in the day which was felt to be near at hand, when an independent people would shape the permanent institutions of a continent. Under a conservative influence, the motion prevailed to supersede the old committee of correspondence by a new one of fifty, and its members were selected by open nomination. The choice included men from all classes. Nearly a third part were of those who followed the British standard to the last; others were lukewarm, unsteady, and blind to the nearness of revolution; others again were enthusiastic Sons of Liberty. The friends to government claimed that the majority was inflexibly loyal; the control fell into the hands of men who still aimed at reconciling a continued dependence on England with the just freedom of the colonies.

The port act was rapidly circulated through the country. In some places it was printed upon paper with a black border, and cried about the streets as a barbarous murder; in others, it was burnt in the presence of a crowd of the people. On the seventeenth, the representatives of Connecticut made a declaration of rights. "Let us play the man," said they, "for the cause of our country; and trust the event to Him who orders all events for the best good of his people." On the same day, the freemen of the town of Providence, unsolicited from abroad and after full discussion, voted to promote "a congress of the representatives of all the North American colonies." Declaring "personal liberty an essential part of the natural rights of mankind," they expressed the wish to prohibit the importation of negro slaves, and to set free all negroes born in the colony.

On the nineteenth, the city and county of New York inaugurated their new committee with the formality of public approval. Two parties appeared in array: on the one side, men of property; on the other, tradesmen and mechanics. Foreboding a revolution, they seemed to contend in advance whether their future government should be formed upon the basis of property or on purely popular principles. The mass of the people were ready to found a new social order in which they would rule; but on that day they chose to follow the wealthier class if it would but make with them a common cause; and the nomination of the committee was accepted, even with the addition of Isaac Low as its chairman, who was more of a loyalist than a patriot.

In Philadelphia, where Wedderburn and Hutchinson had been burnt in effigy, the letter from the New York Sons of Liberty had been received, and when, on the nineteenth, the messenger from Boston arrived with despatches, he found Charles Thomson, Thomas

Mifflin, Joseph Reed, and others preparing to call a public meeting on the evening of the next day.

On the morning of the twentieth, the king gave in person his assent to the act which made the British commander-in-chief in America, his army, and the civil officers, no longer amenable to American courts of justice; and to the act which mutilated the charter of Massachusetts, and destroyed the freedom of its town-meetings. "The law," wrote Garnier, "the extremely intelligent" French chargé, "must either lead to the complete reduction of the colonies, or clear the way for their independence." "I wish from the bottom of my heart," said the duke of Richmond, during a debate in the house of lords, "that the Americans may resist, and get the better of the forces sent against them." Four years later, Fox observed: "The alteration of the government of Massachusetts was certainly a most capital mistake, because it gave the whole continent reason to think that their government was liable to be subverted at our pleasure and rendered entirely despotic. From thence all were taught to consider the town of Boston as suffering in the common cause."

While the king, in the presence of parliament, was accepting the laws which began a civil war, in Philadelphia the Presbyterians, true to their traditions, held it right to resist tyranny; "the Germans, who composed a large part of the inhabitants of the province, were all on the side of liberty"; the merchants refused to sacrifice their trade; the Quakers in any event scrupled to use arms; a numerous class, like Reed, cherished the most passionate desire for a reconciliation with the mother country. The cause of America needed intrepid counsellors; but the great central state fell under the influence of Dickinson. His claims to public respect were indisputable. He was honored for spotless morals, eloquence, and good service in the colonial legislature. His writings had endeared him to America as a sincere friend of liberty. Residing at a country seat which overlooked Philadelphia and the Delaware river, he delighted in study and repose, and wanted boldness of will. "He had an excellent heart, and the cause of his country lay near it"; "he loved the people of Boston with the tenderness of a brother"; yet he was more jealous of their zeal than touched by their sorrows. "They will have time enough to die," were his words on that morning. "Let them give the other provinces opportunity to think and resolve. If they expect to drag them by their own violence into mad measures, they will be left to perish by themselves, despised by their enemies, and almost detested by their friends." Having matured his scheme in solitude, he received at dinner Thomson, Mifflin, and Reed, who, for the sake of his public co-operation, acquiesced in his delays.

In the evening, about three hundred of the principal citizens of Philadelphia assembled in the long room of the City Tavern. The letter from the Sons of Liberty of New York was read aloud, as well as the letters from Boston. Two measures were thus brought under discussion: that of New York for a congress, that of Boston for an immediate cessation of trade. The latter proposition was received with loud and general murmurs. Dickinson, having conciliated the wavering merchants by expressing himself strongly against it, was heard with applause as he spoke for a general congress. He insisted, however, on a preliminary petition to his friend John Penn, the proprietary governor, to call together the legislature of the colony. This request every one knew would be refused. But then, reasoned Mifflin and the ardent politicians, a committee of correspondence, after the model of Boston, must, in consequence of the refusal, be named for the several counties in the province. Delegates will then be appointed to a general congress; "and, when the colonies are once united in councils, what may they not effect?" At an early hour Dickinson retired from the meeting, of which the spirit far exceeded his own; but even the most zealous acknowledged the necessity of deferring to his advice. Accepting, therefore, moderation and prudence as their watchwords, they did little more than resolve that Boston was suffering in the general cause; and they appointed a committee of intercolonial correspondence, with Dickinson as its chief.

On the next day, the committee, at a meeting from which Dickinson stayed away, in a letter to Boston drafted mainly by William Smith, embodied the system which, for the coming year, was to control the counsels of America. It proposed a general congress of deputies from the different colonies, who, in firm but dutiful terms, should make to the king a petition of their rights. This, it was believed, would be granted through the influence of the wise and good in the mother country; and the most sanguine predicted that the very idea of a general congress would compel a change in the policy of Great Britain.

In like manner, the fifty-one who now represented the city and county of New York adopted from their predecessors the plan of a continental congress, and to that body they referred all questions relating to commerce, thus postponing the proposal for an immediate suspension of trade, but committing themselves irrevocably to union and resistance. At the same time, they invited every county in the colony to make choice of a committee.

The messenger, on his return with the letters from Philadelphia and New York, found the people of Connecticut anxious for a congress, even if it should not at once embrace the colonies south of the Potomac; and their committee wisely entreated Massachusetts to fix the place and time for its meeting.

At Boston, the agents and supporters of the British ministers strove to bend the firmness of its people by holding up to the tradesmen the grim picture of misery and want; while Hutchinson promised to obtain in England a restoration of trade, if the town would but pay the first cost of the tea. Before his departure, one hundred and twenty-three merchants and others of Boston addressed him, "lamenting the loss of so good a governor," confessing the propriety of indemnifying the East India company, and appealing to his most benevolent disposition to procure by his representations some speedy relief; but at a full meeting of the merchants and traders the address was disclaimed. Thirty-three citizens of Marblehead, who signed a similar paper, brought upon themselves the public reprobation of their townsmen. Twenty-four lawyers, including judges of admiralty and attorneys of the crown, subscribed an extravagant panegyric of Hutchinson's general character and conduct; but those who for learning and integrity most adorned their profession, withheld their names.

On the other hand, the necessity of a response to the courage of the people, the hearty adhesion of the town of Providence, and the cheering letter from the old committee of New York, animated a majority of the merchants of Boston, and through their example those of the province, to an engagement to cease all importations from England. Confidence prevailed that their brethren, at least as far south as Philadelphia, would embrace the same mode of peaceful resistance. The letter from that city was received with impatience. But Samuel Adams suppressed all murmurs. "I am fully of the Farmer's sentiments," said he; "violence and submission would at this time be equally fatal"; but he exerted himself the more to promote the immediate suspension of commerce.

The legislature of Massachusetts, on the last Wednesday of May, organized the government for the year by the usual election of councillors; of these, the governor negatived thirteen, among them James Bowdoin, Samuel Dexter, William Phillips, and John Adams, than whom the province could not show purer or abler men. The desire of the assembly that he would appoint a fast was refused; "for," said he to Dartmouth, "the request was only to give an opportunity for sedition to flow from the pulpit." On Saturday, the twenty-eighth, Samuel Adams was on the point of proposing a general congress, when the assembly was unexpectedly prorogued, to meet after ten days at Salem.

The people of Boston, then the most flourishing commercial town on the continent, never regretted their being the principal object of ministerial vengeance. "We shall suffer in a good cause," said the thousands who depended on their daily labor for bread; "the righteous Being, who takes care of the ravens that cry unto him, will provide for us and ours."

Hearts glowed warmly on the banks of the Patapsco. That admirable site for commerce—whose river-side and hill-tops are now covered with stately warehouses, mansions, and monuments, whose bay sparkles round the prows of the swiftest barks, whose wharfs invite the wealth of the West Indies and South America, and whose happy enterprise, availing itself of its nearness to the west, sends across the mountains its iron pathway of many arms—had for a century been tenanted only by straggling cottages. But its convenient proximity to the border counties of Pennsylvania and Virginia had been observed by Scotch-Irish Presbyterians and others; and within a few years they had created the town of Baltimore, which already was the chief emporium within the Chesapeake bay. When the messages from the old committee of New York, from Philadelphia, and from Boston, reached its inhabitants, they could not "see the least grounds for expecting relief from a petition and remonstrance." Calling to mind the contempt with which for ten years their petitions had been thrust aside, they were "convinced that something more sensible than supplications would best serve their purpose."

After consultation with the men of Annapolis, who promptly resolved to stop all trade with Great Britain, the inhabitants of the city and county of Baltimore advocated suspending commerce with Great Britain and the West Indies, chose deputies to a colonial convention, recommended a continental congress, appointed a numerous committee of correspondence, and sent cheering words to their "friends" at Boston. "The Supreme Disposer of all events," said they, "will terminate this severe trial of your patience in a happy confirmation of American freedom." For this spirited conduct, Baltimore was applauded as the model; and its example kindled new life in New York.

On the twenty-eighth, the assembly of New Hampshire, though still desiring to promote harmony with the parent land, began its organization for resisting encroachments on American rights.

Three days later, the people of New Jersey declared for a suspension of trade and a congress, and claimed "to be fellow-sufferers with Boston in the cause of liberty."

For South Carolina, the character of its labor forbade all thought of rivalling British skill in manufactures. Its wealthy inhabitants, shunning the occupations of city life, loved to reside in hospitable elegance on their large and productive estates. Its annual exports to the northern provinces were of small account, while to Great Britain they exceeded two millions of dollars in value. Enriched by this commerce, its people cherished a warm affection for the mother country, and delighted in sending their sons "home," as England was called, for their education. The harbor of Charleston was almost unguarded, except by the sand-bar at its entrance. The Creeks and Cherokees on the frontier, against whom the English government had once been solicited by South Carolina herself to send over a body of troops as a protection, were still numerous and warlike. The negro slaves, who in the country near the ocean very far outnumbered the free, were so many hostages for the allegiance of their masters. The trade of Charleston was in the hands of British factors, some of whom speculated already on the coming confiscation of the rice-swamps and indigo-fields of "many a bonnie rebel." The upland country was numerously peopled by loyal men who felt no grievances. And yet the planters refused to take counsel of their interests or their danger. "Boston," said they, "is but the first victim at the altar of tyranny." Reduced to the dilemma either to hold their liberties as tenants at will of the British house of commons, or to prepare for resistance, their choice was never in doubt. "The whole continent," they said, "must be animated with one great soul, and all Americans must resolve to stand by one another even unto death. Should they fail, the constitution of the mother country itself would lose its excellence." They knew the imminent ruin which they risked; but they "remembered that the happiness of many generations and many millions depended on their spirit and constancy."

The burgesses of Virginia sat as usual in May. The extension of the province to the west and north-west was their great ambition, which the governor, greedy of a large possession of land and of fees for conniving at the acquisitions of others, selfishly seconded in flagrant disregard of his instructions. To Lady Dunmore, who had just arrived, the assembly voted a congratulatory address, and its members invited her to a ball. The thought of revolution was not harbored; but they none the less held it their duty to resist the systematic plan of parliamentary despotism; and, without waiting for an appeal from Boston, they resolved on its deliverance. First among them as an orator stood Patrick Henry. But eloquence was his least merit: he was revered as the ideal of a patriot of Rome in its austerest age. At the approach of danger his language gained the boldness of prophecy. He was borne up by the strong support of Richard Henry Lee and Washington. It chanced that George Mason was then at Williamsburg, a man of strong and true affections; learned in constitutional law; a profound reasoner; honest and fearless in council; shunning the ways of ambition from sorrow at the death of his wife for whom he never ceased to mourn; but earnestly mindful of his country, as became one whose chastened spirit looked beyond the interests of the moment. After deliberation with these associates, Jefferson prepared the resolution which, on the twenty-fourth, at the instance of Robert Carter Nicholas, the house of burgesses adopted. In the name of Virginia it recommended to their fellow-citizens that the day on which the Boston port act was to take effect should be set apart "as a day of fasting and prayer, devoutly to implore the divine interposition for averting the dreadful calamity which threatened destruction to their civil rights, and the evils of a civil war; and to give to the American people one heart and one mind firmly to oppose, by all just and proper means, every injury to American rights." The resolve, which bound only the members themselves, was distributed by express through their respective counties as a general invitation to the people. Especially Washington sent the notice to his constituents; and Mason charged his little household of sons and daughters to keep the day strictly, and attend church clad in mourning.

On the morning which followed the adoption of this measure Dunmore dissolved the house. The burgesses immediately repaired to the Raleigh tavern, about one hundred paces from the capitol; and with Peyton Randolph, their late speaker, in the chair, voted that the attack on Massachusetts was an attack on all the colonies, to be opposed by the united wisdom of all. In conformity with this declaration, they advised for future time an annual continental congress. They named Peyton Randolph, with others, a committee of correspondence to invite a general concurrence in this design. As yet social relations were not imbittered. Washington, of whom Dunmore sought information respecting western affairs, continued his visits at the governor's house; the ball in honor of Lady Dunmore was well attended. Not till the offices of courtesy and of patriotism were fulfilled did most of the burgesses return home, leaving their committee on duty.

On the afternoon of Sunday, the twenty-ninth, the letters from Boston reached Williamsburg. So important did they appear that the next morning, at ten o'clock, the committee, having called to their aid Washington and all other burgesses who were still in town, inaugurated a revolution. Being but twenty-five in number, they refused to assume the responsibility of definite measures of resistance; but, as the province was without a legislature, they summoned a convention of delegates to be elected by the several counties, and to meet at the capitol on the first day of the ensuing August.

The rescue of freedom even at the cost of a civil war, a convention of the people for the regulation of their own internal affairs, an annual congress of all the colonies for the perpetual assertion of common rights, were the policy of Virginia. When the report of her measures reached England, the startled ministers called to mind how often she had been the model for other colonies. Her influence continued undiminished; and her system was promptly adopted by the people of North Carolina.

"Lord North had no expectation that we should be thus sustained," said Samuel Adams; "he trusted that Boston would be left to fall alone." In three weeks after the receipt of the port act, less time than was taken by the unanimous British parliament for its enactment, the continent, as "one great commonwealth," made the cause of Boston its own.

John Fiske (1842–1901),
Popularizer of History

One of the most influential lecturers and popular historical writers of his day was John Fiske, who compromised, to some extent, his imaginative capacity for original historical scholarship with a desire to make history writing a profitable source of income. He was born in Hartford, Connecticut, and baptized Edmund Fisk Green, a name he later changed. His father was a lawyer and Whig journalist who once served as Henry Clay's private secretary. His mother was a schoolteacher widowed in 1852, but her remarriage to a well-to-do lawyer and diplomat made it possible to finance John during his early years of marriage. Fiske may not have been quite the child prodigy that he was said to be, but there is no question that he developed unusual bookish tastes, kept apart from other boys, and was influenced by the elderly folk who reared him. He showed an aptitude for languages, history, and literature, but the inflexible Harvard curriculum and methods dispirited him and led him to study independently.

Profoundly influenced by Darwin and Spencer as well as by the philologists, he became increasingly rationalistic in his religious views and was regarded as a heretical young man. Anxious to write, he experimented with articles in philosophy, history, and the evolution of languages, dropping his earlier plans to practice law. Harvard failed to grant him a tutorship, partly because of his religious positivism and partly because there was little demand for his philological specialties, which disappointed him, but he did serve during the 1870's as a Harvard librarian.

Fiske became a national lecturer and popular writer in an effort to support his growing family without further subsidies from his mother. He turned down a Cornell lectureship because the salary seemed small, and conservatives kept him out of a permanent Harvard post. But he could not afford the time needed for meticulous research, though his creative and imaginative syntheses gave his histories a considerable reputation. Unfortunately, too many of his books were merely an elaboration of popular lectures sponsored by wealthy dowagers. Yet there were those who agreed with the amateur historian Theodore Roosevelt who, in his presidential address of 1912 before the American Historical Association, insisted that the task of history should be divided between the intensive historical investigator and the gifted writer such as Fiske. Among Fiske's scattered contributions was one in educational psychology regarding the significance of prolonged human infancy for schooling and directed culture. John Dewey praised Fiske's idea, although he noted that it had been held by classical writers.

Charles Beard in his *Economic Interpretation of the Constitution* was to attack Fiske's best-known work, *The Critical Period of American History 1783-1789* (1888), because it held that the Constitution was a popularly desired creation, sought after a decade of anarchic national affairs. Beard (and Merrill Jensen after him) looked upon Fiske's ideas as conservative and indifferent to economic facts. However, recent revisionists like Robert Brown may bring us back to a modified version of the Fiske thesis.

Of his histories, there is perhaps the largest measure of originality in *The Discovery of America* (1892), which uses the then-popular social evolutionary approach beginning with primitive society and treats comparatively the various early cultures in Europe and America. The selection dealing with Las Casas reprinted here shows that Fiske judged correctly the nature of the myth regarding the noted apostle who was charged with imposing African slavery as a substitute for Indian slavery in the New World.

Generally, Fiske's social ideas were conservative, and he inclined to an individualistic Spencerian version of Darwinism. His *Old Virginia and Her Neighbors* (1897) popularized the Southern ante-bellum myth that the Cavaliers contributed to the elite stock of Old Virginia, and he praised genealogy as a major tool for historians. As president of the powerful Immigration Restriction League he urged the restriction of newcomers from southern and eastern Europe and the strengthening of Anglo-Saxon elements. Like some literary historians, he tended to minimize economic forces in favor of drama, politics, and war.

The Discovery of America

[LAS CASAS]

. . . There were such atrocities as would seem incredible were they not recounted by a most intelligent and faithful witness who saw with his own eyes many of the things of which he tells us. Bartolomé de Las Casas was born in Seville in 1474.[1] His family, one of the noblest in Spain, was of French origin, descended from the viscounts of Limoges.[2] They were already in Spain before the thirteenth century, and played a distinguished part in the conquest of Seville from the Moors by Ferdinand III of Castile, in 1252. From that time forward, members of the family were to be found in positions of trust, and among their marked traits of character were invincible courage and spotless integrity. By birth and training Bartholomew was an aristocrat to the very tips of his fingers. For the earlier part of his life dates can hardly be assigned, but the news of the triumphant return of Columbus from his first voyage across the Sea of Darkness may probably have found him at the university of Salamanca, where for several years he studied philosophy, theology, and jurisprudence, and obtained a licentiate's degree. His father, Don Francisco de Las Casas, accompanied Columbus on the second voyage, and returned to Seville in 1497 with a young Indian slave whom Columbus had given him.

Volume I, pages 437–41, 451–8 (Houghton Mifflin, 1892).

It was on this occasion that Isabella asked, with some indignation, "Who has empowered my admiral thus to dispose of my subjects?" The elder Las Casas gave the Indian to his son, who soon became warmly interested in him and in his race; and as the father retained an estate in Hispaniola, the son came out with Ovando in 1502 and settled in that island.[3] He was then twenty-eight years old. Little is known of his first occupations there, except that he seems to have been more or less concerned in money-making, like all the other settlers. But about 1510 he was ordained as a priest. He seems to have been the first Christian clergyman ordained in the New World. He was a person of such immense ability and strength of character that in whatever age of the world he had lived he would undoubtedly have been one of its foremost men. As a man of business he had rare executive power; he was a great diplomatist and an eloquent preacher, a man of Titanic energy, ardent but self-controlled, of unconquerable tenacity, warm-hearted and tender, calm in his judgments, shrewdly humorous, absolutely fearless, and absolutely true. He made many and bitter enemies, and some of them were unscrupulous enough; but I believe no one has ever accused him of any worse sin than extreme fervour of temperament. His wrath could rise to a white heat, and indeed there was occasion enough for it. He was also very apt to call a spade a spade and to proclaim unpleasant truths with pungent emphasis. But his justice is conspicuously displayed in his voluminous writings. He was one of the best historians of his time, and wrote a most attractive Spanish style, quaint, pithy, and nervous,—a style which goes straight to the mark and rings like true metal.[4] It is impossible to doubt the accuracy of his statements about the matters of fact which were within the range of his personal knowledge. His larger statistics, as to the numbers of the Indian populations exterminated, have been doubted with good reason; statistics are a complicated affair, in which it is easy to let feelings make havoc with figures.[5] But with regard to particular statements of fact one cannot help believing Las Casas, because his perfect sincerity is allied with a judgment so sane and a charity so broad as to constrain our assent. He is almost always ready to make allowances, and very rarely lets his hatred of sin blind him to any redeeming qualities there may be in the sinner. It was he that said, in his crisp way, of Ovando, that he was a good governor, but not for Indians. What Las Casas witnessed under the administration of Ovando and other governors, he published in 1552, in his "Brief Relation of the Destruction of the Indies," a book of which there are copies in several languages, all more or less rare now.[6] It is one of the most grewsome books ever printed.

We have seen how by the year 1499 communities of Indians were assigned in *repartimiento* to sundry Spaniards, and were thus reduced to a kind of villenage. Queen Isabella had disapproved of this, but she was persuaded to sanction it, and presently in 1503 she and Ferdinand issued a most disastrous order. They gave discretionary power to Ovando to compel Indians to work, but it must be for wages. . . .

There must be a stop put to this, said Las Casas. We have started wrong. Here are vast countries which Holy Church has given to the Spaniards in trust, that the heathen may be civilized and brought into the fold of Christ; and we have begun by making Hispaniola a hell. This thing must not be suffered to grow with the growth of Spanish conquest. There was but one remedy. The axe must be put to the root of the tree. Slavery must be abolished.

Las Casas began by giving up his own slaves. He had reason enough to know that others might not treat them so well as he, but he was not the man to preach what he did not practise. His partner, Pedro de Renteria, was a man of noble nature and much under his influence, so that there was no difficulty there. Then Las Casas went into the pulpit and preached to his congregation that their souls were in danger so long as they continued to hold their *encomiendas* of Indians. "All were amazed," he says; "some were struck with compunction; others were as much surprised to hear it called a sin to make use of the Indians, as if they had been told it were sinful to make use of the beasts of the field."

Too many were of this latter mood, and finding his people incorrigible, Las Casas sold what worldly goods he had left, and went to Spain to lay the case before King Ferdinand. First he visited Bishop Fonseca, as the most important member of the Council for the Indies.

From this coarse man, with his cynical contempt for philanthropists, Las Casas got such a reception as might have been expected. It will be remembered that Ovando was one of Fonseca's creatures. When Las Casas told how 7,000 children had cruelly perished in Hispaniola within three months, he doubtless overstated the case, and clearly Fonseca did not believe him. He answered roughly, "Look here, you droll fool, what is all this to me, and what is it to the king?" This fairly took our poor priest's breath away. He only exclaimed, "O great and eternal God! to whom, then, is it of any concern?" and so he turned upon his heel and left the room.

On arriving at Seville, he learned that the king had just died, January 23, 1516. Ferdinand's daughter Joanna, queen of Castile and heiress to the throne of Aragon, was still insane, and both thrones descended practically to her illustrious son Charles, a boy of sixteen, who was then in Flanders. For the present the great cardinal Ximenes was regent of Spain, and to him went Las Casas with his tale of woe. From the cardinal he obtained ready and cordial sympathy. It was a fortunate circumstance that at this juncture brought two such men together. Las Casas knew well that the enslavement of Indians was not contemplated in the royal orders of 1503, except so far as concerned cannibals taken in war; but the evil had become so firmly established that at first he hesitated about the policy of using this line of argument. He prudently shaped his question in this wise: "With what justice can such things be done, whether the Indians are free or not?" Here, to his joy, the cardinal caught him up vehemently. "With no justice whatever: what, are not the Indians free? who doubts about their being free?" This was a great point gained at the start, for it put the official theory of the Spanish government on the side of Las Casas, and made the Spaniards in America appear in the light of transgressors. The matter was thoroughly discussed with Ximenes and that amiable Dutchman, Cardinal Adrian, who was afterwards pope. A commission of Hieronymite friars was appointed to accompany Las Casas to the West Indies, with minute instructions and ample powers for making investigations and enforcing the laws. Ximenes appointed Las Casas Protector of the Indians, and clothed him with authority to

impeach delinquent judges or other public officials. The new regulations, could they have been carried out, would have done much to
mitigate the sufferings of the Indians. They must be paid wages, they
must be humanely treated and taught the Christian religion. But as
the Spanish government needed revenue, the provision that Indians
might be compelled to work in the mines was not repealed. The
Indians must work, and the Spaniards must pay them. Las Casas
argued correctly that so long as this provision was retained the work
of reform would go but little way. Somebody, however, must work
the mines; and so the talk turned to the question of sending out white
labourers or negroes.

Here we come to the statement, often repeated, that it was Las
Casas who first introduced negro slavery and the African slave-trade
into the New World. The statement is a good specimen of the headlong, helter-skelter way in which things get said and believed in this
superficial world. As first repeated, there was probably an agreeable
tinge of paradox in representing the greatest of philanthropists as the
founder of one of the vilest systems of bondage known to modern
times. At length it has come to pass that people who know nothing
about Las Casas, and have absolutely no other idea associated with his
name, still vaguely think of him as the man who brought negro slaves
to America as substitutes for Indians,—the man who sacrificed one
race of his fellow-creatures to another, and thus paid Peter by robbing
Paul.

There could not be a grosser historical blunder than this notion,
and yet, like most such blunders, it has arisen from a perversion of
things that really were said if not done. In order to arrive at historical
truth, it is not enough to obtain correct items of fact; it is necessary
to group the items in their causal relations and to estimate the precise
weight that must be accorded to each in the total result. To do this is
often so difficult that half-truths are very commonly offered us in
place of whole truths; and it sometimes happens that of all forms of
falsehood none is so misleading as the half-truth.

The statement about Las Casas, with which we are here concerned,
properly divides itself into a pair of statements. It is alleged, in the

first place, that it was Las Casas who first suggested the employment of negroes as substitutes for Indians; and in the second place, that the origin, or at any rate the steady development, of negro slavery in America was due to this suggestion. These are two different propositions and call for different comments.

With regard to the first, it is undoubtedly true that Las Casas at one time expressed the opinion that if there must be slave labour, the enslavement of blacks might perhaps be tolerated as the smaller of two evils, inasmuch as the negroes were regarded as a hardier race than the Indians and better able to support continuous labour. At one time the leading colonists of Hispaniola had told Las Casas that if they might have license to import each a dozen negroes, they would coöperate with him in his plans for setting free the Indians and improving their condition. When Las Casas at the Spanish court was confronted with the argument that there must be somebody to work the mines, he recalled this suggestion of the colonists, and proposed it as perhaps the least odious way out of the difficulty. It is therefore evident that at that period in his life he did not realize the wickedness of slavery so distinctly in the case of black men as in the case of red men. In other words, he had not yet outgrown that mediæval habit of mind which regarded the right to "life, liberty, and the pursuit of happiness," and other rights, not as common to all mankind, but as parcelled out among groups and classes of men in a complicated way that to our minds, on the eve of the twentieth century, has become wellnigh unintelligible. It was the great French writers of the eighteenth century who first gave distinct expression to the notion of "unalienable rights," with which mankind has been endowed by the Creator. This notion has become so familiar to our minds that we sometimes see the generalizations of Rousseau and Diderot, or whatever remains sound in them, derided as mere platitudes, as if it had never been necessary to preach such self-evident truths. But these "platitudes" about universal rights were far enough from being self-evident in the sixteenth century. On the contrary, they were extremely unfamiliar and abstruse conceptions, toward which the most enlightened minds could only grope their way by slow degrees.[7] In Las Casas it is interesting to trace such a development. He had gradually risen to the perception of the full wickedness of slavery in the form in which he had become familiar with it; but he had not yet extended his generalizations, as a modern thinker would do, to remote cases, and in order to gain a point, the supreme importance of which he keenly felt, he was ready to make concessions. In later years he blamed himself roundly for making any such concessions. Had he "sufficiently considered the matter," he would not for all the world have entertained such a suggestion for a moment; for, said he, the negroes "had been made slaves unjustly and tyrannically, and the same reason holds good of them as of the Indians." [8]

With regard to the second of the statements we are considering, the question arises how far did this suggestion, for which Las Casas afterward so freely blamed himself, have any material effect in setting on foot the African slave-trade or in enlarging its dimensions? The reply is that it had no such effect whatever. As for the beginnings negroes had been carried to Hispaniola in small numbers as early as 1501; and in the royal instructions drawn up at that time for Ovando, he was forbidden to take to the colony Moors, Jews, new converts from Islam or Judaism, monks not Spanish, and the children of persons burned at the stake for heresy, but he might take negro slaves.[9] Official documents prove that at various times between 1500 and 1510 negroes were sent over to work in the mines, but not in large numbers.[10] As for the extensive development of negro slavery in the West Indies, it did not begin for many years after that period in the career of Las Casas with which we are now dealing, and there is nothing to show that his suggestion or concession was in any way concerned in bringing it about. If, on the other hand, instead of confining our attention to this single incident in his life, the importance of which has been egregiously exaggerated, we consider the general effect of his life-work, that effect was clearly adverse to the development of the African slave-trade. For if the depopulation of the New World had continued, which Las Casas did so much to check, it cannot be doubted that the importation of negroes to Spanish America would have been immeasurably greater than it has been. The African slave-trade would have assumed much larger proportions than it has ever known, and its widely ramifying influence for evil, its poisonous effects upon the character of European society in the New World, whether Spanish or English, would probably have surpassed anything that we can now realize. When the work of Las Casas is deeply considered, we cannot make him anything else but an antagonist of human slavery in all its forms, and the mightiest and most effective antagonist, withal, that has ever lived. Subtract his glorious life from the history of the past, and we might still be waiting, sick with hope deferred, for a Wilberforce, a Garrison, and a Lincoln.

NOTES

[1] The life of Las Casas is beautifully and faithfully told by Sir Arthur Helps, in his *History of the Spanish Conquest in America*, London, 1855–61, in 4 vols., a book which it does one's soul good to read. The most recent and elaborate biography is by Don Antonio Fabié, *Vida y escritos de Fray Bartolomé de Las Casas*, Madrid, 1879, in 2 vols. See also Llorente, *Vie de Las Casas*, prefixed to his *Œuvres de Las Casas*, Paris, 1822, tom. i. pp. ix.–cx.; Remesal, *Historia de Chyapa y de Guatemala*, Madrid, 1619. References may also be found in Oviedo, Gomara, Herrera, Torquemada, and other historians. One should above all read the works of Las Casas himself, concerning which much information may be obtained from Sabin's *List of the Printed Editions of the Works of Fray Bartholomé de Las Casas, Bishop of Chiapa*, New York, 1870. The book contains also a notice of the MSS.—The *Life of Las Casas*, by Sir Arthur Helps, London, 1868, consists of passages extracted from his larger work, and suffers seriously from the removal of the context.

[2] Argote, *Nobleza de Andalucia*, fol. 210. According to Llorente (*Vie de Las Casas*, p. xcviii.) a branch of the Seville family returned to France. Don Carlos de Las Casas was one of the grandees who accompanied Blanche of Castile when she went to France in the year 1200, to marry the prince, afterward Louis VIII. From this nobleman was descended Napoleon's faithful chamberlain the Marquis de Las Cases. The migration of the French family to Spain probably antedated the custom of giving surnames, which was growing up in the eleventh and twelfth centuries. The name Las Casas was of course acquired in Spain, and afterward the branch of the family which had returned to France changed the spelling to Las Cases.

[3] According to Llorente, the elder Las Casas accompanied Columbus on his

first voyage in 1492, and Bartholomew was with him on his third voyage in 1498, but this has been disproved. See Humboldt, *Examen critique,* tom. iii. p. 286.

[4] I do not mean to be understood as calling it a *literary* style. It is not graceful like that of great masters of expression such as Pascal or Voltaire. It is not seldom cumbrous and awkward, usually through trying to say too much at once. But in spite of this it is far more attractive than many a truly artistic literary style. There is a great charm in reading what comes from a man brimful of knowledge and utterly unselfish and honest. The crisp shrewdness, the gleams of gentle humour and occasional sharp flashes of wit, and the fervid earnestness in the books of Las Casas, combine to make them very delightful. It was the unfailing sense of humour, which is so often wanting in reformers, that kept Las Casas from developing into a fanatic. . . .

[5] The arithmetic of Las Casas is, however, no worse than that of all the Spanish historians of that age. With every one of them the nine digits seem to have gone on a glorious spree.

[6] I have never seen any of the English versions. Sabin mentions four, published in London in 1583, 1656, 1687, and 1699. *List of the Printed Editions,* etc., pp. 22–24. The edition which I use is the Latin one published at Heidelberg, 1664, small quarto.

[7] As Mr. John Morley observes, "the doctrine of moral obligations toward the lower races had not yet taken its place in Europe." *Diderot and the Encyclopædists,* London, 1880, p. 386. Mr. Morley's remarks on the influence of Raynal's famous book, *Histoire des deux Indes* in this connection, are admirable.

[8] Las Casas, *Hist. de las Indias,* tom. iv. p. 380.

[9] Navarrete, *Coleccion de viages,* tom. ii. doc. 175.

[10] Herrera, *Hist. de las Indias,* tom. i. pp. 274–276.

The Critical Period of American History

"The times that tried men's souls are over," said Thomas Paine in the last number of the "Crisis," which he published after hearing that the negotiations for a treaty of peace had been concluded. The preliminary articles had been signed at Paris on the 20th of January, 1783. The news arrived in America on the 23d of March, in a letter to the president of Congress from Lafayette, who had returned to France soon after the victory at Yorktown. A few days later Sir Guy Carleton received his orders from the ministry to proclaim a cessation of hostilities by land and sea. A similar proclamation made by Congress was formally communicated to the army by Washington on the 19th of April, the eighth anniversary of the first bloodshed on Lexington green. Since Wayne had driven the British from Georgia, early in the preceding year, there had been no military operations between the regular armies. Guerrilla warfare between Whig and Tory had been kept up in parts of South Carolina and on the frontier of New York, where Thayendanegea was still alert and defiant; while beyond the mountains the tomahawk and scalping-knife had been busy, and Washington's old friend and comrade, Colonel Crawford, had been scorched to death by the firebrands of the red demons; but the armies had sat still, awaiting the peace which every one felt sure must speedily come. After Cornwallis's surrender, Washington marched his army back to the Hudson, and established his headquarters at Newburgh. Rochambeau followed somewhat later, and in September joined the Americans on the Hudson; but in December the French army marched to Boston, and there embarked for France. After the formal cessation of hostilities on the 19th of April, 1783, Washington granted furloughs to most of his soldiers; and these weather-beaten veterans trudged homeward in all directions, in little groups of four or five, depending largely for their subsistence on the hospitality of

Pages 50–70 (Houghton Mifflin, 1892).

the farm-houses along the road. Arrived at home, their muskets were hung over the chimney-piece as trophies for grandchildren to be proud of, the stories of their exploits and their sufferings became household legends, and they turned the furrows and drove the cattle to pasture just as in the "old colony times." Their furloughs were equivalent to a full discharge, for on the 3d of September the definitive treaty was signed, and the country was at peace. On the 3d of November the army was formally disbanded, and on the 25th of that month Sir Guy Carleton's army embarked from New York. Small British garrisons still remained in the frontier posts of Ogdensburg, Oswego, Niagara, Erie, Sandusky, Detroit, and Mackinaw, but by the terms of the treaty these places were to be promptly surrendered to the United States. On the 4th of December a barge waited at the South Ferry in New York to carry General Washington across the river to Paulus Hook. He was going to Annapolis, where Congress was in session, in order to resign his command. At Fraunces's Tavern, near the ferry, he took leave of the officers who so long had shared his labours. One after another they embraced their beloved commander, while there were few dry eyes in the company. They followed him to the ferry, and watched the departing boat with hearts too full for words, and then in solemn silence returned up the street. At Philadelphia he handed to the comptroller of the treasury a neatly written manuscript, containing an accurate statement of his expenses in the public service since the day when he took command of the army. The sums which Washington had thus spent out of his private fortune amounted to $64,315. For his personal services he declined to take any pay. At noon of the 23d, in the presence of Congress and of a throng of ladies and gentlemen at Annapolis, the great general gave up his command, and requested as an "indulgence" to be allowed to retire into private life. General Mifflin, who during the winter of Valley Forge had conspired with Gates to undermine the confidence of the people in Washington, was now president of Congress, and it was for him to make the reply. "You retire," said Mifflin, "from the theatre of action with the blessings of your fellow-citizens, but the glory of your virtues will not terminate with your military command; it will continue to

animate remotest ages." The next morning Washington hurried away
to spend Christmas at his pleasant home at Mount Vernon, which,
save for a few hours in the autumn of 1781, he had not set eyes on
for more than eight years. His estate had suffered from his long
absence, and his highest ambition was to devote himself to its simple
interests. To his friends he offered unpretentious hospitality. "My
manner of living is plain," he said, "and I do not mean to be put out
of it. A glass of wine and a bit of mutton are always ready, and such
as will be content to partake of them are always welcome. Those who
expect more will be disappointed." To Lafayette he wrote that he was
now about to solace himself with those tranquil enjoyments of which
the anxious soldier and the weary statesman know but little. "I have
not only retired from all public employments, but I am retiring within
myself, and shall be able to view the solitary walk and tread the paths
of private life with heartfelt satisfaction. Envious of none, I am determined to be pleased with all; and this, my dear friend, being the
order of my march, I will move gently down the stream of life until I
sleep with my fathers."

In these hopes Washington was to be disappointed. "All the world
is touched by his republican virtues," wrote Luzerne to Vergennes,
"but it will be useless for him to try to hide himself and live the life
of a private man: he will always be the first citizen of the United
States." It indeed required no prophet to foretell that the American
people could not long dispense with the services of this greatest of
citizens. Washington had already put himself most explicitly on record
as the leader of the men who were urging the people of the United
States toward the formation of a more perfect union. The great lesson
of the war had not been lost on him. Bitter experience of the evils
attendant upon the weak government of the Continental Congress
had impressed upon his mind the urgent necessity of an immediate
and thorough reform. On the 8th of June, in view of the approaching
disbandment of the army, he had addressed to the governors and
presidents of the several states a circular letter, which he wished to
have regarded as his legacy to the American people. In this letter he
insisted upon four things as essential to the very existence of the

United States as an independent power. First, there must be an indissoluble union of all the states under a single federal government, which must possess the power of enforcing its decrees; for without such authority it would be a government only in name. Secondly, the debts incurred by Congress for the purpose of carrying on the war and securing independence must be paid to the uttermost farthing. Thirdly, the militia system must be organized throughout the thirteen states on uniform principles. Fourthly, the people must be willing to sacrifice, if need be, some of their local interests to the common weal; they must discard their local prejudices, and regard one another as fellow-citizens of a common country, with interests in the deepest and truest sense identical.

The unparalleled grandeur of Washington's character, his heroic services, and his utter disinterestedness had given him such a hold upon the people as scarcely any other statesman known to history, save perhaps William the Silent, has ever possessed. The noble and sensible words of his circular letter were treasured up in the minds of all the best people in the country, and when the time for reforming the weak and disorderly government had come it was again to Washington that men looked as their leader and guide. But that time had not yet come. Only through the discipline of perplexity and tribulation could the people be brought to realize the indispensable necessity of that indissoluble union of which Washington had spoken. Thomas Paine was sadly mistaken when, in the moment of exultation over the peace, he declared that the trying time was ended. The most trying time of all was just beginning. It is not too much to say that the period of five years following the peace of 1783 was the most critical moment in all the history of the American people. The dangers from which we were saved in 1788 were even greater than the dangers from which we were saved in 1865. In the War of Secession the love of union had come to be so strong that thousands of men gave up their lives for it as cheerfully and triumphantly as the martyrs of older times, who sang their hymns of praise even while their flesh was withering in the relentless flames. In 1783 the love of union, as a sentiment for which men would fight, had scarcely come into existence

among the people of these states. The souls of the men of that day
had not been thrilled by the immortal eloquence of Webster, nor
had they gained the historic experience which gave to Webster's
words their meaning and their charm. They had not gained control
of all the fairest part of the continent, with domains stretching more
than three thousand miles from ocean to ocean, and so situated in
geographical configuration and commercial relations as to make the
very idea of disunion absurd, save for men in whose minds fanaticism for the moment usurped the place of sound judgment. The men
of 1783 dwelt in a long, straggling series of republics, fringing the
Atlantic coast, bordered on the north and south and west by two
European powers whose hostility they had some reason to dread. But
nine years had elapsed since, in the first Continental Congress, they
had begun to act consistently and independently in common, under
the severe pressure of a common fear and an immediate necessity of
action. Even under such circumstances the war had languished and
come nigh to failure simply through the difficulty of insuring concerted action. Had there been such a government that the whole power
of the thirteen states could have been swiftly and vigorously wielded
as a unit, the British, fighting at such disadvantage as they did, might
have been driven to their ships in less than a year. The length of the
war and its worst hardships had been chiefly due to want of organization. Congress had steadily declined in power and in respectability;
it was much weaker at the end of the war than at the beginning; and
there was reason to fear that as soon as the common pressure was
removed the need for concerted action would quite cease to be felt,
and the scarcely formed Union would break into pieces. There was
the greater reason for such a fear in that, while no strong sentiment
had as yet grown up in favour of union, there was an intensely powerful sentiment in favour of local self-government. This feeling was
scarcely less strong as between states like Connecticut and Rhode
Island, or Maryland and Virginia, than it was between Athens and
Megara, Argos and Sparta, in the great days of Grecian history. A
most wholesome feeling it was, and one which needed not so much
to be curbed as to be guided in the right direction. It was a feeling

which was shared by some of the foremost Revolutionary leaders, such as Samuel Adams and Richard Henry Lee. But unless the most profound and delicate statesmanship should be forthcoming, to take this sentiment under its guidance, there was much reason to fear that the release from the common adhesion to Great Britain would end in setting up thirteen little republics, ripe for endless squabbling, like the republics of ancient Greece and mediæval Italy, and ready to become the prey of England and Spain, even as Greece became the prey of Macedonia.

As such a lamentable result was dreaded by Washington, so by statesmen in Europe it was generally expected, and by our enemies it was eagerly hoped for. Josiah Tucker, Dean of Gloucester, was a far-sighted man in many things; but he said, "As to the future grandeur of America, and its being a rising empire under one head, whether republican or monarchical, it is one of the idlest and most visionary notions that ever was conceived even by writers of romance. The mutual antipathies and clashing interests of the Americans, their difference of governments, habitudes, and manners, indicate that they will have no centre of union and no common interest. They never can be united into one compact empire under any species of government whatever; a disunited people till the end of time, suspicious and distrustful of each other, they will be divided and subdivided into little commonwealths or principalities, according to natural boundaries, by great bays of the sea, and by vast rivers, lakes, and ridges of mountains." Such were the views of a liberal-minded philosopher who bore us no ill-will. George III. said officially that he hoped the Americans would not suffer from the evils which in history had always followed the throwing off of monarchical government: which meant, of course, that he hoped they *would* suffer from such evils. He believed we should get into such a snarl that the several states, one after another, would repent and beg on their knees to be taken back into the British empire. Frederick of Prussia, though friendly to the Americans, argued that the mere extent of country from Maine to Georgia would suffice either to break up the Union, or to make a monarchy necessary. No republic, he said, had ever long existed on so great a scale. The Roman republic had been transformed into a despotism mainly by the excessive enlargement of its area. It was only little states, like Venice, Switzerland, and Holland, that could maintain a republican government. Such arguments were common enough a century ago, but they overlooked three essential differences between the Roman republic and the United States. The Roman republic in Cæsar's time comprised peoples differing widely in blood, in speech, and in degree of civilization; it was perpetually threatened on all its frontiers by powerful enemies; and representative assemblies were unknown to it. The only free government of which the Roman knew anything was that of the primary assembly or town meeting. On the other hand, the people of the United States were all English in speech, and mainly English in blood. The differences in degree of civilization between such states as Massachusetts and North Carolina were considerable, but in comparison with such differences as those between Attika and Lusitania they might well be called slight. The attacks of savages on the frontier were cruel and annoying, but never since the time of King Philip had they seemed to threaten the existence of the white man. A very small military establishment was quite enough to deal with the Indians. And to crown all, the American people were thoroughly familiar with the principle of representation, having practised it on a grand scale for four centuries in England, and for more than a century in America. The governments of the thirteen states were all similar, and the political ideas of one were perfectly intelligible to all the others. It was essentially fallacious, therefore, to liken the case of the United States to that of ancient Rome.

But there was another feature of the case which was quite hidden from the men of 1783. Just before the assembling of the first Continental Congress James Watt had completed his steam-engine; in the summer of 1787, while the Federal Convention was sitting at Philadelphia, John Fitch launched his first steamboat on the Delaware River; and Stephenson's invention of the locomotive was to follow in less than half a century. Even with all other conditions favourable, it is doubtful if the American Union could have been preserved to the present time without the railroad. But for the military aid of railroads our government would hardly have succeeded in putting down the rebellion of the southern states. In the debates on the Oregon Bill in the United States Senate in 1843, the idea that we could ever have an interest in so remote a country as Oregon was loudly ridiculed by some of the members. It would take ten months—said George Mc-Duffie, the very able senator from South Carolina—for representatives to get from that territory to the District of Columbia and back again. Yet since the building of railroads to the Pacific coast, we can go from Boston to the capital of Oregon in much less time than it took John Hancock to make the journey from Boston to Philadelphia. Railroads and telegraphs have made our vast country, both for political and for social purposes, more snug and compact than little Switzerland was in the Middle Ages or New England a century ago.

At the time of our Revolution the difficulties of travelling formed an important social obstacle to the union of the states. In our time the persons who pass in a single day beween New York and Boston by six or seven distinct lines of railroad and steamboat are numbered by thousands. In 1783 two stage-coaches were enough for all the travellers, and nearly all the freight besides, that went between these two cities, except such large freight as went by sea around Cape Cod. The journey began at three o'clock in the morning. Horses were changed every twenty miles, and if the roads were in good condition some forty miles would be made by ten o'clock in the evening. In bad weather, when the passengers had to get down and lift the clumsy wheels out of deep ruts, the progress was much slower. The loss of life from accidents, in proportion to the number of travellers, was much greater than it has ever been on the railway. Broad rivers like the Connecticut and Housatonic had no bridges. To drive across them in winter, when they were solidly frozen over, was easy; and in pleasant summer weather to cross in a row-boat was not a dangerous undertaking. But squalls at some seasons and floating ice at others were things to be feared. More than one instance is recorded where boats were crushed and passengers drowned, or saved only by scrambling upon ice-floes. After a week or ten days of discomfort and danger the jolted and jaded traveller reached New York. Such was a journey in the most highly civilized part of the United States. The case was still worse in the South, and it was not so very much better in England and France. In one respect the traveller in the United States fared better than the traveller in Europe: the danger from highwaymen was but slight.

Such being the difficulty of travelling, people never made long journeys save for very important reasons. Except in the case of the soldiers, most people lived and died without ever having seen any state but their own. And as the mails were irregular and uncertain, and the rates of postage very high, people heard from one another but seldom. Commercial dealings between the different states were inconsiderable. The occupation of the people was chiefly agriculture. Cities were few and small, and each little district for the most part supported itself. Under such circumstances the different parts of the country knew very little about each other, and local prejudices were intense. It was not simply free Massachusetts and slave-holding South Carolina, or English Connecticut and Dutch New York, that misunderstood and ridiculed each the other; but even between such neighbouring states as Connecticut and Massachusetts, both of them thoroughly English and Puritan, and in all their social conditions almost exactly alike, it used often to be said that there was no love lost. These unspeakably stupid and contemptible local antipathies are inherited by civilized men from that far-off time when the clan system prevailed over the face of the earth, and the hand of every clan was raised against its neighbours. They are pale and evanescent survivals from the universal primitive warfare, and the sooner they die out from human society the better for every one. They should be stigmatized and frowned down upon every fit occasion, just as we frown upon swearing as a symbol of anger and contention. But the only thing which can finally destroy them is the widespread and unrestrained intercourse of different groups of people in peaceful social and commercial relations. The rapidity with which this process is now going on is the most encouraging of all the symptoms of our modern civilization. But a century ago the progress made in this direction had been relatively small, and it was a very critical moment for the American people.

The thirteen states, as already observed, had worked in concert for only nine years, during which their coöperation had been feeble and halting. But the several state governments had been in operation since the first settlement of the country, and were regarded with intense loyalty by the people of the states. Under the royal governors the local political life of each state had been vigorous and often stormy, as befitted communities of the sturdy descendants of English freemen. The legislative assembly of each state had stoutly defended its liberties against the encroachments of the governor. In the eyes of the people it was the only power on earth competent to lay taxes upon them, it was as supreme in its own sphere as the British Parliament itself, and in behalf of this rooted conviction the people had gone to war and won their independence from England. During the war the people of all the states, except Connecticut and Rhode Island, had carefully remodelled their governments, and in the performance of this work had withdrawn many of their ablest statesmen from the Continental Congress; but except for the expulsion of the royal and proprietary governors, the work had in no instance been revolutionary in its character. It was not so much that the American people gained an increase of freedom by their separation from England, as that they kept the freedom they had always enjoyed, that freedom which was the inalienable birthright of Englishmen, but which George III. had foolishly sought to impair. The American Revolution was therefore in no respect destructive. It was the most conservative revolution known to history, thoroughly English in conception from beginning to end. It had no likeness whatever to the terrible popular convulsion which soon after took place in France. The mischievous doctrines of Rousseau had found few readers and fewer admirers among the Americans. The principles upon which their revolution was conducted were those of Sidney, Harrington, and Locke. In remodelling the state governments, as in planning the union of the states, the precedents followed and the principles applied were almost purely English.

We must now pass in review the principal changes wrought in the several states, and we shall then be ready to consider the general structure of the Confederation, and to describe the remarkable series of events which led to the adoption of our Federal Constitution.

It will be remembered that at the time of the Declaration of Independence there were three kinds of government in the colonies. Connecticut and Rhode Island had always been true republics, with governors and legislative assemblies elected by the people. Pennsylvania, Delaware, and Maryland presented the appearance of limited hereditary monarchies. Their assemblies were chosen by the people, but the lords proprietary appointed their governors, or in some instances acted as governors themselves. In Maryland the office of lord proprietary was hereditary in the Calvert family; in Delaware and Pennsylvania, which, though distinct commonwealths with separate legislatures, had the same executive head, it was hereditary in the Penn family. The other eight colonies were viceroyalties, with governors appointed by the king, while in all alike the people elected the legislatures. Accordingly in Connecticut and Rhole Island no change was made necessary by the Revolution, beyond the mere omission of the king's name from legal documents; and their charters, which dated from the middle of the seventeenth century, continued to do duty as state constitutions till far into the nineteenth. During the Revolutionary War all the other states framed new constitutions, but in most essential respects they took the old colonial charters for their model. The popular legislative body remained unchanged even in its name. In North Carolina its supreme dignity was vindicated in its title of the House of Commons; in Virginia it was called the House of Burgesses; in most of the states the House of Representatives. The members were chosen each year, except in South Carolina, where they served for two years. In the New England states they represented the townships, in other states the counties. In all the states except Pennsylvania a property qualification was required of them.

In addition to this House of Representatives all the legislatures except those of Pennsylvania and Georgia contained a second or upper house known as the Senate. The origin of the senate is to be found in the governor's council of colonial times, just as the House of Lords is descended from the Witenagemot or council of great barons summoned by the Old-English kings. The Americans had been used to having the acts of their popular assemblies reviewed by a council, and so they retained this revisory body as an upper house. A higher property qualification was required than for membership of the lower house, and, except in New Hampshire, Massachusetts, and South Carolina, the term of service was longer. In Maryland senators sat for five years, in Virginia and New York four years, elsewhere for two years. In some states they were chosen by the people, in others by the lower house. In Maryland they were chosen by a college of electors, thus affording a precedent for the method of electing the chief magistrate of the union under the Federal Constitution.

Governors were unpopular in those days. There was too much flavour of royalty and high prerogative about them. Except in the two republics of Rhode Island and Connecticut, American political history during the eighteenth century was chiefly the record of interminable squabbles between governors and legislatures, down to the moment when the detested agents of royalty were clapped into jail, or took refuge behind the bulwarks of a British seventy-four. Accordingly the new constitutions were very chary of the powers to be exercised by the governor. In Pennsylvania and Delaware, in New Hampshire and Massachusetts, the governor was at first replaced by an executive council, and the president of this council was first magistrate and titular ruler of the state. His dignity was imposing enough, but his authority was merely that of a chairman. The other states had governors chosen by the legislatures, except in New York where the governor was elected by the people. No one was eligible to the office of governor who did not possess a specified amount of property. In most of the states the governor could not be reëlected, he had no veto upon the acts of the legislature, nor any power of appointing officers. In 1780, in a new constitution drawn up by James Bowdoin and the two Adamses, Massachusetts led the way in the construction of a more efficient executive department. The president was replaced by a governor elected annually by the people, and endowed with the power of appointment and a suspensory veto. The first governor elected under this constitution was John Hancock. In 1783 New Hampshire adopted a similar constitution. In 1790 Pennsylvania added an upper house to its legislature, and vested the executive power in a governor elected by the people for a term of three years, and twice reëligible. He was intrusted with the power of appointment to offices, with a suspensory veto, and with the royal prerogative of reprieving or pardoning criminals. In 1792 similar changes were made in Delaware. In 1789 Georgia added the upper house to its legislature, and about the same time in several states the governor's powers were enlarged.

Thus the various state governments were repetitions on a small scale of what was then supposed to be the triplex government of England, with its King, Lords, and Commons. The governor answered to the king with his dignity curtailed by election for a short period, and by narrowly limited prerogatives. The senate answered to the House of Lords, except in being a representative and not a hereditary body. It was supposed to represent more especially that part of the community which was possessed of most wealth and consideration; and in several states the senators were apportioned with some reference to the amount of taxes paid by different parts of the state. The senate of New York, in direct imitation of the House of Lords, was made a supreme court of errors. On the other hand, the assembly answered to the House of Commons, save that its power was really limited by the senate as the power of the House of Commons is not really limited by the House of Lords. But this peculiarity of the British Constitution was not well understood a century ago; and the misunderstanding, as we shall hereafter see, exerted a very serious influence upon the form of our federal government, as well as upon the constitutions of the several states.

In all the thirteen states the common law of England remained in force, as it does to this day save where modified by statute. British and colonial statutes made prior to the Revolution continued also in force unless expressly repealed. The system of civil and criminal courts, the remedies in common law and equity, the forms of writs, the functions of justices of the peace, the courts of probate, all remained substantially unchanged. In Pennsylvania, Delaware, and New Jersey, the judges held office for a term of seven years; in all the other states they held office for life or during good behaviour. In all the states save Georgia they were appointed either by the governor or by the legislature. It was Georgia that in 1812 first set the pernicious example of electing judges for short terms by the people,*—a practice which is responsible for much of the degradation that the courts have suffered in many of our states, and which will have to be abandoned before a proper administration of justice can ever be secured.

In bestowing the suffrage, the new constitutions were as conservative as in all other respects. The general state of opinion in America at that time, with regard to universal suffrage, was far more advanced than the general state of opinion in England, but it was less advanced than the opinions of such statesmen as Pitt and Shelburne and the Duke of Richmond. There was a truly English irregularity in the provisions which were made on this subject. In New Hampshire, Pennsylvania, Delaware, and South Carolina, all resident freemen who paid taxes could vote. In North Carolina all such persons could vote for members of the lower house, but in order to vote for senators a freehold of fifty acres was required. In Virginia none could vote save those who possessed such a freehold of fifty acres. To vote for governor or for senators in New York, one must possess a freehold of $250, clear of mortgage, and to vote for assemblymen one must either have a freehold of $50, or pay a yearly rent of $10. The pettiness of these sums was in keeping with the time when two daily coaches sufficed for the traffic between our two greatest commercial cities. In Rhode Island an unincumbered freehold worth $134 was required; but in Rhode Island and Pennsylvania the eldest sons of qualified freemen could vote without payment of taxes. In all the other states the possession of a small amount of property, either real or personal, varying from $33 to $200, was the necessary qualification for voting. Thus slowly and irregularly did the states drift toward universal suffrage; but although the impediments in the way of voting were

* In recent years Georgia has been one of the first states to abandon this bad practice.

more serious than they seem to us in these days when the community is more prosperous and money less scarce, they were still not very great, and in the opinion of conservative people they barely sufficed to exclude from the suffrage such shiftless persons as had no visible interest in keeping down the taxes. . . .

Henry Adams (1838–1918) and the
Search for a Science of History

Perhaps the most scintillating of all American historians, Henry Adams was the Boston-born son of the reformist statesman, Charles Francis Adams, Lincoln's minister to England during the Civil War. He was the grandson of President John Quincy Adams and the great-grandson of President John Adams—a heritage that greatly influenced his outlook. His brothers, Brooks and Charles Francis, Jr., shared his lifelong interest in writing history and the philosophy of history. As secretary to his father at the Court of St. James he learned much about diplomacy, met the most famous British scientists as well as statesmen, and broadened the education that he had acquired at Harvard. He studied law, but he quickly gave up the idea of practice and turned to journalism, writing critical articles on Jay Gould, Jim Fiske, and the corruption of business and politics.

In 1870 he accepted with some lack of enthusiasm Harvard's invitation to teach medieval history, and he soon added courses in early American history. Several years later he was engrossed in a magnum opus entitled *The History of the United States during the Administrations of Jefferson and Madison* (9 vols., 1889–91). He also wrote an excellent and appreciative biography of Albert Gallatin in 1879 and an unsympathetic one of the eccentric John Randolph in 1882.

His famous *History,* as one might expect, was particularly expert in diplomatic affairs, and covered the War of 1812 thoroughly. More impressive to present-day historians is his mastery of social history, which he handled philosophically as well as descriptively. He displayed the Adams family bias toward Jefferson, but this did not affect the general accuracy or thoughtfulness of his presentation. His extensive original sources were drawn from foreign as well as American archives and his synthesis was to remain substantially accepted for

many decades. There were already clear suggestions of his search for
a positivist philosophy of history based on the natural sciences. He
had considered the possibilities of Darwinism as an evolutionary clue
to historical development, but he had become deeply interested in the
potentialities of the New Physics as a tool of historical analysis. Most
impressive to him, as the years went by, were the implications of the
New Physics with its Second Law of Thermodynamics concerning
the conservation of energy and the equilibration of force—which he
thought could eventually be reduced to a helpful mathematical
formula applicable to history.

His search for a scientific philosophy of history soon overshadowed
and replaced his empirical research in American history. He speculated at length upon the Virgin in medieval Christianity as a focal
source of all-pervading energy, particularly in *Mont Saint Michel and
Chartres* (1904), which was hailed as a pioneer work by Ralph Adams
Cram, the leading neo-medieval architect. Later, he saw a great force
in the dynamo as a symbol of the modern technological spirit. This
was imaginatively expressed in his remarkable autobiography, written
in the third person, *The Education of Henry Adams* (1907). But his
incessant urging to teachers and historians to seek a philosophy of
history based upon the New Physics left professionals cold, although
his gifted brother Brooks did use natural science ideas in his own
historical writings. Historians, however, admired his *History* and
elected him president of the American Historical Association.

The following selections illustrate Henry Adams's skill in social
history, and show his obvious superiority in analysis to the technique
of McMaster (pages 217–53). The article on John Smith's trustworthiness regarding the Pocahontas episode is a model of historical analysis
in the tradition of Ranke, although his unfavorable conclusions have
been challenged by certain historians.

Historical Essays

CAPTAINE JOHN SMITH

Captain John Smith belonged to the extraordinary school of adventurers who gave so much lustre to the reign of Elizabeth, and whose most brilliant leader King James brought to the Tower and the block. Like Raleigh, though on a much lower level, Smith sustained many different characters. He was a soldier or a sailor indifferently, a statesman when circumstances gave him power, and an author when occasion required. Born in Lincolnshire in 1579, of what is supposed to have been a good Lancashire family, at a very early age he became a soldier of fortune in the Low Countries, and drifted into the Austrian service, where he took part in the campaign of 1600 against the Turks. Afterward he reappeared as a soldier of the Prince of Transylvania, who gave him a coat-of-arms, which was registered at the Herald's College in London. His extraordinary adventures during the three or four years of his life in Eastern Europe were related in his Autobiography, or "True Travels," a work published in London in 1630, near the close of his life. Dr. Palfrey's History of New England contains the earliest critical examination of this portion of Smith's story from an historical and geographical point of view, with a result not on the whole unfavorable to Smith.[1]

In 1604 Smith was again in England, where he soon began to interest himself in the enterprise of colonizing America.

On the 10th of April, 1606, King James conferred a charter upon certain persons in England, who took the title of the Virginia Company, and who proceeded to fit out an expedition of three small vessels, containing, in addition to their crews, one hundred and five colonists, headed by a Council, of which Edward Maria Wingfield was chosen President, and Captains Bartholomew Gosnold, John Smith, John Ratcliffe, John Martin, and George Kendall were the

Pages 42–70 (Scribner's, 1891). Originally printed in the *North American Review* for January, 1867.

other members. After various delays this expedition dropped down
the Thames December 20 of the same year, but was kept six weeks in
sight of England by unfavorable winds. After a long and difficult
voyage, and a further delay of three weeks among the West India
Islands, the headlands of Chesapeake Bay were passed April 26, 1607.
On the 14th of May following, the colonists formally founded Jamestown.

In the mean while trouble had risen between Smith and his colleagues. Smith's story was told in the "Generall Historie" as follows:—

Now, Captain Smith, who all this time from their departure from the
Canaries was restrained as a prisoner upon the scandalous suggestions of
some of the chiefe, (envying his repute), who fained he intended to usurpe
the Government, murther the Councell, and make himselfe King; that his
confederats were dispersed in all the three ships, and that divers of his
confederats that revealed it would affirm it. For this he was committed as
a prisoner. Thirteen weeks he remained thus suspected, and by that time
the ships should returne, they pretended out of their commisserations to
refer him to the Councell in England to receive a check, rather then by
particulating his designes make him so odious to the world, as to touch
his life, or utterly overthrow his reputation.

Captain Newport, who was about to return to England, exerted his
influence so strongly in favor of harmony that Smith was allowed to
resume his seat among the Council; but he was not liked by the
persons in control of the expedition, and some little light on the causes
of their dislike or suspicion may be found in a passage of Wingfield's
"Discourse," which said of Smith that "it was proved to his face that
he begged in Ireland, like a rogue without a lycence,"—and he adds,
"To such I would not my name should be a companyon." If Smith
was accused of conspiring to obtain power, the dark events and questionable expedients of his varied and troubled career might well be
flung in his face, and produce a considerable influence on the minds
of his judges. Harmony was a blessing little known among the unhappy colonists, and before the close of the year, Captain George
Kendall, another of the members of the Council, was accused of the

same crime with which Smith had been charged, and was tried, convicted, and actually executed.

Newport, who had great influence over the colonists, sailed for England June 22, leaving three months' supplies behind him, and promising to return in seven months with a new company of settlers. His departure was followed by disasters and troubles of every description. The mortality was frightful. More than forty deaths took place before September, some caused by fevers and sickness, some by the Indians, but the larger number by famine. The kindness of the Indians alone, according to the express statement of Percy, who was among the survivors, preserved the remaining colonists from the fate of the lost Roanoke settlement of 1585.

Even this condition of the colony, though during five months together not five able-bodied men could mount the defences, had no effect in quieting the jealousies and dissensions of the leaders. Captain Gosnold died, leaving only Wingfield, Ratcliffe, Smith, and Martin in the Council. The last three combined to depose Wingfield; and this revolution took place September 10, without resistance. Ratcliffe, as the next in order, was chosen President.

"As at this time," said Smith, "were most of our chiefest men either sicke or discontented, the rest being in such dispaire as they would rather starve and rot with idleness than be perswaded to do anything for their owne reliefe without constraint,—our victualles being now within eighteene dayes spent, and the Indians' trade decreasing, I was sent to the mouth of ye river to trade for Corne, and try the River for Fish; but our fishing we could not effect by reason of the stormy weather." Fortunately the Indians were found willing to trade for corn, and by means of their supplies the lives of the settlers were saved. On the 9th of November, Smith made a longer excursion, partially exploring the Chickahominy, and was received with much kindness by the Indians, who supplied him with corn enough to have "laded a ship." Elated by his success and encouraged by the friendly attitude of the savages,—or, according to his own account, eager "to discharge the imputation of malicious tungs, that halfe suspected I durst not, for so long delaying,"—he determined to carry on his ex-

ploration of the Chickahominy to its source. On the 10th of December
he started in the pinnace, which he left at a place he called Apocant,
forty miles above the mouth of the Chickahominy, and continued
his journey in a barge. Finally, rather than endanger the barge, he
hired a canoe and two Indians to row it, and with two of his own
company, named Robinson and Emry, went twenty miles higher.
"Though some wise men may condemn this too bould attempt of
too much indiscretion, yet if they well consider the friendship of the
Indians in conducting me, the desolatenes of the country, the
propabilitie of [discovering] some lacke, and the malicious judges of
my actions at home, as also to have some matters of worth to incourage
our adventurers in England, might well have caused any honest
minde to have done the like, as wel for his own discharge as for the
publike good."

At length they landed to prepare their dinner, and Smith with one
Indian walked on along the course of the river, while Robinson and
Emry with the other Indian remained to guard the canoe. Within a
quarter of an hour he heard a hallooing of Indians and a loud cry,
and fearing treachery, he seized his guide, whose arm he bound fast
to his own hand, while he prepared his pistol for immediate use. As
they "went discoursing," an arrow struck him on the right thigh,
but without harm. He soon found himself attacked by some two
hundred savages, against whose arrows he used his guide as a shield,
discharging his pistol three or four times. The Indian chief, Opechankanough, then called upon him to surrender, and the savages laid
their bows on the ground, ceasing to shoot.

My hinde treated betwixt them and me of conditions of peace; he discovered me to be the Captaine. My request was to retire to ye boate; they
demaunded my armes; the rest they saide were slaine, only me they would
reserve; the Indian importuned me not to shoot. In retiring, being in the
midst of a low quagmire, and minding them more then my steps, I stept
fast into the quagmire, and also the Indian in drawing me forth. Thus
surprised, I resolved to trie their mercies; my armes I caste from me, till
which none durst approach me. Being ceazed on me, they drew me out
and led me to the King.

Thus far, to avoid confusion, the account has followed the "True Relation," written by Smith, and published in London in 1608, the year after the events described.[2] In 1624 Smith published in London his "Generall Historie," which contained a version of the story varying essentially from that of the "True Relation." In continuing the account of his captivity, the two narratives will be placed side by side, for convenience of comparison, and the principal variations will be printed in Italics.

After describing the circumstances of his capture, which took place far up the Chickahominy River, Smith continued in his double narrative:—

A TRUE RELATION.
1608.

"They drew me out and led me to the King. I presented him with a compasse diall. . . . With kinde speeches and bread he requited me, conducting me where the Canow lay, and John Robinson slaine, with 20 or 30 arrowes in him. Emry I saw not. I perceived by the aboundance of fires all over the woods, *at each place I expected when they would execute me, yet they used me with what kindnes they could.* Approaching their Towne, which was within 6 miles where I was taken, . . . the Captaine conducting me to his lodging, a quarter of venison and some ten pound of bread I had for supper; what I left was reserved for me, and sent with me to my lodging. Each morning 3 women presented me three great platters of fine bread; *more venison than ten men could devour I had;* my gowne, points and garters, my compas and a tablet they gave me again; though 8 ordinarily guarded

THE GENERALL HISTORIE.
1624.

"Then according to their composition they drew him forth and led him to the fire where his men were slaine. Diligently they chafed his benumbed limbs. He demanding for their Captaine they showed him Opechankanough king of Pamaunkee, to whom he gave a round ivory double-compass Dyall. Much they marvailed at the playing of the Fly and Needle. . . . *Notwithstanding, within an houre after they tied him to a tree, and as many as could stand about him prepared to shoot him,* but the King holding up the Compass in his hand, they all laid down their bowes and arrowes, and in a triumphant manner led him to Orapaks, where he was after their manner kindly feasted and well used. . . . Smith they conducted to a long house where *thirtie or fortie tall fellowes did guard him,* and ere long *more bread and venison was brought him than would have served twentie men.* I me, I wanted not what they could devise to content me; and still our longer acquaintance increased our better affection. . . . I desired he [the King] would send a messenger to Paspahegh [Jamestown] with a letter I would write, by which they shold understand how kindly they used me, and that I was well, least they should revenge my death; this he granted, and sent three men, in such weather as in reason were unpossible by any naked to be endured. . . . The next day after my letter came a salvage to my lodging with his sword to have slaine me. . . . This was the father of him I had slayne, whose fury to prevent, the King presently conducted me to another Kingdome, upon the top of the next northerly river, called Youghtanan. Having feasted me, he further led me to another branch of the river called Mattapament; to two other hunting townes they led me, and to each of these countries a house of the great Emperor of Pewhakan, whom as yet I supposed to bee at the Fals; *to him I told him I must goe, and so returne to Paspahegh.* After this foure or five dayes march, we returned to Rasawrack, the first towne they brought me too, where binding the Mats in bundles, they marched two dayes journey and crossed the river of Youghtanan where it was as broad as Thames; so conducting me to a place called Menapacute in Pamaunke, where yᵉ King inhabited. . . .

"From hence this kind King con-

think his stomach at that time was not very good; what he left they put in baskets and tyed over his head; about midnight they set the meat again before him. All this time not one of them would eat a bit with him, till the next morning they brought him as much more, and then did they eate all the olde, and reserved the newe as they had done the other; which made him think they would fat him to eate him. Yet in this desperate estate to defend him from the cold, one Maocassater brought him his gowne in requitall of some beads and toyes Smith had given him at his first arrival in Virginia.

"Two dayes after, a man would have slaine him (but that the guard prevented it) for the death of his sonne, to whom they conducted him to recover the poore man then breathing his last. . . . In part of a Table booke he writ his minde to them at the Fort, and . . . the messengers . . . according to his request went to Jamestowne in as bitter weather as could be of frost and snow, and within three dayes returned with an answer.

"Then they led him to the Youthtanunds, the Mattaponients, the Payankatanks, the Nantaughtacunds, and Omawmanients upon the rivers of Rapahannock and *Patawomeck, over all those rivers* and back againe by divers other severall nations to the King's habitation at Pamaunkee, where they entertained him with most strange and fearfull Conjurations. . . .

ducted mee to a place called Topa-hanocke, a kingdome upon another River northward. The cause of this was, that the yeare before, a shippe had beene in the River of Pamaunke, who having been kindly entertained by Powhatan their Emperour, they returned thence, and discovered the River of Topahanocke, where being received with like kindnesse, yet he slue the King and tooke of his people; and they supposed I were hee, but the people reported him a great man that was Captaine, and using mee kindly, the next day we departed. . . .

"The next night I lodged at a hunting town of Powhatams, and the next day arrived at Waranacomoco upon the river of Pamauncke, where the great king is resident. . . .

"Arriving at Weramocomoco, their Emperour . . . kindly welcomed me with good wordes and great Platters of sundrie Victuals, *assuring mee his friendship, and my libertie within foure dayes.* . . . Hee desired mee to forsake Paspahegh, and to live with him upon his River,—a Countrie called Capa Howasicke; hee promised to give me Corne, Venison, or what I wanted to feede us; Hatchets and Copper wee should make him, and none should disturbe us. This request I promised to performe; and thus having with all the kindnes hee could devise, sought to content me, hee sent me home *with 4 men,* one that usually carried my Gowne and Knapsacke after me, two other

"At last they brought him to Meronocomoco, where was Powhatan their Emperor. Here more than two hundred of those grim Courtiers stood wondering at him, as he had been a monster; till Powhatan arrd his trayne had put themselves in their greatest braveries. . . . At his entrance before the King, all the people gave a great shout. The Queene of Appamatuck was appointed to bring him water to wash his hands, and another brought him a bunch of feathers, instead of a Towell to dry them. *Having feasted him after their best barbarous manner they could, a long consultation was held; but the conclusion was, two great stones were brought before Powhatan; then as many as could lay their hands on him dragged him to them, and thereon laid his head; and being ready with their clubs to beate out his braines, Pocahontas the King's dearest daughter, when no intreaty could prevaile, got his head in her armes, and laid her owne upon his to save him from death; whereat the Emperour was contented he should live to make him hatchets, and her bells, beads, and copper.* . . .

"Two dayes after, Powhatan having disguised himselfe in the most fearfullest manner he could . . . more like a devil than a man, with some two hundred more as blacke as himselfe, came unto him and told him now they were friends, and presently he should goe to Jamestowne, to send him two great gunnes and a gryndstone, for which loded with bread, and one to accompanie me. . . .

"From Weramocomoco is but 12 miles, yet the Indians trifled away that day, and would not goe to our Forte by any perswasions; but in certaine olde hunting houses of Paspahegh we lodged all night. The next morning ere Sunne rise, we set forward for our Fort, where we arrived within an houre, where each man with truest signes of joy they could expresse welcomed mee, except M. Archer, and some 2 or 3 of his, who was then in my absence sworne Counsellour, though not with the consent of Captaine Martin. Great blame and imputation was laide upon mee by them for the losse of our two men which the Indian slew; insomuch that they purposed to depose me; but *in the midst of my miseries it pleased God to send Captaine Nuport, who arriving there the same night so tripled our joy as for a while these plots against me were deferred,* though with much malice against me, which Captain Newport in a short time did plainly see."

he would give him the Country of Capahowosick, and for ever esteeme him as his sonne Nantaquoud. So to Jamestowne *with 12 guides* Powhatan sent him, *he still expecting (as he had done all this long time of his imprisonment) every houre to be put to one death or other, for all their feasting.* But almightie God (by his divine providence) had mollified the hearts of those sterne Barbarians with compassion. The next morning betimes they came to the Forte. . . .

"*Now in Jamestowne they were all in combustion, the strongest preparing once more to run away with the Pinnace; which with the hazzard of his life, with Sabre, falcon, and musket shot, Smith forced now the third time to stay or sinke.* Some, no better than they should be, had plotted with the President the next day to have put him to death by the Leviticall law, for the lives of Robinson and Emry, pretending the fault was his that had led them to their ends: but *he quickly tooke such order with such lawyers, that he layd them by the heels till he sent some of them prisoners for England.* . . .

"Newport got in and arrived at James Towne not long after the redemption of Captaine Smith. . . .

"Written by Thomas Studley, the first Cape Merchant in Virginia, Robert Fenton, Edward Harrington, and J. S."

Comparison of the two narratives thus for the first time placed side by side, betrays a tone of exaggeration in the later story. Eight guards, which had been sufficient in 1608, were multiplied into thirty or forty tall fellows in 1624. What was enough for ten men at the earlier time would feed twenty according to the later version. In 1608 four guides were an ample escort to conduct Smith to Jamestown, but they were reinforced to the number of twelve sixteen years afterward. With the best disposition toward Smith, one cannot forget that he belonged to the time when Falstaff and his misbegotten knaves in Kendal Green appeared upon the stage. The execution wrought upon the lawyers who wished to try Smith for his life on his return to Jamestown was prompt and decisive according to the story of 1624, but in 1608 "in the midst of my miseries it pleased God to send" Captain Newport to defer the plots of Smith's enemies. With sabre, falcon, and musket-shot he forced the mutinous crew of the pinnace to stay or sink, according to the "Generall Historie," while the "True Relation" was silent as to any feat of arms, but simply said that Captain Newport arrived the same evening.

The same exaggeration marked the account of Smith's treatment among the savages. According to the story written a few months after the event, a people was described, savage, but neither cruel nor blood-thirsty; reckless perhaps of life in battle, but kind and even magnanimous toward their captive. The "True Relation" implied that no demonstration was made against Smith's life, such as he described in 1624 as occurring within an hour after his capture. Only a few days after he was taken prisoner, he directed Opechankanough to take him to Powhatan, and even then he knew that he was to be allowed to return to Jamestown. "To him I told him I must go, and so return to Paspahegh." Powhatan received him with cordiality, and having sought to content him with all the kindness he could devise, sent him with a guard of honor back to his friends. In the "True Relation," the behavior of the Indians toward Smith was more humane than he would have received at the hands of civilized peoples. He found no cause to fear for his life, except from a savage whose son he had killed, and from whom Opechankanough protected him. One line indeed alluded to a fear that they fed him so fat as to make him much doubt they meant to sacrifice him; but this evidence of the kindness of the Indians implied that he believed himself to have been mistaken in having entertained the suspicion. Yet in 1624, throughout his long imprisonment, he was still expecting every hour to be put to one death or another.

These variations would not concern the ordinary reader of colonial history, if they stopped at trifling inconsistencies. They would merely prove the earlier narrative to be the safer authority for historians to follow, which is an established law of historical criticism. The serious divergence occurred in Smith's account of his visit to Powhatan, which in 1608 was free from thè suspicion of danger to his life, but in 1624 introduced Pocahontas as his savior from a cruel execution. The absence of Pocahontas, and of any allusion to her interference, or of reference to the occasion on which she interfered, makes the chief characteristic of the earlier story, and if the law of evidence is sound, requires the rejection of the latter version as spurious.

Smith's silence in 1608 about his intended execution and his preservation by Pocahontas was the more remarkable, because the "True Relation" elsewhere mentioned Pocahontas, with every appearance of telling the whole share she had in Smith's affairs. Smith's captivity occurred in December. In the following month of May, Smith imprisoned at Jamestown some Indians whom he suspected of treachery. The "True Relation" continued:—

Powhatan, understanding we detained certaine Salvages, sent his daughter, a child of tenne yeares old, which not only for feature, countenance, and proportion much exceedeth any of the rest of his people, but for wit and spirit the only Nonpareil of his Country: this he sent by his most trustie messenger, called Rawhunt, as much exceeding in deformitie of person, but of a subtill wit and crafty understanding. He with a long circumstance told me how well Powhatan loved and respected mee, and in that I should not doubt any way of his kindnesse he had sent his child, which he most esteemed, to see me: . . . his little daughter he had taught this lesson also.

Smith regarded Pocahontas as a person so much worth winning to his interests that he surrendered the prisoners to her.

We guarded them as before to the Church, and after prayer gave them to Pocahontas, the King's Daughter, in regard of her father's kindnesse in sending her. . . . Pocahontas also we requited, with such trifles as contented her, to tel that we had used the Paspaheyans very kindly in so releasing them.

Had Pocahontas saved Smith's life four months before, Smith would have been likely to surrender the prisoners out of gratitude to her, rather than "in regard of her father's kindnesse in sending" his favorite child to ask a return for his own hospitality.

No American needs to learn that Pocahontas is the most romantic character in the history of his country. Her name and story are familiar to every schoolboy, and families of the highest claim to merit trace their descent from the Emperor's daughter that saved the life of Captain John Smith. In the general enthusiasm, language and perhaps commonsense have been strained to describe her attributes. Her beauty and wild grace, her compassion and disinterestedness, her Christian life and pure character, have been dwelt upon with warmth the more natural as the childhood of the nation furnished little latitude to imagination. One after another, American historians have contented themselves with repeating the words of the "Generall Historie," heaping praises which no critics were cynical enough to gainsay, now on the virtues of Pocahontas, and now on the courage and constancy of Smith.

The exclusive share of the later narrative in shaping popular impressions was well shown by the standard authority for American history. In the early editions of Bancroft's "History of the United States," the following version of Smith's adventure was given:—

The gentle feelings of humanity are the same in every race, and in every period of life; they bloom, though unconsciously, even in the bosom of a child. Smith had easily won the confiding fondness of the Indian maiden; and now, the impulse of mercy awakened within her breast, she clung firmly to his neck, as his head was bowed to receive the strokes of the tomahawk. Did the childlike superstition of her kindred reverence her interference as a token from a superior power? Her fearlessness and her entreaties persuaded the council to spare the agreeable stranger, who might make hatchets for her father, and rattles and strings of beads for herself, the favorite child. The barbarians, whose decision had long been held in suspense by the mysterious awe which Smith had inspired, now resolved to receive him as a friend, and to make him a partner of their councils. They tempted him to join their bands, and lend assistance in an attack upon the white men at Jamestown; and when his decision of character succeeded in changing the current of their thoughts, they dismissed him with mutual promises of friendship and benevolence.

In a note appended to these paragraphs the author quoted:—

Smith, I. 158–162, and II. 29–33. The account is fully contained in the oldest book printed on Virginia, in our Cambridge library. It is a thin quarto, in black-letter, by John Smith, printed in 1608,—A True Relation, etc.

The story, in passing through the medium of Mr. Bancroft's mind, gained something which did not belong to the original, or belonged to it only in a modified degree. The spirit of Smith infused itself into the modern historian, as it had already infused itself into the works of his predecessors. The lights were intensified; the shadows deepened; the gradations softened. The copy surpassed its model. This tendency went so far that the author quoted the "True Relation" as the full authority for what was to be found only in the "Generall Historie," if indeed it was all to be found even there. When Mr. Bancroft collated his version of the story with the black-letter pamphlet in the Cambridge library, the popular reputation of Smith had already created an illusion in his mind resembling the optical effect of refracted light. He saw something which did not exist,—the exaggerated image of a figure beyond.

The labors of Charles Deane have made necessary a thorough examination into the evidence bearing on Smith's story; and Deane's notes make such an inquiry less laborious than the mass of material seemed to threaten. With that aid, an analysis of the evidence can be brought within narrow compass.

The first President of the colony was Edward Maria Wingfield, who in September, 1607, was deprived of his office, and placed in confinement by Smith and the other members of the Council. When Newport—who with a new company of settlers arrived at Jamestown Jan. 8, 1608, immediately after Smith's release—began his second return voyage to London, he took the deposed President Wingfield with him, and they arrived safely at Blackwall on the 21st of May. Wingfield kept a diary during his stay in Virginia, and after his return he wrote with its assistance a defence of himself and his administration, privately circulated in manuscript, and at a later period used by Purchas, but afterward forgotten and hidden in the dust of the Lambeth Library. From this obscurity it was drawn by Mr. Deane, who published it with notes in the fourth volume of the Archæologia Americana in 1860.[3] Excepting a few papers of little consequence, this is the earliest known writing which came directly from the colony. The manuscript of Smith's "True Relation," its only possible rival, could not have reached England before the month of July, while Wingfield's manuscript was intended for immediate circulation in May or June. Wingfield's work, which was called "A Discourse of Virginia," is therefore new authority on the early history of the colony, and has peculiar value as a test for the correctness of the "True Relation." Its account of Smith's captivity could only have been gained from his own mouth, or from those to whom he told the story, and its accuracy can be tested by the degree of its coincidence with the "True Relation."

A number of passages in this short pamphlet would be worth extracting; but the inquiry had best be narrowed to the evidence in regard to Pocahontas. The passage from Wingfield, telling of Smith's adventures among the Indians, ran as follows:—

Dec. The 10th of December Mr. Smith went up the ryver of the Chechohomynies to trade for corne. He was desirous to see the heade of that river; and when it was not passible with the shallop, he hired a cannow and an Indian to carry him up further. The river the higher grew worse and worse. Then he went on shoare with his guide, and left Robinson and Emmery, twoe of our men in the cannow, which were presently slaine by the Indians, Pamaonke's men, and he himself taken prysoner; and by the means of his guide his lief was saved. And Pamaonche haveing him prisoner, carryed him to his neybors wyroances to see if any of them knewe him for one of those which had bene, some two or three yeres before us, in a river amongst them Northward, and taken awaie some Indians from them by force. At last he brought him to the great Powaton (of whome before wee had no knowledg), who sent him home to our towne the viii^th of January. . . .

Mr. Archer sought how to call Mr. Smith's lief in question, and had indited him upon a chapter in Leviticus for the death of his twoe men. He had had his tryall the same daie of his retorne, and I believe his hanging the same or the next daie, so speedie is our law there; but it pleased God to send Captn. Newport unto us the same evening to our unspeakable comfort, whose arrivall saved Mr. Smyth's life and mine.

Deane, in editing Wingfield in 1860, furnished a note upon this passage, in which for the first time a doubt was thrown upon the story of Pocahontas's intervention. Yet the discovery of Wingfield's narrative added little to the evidence contained in the "True Relation,"—always a well-known work. The "Discourse" supplied precise dates, fixing Smith's departure on the 10th of December, and his return on the 8th of January, his absence being exactly four weeks in length; it said that Smith's guide saved his life, which might be a variation from the story of the "True Relation"; it dwelt on the danger Smith ran, from the enmity of Archer, which might be only the result of Wingfield's dislike of that person. In general, this new evidence, though clearly independent of the "True Relation," confirmed it in essentials, and especially in the omission of reference to Pocahontas. So remarkable an incident as her protection of Smith, if known to Wingfield, would scarcely have been omitted in this narrative, which must have contained the version of Smith's adventures current among the colonists after his return to Jamestown.

These two works are the only contemporaneous authority for the first year of the colonial history. A wide gap intervenes between them and the next work; and the strength of Deane's case rests so largely on the negative evidence offered by the "True Relation" and the "Discourse," that for his purpose further search was useless. Every one, whether believing or disbelieving the "Generall Historie," must agree that Pocahontas was not mentioned, either by name or by implication, as the preserver of Smith's life either by Smith in the "True Relation" or by Wingfield in his "Discourse." The inquiry might stop here, and each reader might be left to form his own opinion as to the relative value of the conflicting narratives; but the growth of a legend is as interesting as the question of its truth.

Newport returned to England April 10, 1608, carrying Wingfield with him, and leaving Ratcliffe President of the Colony, with Martin, Smith, and Archer in the Council, together with a new member, Matthew Scrivener, who had arrived with Newport. Smith in June explored successfully a part of Chesapeake Bay, and returning July 21, found, according to the "Generall Historie," the colonists in a miserable condition, unable to do anything but complain of Ratcliffe, whose principal offence appears to have been his obliging the colonists to build him "an unnecessary building for his pleasure in the woods." Ratcliffe, whose real name was Sicklemore, was a poor creature, if the evidence in regard to him can be believed. He was deposed, and Scrivener, Smith's "deare friend," though then exceedingly ill, succeeded him as President. This revolution was rapidly effected; for three days later, July 24, Smith again set out with twelve men, to finish his explorations, and made a complete tour round the bay, which supplied his materials for the map published at Oxford in 1612. He did not return to Jamestown till the 7th of September, and on the 10th he assumed the Presidency, "by the Election of the Councell and request of the Company." Scrivener appears merely to have held the office during Smith's pleasure, and voluntarily resigned it into his hands.

The history of Smith's administration of the colony from Sept. 10, 1608, till the end of September, 1609, is given in the "Generall Historie," and may be studied with advantage as an example of Smith's style. Whatever may have been the merits of his government, he had no better success than his predecessors, and he not only failed to command obedience, but was left almost or quite without a friend. He was ultimately deposed and sent to England under articles of complaint. The precise tenor of these articles is unknown; but Mr. Deane has found in the Colonial Office a letter of Ratcliffe, alias Sicklemore, dated Oct. 4, 1609, in which he announced to the Lord Treasurer that "this man [Smith] is sent home to answere some misdemeanors whereof I perswade me he can scarcely clear himselfe

from great imputation of blame." Beyond a doubt the difficulties of
the situation were very great, and the men Smith had to control were
originally poor material, and were made desperate by their trials;
but certainly his career in Virginia terminated disastrously, both for
himself and for the settlement. The Virginia Company, notwithstanding his applications, never employed him again.

The colony went from bad to worse. George Percy, a brother of
the Earl of Northumberland, succeeded Smith in the Presidency. The
condition of the colonists between Smith's departure in October, 1609,
and the arrival of Sir Thomas Gates in May, 1610, was terrible. Percy
was so "sicke hee could neither goe nor stand." Ratcliffe, with a number of others, was killed by Indians. The remainder fed on roots,
acorns, fish, and actually on the savages whom they killed, and on
each other,—one man murdering his wife and eating her. Out of the
whole number, said to have been five hundred, not more than sixty
were living when Gates arrived; and he immediately took them on
board ship, and abandoning Jamestown, set sail for England. Only
by accident they met a new expedition under Lord Delaware, at the
mouth of the river, which brought a year's provisions, and restored
the fortunes of the settlement. In spite of the discouragement produced in England by these disasters, the Company renewed its efforts,
and again sent out Sir Thomas Gates with six vessels and three
hundred men, who arrived in August, 1611. The government was
then in the hands of Sir Thomas Dale, who assumed it in May, 1611,
and retained it till 1616. If the ultimate success of the colony was
due to any single man, the merit appears to belong to Dale; for his
severe and despotic rule crushed the insubordination that had been
the curse of the State, compelled the idle to work, and maintained
order between the colonists and the Indians.

In the mean while Smith, who had taken final leave of the colony,
appears to have led a quiet life in London during several years. Lost
from sight during the years 1610 and 1611, he appeared again in
1612 busied in the same direction as before. In that year he published
at Oxford a short work called "A Map of Virginia. With a Description of the Countrey, the Commodities, People, Government, and

Religion. Written by Captaine Smith, sometimes Governour of the Countrey. Whereunto is annexed the proceedings of those Colonies, &c., by W. S." The latter part of the publication, which purported to be drawn from the writings of certain colonists, was afterward reprinted, with alterations, as the Third Book of the "Generall Historie," from the title of which it appears that "W. S." stood for the initials of William Simons, Doctor of Divinity.

In this tract only one passage bore upon Smith's story of Pocahontas. Among the customs described as peculiar to the Indians was the form of execution practised against criminals. Their heads, Smith said, were placed upon an altar, or sacrificing-stone, while "one with clubbes beates out their braines." During his captivity Smith added, not indeed that he had actually seen this mode of execution, but that an Indian had been beaten in his presence till he fell senseless, without a cry or complaint. The passage is remarkable for more than one reason. In the first place, the mode of execution there described was uncommon, if not unknown, among the Indians of the sea-coast; in the second place, the passage contained the germ of Smith's later story. Practised lawyers may decide whether, under the ordinary rules of evidence, this passage implies that Smith had himself not been placed in the position described, and future students may explain why Smith should have suppressed his own story, supposing it to have been true. The inference is strong that if anything of the sort had occurred, it would have been mentioned here; and this argument is strengthened by a short narration of his imprisonment given in the second part of the pamphlet, for which Dr. Simons was the nominal authority. This version ran as follows:—

A month those barbarians kept him prisoner. Many strange triumphs and conjurations they made of him; yet he so demeened himself amongst them as he not only diverted them from surprising the fort, but procured his own liberty, and got himself and his company such estimation among them that those savages admired him as a Demi God. So returning safe to the Fort, once more stayed the pinnace her flight for England.

This work was, as above mentioned, afterward reprinted, under the author's name, as the Third Book of the "Generall Historie." The passage just quoted was there reproduced with the evidently intentional substitution of "six or seven weekes" for "a month," as in the original. In the "Generall Historie" the concluding paragraph was omitted, and in its place stood, "The manner how they used and delivered him is as followeth." Then, breaking abruptly into the middle of the old narrative, the story which has been quoted was interpolated.

The narrative in the second part of the "Map of Virginia," of which the above extract forms a part, was signed by the name of Thomas Studley alone, while in the "Generall Historie" the enlarged account bore also the signatures of Edward Harrington, Robert Fenton, and Smith himself. A question may arise as to the extent to which these persons should be considered as dividing with Smith the responsibility for the story. Thomas Studley died on the 28th of August, 1607. Both he and Edward Harrington had lain four months in their graves before Smith ever heard of Powhatan or Pocahontas. The date of Robert Fenton's death is not so clear, but there is no reason to suppose that he had any share in the narration of events which Smith alone witnessed.

The argument so far as the Oxford tract is concerned would be strong enough, if it went no further; but it becomes irresistible when this tract not only mentions Pocahontas, but introduces her as the savior of Smith's life, although it says no word of her most famous act in this character. The allusion occurred toward the end of the pamphlet, where the assumed writer took occasion to defend Smith against certain charges, one of them being an alleged scheme on his part of marrying Powhatan's daughter Pocahontas in order to acquire a claim to the throne. The writer denied the charge, and added:—

It is true she was the very nonparell of his kingdome, and at most not past 13 or 14 yeares of age. Very often shee came to our fort with what shee could get for Captaine Smith, that ever loved and used all the countrie well, but her especially he ever much respected; and she so well requited it that when her father intended to have surprised him, shee, by stealth in the darke night, came through the wild woods and told him of it.

The Oxford tract of 1612 may be considered decisive that down to that date the story of Pocahontas had not been made public. Here we take leave of Smith as an authority for a period of some ten years, during which he published but one work, not relating to the present subject. An entirely new class of colonists had in 1610–1611 taken the place of the first settlers, almost exterminated by the disasters of 1609–1610. Among the new-comers in the train of Lord Delaware, in 1610, was William Strachey, who held the office of Secretary of the Colony. Little is known of Strachey, except that after his return to England he compiled a work called the "Historie of Travaile into Virginia," never completed in its original plan, but still extant in two neatly written manuscripts, printed by the Hakluyt Society in 1849. The date of its composition was probably about the year 1615. It consisted largely of extracts from Smith's previous works, though without acknowledgment of their origin; it also contained original matter, and especially some curious references to Pocahontas,[4] but no reference, direct or indirect, to her agency in saving Smith's life, and no trace of the high esteem which such an act would have won for her.

Next in order after Strachey's manuscript comes a work which is quite original, and gives perhaps the best account of the colony ever made public by an eye-witness. This is a small volume in quarto, printed in London in 1615, and called "A True Discourse of the Present Estate of Virginia . . . till the 18th of June, 1614, together with . . . the Christening of Powhatan's daughter and her Marriage with an Englishman. Written by Raphe Hamor, late Secretarie in the Colonie." It contains a minute and graphic story how "Pocahuntas, King Powhatan's daughter, whose fame has spread even to England, under the name of Non Parella," while staying with some tribe, subject to her father, on the Potomac, was seized and carried away by Captain Argol, who had sailed up that river on a trading expedition. Her imprisonment as a hostage at Jamestown, her visit to her father's residence with Sir Thomas Dale and a strong force of English, Powhatan's failure to redeem her, and her subsequent marriage to John Rolfe April 5, 1613, are all circumstantially narrated; and finally an extremely interesting account is given of a visit which Hamor made to Powhatan, and of the conversation he had with that extraordinary savage. Besides this work of Hamor, the volume also contains several letters from persons in Virginia, one of which is by John Rolfe, written with the object of justifying his marriage. Afterward, when the arrival of Pocahontas in England had excited an interest throughout Europe in her story, Hamor's book was translated and published in Germany.

Although repeated allusions to Pocahontas occur in the works already mentioned, in Hamor she makes, for the first time, her appearance as a person of political importance. In the "True Relation" Smith represented her as a pretty and clever child ten years old, once sent with a trusted messenger by Powhatan to the fort to entreat the liberation of some Indians whom Smith had seized. The Oxford tract mentioned her as a friend of Smith, but a mere child. Strachey gave a curious description of her intimate relations with the colony during his residence there:—

Pocahuntas, a well featured but wanton yong girle, Powhatan's daughter, sometymes resorting to our fort, of the age then of eleven or twelve yeares, would get the boyes forth with her into the markett place, and make them wheele, falling on their hands, turning up their heeles upwards, whome she would followe and wheele so her self, naked as she was, all the fort over.

Pocahontas was then apparently considered as a child like any other; but from the time when Argol treacherously seized her she took an important position,—in the first place, as the guaranty of a peace which Powhatan promised, and preserved during the remainder of her life and of his own; in the second place, as a person calculated to excite interest in England in behalf of the colony; and finally, as an eminent convert to the English Church, through whom a religious influence might be exercised among her father's subjects. Hamor's book was filled with her history, and Rolfe's letter showed much anxiety to prove the propriety of his course in marrying her. Both writers were interested in exciting as much sympathy for her as could be roused. Yet neither the one nor the other alluded to the act which has since become her first claim to praise, and which has almost thrown the rest of her story out of sight. There is no reason to suppose that in Virginia in 1614 the persons best informed were yet aware that Pocahontas had saved Smith's life.

In the month of June, 1616, Sir Thomas Dale arrived at Plymouth on his return home, bringing with him among his suite the baptized Pocahontas, then called Rebecca Rolfe, who with her husband and child came at the charge of the Company to visit England, and to prove to the world the success of the colony. She became at once the object of extraordinary attention, and in the following winter she was the most distinguished person in society. Her portrait taken at that time still exists, and shows a somewhat hard-featured figure, with a tall hat and ruff, appearing ill at ease in the stiff and ungraceful fashions of the day. Gentlemen of the court sent the engraving, as the curiosity of the season, in their letters to correspondents abroad. The Church received her with great honor, and the Bishop of London gave her an entertainment, celebrated in enthusiastic terms by Purchas. At the court masque in January, 1617, Pocahontas was among the most conspicuous guests. The King and Queen received her in special audiences; and to crown all, tradition reports, with reasonable foundation, that King James, in his zeal for the high principles of divine right and the sacred character of royalty, expressed his serious displeasure that Rolfe, who was at best a simple gentleman, should have ventured so far beyond his position as to ally himself with one who was of imperial blood.

Just at that time, when the influence of London society had set its stamp of fashion on the name of the Indian girl, and when King James had adopted her as rightfully belonging within the pale of the divinity that hedges a king, Samuel Purchas, "Parson of St. Martin's by Ludgate," published the third edition of his "Pilgrimage." Purchas, although not himself an explorer, was an enthusiast on the subject of travels and adventures; and in compiling the collection now so eagerly sought and so highly valued by collectors of books, he had, so far as related to Virginia, the direct assistance of personal witnesses, and also of manuscripts now unhappily lost except for his extracts. He was well acquainted with Smith, who "gently communicated" his notes to him, and who was in London, and visited Pocahontas at Brentford. Purchas himself saw Pocahontas. He was present when "my Honble. and Rev^d. Patron the Lord Bishop of London, D^r. King, entertained her with festivall state and pompe beyond what I have seen in his great hospitalitie afforded to other ladies," in his "hopefull zeale by her to advance Christianitie." He knew Tomocomo, an Indian of Powhatan's tribe, who came with her to England. "With this savage I have often conversed at my good friend's Master Doctor Goldstone, where he was a frequent guest; and where I have both seen him sing and dance his diabolicall measures, and heard him discourse of his countrey and religion, Sir Thomas Dale's man being the interpretour." He knew Rolfe also, who lent him his manuscript Discourse on Virginia. Yet Purchas's book contained no allusion to the heroic intervention on behalf of Smith, the story of whose captivity is simply copied from Simons's quarto of 1612; the diffuse comments on men and manners in Virginia contain no trace of what would have been correctly regarded as the most extraordinary incident in colonial history.

Silence in a single instance, as in Wingfield or in Strachey, might be accounted for, or at all events might be overlooked; but silence during a long period of years and under the most improbable circumstances, cannot be ignored. Wingfield, Smith himself, Simons, Strachey, Hamor, Rolfe, and Purchas, all the authorities without exception known to exist, are equally dumb when questioned as to a circumstance which since 1624 has become the most famous part of colonial history. The field is exhausted. No other sources exist from which to draw authentic information. Nothing remains but to return to Smith, and to inquire when it was that this extraordinary story first made its appearance, and how it obtained authority.

The blaze of fashionable success that surrounded Pocahontas in London lighted the closing scene of her life. She was obliged, against her will as was believed, to set out on her return to Virginia, but she never actually left the shores of England. Detained in the Thames by several weeks of contrary winds, her failing strength altogether gave way; and in March, 1617, in the word-play of Purchas, "she came at Gravesend to her end and grave." Her father, Powhatan, survived her less than a year.

Smith in the meanwhile was busied with projects in regard to New England and the fisheries. His efforts to form a colony there and to create a regular system of trade had little success; but to spread a knowledge of the new country among the people of England, he printed, in 1616, a small quarto, called "A Description of New England," and in 1620 he published another pamphlet, entitled "New England's Trials," a second and enlarged edition of which appeared in 1622. There at last, in 1622, the long-sought allusion to his captivity occurred in the following words:—

For wronging a soldier but the value of a penny I have caused Powhatan [to] send his own men to Jamestowne to receive their punishment at my discretion. It is true in our greatest extremitie they shot me, slue three of my men, and by the folly of them that fled took me prisoner; yet God made Pocahontas the King's daughter the means to deliver me; and thereby taught me to know their treacheries to preserve the rest.

The first appearance of this famous story can therefore be fixed within five years,—between 1617 and 1622,—although the complete account is only to be found in the "Generall Historie," printed in 1624, from which copious extracts have already been quoted. Only one point of difficulty still requires attention.

Smith there said (pp. 121–123) that when Pocahontas came to England he wrote for her a sort of letter of introduction to the Queen, or, in his own words, "a little booke to this effect to the Queen, an abstract whereof followeth."

Some ten yeeres agoe, being in Virginia and taken prisoner by the power of Powhatan their chiefe King, . . . I cannot say I felt the least occasion of want that was in the power of those my mortall foes to prevent, notwithstanding al their threats. After some six weeks fatting amongst those

Salvage Courtiers, at the minute of my execution, she hazarded the beating out of her owne braines to save mine, and not onely that, but so prevailed with her father that I was safely conducted to Jamestowne.

This letter rests on the authority of the "Generall Historie," and has neither more nor less weight than that work gives it. Smith's "abstract of the effect" of the little book was as liable to interpolations as the text of the "Generall Historie" elsewhere. At the time it was published, in 1624, not only had Pocahontas long been dead, but Queen Anne herself had in 1619 followed her to the grave, and Smith remained alone to vouch for his own accuracy. The Virginia Company had no interest in denying the truth of a story so well calculated to draw popular sympathy toward the colony.

Smith's character was always a matter of doubt. Thomas Fuller, one of Smith's contemporaries, published the "Worthies of England" some thirty years after Smith's death, when the civil wars had intervened to obliterate the recollection of personal jealousies, and when Smith must have been little remembered. Fuller devoted a page to Smith's history in the following vein:—

From the Turks in Europe he passed to the Pagans in America, where, towards the latter end of the reign of Queen Elizabeth, such his perils, preservations, dangers, deliverances, they seem to most men above belief, to some beyond truth. Yet have we two witnesses to attest them, the prose and the pictures, both in his own book; and it soundeth much to the diminution of his deeds that he alone is the herald to publish and proclaim them.

The essential evidence on each side of this curious question has now been exhausted, although it would be easy to argue indefinitely in regard to Smith's general character. This must be done by the first historian who attempts again to deal with the history of the Virginia Colony. The argument may be left for future and final judgment, but some reasonable theory is still required to explain the existence of the story assumed to be false. Deane, like Palfrey, hints that Smith in the latter part of his life fell into the hands of hack-writers, who adapted history for popular effect. Perhaps the truth may be somewhat as follows.

The examination of Smith's works has shown that his final narrative was the result of gradual additions. The influence exercised by Pocahontas on the affairs of the colony, according to the account given in 1608, was slight. In 1612 she first appeared in her heroic character. Her capture and her marriage to Rolfe gave her importance. Her visit to England made her the most conspicuous figure in Virginia, and romantic incidents in her life were likely to be created, if they did not already exist, by the exercise of the popular imagination, attracted by a wild and vigorous picture of savage life.

The history of the emperor's daughter became, as Smith implied, a subject for the stage. Nothing was more natural or more probable. It is not even necessary to assume that Smith invented the additions to his own story. He may have merely accepted them after they had obtained a hold on the minds of his contemporaries.

In the meanwhile Smith's own career had failed, and his ventures ended disastrously, while in most cases he did not obtain the employment which he continued to seek with unrelaxed energy. In 1622 a disaster occurred in Virginia which roused the greatest interest and sympathy in England, and gave occasion for renewed efforts in behalf of the colony. The Indians rose against the English, and in the month of May a massacre took place around Jamestown. The opportunity was one not to be lost by a man who like Smith, while burning to act, was still smarting under what he considered undeserved neglect, and he hastened to offer his services to the Company, with a plan for restoring peace; but his plan and his offer of services were again declined. Still, the resource which he had frequently used remained, and by publishing the "Generall Historie" he made a more ambitious appeal to the public than any he had yet attempted. In this work he embodied everything that could tend to the increase of his own reputation, and drew material from every source that could illustrate the history of English colonization. Pocahontas was made to appear in it on every possible occasion, and his own share in the affairs of the colony was magnified at the expense of his companions. None of those whose reputations he treated with harshness appeared to vindicate their own characters, far less to assert their knowledge in regard to Pocahontas. The effort indeed failed of its object, for he remained unemployed and without mark of distinction. "He led his old age in London, where his having a Prince's mind imprisoned in a poor man's purse rendered him to the contempt of such who were not ingenuous. Yet he efforted his spirits with the remembrance and relation of what formerly he had been and what he had done." So Fuller wrote, who might have known him in his later years. Smith died quietly in his bed, in London, in June, 1631. His will has been published by Deane, but furnishes little new information. In the absence of criticism, his book survived to become the standard authority on Virginian history. The readiness with which it was received is scarcely so remarkable as the credulity which has left it unquestioned almost to the present day.

NOTES

[1] Palfrey's History of New England, i. pp. 89–92, note.

[2] *A True Relation of Virginia.* By Captain John Smith. With an Introduction and Notes, by Charles Deane. Boston. 1866.

[3] *A Discourse of Virginia.* By Edward Maria Wingfield, the First President of the Colony. Edited by Charles Deane, Member of the American Antiquarian Society, and of the Massachusetts Historical Society. Boston: Privately printed. 1860.

[4] See Deane's edition of the True Relation, p. 72.

History of the United States during the Administrations of Jefferson and Madison

[POPULAR CHARACTERISTICS]

The growth of character, social and national,—the formation of men's minds,—more interesting than any territorial or industrial growth, defied the tests of censuses and surveys. No people could be expected, least of all when in infancy, to understand the intricacies of its own character, and rarely has a foreigner been gifted with insight to explain what natives did not comprehend. Only with diffidence could the best-informed Americans venture, in 1800, to generalize on the subject of their own national habits of life and thought. Of all American travellers President Dwight * was the most experienced; yet his four volumes of travels were remarkable for no trait more uniform than their reticence in regard to the United States. Clear and emphatic wherever New England was in discussion, Dwight claimed no knowledge of other regions. Where so good a judge professed ignorance, other observers were likely to mislead; and Frenchmen like Liancourt, Englishmen like Weld, or Germans like Bülow, were almost equally worthless authorities on a subject which none understood. The newspapers of the time were little more trustworthy than the books of travel, and hardly so well written. The literature of a higher kind was chiefly limited to New England, New York, and Pennsylvania. From materials so poor no precision of result could be expected. A few customs, more or less local; a few prejudices, more or less popular; a few traits of thought, suggesting habits of mind,—must form the entire material for a study more important than that of politics or economics.

The standard of comfort had much to do with the standard of character; and in the United States, except among the slaves, the laboring class enjoyed an ample supply of the necessaries of life. In

Volume I, pages 41–68, 72–3 (Scribner's, 1889).
[* Timothy Dwight of Yale]

this respect, as in some others, they claimed superiority over the laboring class in Europe, and the claim would have been still stronger had they shown more skill in using the abundance that surrounded them. The Duc de Liancourt, among foreigners the best and kindest observer, made this remark on the mode of life he saw in Pennsylvania:—

There is a contrast of cleanliness with its opposite which to a stranger is very remarkable. The people of the country are as astonished that one should object to sleeping two or three in the same bed and in dirty sheets, or to drink from the same dirty glass after half a score of others, as to see one neglect to wash one's hands and face of a morning. Whiskey diluted with water is the ordinary country drink. There is no settler, however poor, whose family does not take coffee or chocolate for breakfast, and always a little salt meat; at dinner, salt meat, or salt fish, and eggs; at supper again salt meat and coffee. This is also the common regime of the taverns.

An amusing, though quite untrustworthy Englishman named Ashe, who invented an American journey in 1806, described the fare of a Kentucky cabin:—

The dinner consisted of a large piece of salt bacon, a dish of hominy, and a tureen of squirrel broth. I dined entirely on the last dish, which I found incomparably good, and the meat equal to the most delicate chicken. The Kentuckian eat nothing but bacon, which indeed is the favorite diet of all the inhabitants of the State, and drank nothing but whiskey, which soon made him more than two-thirds drunk. In this last practice he is also supported by the public habit. In a country, then, where bacon and spirits form the favorite summer repast, it cannot be just to attribute entirely the causes of infirmity to the climate. No people on earth live with less regard to regimen. They eat salt meat three times a day, seldom or never have any vegetables, and drink ardent spirits from morning till night. They have not only an aversion to fresh meat, but a vulgar prejudice that it is unwholesome. The truth is, their stomachs are depraved by burning liquors, and they have no appetite for anything but what is high-flavored and strongly impregnated by salt.

Salt pork three times a day was regarded as an essential part of American diet. In the "Chain-bearer," Cooper described what he called American poverty as it existed in 1784. "As for bread," said the mother, "I count that for nothing. We always have bread and potatoes enough; but I hold a family to be in a desperate way when the mother can see the bottom of the pork-barrel. Give me the children that's raised on good sound pork afore all the game in the country. Game's good as a relish, and so's bread; but pork is the staff of life . . . My children I calkerlate to bring up on pork."

Many years before the time to which Cooper referred, Poor Richard asked: "Maids of America, who gave you bad teeth?" and supplied the answer: "Hot soupings and frozen apples." Franklin's question and answer were repeated in a wider sense by many writers, but none was so emphatic as Volney:—

I will venture to say [declared Volney] that if a prize were proposed for the scheme of a regimen most calculated to injure the stomach, the teeth, and the health in general, no better could be invented than that of the Americans. In the morning at breakfast they deluge their stomach with a quart of hot water, impregnated with tea, or so slightly with coffee that it is mere colored water; and they swallow, almost without chewing, hot bread, half baked, toast soaked in butter, cheese of the fattest kind, slices of salt or hung beef, ham, etc., all which are nearly insoluble. At dinner they have boiled pastes under the name of puddings, and the fattest are esteemed the most delicious; all their sauces, even for roast beef, are melted butter; their turnips and potatoes swim in hog's lard, butter, or fat; under the name of pie or pumpkin, their pastry is nothing but a greasy paste, never sufficiently baked. To digest these viscous substances they take tea almost instantly after dinner, making it so strong that it is absolutely bitter to the taste, in which state it affects the nerves so powerfully that even the English find it brings on a more obstinate restlessness than coffee. Supper again introduces salt meats or oysters. As Chastellux says, the whole day passes in heaping indigestions on one another; and to give tone to the poor, relaxed, and wearied stomach, they drink Madeira, rum, French brandy, gin, or malt spirits, which complete the ruin of the nervous system.

An American breakfast never failed to interest foreigners, on account of the variety and abundance of its dishes. On the main lines of travel, fresh meat and vegetables were invariably served at all meals; but Indian corn was the national crop, and Indian corn was eaten three times a day in another form as salt pork. The rich alone could afford fresh meat. Ice-chests were hardly known. In the country fresh meat could not regularly be got, except in the shape of poultry or game; but the hog cost nothing to keep, and very little to kill and preserve. Thus the ordinary rural American was brought up on salt pork and Indian corn, or rye; and the effect of this diet showed itself in dyspepsia.

One of the traits to which Liancourt alluded marked more distinctly the stage of social development. By day or by night, privacy was out of the question. Not only must all men travel in the same coach, dine at the same table, at the same time, on the same fare, but even their beds were in common, without distinction of persons. Innkeepers would not understand that a different arrangement was possible. When the English traveller Weld reached Elkton, on the main road from Philadelphia to Baltimore, he asked the landlord what accommodation he had. "Don't trouble yourself about that," was the reply; "I have no less than eleven beds in one room alone." This primitive habit extended over the whole country from Massachusetts to Georgia, and no American seemed to revolt against the tyranny of innkeepers.

"At New York I was lodged with two others, in a back room on the ground floor," wrote, in 1796, the Philadelphian whose complaints have already been mentioned. "What can be the reason for that vulgar, hoggish custom, common in America, of squeezing three, six, or eight beds into one room?"

Nevertheless, the Americans were on the whole more neat than their critics allowed. "You have not seen the Americans," was Cobbett's reply, in 1819, to such charges; "you have not seen the nice, clean, neat houses of the farmers of Long Island, in New England, in the Quaker counties of Pennsylvania; you have seen nothing but the smoke-dried ultra-montanians." Yet Cobbett drew a sharp contrast between the laborer's neat cottage familiar to him in Surrey and Hampshire, and the "shell of boards" which the American occupied, "all around him as barren as a sea-beach." He added, too, that "the example of neatness was wanting"; no one taught it by showing its charm. Felix de Beaujour, otherwise not an enthusiastic American, paid a warm compliment to the country in this single respect, although he seemed to have the cities chiefly in mind:—

American neatness must possess some very attractive quality, since it seduces every traveller; and there is no one of them who, in returning to his own country, does not wish to meet again there that air of ease and neatness which rejoiced his sight during his stay in the United States.

Almost every traveller discussed the question whether the Americans were a temperate people, or whether they drank more than the English. Temperate they certainly were not, when judged by a modern standard. Every one acknowledged that in the South and West drinking was occasionally excessive; but even in Pennsylvania and New England the universal taste for drams proved habits by no means strict. Every grown man took his noon toddy as a matter of course; and although few were seen publicly drunk, many were habitually affected by liquor. The earliest temperance movement, ten or twelve years later, was said to have had its source in the scandal caused by the occasional intoxication of ministers at their regular meetings. Cobbett thought drinking the national disease; at all hours of the day, he said, young men, "even little boys, at or under twelve years of age, go into stores and tip off their drams." The mere comparison with England proved that the evil was great, for the English and Scotch were among the largest consumers of beer and alcohol on the globe.

In other respects besides sobriety American manners and morals were subjects of much dispute, and if judged by the diatribes of travellers like Thomas Moore and H. W. Bülow, were below the level of Europe. Of all classes of statistics, moral statistics were least apt to be preserved. Even in England, social vices could be gauged only by the records of criminal and divorce courts; in America, police was wanting and a divorce suit almost, if not quite, unknown. Apart from some coarseness, society must have been pure; and the coarseness was mostly an English inheritance. Among New Englanders, Chief-Justice Parsons was the model of judicial, social, and religious propriety; yet Parsons, in 1808, presented to a lady a copy of "Tom Jones," with a letter calling attention to the adventures of Molly Seagrim and the usefulness of describing vice. Among the social sketches in the "Portfolio" were many allusions to the coarseness of Philadelphia society, and the manners common to tea-parties. "I heard from married ladies," said a writer in February, 1803, "whose station as mothers demanded from them a guarded conduct,—from young ladies, whose age forbids the audience of such conversation, and who using it modesty must disclaim,—indecent allusions, indelicate expressions, and even at times immoral innuendoes. A loud laugh or a coarse exclamation followed each of these, and the young ladies generally went through the form of raising their fans to their faces."

Yet public and private records might be searched long, before they revealed evidence of misconduct such as filled the press and formed one of the commonest topics of conversation in the society of England and France. Almost every American family, however respectable, could show some victim to intemperance among its men, but few were mortified by a public scandal due to its women.

If the absence of positive evidence did not prove American society to be as pure as its simple and primitive condition implied, the same conclusion would be reached by observing the earnestness with which critics collected every charge that could be brought against it, and by noting the substance of the whole. Tried by this test, the society of 1800 was often coarse and sometimes brutal, but, except for intemperance, was moral. Indeed, its chief offence, in the eyes of Europeans, was dulness. The amusements of a people were commonly a fair sign of social development, and the Americans were only beginning to amuse themselves. The cities were small and few in number, and the diversions were such as cost little and required but elementary knowledge. In New England, although the theatre had gained a firm foothold in Boston, Puritan feelings still forbade the running of horses.

The principal amusements of the inhabitants [said Dwight] are visiting, dancing, music, conversation, walking, riding, sailing, shooting at a mark, draughts, chess, and unhappily, in some of the larger towns, cards and dramatic exhibitons. A considerable amusement is also furnished in many places by the examination and exhibitions of the superior schools; and a more considerable one by the public exhibitions of colleges. Our country-men also fish and hunt. Journeys taken for pleasure are very numerous, and are a very favorite object. Boys and young men play at foot-ball, cricket, quoits, and at many other sports of an athletic cast, and in the winter are peculiarly fond of skating. Riding in a sleigh, or sledge, is also a favorite diversion in New England.

President Dwight was sincere in his belief that college commence-ments and sleigh-riding satisfied the wants of his people; he looked upon whist as an unhappy dissipation, and upon the theatre as im-moral. He had no occasion to condemn horse-racing, for no race-course was to be found in New England. The horse and the dog existed only in varieties little suited for sport. In colonial days New England produced one breed of horses worth preserving and develop-ing,—the Narragansett pacer; but, to the regret even of the clergy, this animal almost disappeared, and in 1800 New England could show nothing to take its place. The germ of the trotter and the trotting-match, the first general popular amusement, could be seen in almost any country village, where the owners of horses were in the habit of trotting what were called scratch-races, for a quarter or half a mile from the door of the tavern, along the public road. Per-haps this amusement had already a right to be called a New-England habit, showing defined tastes; but the force of the popular instinct was not fully felt in Massachusetts, or even in New York, although there it was given full play. New York possessed a race-course, and made in 1792 a great stride toward popularity by importing the famous stallion "Messenger" to become the source of endless interest for future generations; but Virginia was the region where the Ameri-can showed his true character as a lover of sport. Long before the Revolution the race-course was commonly established in Virginia and Maryland; English running-horses of pure blood—descendants of the Darley Arabian and the Godolphin Arabian—were imported, and racing became the chief popular entertainment. The long Revolu-tionary War, and the general ruin it caused, checked the habit and

deteriorated the breed; but with returning prosperity Virginia showed
that the instinct was stronger than ever. In 1798 "Diomed," famous
as the sire of racers, was imported into the State, and future rivalry
between Virginia and New York could be foreseen. In 1800 the Virginia race-course still remained at the head of American popular
amusements.

In an age when the Prince of Wales and crowds of English gentlemen attended every prize-fight, and patronized Tom Crib, Dutch
Sam, the Jew Mendoza, and the negro Molyneux, an Englishman
could hardly have expected that a Virginia race-course should be
free from vice; and perhaps travellers showed best the general morality
of the people by their practice of dwelling on Virginia vices. They
charged the Virginians with fondness for horse-racing, cock-fighting,
betting, and drinking; but the popular habit which most shocked
them, and with which books of travel filled pages of description, was
the so-called rough-and-tumble fight. The practice was not one on
which authors seemed likely to dwell; yet foreigners like Weld, and
Americans like Judge Longstreet in "Georgia Scenes," united to give
it a sort of grotesque dignity like that of a bull-fight, and under their
treatment it became interesting as a popular habit. The rough-and-
tumble fight differed from the ordinary prize-fight, or boxing-match,
by the absence of rules. Neither kicking, tearing, biting, nor gouging
was forbidden by the law of the ring. Brutal as the practice was, it
was neither new nor exclusively Virginian. The English travellers
who described it as American barbarism, might have seen the same
sight in Yorkshire at the same date. The rough-and-tumble fight was
English in origin, and was brought to Virginia and the Carolinas in
early days, whence it spread to the Ohio and Mississippi. The habit
attracted general notice because of its brutality in a society that showed
few brutal instincts. Friendly foreigners like Liancourt were honestly
shocked by it; others showed somewhat too plainly their pleasure at
finding a vicious habit which they could consider a natural product
of democratic society. Perhaps the description written by Thomas
Ashe showed best not only the ferocity of the fight but also the
antipathies of the writer, for Ashe had something of the artist in his

touch, and he felt no love for Americans. The scene was at Wheeling. A Kentuckian and a Virginian were the combatants.

Bulk and bone were in favor of the Kentuckian; science and craft in that of the Virginian. The former promised himself victory from his power; the latter from his science. Very few rounds had taken place or fatal blows given, before the Virginian contracted his whole form, drew up his arms to his face, with his hands nearly closed in a concave by the fingers being bent to the full extension of the flexors, and summoning up all his energy for one act of desperation, pitched himself into the bosom of his opponent. Before the effects of this could be ascertained, the sky was rent by the shouts of the multitude; and I could learn that the Virginian had expressed as much beauty and skill in his retraction and bound, as if he had been bred in a menagerie and practised action and attitude among panthers and wolves. The shock received by the Kentuckian, and the want of breath, brought him instantly to the ground. The Virginian never lost his hold. Like those bats of the South who never quit the subject on which they fasten till they taste blood, he kept his knees in his enemy's body; fixing his claws in his hair and his thumbs on his eyes, gave them an instantaneous start from their sockets. The sufferer roared aloud, but uttered no complaint. The citizens again shouted with joy.

Ashe asked his landlord whether this habit spread down the Ohio.

I understand that it did, on the left-hand side, and that I would do well to land there as little as possible. . . . I again demanded how a stranger was to distinguish a good from a vicious house of entertainment. "By previous inquiry, or, if that was impracticable, a tolerable judgment could be formed from observing in the landlord a possession or an absence of ears."

The temper of the writer was at least as remarkable in this description as the scene he pretended to describe, for Ashe's Travels were believed to have been chiefly imaginary; but no one denied the roughness of the lower classes in the South and Southwest, nor was roughness wholly confined to them. No prominent man in Western society bore himself with more courtesy and dignity than Andrew Jackson of Tennessee, who in 1800 was candidate for the post of major-general of State militia, and had previously served as Judge on the Supreme Bench of his State; yet the fights in which he had been engaged exceeded belief.

Border society was not refined, but among its vices, as its virtues, few were permanent, and little idea could be drawn of the character that would at last emerge. The Mississippi boatman and the squatter on Indian lands were perhaps the most distinctly American type then existing, as far removed from the Old World as though Europe were a dream. Their language and imagination showed contact with Indians. A traveller on the levee at Natchez, in 1808, overheard a quarrel in a flatboat near by:—

"I am a man; I am a horse; I am a team," cried one voice; "I can whip any man in all Kentucky, by God!" "I am an alligator," cried the other; "half man, half horse; can whip any man on the Mississippi, by God!" "I am a man," shouted the first; "have the best horse, best dog, best gun, and handsomest wife in all Kentucky, by God!" "I am a Mississippi snapping-turtle," rejoined the second; "have bear's claws, alligator's teeth, and the devil's tail; can whip *any* man, by God!"

And on this usual formula of defiance the two fire-eaters began their fight, biting, gouging, and tearing. Foreigners were deeply impressed by barbarism such as this, and orderly emigrants from New England and Pennsylvania avoided contact with Southern drinkers and fighters; but even then they knew that with a new generation such traits must disappear, and that little could be judged of popular character from the habits of frontiersmen. Perhaps such vices deserved more attention when found in the older communities, but even there they were rather survivals of English low-life than products of a new soil, and they were given too much consequence in the tales of foreign travellers.

This was not the only instance where foreigners were struck by what they considered popular traits, which natives rarely noticed. Idle curiosity was commonly represented as universal, especially in the Southern settler who knew no other form of conversation:—

"Frequently have I been stopped by one of them," said Weld, "and without further preface asked where I was from, if I was acquainted with any news, where bound to, and finally my name. 'Stop, Mister! why, I guess now you be coming from the new State?' 'No, sir.' 'Why, then, I guess as how you be coming from Kentuck?' 'No, sir.' 'Oh, why, then, pray now where might you be coming from?' 'From the low country.' 'Why, you must have heard all the news, then; pray now, Mister, what might the price of bacon be in those parts?' 'Upon my word, my friend, I can't inform you.' 'Ay, ay; I see, Mister, you be'ent one of us. Pray now, Mister, what might your name be?' "

Almost every writer spoke with annoyance of the inquisitorial habits of New England and the impertinence of American curiosity. Complaints so common could hardly have lacked foundation, yet the Americans as a people were never loquacious, but inclined to be somewhat reserved, and they could not recognize the accuracy of the description. President Dwight repeatedly expressed astonishment at the charge, and asserted that in his large experience it had no foundation. Forty years later, Charles Dickens found complaint with Americans for taciturnity. Equally strange to modern experience were the continual complaints in books of travel that loungers and loafers, idlers of every description, infested the taverns, and annoyed respectable travellers both native and foreign. Idling seemed to be considered a popular vice, and was commonly associated with tippling. So completely did the practice disappear in the course of another generation that it could scarcely be recalled as offensive; but in truth less work was done by the average man in 1800 than in aftertimes, for there was actually less work to do. "Good country this for lazy fellows," wrote Wilson from Kentucky; "they plant corn, turn their pigs into the woods, and in the autumn feed upon corn and pork. They lounge about the rest of the year." The roar of the steam-engine had never been heard in the land, and the carrier's wagon was three weeks between Philadelphia and Pittsburg. What need for haste when days counted for so little? Why not lounge about the tavern when life had no better amusement to offer? Why mind one's own business when one's business would take care of itself?

Yet however idle the American sometimes appeared, and however large the class of tavern loafers may have actually been, the true

American was active and industrious. No immigrant came to America for ease or idleness. If an English farmer bought land near New York, Philadelphia, or Baltimore, and made the most of his small capital, he found that while he could earn more money than in Surrey or Devonshire, he worked harder and suffered greater discomforts. The climate was trying; fever was common; the crops ran new risks from strange insects, drought, and violent weather; the weeds were annoying; the flies and mosquitoes tormented him and his cattle; laborers were scarce and indifferent; the slow and magisterial ways of England, where everything was made easy, must be exchanged for quick and energetic action; the farmer's own eye must see to every detail, his own hand must hold the plough and the scythe. Life was more exacting, and every such man in America was required to do, and actually did, the work of two such men in Europe. Few English farmers of the conventional class took kindly to American ways, or succeeded in adapting themselves to the changed conditions. Germans were more successful and became rich; but the poorer and more adventurous class, who had no capital, and cared nothing for the comforts of civilization, went West, to find a harder lot. When, after toiling for weeks, they reached the neighborhood of Genessee or the banks of some stream in southern Ohio or Indiana, they put up a rough cabin of logs with an earthen floor, cleared an acre or two of land, and planted Indian corn between the tree-stumps,—lucky if, like the Kentuckian, they had a pig to turn into the woods. Between April and October, Albert Gallatin used to say, Indian corn made the penniless immigrant a capitalist. New settlers suffered many of the ills that would have afflicted an army marching and fighting in a country of dense forest and swamp, with one sore misery besides,— that whatever trials the men endured, the burden bore most heavily upon the women and children. The chance of being shot or scalped by Indians was hardly worth considering when compared with the certainty of malarial fever, or the strange disease called milk-sickness, or the still more depressing home-sickness, or the misery of nervous prostration, which wore out generation after generation of women and children on the frontiers, and left a tragedy in every log-cabin. Not for love of ease did men plunge into the wilderness. Few laborers of the Old World endured a harder lot, coarser fare, or anxieties and responsibilities greater than those of the Western emigrant. Not merely because he enjoyed the luxury of salt pork, whiskey, or even coffee three times a day did the American laborer claim superiority over the European.

A standard far higher than the average was common to the cities; but the city population was so small as to be trifling. Boston, New York, Philadelphia, and Baltimore together contained one hundred and eighty thousand inhabitants; and these were the only towns containing a white population of more than ten thousand persons. In a total population of more than five millions, this number of city people, as Jefferson and his friends rightly thought, was hardly American, for the true American was supposed to be essentially rural. Their comparative luxury was outweighed by the squalor of nine hundred thousand slaves alone.

From these slight notices of national habits no other safe inference could be drawn than that the people were still simple. The path their development might take was one of the many problems with which their future was perplexed. Such few habits as might prove to be fixed, offered little clew to the habits that might be adopted in the process of growth, and speculation was useless where change alone could be considered certain.

If any prediction could be risked, an observer might have been warranted in suspecting that the popular character was likely to be conservative, for as yet this trait was most marked, at least in the older societies of New England, Pennsylvania, and Virginia. Great as were the material obstacles in the path of the United States, the greatest obstacle of all was in the human mind. Down to the close of the eighteenth century no change had occurred in the world which warranted practical men in assuming that great changes were to come. Afterward, as time passed, and as science developed man's capacity to control Nature's forces, old-fashioned conservatism vanished from society, reappearing occasionally, like the stripes on a mule, only to prove its former existence; but during the eighteenth century the progress of America, except in political paths, had been less rapid than ardent reformers wished, and the reaction which followed the French Revolution made it seem even slower than it was. In 1723 Benjamin Franklin landed at Philadelphia, and with his loaf of bread under his arm walked along Market Street toward an immortality such as no American had then conceived. He died in 1790, after witnessing great political revolutions; but the intellectual revolution was hardly as rapid as he must, in his youth, have hoped.

In 1732 Franklin induced some fifty persons to found a subscription library, and his example and energy set a fashion which was generally followed. In 1800 the library he founded was still in existence; numerous small subscription libraries on the same model, containing fifty or a hundred volumes, were scattered in country towns; but all the public libraries in the United States—collegiate, scientific, or popular, endowed or unendowed—could hardly show fifty thousand volumes, including duplicates, fully one third being still theological.

Half a century had passed since Franklin's active mind drew the lightning from heaven; and decided the nature of electricity. No one in America had yet carried further his experiments in the field which he had made American. This inactivity was commonly explained as a result of the long Revolutionary War; yet the war had not prevented population and wealth from increasing, until Philadelphia in 1800 was far in advance of the Philadelphia which had seen Franklin's kite flying among the clouds.

In the year 1753 Franklin organized the postal system of the American colonies, making it self-supporting. No record was preserved of the number of letters then carried in proportion to the population, but in 1800 the gross receipts for postage were $320,000, toward which Pennsylvania contributed most largely,—the sum of $55,000. From letters the Government received in gross $290,000. The lowest rate of letter-postage was then eight cents. The smallest charge for letters carried more than a hundred miles was twelve and a half cents. If on an average ten letters were carried for a dollar, the whole number of letters was 2,900,000,—about one a year for every grown inhabitant.

Such a rate of progress could not be called rapid even by conservatives, and more than one stanch conservative thought it unreasonably slow. Even in New York, where foreign influence was active and the rewards of scientific skill were comparatively liberal, science hardly kept pace with wealth and population.

Noah Webster, who before beginning his famous dictionary edited the "New York Commercial Advertiser," and wrote on all subjects with characteristic confidence, complained of the ignorance of his countrymen. He claimed for the New Englanders an acquaintance with theology, law, politics, and light English literature; "but as to classical learning, history (civil and ecclesiastical), mathematics, astronomy, chemistry, botany, and natural history, excepting here and there a rare instance of a man who is eminent in some one of these branches, we may be said to have no learning at all, or a mere smattering." Although defending his countrymen from the criticisms of Dr. Priestley, he admitted that "our learning is superficial in a shameful degree, . . . our colleges are disgracefully destitute of books and philosophical apparatus, . . . and I am ashamed to own that scarcely a branch of science can be fully investigated in America for want of books, especially original works. This defect of our libraries I have experienced myself in searching for materials for the History of Epidemic Diseases. . . . As to libraries, we have no such things. There are not more than three or four tolerable libraries in America, and these are extremely imperfect. Great numbers of the most valuable authors have not found their way across the Atlantic."

This complaint was made in the year 1800, and was the more significant because it showed that Webster, a man equally at home in Philadelphia, New York, and Boston, thought his country's deficiencies greater than could be excused or explained by its circumstances. George Ticknor felt at least equal difficulty in explaining the reason why, as late as 1814, even good schoolbooks were rare in Boston, and a copy of Euripides in the original could not be bought at any book-seller's shop in New England. For some reason, the

American mind, except in politics, seemed to these students of
literature in a condition of unnatural sluggishness; and such complaints were not confined to literature or science. If Americans agreed
in any opinion, they were united in wishing for roads; but even on
that point whole communities showed an indifference, or hostility,
that annoyed their contemporaries. President Dwight was a somewhat extreme conservative in politics and religion, while the State
of Rhode Island was radical in both respects; but Dwight complained
with bitterness unusual in his mouth that Rhode Island showed no
spirit of progress. The subject of his criticism was an unfinished
turnpike-road across the State.

The people of Providence expended upon this road, as we are informed,
the whole sum permitted by the Legislature. This was sufficient to make
only those parts which I have mentioned. The turnpike company then
applied to the Legislature for leave to expend such an additional sum as
would complete the work. The Legislature refused. The principal reason
for the refusal, as alleged by one of the members, it is said, was the following: that turnpikes and the establishment of religious worship had their
origin in Great Britain, the government of which was a monarchy and the
inhabitants slaves; that the people of Massachusetts and Connecticut were
obliged by law to support ministers and pay the fare of turnpikes, and were
therefore slaves also; that if they chose to be slaves they undoubtedly had
a right to their choice, but that free-born Rhode Islanders ought never to
submit to be priest-ridden, nor to pay for the privilege of travelling on the
highway. This demonstrative reasoning prevailed, and the road continued
in the state which I have mentioned until the year 1805. It was then completed, and free-born Rhode Islanders bowed their necks to the slavery of
travelling on a good road.

President Dwight seldom indulged in sarcasm or exaggeration
such as he showed in this instance; but he repeated only matters of
notoriety in charging some of the most democratic communities with
unwillingness to pay for good roads. If roads were to exist, they
must be the result of public or private enterprise; and if the public
in certain States would neither construct roads nor permit corporations to construct them, the entire Union must suffer for want of
communication. So strong was the popular prejudice against paying

for the privilege of travelling on a highway that in certain States, like Rhode Island and Georgia, turnpikes were long unknown, while in Virginia and North Carolina the roads were little better than where the prejudice was universal.

In this instance the economy of a simple and somewhat rude society accounted in part for indifference; in other cases, popular prejudice took a form less easily understood. So general was the hostility to Banks as to offer a serious obstacle to enterprise. The popularity of President Washington and the usefulness of his administration were impaired by his support of a national bank and a funding system. Jefferson's hostility to all the machinery of capital was shared by a great majority of the Southern people and a large minority in the North. For seven years the New York legislature refused to charter the first banking company in the State; and when in 1791 the charter was obtained, and the Bank fell into Federalist hands, Aaron Burr succeeded in obtaining banking privileges for the Manhattan Company only by concealing them under the pretence of furnishing a supply of fresh water to the city of New York.

This conservative habit of mind was more harmful in America than in other communities, because Americans needed more than older societies the activity which could alone partly compensate for the relative feebleness of their means compared with the magnitude of their task. Some instances of sluggishness, common to Europe and America, were hardly credible. For more than ten years in England the steam-engines of Watt had been working, in common and successful use, causing a revolution in industry that threatened to drain the world for England's advantage; yet Europe during a generation left England undisturbed to enjoy the monopoly of steam. France and Germany were England's rivals in commerce and manufactures, and required steam for self-defense; while the United States were commercial allies of England, and needed steam neither for mines nor manufactures, but their need was still extreme. Every American knew that if steam could be successfully applied to navigation, it must produce an immediate increase of wealth, besides an ultimate settlement of the most serious material and political difficulties of the Union. Had both the national and State Governments devoted millions of money to this object, and had the citizens wasted, if necessary, every dollar in their slowly filling pockets to attain it, they would have done no more than the occasion warranted, even had they failed; but failure was not to be feared, for they had with their own eyes seen the experiment tried, and they did not dispute its success. For America this question had been settled as early as 1789, when John Fitch—a mechanic, without education or wealth, but with the energy of genius—invented engine and paddles of his own, with so much success that during a whole summer Philadelphians watched his ferry-boat plying daily against the river current. No one denied that his boat was rapidly, steadily, and regularly moved against wind and tide, with as much certainty and convenience as could be expected in a first experiment; yet Fitch's company failed. He could raise no more money; the public refused to use his boat or to help him build a better; they did not want it, would not believe in it, and broke his heart by their contempt. Fitch struggled against failure, and invented another boat moved by a screw. The Eastern public still proving indifferent, he wandered to Kentucky, to try his fortune on the Western waters. Disappointed there, as in Philadelphia and New York, he made a deliberate attempt to end his life by drink; but the process proving too slow, he saved twelve opium pills from the physician's prescription, and was found one morning dead.

Fitch's death took place in an obscure Kentucky inn, three years before Jefferson, the philosopher president, entered the White House. Had Fitch been the only inventor thus neglected, his peculiarities and the defects of his steamboat might account for his failure; but he did not stand alone. At the same moment Philadelphia contained another inventor. Oliver Evans, a man so ingenious as to be often called the American Watt. He, too, invented a locomotive steam-engine which he longed to bring into common use. . . .

Possibly Fulton and Fitch, like other inventors, may have exaggerated the public apathy and contempt; but whatever was the precise force of the innovating spirit, conservatism possessed the world by right. Experience forced on men's minds the conviction that what had ever been must ever be. At the close of the eighteenth century nothing had occurred which warranted the belief that even the material difficulties of America could be removed. Radicals as extreme as Thomas Jefferson and Albert Gallatin were contented with avowing no higher aim than that America should reproduce the simpler forms of European republican society without European vices; and even this their opponents thought visionary. The United States had thus far made a single great step in advance of the Old World,— they had agreed to try the experiment of embracing half a continent in one republican system; but so little were they disposed to feel confidence in their success, that Jefferson himself did not look on this American idea as vital; he would not stake the future on so new an invention. "Whether we remain in one confederacy," he wrote in 1804, "or form into Atlantic and Mississippi confederations, I believe not very important to the happiness of either part." Even over his liberal mind history cast a spell so strong, that he thought the solitary American experiment of political confederation "not very important" beyond the Alleghanies.

The task of overcoming popular inertia in a democratic society was new, and seemed to offer peculiar difficulties. Without a scientific class to lead the way, and without a wealthy class to provide the means of experiment, the people of the United States were still required, by the nature of their problems, to become a speculating and scientific nation. They could do little without changing their old habit of mind, and without learning to love novelty for novelty's sake. Hitherto their timidity in using money had been proportioned to the scantiness of their means. Henceforward they were under every inducement to risk great stakes and frequent losses in order to win occasionally a thousand fold. In the colonial state they had naturally accepted old processes as the best, and European experience as final authority. As an independent people, with half a continent to civilize, they could not afford to waste time in following European examples, but must devise new processes of their own. A world which assumed that what had been must be, could not be scientific; yet in order to make the Americans a successful people, they must be roused to feel the necessity of scientific training. Until they were satisfied that knowledge was money, they would not insist upon high education; nor until they saw with their own eyes stones turned into gold, and vapor into cattle and corn, would they learn the meaning of science.

John Bach McMaster (1852–1932) and the New Social History

It may seem surprising that John Bach McMaster, a conventional Whig, rather than George Bancroft, apostle of the Common Man, became the American pioneer of social history. But, McMaster was a product of the New York public schools, a native of Walt Whitman's Brooklyn, and a graduate of what is today the City College of New York and even his father, a New Orleans banker, a Louisiana sugar planter, and a merchant with ties abroad, did not influence his democratic, if somewhat upper-class, sympathies.

He had sufficient technical training at college to become a practicing civil engineer and an instructor in engineering at the College of New Jersey (later Princeton). His historical interests were stimulated by technical map-making for a Civil War biographer and by scientific expeditions to the Bad Lands of Wyoming in search of fossils. He was particularly impressed by his readings in Buckle, Macaulay, and Green with their emphasis upon social history. Buckle's effort to create a science of history encouraged his belief that one could study man scientifically by dealing with large groups rather than exceptional individuals. The rising vogue of Darwinism and the idea of inevitable progress were to be reflected in McMaster's optimistic interpretation of human development toward a better world.

In 1883 Appleton published the first volume of his eight-volume *A History of the People of the United States from the Revolution to the Civil War*. The selection given here, "The State of America in 1784," suggests the inspiration of Macaulay's third chapter which deals with the condition of England since 1685. Here was indeed a history of people rather than of rulers alone, although McMaster did not omit elections, wars, diplomacy, and other staples of history books. Unlike the New England historians, with a few exceptions like Parkman, he gave considerable attention to Western history, but he did not depart from a heavily nationalistic viewpoint. He even solicited the strongly nationalistic veterans group, the Grand Army of the Republic, to examine a school textbook of his for their approval as to orthodoxy. Unfortunately, too much of his social history was either pageantry or cumulative facts rather than scholarly evaluations of the social institutions and habits, which he described but did not relate to their social economic environment. Still there remained sufficient substance in his books for their wide use by academicians even in the second half of the twentieth century.

Shortly after the appearance of the first volume, McMaster was invited by the University of Pennsylvania to a chair in American history. For his fellow historians, he (together with Hermann von Holst and James Ford Rhodes) made the large-scale use of newspaper sources quite respectable, although he did not forsake the older types of documentation. The high prestige of the journalist in that day of emergent suffrage reform and growing mass literacy made this development understandable. McMaster's seventeen books are of uneven quality, although his pioneer business biography of Stephen Girard won warm praise. Readers enjoyed the freshness of his narrative, which was bolstered by human interest material from the newspapers. Teachers were encouraged to devote more attention to social history; and younger scholars went on to refine the techniques of writing the history of social institutions.

The second selection given here, "The Common School in the First Half Century," praises the American free school system as a great institution and tells a story that was not too well known at that time.

History of the People of the United States

The subject of my narrative is the history of the people of the United States of America from the close of the war for independence down to the opening of the war between the States. In the course of this narrative much, indeed, must be written of wars, conspiracies, and rebellions; of presidents, of congresses, of embassies, of treaties, of the ambition of political leaders in the senate-house, and of the rise of great parties in the nation. Yet the history of the people shall be the chief theme. At every stage of the splendid progress which separates the America of Washington and Adams from the America in which we live, it shall be my purpose to describe the dress, the occupations, the amusements, the literary canons of the times; to note the changes of manners and morals; to trace the growth of that humane spirit which abolished punishment for debt, which reformed the discipline of prisons and jails, and which has, in our own time, destroyed slavery and lessened the miseries of dumb brutes. Nor shall it be less my aim to recount the manifold improvements which, in a thousand ways, have multiplied the conveniences of life and ministered to the happiness of our race; to describe the rise and progress of that long series of mechanical inventions and discoveries which is now the admiration of the world, and our just pride and boast; to tell how, under the benign influence of liberty and peace, there sprang up, in the course of a single century, a prosperity unparalleled in the annals of human affairs; how, from a state of great poverty and feebleness, our country grew rapidly to one of opulence and power; how her agriculture and her manufactures flourished together; how, by a wise system of free education and a free press, knowledge was disseminated, and the arts and sciences advanced; how the ingenuity of her people became fruitful of wonders far more astonishing than any of which the alchemists had ever dreamed.

Volume I, pages 1–8; Volume V, pages 343–72 (Appleton, 1885).

Such a mingling of social with political history is necessary to a correct understanding of the peculiar circumstances under which our nation was formed and grew up. Other people in other times have become weary of their rulers, have thrown off the yoke, have come out of the house of bondage and set up that form of government which has always been thought the freest and most perfect. But our ancestors were indeed a highly favored people. They were descended from the most persevering, the most energetic, the most thrifty of races. They enjoyed the highest form of civilization; their climate was salubrious; their soil rich; their country boundless; they were hampered by no traditions; they were surrounded by no nations of whom they stood in fear. Almost alone, in a new land, they were free to work out their own form of government in accordance with their own will. The consequence has been such a moral and social advancement as the world has never seen before. The Americans who, toward the close of 1783, celebrated with bonfires, with cannon, and with bell-ringing, the acknowledgment of independence and the return of peace, lived in a very different country from that with which their descendants are familiar. Indeed, could we, under the potent influence of some magician's drugs, be carried back through the hundred years, we should find ourselves in a country utterly new to us. Rip Van Winkle, who fell asleep when his townsmen were throwing up their hats and drinking their bumpers to good King George, and awoke when a generation that knew him not was shouting the names of men and parties unknown to him, did not find himself in a land more strange. The area of the republic would shrink to less than half its present extent. The number of the States would diminish to thirteen, nor would many of them be contained in their present limits or exhibit their present appearance. Vast stretches of upland, which are now an endless succession of wheat-fields and corn-fields and orchards, would appear overgrown with dense forests abandoned to savage beasts and yet more savage men. The hamlets of a few fishermen would mark the sites of wealthy havens now bristling with innumerable masts, and the great cities themselves would dwindle to dimensions scarce exceeding those of some rude settlement far to the west of the Colorado river. Of the inventions and discoveries which abridge distance, which annihilate time, which extend commerce, which aid agriculture, which save labor, which transmit speech, which turn the darkness of the night into the brilliancy of the day, which alleviate pain, which destroy disease, which lighten even the infirmities of age, not one existed. Fulton was still a portrait-painter, Fitch and Rumsey had not yet begun to study the steam-engine, Whitney had not yet gone up to college. Howe and Morse, M'Cormick and Fairbanks, Goodyear and Colt, Dr. Morton and Dr. Bell, were yet to be born.

By the treaty which secured the independence of the colonies, the boundaries of the region given up by the mother country were clearly defined. The territory ceded stretched from the Atlantic Ocean westward to the banks of the Mississippi, and from a line running along the great lakes on the north it spread southward to the thirty-first parallel and the southern border of Georgia. This vast tract was parcelled out among the thirteen original States. Of the thirteen, seven had well-defined boundaries; of the remaining six, some laid claim to lands since given to other States, while a few would content themselves with no limits short of the waters of the Mississippi river.

But, though the Fourth of July orators then boasted that their country extended over fifteen hundred miles in length, and spread westward across plains of marvellous fertility into regions yet unexplored by man, they had but to look about them to see that the States were indeed but little better than a great wilderness. A narrow line of towns and hamlets extended, with many breaks, along the coast from the province of Maine to Georgia. Maine was still owned by Massachusetts, and did not contain one hundred thousand souls. Portland existed, then Falmouth, and along the shore were a few fishers' cots, built of rough-hewn logs, and thatched with seaweed. But an almost unbroken solitude lay between Portland and the St. Lawrence. In New Hampshire a few hardy adventurers had marked out the sites of villages in the White Mountains. In New York, Albany was settled, and Schenectady; but the rich valleys through which the Mohawk and the Genesee flow down to join the Hudson and the lake, were the hunting-grounds of the Oneidas, the Mohawks, the Cayugas. In Pennsylvania, dense forests and impassable morasses covered that region where rich deposits of iron and of coal have since produced the Birmingham of America. In Virginia, a straggling village or two was to be found about the headwaters of the Potomac and the James. Beyond the Blue Ridge, Daniel Boone was fighting the Cherokees in the canebrakes of Kentucky. Some villages of log huts surrounded by stockades were rising on the fertile plains of western Tennessee. A handful of pioneers had settled at Natchez. Pittsburgh was a military post. St. Louis was begun, but the very name of the village was unknown to nine tenths of the Americans. So late as 1795, Cincinnati consisted of ninety-five log cabins and five hundred souls. In truth, that splendid section of our country drained by the Ohio and the Tennessee was one vast solitude. Buffaloes wandered in herds over the rich plains now the granaries of Europe. Forests of oak and sycamore grew thick on the site of many great and opulent cities whose population now exceeds that of Virginia during the revolution, and whose names are spoken in the remotest corner of the civilized world. No white man had yet beheld the source of the Mississippi river. Of the country beyond the Mississippi little more was known than of the heart of Africa. Now and then some weather-beaten trapper came from it to the frontiers of the States with stories of great plains as level as the floor, where the grass grew higher than the waist, where the flowers were more beautiful than in the best kept garden, where trees were never seen, and where the Indians still looked upon the white man as a god. But this country lay far to the west of the frontier, and the frontier was wilder then than Wyoming is now. There the white man lived in an unending war with the red man.

The opinion which many careful and just-minded persons of our time have formed touching the Indians of whom the settlers in the border-land then stood in constant dread, is a singular mixture of truth and romance. Time and absence have softened all that is vile and repulsive in his character, and left in full relief all that is good and alluring. We are in no danger of being tomahawked. We are not terrified by his war-whoop. An Indian in his paint and feathers is now a much rarer show than a Bengal tiger or a white bear from the Polar sea. Of the fifty millions of human beings scattered over the land, not five millions have ever in their lives looked upon an Indian. We are therefore much more disposed to pity than to hate. But, one hundred years ago, there were to be found, from Cape Ann to Georgia, few men who had not many times in their lives seen numbers of Indians, while thousands could be found scattered through every State, whose cattle had been driven off, and whose homes had been laid in ashes by the braves of the Six Nations, who had fought with them from behind trees and rocks, and carried the scars of wounds received in hand-to-hand encounters. In every city were to be seen women who had fled at the dead of night from their burning cabins; who had, perhaps, witnessed the destruction of Schenectady; or were by a merciful Providence spared in the massacre of the Minisink; whose husbands had gone down in the universal slaughter of Wyoming; or whose children had, on that terrible day when Brant came into Orange county, stood in the door of the school-house when the master was dragged out, when their playmates were scalped, when their aprons were marked with the black mark which, like the blood upon the door-posts, a second time staid the hand of the Angel of Death. The opinions which such men and women held of the noble red man was, we may be sure, very different from those current among the present generation, and formed on no better authority than the novels of Cooper, and the lives of such warriors as Red Jacket and Brant.

Of the true character of the Indian it is difficult to give any notion to those who are acquainted with it only as it appears exalted or debased in the pages of fiction. In him were united in a most singular manner all the vices and all the arts which form the weapons, offensive and defensive, of the weak, with many of those high qualities which are always found associated with courage and strength. He was, essentially, a child of Nature, and his character was precisely such as circumstances made it. His life was one long struggle for food. His daily food depended not on the fertility of the soil or the abundance of the crops, but on the skill with which he used his bow; on the courage with which he fought, single-handed, the largest and fiercest of beasts; on the quickness with which he tracked, and the cunning with which he outwitted the most timid and keen-scented of creatures. His knowledge of the habits of animals surpassed that of Audubon. The shrewd devices with which he snared them would have elicited the applause of Ulysses; the clearness of his vision excelled that of the oldest sailor; the sharpness of his hearing was not equalled by that of the deer. Men of a less-gifted race were astounded at the rapidity with which he followed the most obscure trail over the most difficult ground; at the perfection with which he imitated the bark of the wolf, the hoot of the owl, the whistle of the whippoorwill; at the cat-like tread with which, over beds of autumn-leaves and heaps of dried twigs, he walked to the very side of the grazing deer. Nor was his success in the hunt without its effect. Many of the qualities of the creatures he hunted were, as he believed, imbibed with their blood. Courage, such as enables a man to go through a campaign or a battle with credit, such as makes him first in the breach and last in the retreat, and sends him, with a measured step and cool head, to the cannon's mouth, the brave possessed in the highest degree. Nor did he lack a more exalted fortitude. While he underwent the most excruciating torture the ingenuity of his enemies could devise, while his ears were being lopped off, while his nose was being slit, while slices of flesh were being cut from his body and the bleeding wounds smeared with hot ashes, while his feet were roasting, while his limbs were being torn with hot splinters, while the flames leaped high about him, he shouted his death-song with a steady voice till his tormentors plucked out his tongue or brained him with a tomahawk.

Yet this man whose courage was unquestionable, was given to the dark and crooked ways which are the resort of the cowardly and the weak. Much as he loved war, the fair and open fight had no charms for him. To his mind it was madness to take the scalp of an enemy at the risk of his own, when he might waylay him in an ambuscade, or shoot him with a gun or an arrow from behind a tree. He was never so happy as when, at the dead of night, he roused his sleeping enemies with an unearthly yell, and massacred them by the light of their burning- homes. Cool and brave men who have heard that whoop, have left us a striking testimony of its nature; how that no number of repetitions could strip it of its terrors; how that, to the very last, at the end of it the blood curdled, the heart ceased to beat, and a strange paralysis seized upon the body. The contrast between the savage on the war-path and the savage in his wigwam was indeed striking. When the hatchet was dug up, when the war-paint was put on, when the peace-pipe was broken, the idle, shiftless savage was all activity. Patient of hunger, patient of cold, he would march all day through the snow, with the thermometer far below zero; and at night, rolled in buffalo robes, go hungry to sleep. But when the chase was over, when the war was done, and the peace-pipe smoked out, he abandoned himself to debauchery and idleness. To sleep all day in a wigwam of painted skins, filthy and blackened with smoke, adorned with scalps, and hung with tomahawks and arrows, to dance in the shine of the new moon to music made from the skin of snakes, to tell stories of witches and evil spirits, to gamble, to sing, to jest, to boast of his achievements in war, and to sit with a solemn gravity at the councils of his chief, constituted his most serious employment. His squaw was his slave. With no more affection than a coyote feels for its mate, he brought her to his wigwam that she might gratify the basest of his passions and administer to his wants. It was Starlight or Cooing Dove that brought the wood for his fire and the water for his drink, that ploughed the field and sowed the maize. The bead-work which adorned his moccasins, the porcupine quills which set off his cloak, were arranged by her hands. When he travelled she trudged along with the pappoose on her back beside the led-horse that carried the wigwam and the few pots and jars of sun-baked clay.

The mental attainments of the Indian were quite of a piece with his character. His imagination was singularly strong, his reason singularly weak. He was as superstitious as a Hottentot negro and as unreasonable as a child. When a long succession of fasts and gorgings, when bad food and fire-water had done their worst, he awoke screaming from his dreams to assert that a wolf had sat upon his breast, that he had been in the clutches of Pauguk. Every twig that fell upon him in the forest was an omen. The simplest occurrences of life were full of significance. If he were sick some enemy had brought it on him. If misfortune overtook him it was the work of a medicine man or a witch whose anger he had excited. Then it was that, in his hour of need, he betook himself to the magic of his medicine bag and the skill of the medicine man, and, during incantations and strange mutterings and exorcisms, was beaten and bruised from head to foot and finally made to believe that a toad or a bright stone had been taken out of him, and was the cause of his ills. Gay colors pleased him beyond expression. Over a red blanket or a patchwork quilt the sedate and dignified savage would go into raptures of delight. To possess it he would gladly part with a bundle of skins which exceeded it many times in value, or with a hundred bushels of Indian corn.

Thus hemmed in on the east by the waters of the ocean, and on the west by a crafty and ever vigilant foe, were scattered the inhabitants of the thirteen States. Unfortunately the precise number of the population cannot now be ascertained with any high degree of certainty. But from such information as we have, it is safe to say that, in 1784, the number could not have been far from three millions and a quarter. It has been estimated that at the opening of the war there were in the country, both white and black, 2,750,000 souls.[1] . . .

THE COMMON SCHOOL IN THE FIRST HALF CENTURY

In the long list of institutions of which our countrymen have just cause to be proud, few hold so high a place in the estimation of the people, or show so marvellous a progress, as the American common school. To-day, in the five-and-forty States comprising the Union, more than fourteen millions of children are being educated at public expense by an army of four hundred thousand teachers, and at an annual cost of one hundred and seventy millions of dollars. When John Quincy Adams took the oath of office as President of the United

States there were not fourteen million inhabitants in our entire country, nor did the common school exist as an American institution. In some States it was slowly struggling into existence; in others it was quite unknown. Here the maintenance was voluntary. There free education was limited to children of paupers or of parents too poor to educate their sons and daughters at their own expense. Elsewhere State aid was coupled with local taxation. Scarcely anywhere did the common-school system really flourish. Parents were indifferent. Teachers as a class were ill-fitted for the work before them, and many a plan which seemed most promising as displayed in the laws accomplished little for the children of the State.

The story of the rise and development of the common school in the United States may well begin with the passage of an act by the General Court of Massachusetts as far back as 1647. Each township of fifty householders was then required to employ some one to teach reading and writing to such children as might come to him, and each township of one hundred householders to set up a grammar-school and hire such masters as could fit youth for the university. A previous law, enacted in 1742 [1642], made it the duty of parents and masters to teach their children and apprentices to read the English tongue, to know the capital laws, and to be able to repeat by rote some orthodox catechism. These two acts—the one requiring parents to see to it that their children had the rudiments of education, and the other requiring towns to provide schools—form together the foundation of the earliest common-school system in our country.

As time passed and population increased and towns grew in size, the provisions of 1647 seemed to be too meagre, whereupon it was ordered, in 1683, that in every town of more than five hundred families two grammar and two writing-schools (primary they would now be called) should be maintained. But this was a step too far in advance. The number of parents who wished to give their children more than the plainest sort of an education did not increase rapidly with the growth of population, the grammar-schools became a burden on the people and after the union of the Plymouth Colony and Eastern Maine with Massachusetts a step backward was taken and their maintenance was no longer required.

Each town of fifty householders must, however, have one reading-and-writing school. This gave the people all they desired, and when the Revolution opened there was not a school of any importance in Massachusetts save one, which was not founded and supported by the people.

With the Revolution came the transition from colony to Commonwealth, the adoption in 1780 of a written Constitution which made it the duty of the General Court to cherish public and grammarschools, and nine years later the enactment of a law which arranged the towns in four great classes,[2] specified the kind and number of schools that each must support, and planted the district system in New England. In many parts of Massachusetts the people were scattered far and wide. To force the children to come long distances over bad roads and in foul weather to attend one school would be such a hardship that the framers of the law most wisely provided that the inhabitants of each town should mark out as many districts as they saw fit, establish one school in each, and pay the salary of the master by a tax on polls and ratable estates. Not till 1800 were the towns authorized to raise money to build and furnish school-houses. Prior to that year, and indeed long after, district schools were kept in the basements of churches or in rude cabins erected by the voluntary labor of the people.

Funds for school uses were raised by a tax laid by the legal voters in town meeting assembled. At these gatherings each freeman might propose such a sum as he thought sufficient, and on the amounts so named the mind of the town was taken, beginning with the highest and going down in order till one received the approval of the majority. The tax so voted was then assessed on property within the town, was collected in the usual way, and the money divided among the districts in proportion to the number of children of school age, and paid to the trustees. These officials, one for each district, were elected by the people in public meeting at the school-house, and charged with the duty of hiring the teachers, caring for the school property, and receiving and expending the school money. Two school sessions were held each year. That in summer was for young children and girls, was conducted by a young woman, and extended over a term of from five to thirteen weeks, during which the subjects taught were reading, writing, and spelling. That in the winter was kept by a young man, and was attended by both girls and boys, who received instruction in reading, writing, arithmetic, English grammar, geography, the Constitution of the United States, the Constitution of Massachusetts, and the dictionary. From time to time poems, fragments of orations, and extracts from plays were committed to memory and delivered by some scholar in the upper class as an exercise in public speaking.

Prior to 1800 there were few text-books deserving of the name. Indeed, at that date, in some subjects there were no text-books used. But a quarter of a century witnessed great changes, and the task of the master was now made easier by the readers and spellers of Noah Webster; the geographies of Woodbridge, Willard, and Morse; the grammars of Murray and Greenleaf; the arithmetics of Adams and Smith; and the fine series of readers prepared by John Pierpont.

Improvement in the appliances for teaching was not accompanied by a like improvement in the art of teaching. As a rule district teachers were not persons trained for their work, nor were they zealous in the cause of education. Some were young men studying at Harvard, or preparing for a profession, or casting about for something to do. These seem to have given satisfaction. But with the work done by another class, those who taught because it was easier to teach than to plough, who became pedagogues because, after many trials in many fields of labor, they despaired of eking out a livelihood in any other, very serious fault was found. The law of 1789 ordered that no one should be a school-master who could not produce evidence of good moral character, who had not been educated at a university or college, or who could not procure a certificate of fitness from a minister settled in the town where the school was to be kept or from two others in the vicinity. But the law was not carefully enforced; men and women utterly unfit for the task were constantly appointed,

sometimes because the district could not afford to hire better, sometimes because the trustee was careless, sometimes because he did not
know the good from the bad. Governor Levi Lincoln stated no more
than the truth when, in 1827, he assured the General Court that the
cause of learning languished both from the indifference of parents
and the incompetence of instructors.

Worse than all was the condition of the grammar-schools. They
had never been popular, but had always been looked on by the people
as costly, unnecessary, and undemocratic. Only a small number could
afford to give their boys and girls any higher education than was
provided for in the common schools. That such as could not should
be taxed for the benefit of such as could was taxing the many for the
benefit of the few, which was unfair, unjust, and contrary to democratic principles. When the educational system was revised in 1789
this feeling was so strong that the provision of the old law was swept
away, and no town of less than two hundred families was required
to support a grammar-school, and even with this not every such town
complied.

The grammar-school, however, was little missed, for its place had
already been taken and its work better done by academies founded
by towns, individuals, or denominations. Some were merely chartered
by the Commonwealth and empowered to hold property and educational funds. Of these, fourteen were flourishing in Massachusetts
before 1800. Others were directly aided with gifts of land or money.[3]

None of them were free, but the cost of tuition was not beyond the
reach of such as chose to strive for it; they were open to girls and boys
alike on equal terms, and fully met the needs of the few who were not
content to end their education with reading, writing, and arithmetic.

Excellent as was the educational system of Massachusetts in theory,
time had shown it faulty in practice. Lack of proper and constant
supervision of the districts led to the employment of unfit teachers.
There was too wide an interval between the common school and the
college, and these two defects the Commonwealth sought to remedy
by the law of 1826. Thenceforth every town of five hundred families
was required to maintain a free English high-school; every town

of four thousand inhabitants a high-school of such grade as to fit students for college; and all towns to elect a school committee of three, or some multiple of three, to which was expressly assigned the duty of examining teachers and supervising the schools in their district. But this law in turn was feebly executed. So late as 1836, out of forty-three towns which ought to have established free high-schools, only fourteen had done so. Many of the committees grew negligent, suffered the buildings to fall out of repair, the children to become irregular in attendance, and went on employing teachers unfit for their work.[4]

Connecticut during two centuries founded free schools on very different principles. To understand her system it must be remembered that in early days the town and the parish were coextensive. The one was the political side, and the other the church side of the same community. As there was but one organization for the government of the town in civil affairs, so there was, at first, but one church society for the management of spiritual affairs. But many of the towns were large in area, and as population spread over them it came about that people living in the outskirts found themselves far removed from the one place of worship. To require large numbers of men, women, and children so situated to travel back and forth over long distances every Sabbath was an unnecessary labor, from which they were relieved by the formation of new church societies and the building of new meeting-houses. Within the limits of one town there might be, and indeed there often were, two or three ecclesiastical societies. If the town had less than seventy families it must maintain a school for at least six months of each year; but if it contained one ecclesiastical society and more than seventy families the term must be extended to eleven months. If, on the other hand, the town was divided into several parishes, such as numbered less than seventy families must have a master for six, and such as numbered more a teacher for eleven months out of twelve. On the head town of every county was laid the duty of supporting a grammar-school wherein Greek, Latin, and English should be well taught. Toward the cost of her compulsory system the State annually paid to each town forty shillings for every thousand pounds in its lists, provided it kept a school according to law. Should the sum so granted be too small, one half of the deficit was to be made up by a tax on the property of the town or parish, and one half by a tuition fee, unless the voters agreed on some other way.

All of this was in colonial days. But the period of dependence on the British Crown passed away, and when Connecticut became a sovereign, free, and independent State she found herself in possession of a vast strip of territory stretching across our country from Pennsylvania to the Mississippi. Much of this was ceded to the Continental Congress in 1786. But a tract of nearly four million acres was retained, and came to be known sometimes as New Connecticut and sometimes as the Western Reserve. A part of it, in 1786, was ordered to be sold, and by way of inducement to emigrants to buy, it was provided that in every town (a plot of land five miles square) five hundred acres should be reserved for the support of churches and a like quantity for schools. But immigration was slow in entering the Reserve, and at the end of eight years only one sale had been effected. Then the State adopted a new policy, ordered all land she possessed in the Reserve to be sold, and set apart the expected proceeds to make a fund, the interest of which was to be divided among ecclesiastical societies of all denominations, to be used for the support of their ministers of the Gospel and their schools in Connecticut.

The measure had been stoutly opposed in the General Assembly, but the feeling there was mild compared with the indignation which burst from pulpit, press, and town meeting after the enactment of the law. Some denounced it as a shameful attempt to establish a permanent provision for "the sacerdotal order." Others ridiculed the idea of disposing of the funds before the land was sold. Still others contended that the money when obtained ought to be spent on the free schools, or given to Yale College, or used to build roads and canals, pay the State debt, or further the interests of the farmer. Even the most conservative admitted that the law had been hastily framed, and in 1795 the General Assembly undid the work of 1793, ordered that the money to be derived from the sale of lands in the Western Reserve should be a permanent and irreducible fund; stripped the church

societies or parishes of all "power to act on the subject of schooling";
authorized "all the inhabitants living within the limits of the located
societies who by law have or may have the right to vote in town
meeting" to assemble annually in October, bade them organize for
the transaction of all business concerning education, and left to these
societies the free use of their shares of the interest yielded annually.

A few months after the enactment of the law the committee, in
whose hands its execution was left sold the land for $1,200,000, pay-
able in five years, and the first State school fund in our history was
created. Interest was allowed to accumulate till 1799, when $60,000
was distributed on the basis of polls and ratable estates.

From 1795 to 1800 the trust was managed by the men who sold the
land; but in 1800 the care of it was assigned to a commission of four,
who seem to have been both unfit and negligent. The investments
were bad, the interest was not collected, and the whole fund threatened with extinction, when the commission was abolished, and James
Hillhouse called from the United States Senate to assume the duty
of "commissioner of the school fund." By him it was finely admin-
istered. Old debts due from the original purchasers of the land were
recovered, overdue interest collected, good securities substituted for
bad, the principal raised in fifteen years to $1,719,000, and more than
three quarters of a million dollars divided among the societies. Education, however, steadily declined. Now that the maintenance of high-
schools was not obligatory, they were no longer founded. The steady
increase of the principal and the large dividends, averaging fifty
thousand dollars a year, made the people less and less inclined to tax
themselves, and more and more disposed to depend on the annual
distribution and the State allowance of two dollars on every one thousand raised by taxation. But in 1820, when the income of the school
fund reached sixty-two thousand dollars, the State abolished the annual allowance from its treasury, and the dividend became practically
the sole means of support. Then the school system went down rapidly,
till it became little more than a number of commonplace district
schools held for a few weeks in summer and a few in winter in
wretched school-houses, taught by teachers of little ability and desti-

tute of aids, and closed when the money obtained from the State was expended.[5]

Between Massachusetts and Connecticut, the earliest Commonwealths to attempt the free education of the people, lay the little State of Rhode Island, where as yet, save in Providence, no free-school system existed. Town records do indeed show that efforts were early made to help the poor to educate their children. Newport, in 1640, set apart a hundred acres and appropriated the income "for a school for encouragement of the poorer sort to train up their youth in learning." Providence, in 1663, ordered that one hundred acres of upland and six acres of meadow, or, in lieu of it, eight acres of lowland, should be laid out, reserved for the maintenance of a school, and the tract called "the school lands of Providence." Bristol, in 1682, voted that parents having children of school age should pay threepence a week to a school-master, and that the town should raise enough more by taxes to make his salary twenty-four pounds a year. Later the license fees paid by keepers of inns and taverns were used for support of the town school. Kingston, in 1696, gave land to Harvard for the education of youths whose parents could not afford to support them. Excellent as all this was, the aid afforded was small, and down almost to the Revolution the private school seems to have been the seat of education. After the close of the French and Indian War, however, the people of Providence thought seriously of founding a free-school system, and went so far as to listen to reports on buildings and on a scheme of management for four schools. But the voters were in nowise inclined to be taxed for such purposes, and, save the erection of one school-house by the joint action of the town and private citizens, nothing was done. Nor was anything done till 1800, when the General Assembly placed on the statute-book the first law providing for the establishment of at least one free school in every town in the State. Four were at once organized at Providence and opened with all possible speed. But elsewhere the law was bitterly denounced. When the General Assembly met again instructions from town after town were read against it, and in 1803 it was repealed. During a quarter of a century the people of Rhode Island went on educating their children in the old way; but at last, in 1828, the State once more came to the rescue, and the free school was permanently established.[6]

New York, at the close of the Revolution, had done less in the cause of education than Rhode Island. There were, indeed, private schools, some parish schools, a few academies, and the remains of King's College; but no common schools within the reach of the great mass of the people. What this meant to a State whose government depended for its stability on the intelligence and good sense of the citizens was fully understood by Governor Clinton. Scarcely a month had passed since the last of the British troops sailed away from Staten Island. The effects of eight years of warfare were weighing heavily on the tax payers, who were in no condition to bear increased expenses. Yet so important and so pressing did the matter seem that the Governor, in his message to the Legislature when it assembled in the half-ruined city of New York, urged it to provide a system of education worthy of the State and the emergency. "Neglect," said he, "of the education of youth is among the evils consequent on war. Perhaps there is scarce anything more worthy your attention than the revival and encouragement of seminaries of learning." The response of the Legislature was the creation of "the Regents of the University of the State of New York," a huge and cumbersome body of perpetual regents, county regents, clerical regents, founder regents, and regents of colleges yet to be created, to whose care was confided the development of an educational system for the State. But the work was not done. The board was too large, the members too widely scattered to attend, and it quickly fell under the control of the friends of the old King's College, now revived and renamed Columbia. The old college had been a distinctly English institution, controlled by the Established Church, serving private interests, and owing no educational duty to the colony, though coming to it time and again for help when its treasury was depleted or its privileges and immunities needed to be extended. In the attempt to restore this old-time condition and make Columbia the educational ruler, the interests of the State at large was utterly neglected, a strong opposition was developed, and in 1787 the law of 1784 was radically altered and the

University of the State of New York established in much the same
form as it exists to-day. The details need not concern us; it is enough
to know that back of this movement was the idea of a system of
education for the people, aided by the State, and controlled by the
State for the good of its citizens.

But how was money for its support to be raised? Taxation was
impossible. Resort was therefore had to public lands and lotteries, and
in 1789 the Legislature ordered the surveyor-general to set apart certain lots in each township within the military district and reserve
them for the use of churches and schools. The help thus afforded
settlers, who were already pouring into central New York and pushing up the Mohawk Valley, was indeed considerable, but towns elsewhere derived no benefit. They were yet to be provided for, and in
their behalf, and as an experiment, a temporary school fund was
created in 1795. For five years to come the State pledged itself to distribute fifty thousand dollars annually among the towns on the basis
of population, and bade the supervisors of each county raise, by taxation, in each town a sum one half that it received from the State.
With the money so provided thirteen hundred and fifty schools, in
which fifty-six thousand children were taught reading, writing, and
arithmetic, were opened in sixteen of the twenty-three counties before
1799. As the five-year limit was then fast expiring, with no prospect
of renewal, a lottery was chartered to raise one hundred thousand
dollars in four drawings.

By this time the school system had utterly collapsed, and Clinton,
the steady friend and unflinching advocate of free education for the
people, once more appealed to the Legislature. "The system of common schools," said he, "having been discontinued and the advantage
to morals, religion, liberty, and good government arising from the
general diffusion of knowledge being universally admitted, permit
me to recommend this subject to your deliberate attention. The failure
of one experiment for the attainment of an important object ought
not to discourage other attempts." But failure did discourage other
attempts, and though Clinton returned to the subject year after year
till he ceased to be Governor, and though his successor took up the

good work where he laid it down, every appeal went unheeded till 1805. In that year Governor Morgan Lewis urged the Legislature to set apart the State lands as a school fund, give the management of the fund to the Regents of the University, authorize them to mark out school-districts, appoint trustees, and levy taxes when needed to supplement the fund. The plan was far too radical for the ideas of the time. Nevertheless the Legislature made bold to take one step, and ordered five hundred thousand acres of vacant land to be sold and the proceeds invested till the annual interest should amount to fifty thousand dollars, when it should be used for the support of free schools.

Meanwhile a band of public-spirited men in New York city, deeply sensible of the importance of educating the horde of children growing up as outcasts in the slums, and weary of waiting for the State to act, formed a society and applied for a charter. "Your memorialists," they assured the Legislature, "have seen with painful anxiety the many evils which have arisen from the neglected education of the children of the poor." Especially deplorable was the condition of such as did not belong to any church and were not provided for by any religious organization. Cared for by no one, neglected by parents who were too indifferent, too intemperate, or too poor to even seek to give them an education, they were growing up in the densest ignorance, a prey to every vice. That something might be done to save these unfortunate little ones it seemed expedient to establish free schools in the city for their education, and for this laudable purpose the petitioners asked to be incorporated. The prayer was willingly granted, and in 1805 "The Society for Establishing a Free School in the City of New York for the Education of such Poor Children as do not belong to or are not provided for by any Religious Society" was created.

An appeal was next made to the public, with such success that it soon became necessary to decide on some scheme of education, and, after due consideration, what was then known as the Lancastrian method was adopted and put in operation for the first time in this country. Joseph Lancaster was born in London in 1778 of well-to-do parents. By nature he belonged to that class of men whose mission it is to labor unrequited for the welfare of their fellows. For one so constituted no better field existed than that afforded by the great city of London. The misery, vice, and crime fostered by ignorance that was itself the product of abject poverty deeply affected him, and, prompted by a strong love of children, he opened a free school in his father's house for the instruction of those whose parents could not pay the cost of education. Success with a few attracted others and still others, till the little room became too small and a school-house was built, in which, it is said, as many as a thousand boys and girls were often gathered.

Increase in numbers of scholars made necessary an increase in the teaching force; but to employ many teachers was beyond the limited means of Lancaster, who therefore met the need by an expedient which at once became the peculiarity of his system. Selecting the brightest of the advanced pupils, he made them monitors and sent them to teach little classes of younger children the rudiments of such knowledge as they had acquired.

In later years, when Lancastrian schools were high in public favor a hot dispute was waged over the merits and defects of the "monitorial or pupil-teacher system." The faults were many; but it should never be forgotten that Lancaster succeeded in deeply interesting in the cause of popular education large numbers of men to whom no other system appealed; that he provided a way of doing the greatest amount of good at the least expense, and that he gave an impetus to the movement in behalf of the public schools at the very moment an impetus was most needed.

Such was the experience of the society at New York. The work done was manifestly good; the Legislature, the city, and the people helped it on, and in 1808 the name was changed to the Free-School Society of New York, and its doors opened to all children who were proper objects of free education.

While the State fund was slowly growing the Legislature bade the Governor appoint five commissioners to plan a general system of State schools, and from them came a report which led to the law of 1812. Electors in each town were authorized to choose three commissioners to mark out as many school-districts as seemed proper. The voters of each district were then to elect three trustees to manage the local school, which was to be supported by the State and the people, for each town was required to raise as much money by taxation as it received from the literary fund. At the head of the system was placed a Superintendent of Education. To the office thus created Gideon Hawley was appointed, and on him, in 1813, fell the duty of putting the system in operation. The task was a hard one, for town after town refused to tax itself, lost its share of the State fund by so doing, and failed to establish a free school. At the urgent request of the Superintendent the tax was therefore made compulsory. Then success attended his efforts, and when, in 1821, the office of State Superintendent was abolished and the free schools placed under the charge of the Secretary of State, three hundred thousand children were receiving instruction in six thousand three hundred school-districts, at an annual cost of two hundred thousand dollars.[7]

In New Jersey there were no common schools. There were private schools of various grades and parochial schools maintained by the several religious bodies. There was a school fund created in 1816 and enlarged in 1817; there was on the statute-book a law authorizing the towns to tax themselves for the tuition of children of paupers and poor parents, but no system of schools open alike to the children of rich and poor without charge and supported by the public treasury.

Delaware was equally backward. There, too, were private and denominational schools, and there, as elsewhere, in colonial times laws were occasionally enacted which may be construed into State aid to education. Nevertheless the first legislation in behalf of popular instruction was a law charging the State Treasurer to set apart all moneys accruing from marriage and tavern licenses for twenty years to come, and such donations, gifts, and bequests as might be received from individuals, as a fund for the establishment of public schools. A little later the law was continued till 1820; but twenty-one years passed away before the first draft was made on the fund and a thousand dollars given each of the three counties to be used for the instruction of children of poor parents in reading, writing, and arithmetic.

The limitation to one class in the community defeated the purpose sought. In the eyes of the people the money was no better than an appropriation for the relief of paupers, and neither the law of 1817 nor a modification of it in 1821 ever met with popular favor. Not till 1829 was the common school really established in Delaware.

Pennsylvania, too, was very slow beginning her system. Her Constitution of 1776 did indeed enjoin it on the Legislature to establish in every county a school for what it termed the correct education of youth and provide for the masters such pay as might enable them to "instruct youth at low prices." But in the stormy days of the Revolution and during the years of distress that immediately followed, the injunction went unheeded. So, too, the Constitution of 1790, which replaced that of 1776, bade the Legislature establish schools throughout the State "in such manner that the poor shall be taught gratis." But this also was disregarded for twelve years, and not till 1802 was the first step taken toward its execution. Then the overseers of the poor in every county were commanded to find out the names of all persons unable to educate their offspring, notify them that their boys and girls might be sent to school at the expense of the State, and to pay the cost with money collected as the poor rates.

The law was regarded as a bold and hazardous experiment, and was to expire in a little more than three years; but ere that day came an amendment was necessary. Teachers, it seems, were not always willing to admit into their schools children they regarded as paupers. Another law, therefore, made it obligatory on all school-masters and school-mistresses who taught reading and writing in the English or German language and arithmetic to receive any child sent by the overseers of the poor or recommended by a justice of the peace and two freeholders.

The purpose of these laws was most praiseworthy. They fell, indeed, far short of establishing a free-school system, yet they were steps in the right direction, and, had the people been so disposed, might have been productive of some good. Most happily they were not so disposed. The law of 1802 was undemocratic; it set off the children of the rich from those children of the poor, invited the parents of the latter to come forward, make a public confession of pauperism, and ask that their boys and girls be sent at State expense to some school to become the object of contempt by both teacher and scholars. In 1804 the people of Northampton County therefore petitioned the Legislature to establish separate schools for the poor, to which their children could go without question. The committee having the petition in charge reported that in their opinion the children of all citizens ought to be taught at public expense, that there ought to be no invidious distinction of rich and poor, that the pay schools were wretchedly conducted, that the larger part of the teachers were utterly ignorant of the language in which they taught, that to acquire any degree of useful knowledge in such institutions required an immense waste of time, and that, considering these facts, it was no wonder so few of the poor had made use of the opportunity to educate their children without cost.

The committee went so far as to outline a plan for a system of free district-schools maintained by the State and open to all children under fourteen. But the report was promptly laid on the table, and, in spite of appeals from the governors and the efforts of the reformers, the old method was continued for twenty years.

Meantime the people took the matter into their own hands, opened Sunday-schools, established the Society for the Free Instruction of Female Children, the Aimwell School Association, the Philadelphia Society for the Establishment and Support of Charity Schools, the Philadelphia Union, the Philadelphia Friends' Association for the Instruction of Poor Children, and put in operation numbers of schools for white children and black. The object lesson thus given was not wasted, and in 1812 the Legislature was persuaded to authorize the county commissioners to establish public schools in such manner as the city council should approve. This too failed, and in 1818 the city and county of Philadelphia was made the first school-district of Pennsylvania and empowered to found free schools on the Lancastrian system for the education of children of indigent parents. Joseph Lancaster was at once sent for, and within a year thirteen schools, with three thousand pupils, were in full operation. Later other school-districts on the same plan were established at Pittsburg and Lancaster.

The history of the Lancastrian schools in Philadelphia, as set forth in the yearly reports of the commissioners, is full of interest. The time of their establishment was one of great commercial and industrial depression, of hard times all over the Union. Years afterward those who passed the dismal period 1816–1820 used to speak of it as "eighteen hundred and starve to death." As no one would take an apprentice, no manufacturing establishment employ a young boy or girl, parents of the better class of working people gladly seized the chance to give their children an education, and by 1820 more than five thousand pupils were on the rolls of the public schools of Philadelphia.[8] But with 1820 came better times. Business was resumed, manufactures were springing up, a demand for child laborers increased, attendance fell off rapidly, and in 1821 less than three thousand boys and girls were in the schools, and the controllers called loudly for legislative action. "If," said they, "the employment of youth in the manufacturing establishments be not accompanied with due attention to their mental and physical health and improvement, they will grow up unfit to discharge the duties of social life, and from bodily infirmities and vicious habits become burdens on the community. Employment of children in factories should be stopped until they have had an opportunity to obtain the rudiments of an education in the public schools." In 1822 the attendance was four hundred and fifty less than in 1821, and in 1823 was less than half what it had been in 1820.

"Of the children who have entered the schools, many," said the controllers, "have been taken away because of the high wages, which vary from fifty cents to a dollar and a quarter a week, according to the demand for labor by the manufacturers. The rising generation may thus sustain irretrievable loss in the abandonment of means for acquiring useful learning. Employers of large numbers of young persons in manufactories should be made to give them a useful education, and care for their health and morals. Something should also be done to rid the streets and wharves of the little children, who as beggars and petty depredators wander about in search of a pittance for the support of idle and worthless parents." An attempt to reach these children was made by associations of charitable persons, and infant schools were opened. But five years passed before the controllers were authorized to establish like institutions as part of the public-school system.

In the Lancastrian schools children were taught the alphabet, spelling, reading, arithmetic, and, when advanced enough, writing on slates and, finally, on paper. To this rudimentary education in the case of the girls was added knitting, useful needlework, plaiting of straw, and sewing on canvas. Down to 1822 none but white children were received; but in that year the controllers grew bold and opened a negro school, and were astonished at the large attendance and capacity of the scholars. Their apology for this daring act throws not a little light on the status of the free negro. "One of the most important acts of the controllers," they say, "since the last annual report, is the opening of a school for colored children." As this was to be the first instance within the district of the extension of the law to "this friendless and degraded portion of society, it became the controllers to examine the ground which they were about to occupy." Legal advice was therefore sought, and under the assurance that the practice was sanctioned in other parts of the State, was not forbidden by the Constitution, and was quite within the limits of the school law, the controllers ventured to make the experiment, trusting that the expediency of the act would not be questioned by the public.

Outside of Philadelphia, Lancaster, and Pittsburg the old system was in use, growing worse and worse each year. A committee appointed by one branch of the Legislature in 1822 to report on the state of education declared that the law of 1809 was not enforced in some counties and was much abused in others; that here the people were paying for the schooling of children whose names were on the registers but whose faces had never been seen in any school-house; that there the gross neglect and incompetency of the teacher defeated the purpose of the law; that elsewhere children were being sent to schools they were not fitted to attend; that it was nobody's business to correct these evils, and that nobody could tell positively whether pupils anywhere were so much as taught their letters. In 1824 reform was once more attempted, the law of 1809 was repealed, and all communities were authorized, if they wished, to establish free schools open to all children and supported by taxation. But before the law could go into effect such a storm of opposition was aroused that in 1826 it was repealed, the old one of 1809 was re-enacted, and the old order of things continued for eight years longer. Once, in 1829, the workingmen in Philadelphia endeavored to break it down, held a mass meeting, and chose a committee to report on the educational methods in Pennsylvania and suggest a remedy. With the exception of the cities of Pittsburg and Lancaster and the city and county of Philadelphia they found the educational system in shocking condition. The elementary schools were irresponsible institutions, owned by individuals, sometimes destitute of all moral character, often grossly ignorant, and always carried on solely with a view to private gain. In some parts of the State there were none even of this sort, and there ignorance and its attendants vice and crime held full sway. The defects of the law of 1809 were thus made worse by local conditions. Sometimes the provisions could not be enforced, for there were no schools. Sometimes to enforce them was but to put children under the influence of an ignorant, brutal, and immoral teacher. Instances were not wanting where the funds appropriated were embezzled or ignorantly misapplied or culpably neglected. Time and again, in order to save a few dollars, county commissioners had deliberately selected the most worthless schools, because they were the cheapest, and made them the only ones open to the poor.

Back of the whole system lay one radical defect. The ruling idea was pauperism. State aid was confined exclusively to the children of the poor. Many a one in consequence went without an education because the parents were too self-respecting to make their offspring an object of public charity, or of such standing in the community that they would not take the benefit of a poor law. The remedy suggested by the workingmen was "a system of universal free and equal public education" [9]—in a word, the common school of to-day.

What was true of Pennsylvania and Delaware was equally true of Maryland. There in every county was at least one academy aided by the State, and in return giving free instruction to a certain number of pupils. There, too, were innumerable pay schools, taught sometimes by men of character, but more generally by vagrant school-masters, redemptioners, or indentured servants. There, too, in Baltimore were all sorts of religious and benevolent associations for the education of boys and girls. There were the Female Humane Association Charity School; the Male Free School, maintained by the Methodists; the Roman Catholic Free School; the school founded by the Carpenters' Humane Society; St. Peter's School; and another for poor girls conducted by the Benevolent Society of the City and County of Baltimore. But not till 1812 did the State begin the foundation of a system of county primary schools for the education of poor children by taxing the capital stock of each State bank, and setting apart the proceeds as a literary fund. In 1816 fifty thousand dollars a year for five years was ordered to be raised by lotteries, and the money added to the fund, and the levy courts of five counties bidden to appoint seven trustees, charge them with the education of poor children in each election district, and assess a property tax of twelve dollars for each child they might assign to any school. In 1819 the Governor laid before the Legislature a plan for raising money without taxation, and urged that an application should be made at once to Congress for a share of the public lands.

Federal aid to education began with the passage of the great land ordinance of 1785, which reserved every sixteenth section for the maintenance of public schools within the township. Not a word was said as to who should establish them, or of what kind or grade they should be. The land was set apart and reserved and nothing more. So, again, in the ordinance of 1787—the famous ordinance for the establishment of government in the territory of the United States northwest of the river Ohio—one article declared that religion, morality, and knowledge being necessary to good government and the happiness of mankind, schools and the means of education should forever be encouraged, and, obedient to this injunction, the Continental Congress ten days later ordained that the sixteenth section should be given perpetually for the purpose of maintaining public schools. But not an acre was actually given till the organization of the State of Ohio in 1802. Then, as one of three considerations offered by Congress in return for the exemption from State taxation, for five years from the date of sale, of land sold by the United States within Ohio, it was promised that the sixteenth section should be granted to the inhabitants of each township for the use of schools. Ohio accepted the conditions, and the next year Congress vested the title to all such sections in the Legislature of Ohio in trust for the use of schools, and for no other use, intent, or purpose whatever. But Congress, not content with this, gave two entire townships to be used by the Legislature for the purposes of a university.

What was done for Ohio was done for Indiana, Illinois, Alabama, and Mississippi. Louisiana over and above her grant had received an additional township of 23,040 acres; Connecticut another for the benefit of her Asylum for Deaf and Dumb; and Tennessee one hundred thousand acres for two colleges, and a like quantity for the founding of one academy in each county. As a result of this wise and liberal policy, great tracts had been ceded to the Western States before 1820, and it was these cessions which suggested to the Governor of Maryland the idea of demanding from the Governments similar grants to the old States.

The committee to which his remarks were sent reported favorably in 1821. The public lands of the United States, the report said, whether acquired by conquest or by cession, by treaty or by purchase, had been secured by the common effort or paid for by the common treasure of all the States, were therefore the common property of all, and ought not to be used for the benefits of any particular set of States to the exclusion of the others. Yet the domain was constantly so used, for never had a State (save Tennessee) or a Territory been carved out of it, but one thirty-sixth part was reserved for the use of schools. Grants, moreover, had been made to Western States for universities, colleges, and academies, till in the course of a generation the Government had parted, or was pledged by precedent to part, with fifteen million acres. Not a foot of this magnificent tract, larger than the State of Ohio, belonged or ever would belong to any State east of the Alleghany Mountains, though some of them gave much of the land in question and all contributed to the fund for the purchase of Louisiana. This, in the opinion of the committee, was unfair and unjust. It was using lands for State, not national purposes. It was converting the common property of the Union to the exclusive benefit of a small section.

Maryland proposed, therefore, to Congress and to her sisters that the Atlantic States, which had never received land to be used for the purposes of education, should be given tracts corresponding to those already granted or pledged to the States beyond the mountains.

In Congress the proposition met with small favor. Ohio, Indiana, and Illinois, Alabama, Mississippi, and Louisiana (Missouri was not yet admitted) said a committee to whom the matter was referred have received the sixteenth section of each surveyed township for schools, and two townships in addition for colleges and academies; Tennessee has been allotted two hundred thousand acres for universities and academies; and Connecticut one whole township in aid of her Asylum for the Deaf and Dumb. Land so disposed of is not subject to taxation by the State in which it lies. If, therefore, this policy be extended to the old States a large part of the soil of the new will be taken up with donation tracts, which cannot be taxed or settled without the consent of the sovereignties that own them. A far wiser course would be to set apart a certain percentage of the money derived from land sales, distribute it among the old States according to population, and subject the land when sold to taxation by the States or Territories in which it happened to be.

The States, on the other hand, were divided in opinion. All in New England save Massachusetts, and all in the middle section save New York, together with Virginia, North Carolina, and Kentucky, heartily approved. Massachusetts dissented because, in her opinion, the public lands are the property of the United States, and no State may claim a share of them, and because the reservation of townships and sections for the support of schools are not donations to the State within whose limits they happened to be, and no other, therefore, is entitled to demand an equivalent.

Failing to secure congressional aid, Maryland fell back on her own resources, and in 1825 adopted a system of district schools which each county was at liberty to adopt or reject. The people at their own cost were to buy the sites, put up the school-buildings, and supply fuel, books, and stationery. The State was to pay the salaries of the teachers. But so strong was the prejudice against taxation for school purposes that six counties rejected the system. Thirteen, indeed, adopted it, but not one ever put it fully into operation, and when, in 1828, the Governor declared the plan a failure, the office of State Superintendent was abolished.

In Virginia the history of popular education, with that of many another movement in behalf of the rights of man, goes back to Thomas Jefferson. To his labors Virginia owes the abolition of primogeniture, the abolition of entail of property, the divorce of Church and state, and the establishment of religious liberty, and had his efforts been attended with a like success she would have owed to him the abolition of slavery and the establishment of the common school. As early as 1779, while the country was still distracted by the Revolution, Jefferson had laid before the House of Burgesses a complete and characteristic plan of universal education. The counties, he urged, should be cut into sections five or six miles square, called hundreds, in each of which there should be a free school for teaching reading, writing, and arithmetic, supported by the people and open to all children. Once a year a "visitor" should pick from each school the brightest boy whose parents were too poor to continue his education, and send him to one of twenty grammar-schools to be founded and scattered over the State. From the batch thus sent annually to each grammar-school one scholar was to be chosen at the end of a year to go on with his studies and the rest dismissed. Six years later the lads thus selected were to be again sifted, one half dropped and one half sent for three years to William and Mary College.

Unhappily, the ruling class in Virginia was not at all disposed to be taxed for the education of the children of poor whites, and the plan was accorded no serious consideration for seventeen years. By that time the rising tide of democracy had reached even Virginia, and in 1796 it was ordained that a majority of the justices of any county, if they saw fit, might establish schools to be maintained by taxation. But they did not see fit so to do, and when the half century of independence closed Virginia was still educating her children in the old way —in "field schools," by the clergy, in academies, and in such colleges as then existed at home or in her sister States.

So was it in North Carolina. She too, like Virginia, had her State university, graduating four or five students each year, and, scattered over the counties, male academies and charity schools, and female academies supported by female benevolent societies, female charitable societies, female orphan societies, aided to a small degree by the State. Towns in which the schools were might grant the use of the common as a building site; money might be raised by lotteries; teachers and scholars were often exempt from military duty; but as yet no common free school existed.

To the great educational movement which spread over our country after 1800 North Carolina was indeed responsive. Governor after governor appealed to the Legislature to spread education into every corner of the State; [10] to put a certain amount of education within the reach of every child in the State; [11] to remember that if the wealthy alone be admitted to the temple of science the most dangerous species of aristocracy may be apprehended.[12] But not till 1816 did the Committee on Education respond with two reports.[13] One came from a member; the other was presented in the name of the committee by Archibald D. Murphy, whose splendid work at a later day earned for him the enviable title of "father of the common schools." After listening to this report, the General Assembly ordered a committee of three to be appointed to digest a system of public instruction, and submit it to the Legislature in 1817. The plan then presented began with the district school and ended with the college. The counties were to be cut into townships, these again, when containing more than one hundred families, were to be parted into wards, in each of which one primary school was to be established. This was a feature plainly borrowed from New England. The next was as plainly taken from the Middle States, for it required those who could to pay, and made the schools free to such and such alone as could not afford to educate their sons and daughters. Even these children were not to receive free instruction for more than three years. Above the primary schools were to be academies, one in each of ten academical districts, and above them the university, then twenty years old. Like many another fine scheme for the public good, the plan of the committee was too far in advance of the means of the State and the ideas of the people, and never took the form of law.

South Carolina, on the other hand, had established what might have been, but was not, a system of free common schools. Her law, enacted in 1811, required the people in each election district to provide as many school-houses as they had representatives in the lower branch of the Legislature, pledged the Legislature to appropriate annually three hundred dollars for the support of each school to be open to all white children, rich and poor alike, but provided that when the sum of money appropriated was too little to pay for the instruction of all who applied, preference should be given to destitute orphans and children of the poor. By this provision the intent of the law is made manifest. Schools were to be founded at public expense for the sole purpose of educating poor children. Only when the funds were sufficient could children of well-to-do parents be admitted. With this excellent intent the State went on year after year appropriating money till, in the course of ten years, three hundred thousand dollars had been drawn from the treasury, without producing any such result as the State desired. The districts took the money given them, rarely made any report on its use, and spent it as they saw fit. Generally they saw fit to expend it on some private or sectarian school, which in return gave free instruction to such poor children as the commissioners were pleased to send, and institutions of this class fed by the State came rapidly into existence. In 1812 there were one hundred and thirty-three, and in 1828 eight hundred and forty. But they were a very different sort from that contemplated by the framers of the law. Instead of free schools for the poor to which children of the rich might be admitted if the funds held out, they were generally private or denominational pay schools, which received the State's money and admitted in return a certain number of poor children sent by the commissioners.

To the educational system thus prevalent in all the States southward of New England, a system which aided with land and money academies and colleges of use to none save the prosperous, and ignored the poor or educated their children as paupers, Georgia affords no exception. The war for independence was scarcely over, indeed the British army was still at New York, when the State entered with zeal on a scheme of public instruction highly creditable to its framers. Land was set apart in Augusta for a university, a thousand acres were granted in each county for the benefit of a free school, and provision made for one academy in each of three counties. The year following the university was founded, endowed with forty thousand acres of wild land, and made the head of an educational body of which all public schools "supported by funds or public money" were parts.

To provide on paper for the creation of schools and colleges was an easy matter. But to actually bring them into existence, to put up the buildings, secure the teachers, and assemble the pupils required money. The money was not to be had, and 1801 came before the university began its career in a one-room building in a city of two houses. A half dozen schools had been started meantime, and a number of county academies, which the State aided as much as it could. But they were all pay schools, were far beyond the reach of the great body of the plain people, who received small consideration before 1817. Then two hundred and fifty thousand dollars, and in 1821 a like sum, was set apart and the interest appropriated "for the support and encouragement of free schools." It was a poor fund for the free schooling of indigent children, was scorned by the people, and, as committees assured the Legislature after ten years of trial, was "wasted," "misapplied," "dissipated with comparatively little benefit."

In the far Northwest, in the region once under the ordinance of 1787, but now parted into the States of Ohio, Indiana, Illinois, and the Territory of Michigan, the sixteenth section of each township had been set aside by the great land ordinance of 1785 for the support of public schools within the township. With so liberal a provision as this it should seem at first sight that from the very start the settled regions of the Northwest Territory ought to have been dotted over with public schools. But this was far from the case, for many causes that could not be foreseen combined to hinder and delay the rise of the common-school system. Great tracts had been reserved by Connecticut and Virginia, and in these the Government did not own one section of land to dedicate to school purposes. Again and again it happened that, for geographical reasons, a township would be but a fraction and would not contain the sixteenth section. Sometimes the section would be swamp land or wholly or in part under water. For many years it was not settled whether the schools endowed with public lands should be controlled and managed by the local or the Federal Government. These obstacles in turn were removed, but others meantime had arisen. Save the emigrants who came from New England in the early days, the mass of the pioneers was composed of people from Pennsylvania and Virginia, who knew nothing of the common school, cared nothing for it, and went on educating their children in the way they themselves had been. The dire poverty of the settlers, the hardships of frontier life, the long Indian wars, the pittance which the lands yielded even when used for school purposes, were all so many hindrances. There were plenty of universities and colleges of the frontier type—a dozen students, a teacher, and a cabin. There were academies quite as good as the needs of the people required; but no common-school system, though the importance of such an institution was again and again urged on the authorities. As early as 1800 the Territorial Legislature, then assembled for the first time, bade the delegate to Congress do his best "to secure equal rights to school lands for all children," poor as well as rich. So strongly did this neglect of the poor appeal to the leaders of the movement for statehood that when Ohio made her first Constitution, in 1802, one section forbade the enactment of any law to deprive the poor of equal rights in the schools, academies, colleges, and universities endowed in whole or in part from the revenue arising from the Government land grants, and required their doors to be open to all scholars, students, and teachers, without any distinction or preference whatsoever.

Unhappily, the provision could not enforce itself, there was nobody to enforce it, and no change for the better is apparent. Here and there was what may be called a district school, but the custom of using the money obtained by selling or leasing the lands to pay for the instruction of poor children at a private school was almost universal. At last, in 1806, part of the State was laid out into districts and the revenue yielded by each sixteenth section was set apart for the support of free schools. But not till 1824 was a law forced through a reluctant Legislature to provide for the establishment of a common-school system supported by taxation.

The story of education in Indiana is but a repetition of that of Ohio. There, too, from the beginning of its separate Territorial existence, what passed for higher education was encouraged, while primary education for the people was neglected. There, too, was a struggling university and a host of academies, but no common schools. The first State constitution, however, required the Legislature to provide by law "for a general system of education, ascending in a regular gradation from township schools to a State university, wherein tuition shall be gratis, and equally open to all"; and under this, in 1816, was made the first attempt at a common-school system. Electors in each township might, if they saw fit, establish schools; but no money was provided, and few came into existence.

In Illinois the struggle was short and decisive. By an act of 1825, voters in any county might create districts, establish schools for white children between the ages of five and twenty, and maintain them by a tax of one-half mill on each dollar of taxable property. The law was not compulsory. Unless a majority of the voters favored a school, none would exist. Yet the idea of a free people being taxed for the support of schools was vigorously resisted, and in 1829 the Legislature repealed so much of the law as provided State aid, and declared that no man should be taxed for the maintenance of schools unless he first gave his consent in writing.

South of the Ohio lay the growing State of Kentucky. There, too, education had never been wholly neglected. From her earliest days schools of the frontier type, academies, and universities were endowed with land grants by Virginia and by her own Legislature. But the first serious effort at the education of the people by the establishment of elementary common schools was the creation of a literary fund in 1821. Into this fund was to go one half the net profits of the Bank of the Commonwealth. But in less than five years the Legislature diverted the money to other purposes, and no good came of the attempt.

Of Tennessee her historian says, with absolute truth, "The history of the common school is the history of her public lands, and the history of her public lands is the history of confusion." [14] Until 1829 no attempt was made to establish them, and that attempt was for many years a failure. Of colleges and universities there was no lack throughout the Union. Sixty-two were in full operation. But the common school, the school for the children of the people, was still to become a great American institution.

NOTES

[1] This estimate is given by De Bow, as made from reliable sources. Vol. iii, p. 404.

[2] In the first class were those of less than fifty families, where no schools were required to be kept. In the second were those of from fifty to one hundred householders, where a school or schools to teach children reading, writing, arithmetic, orthography, the English language, and "decent behavior" must be kept for such time as should be equivalent to six months each year. Towns of from one hundred to one hundred and fifty householders made the third class, and were required not only to maintain the schools of the second class, but in addition to provide masters to give instruction in the English language for such time as should be equivalent to twelve months. Towns and districts of two hundred and more families were further required to support a grammar-school to afford instruction in Latin, Greek, and English.

[3] Before 1797 four such institutions in Maine and three in Massachusetts had received each a township of land. With the immense tracts of forest in Maine to draw on, it was easy to be generous, and in 1797 several other

academies were given half a township of wild land in Maine in order that there might be one academy for every twenty-five thousand people.

[4] For the history of education in Massachusetts see The American Common School in New England. Rev. A. D. Mayo. Report of the Commissioner of Education, 1894–95, chap. xxxix. Remarks on the School Law of the Last Session of the Legislature; and Information Concerning the Common Schools of Massachusetts, New York, and South Carolina. Philadelphia, 1826. Letters to the Hon. William Prescott, LL.D., on the Free Schools of New England, with Remarks upon the Principles of Instruction. By James G. Carter. Boston, 1824. Messages of the Governors of Massachusetts.

[5] The history of education in Connecticut is fully covered by History of Education in Connecticut, by Bernard C. Steiner, Bureau of Education Circular of Information, No. 2, 1893. Barnard's History of Common Schools in Connecticut. The American Journal of Education, vol. iv. The American Common School in New England. Rev. A. D. Mayo. Educational Report, 1894–'95, chap. xxxix. Report of the Connecticut Board of Education for 1876.

[6] History of Higher Education in Rhode Island. William Howe Tolman. Bureau of Education Circular of Information, No. 1, 1894.

[7] The American Common School in New York, New Jersey, and Pennsylvania during the First Half Century of the Republic. Rev. A. D. Mayo. Report, Commissioner of Education, 1895–'96, chap. vi. University of the State of New York. Sidney Sherwood.

[8] Third Annual Report of the Controllers of the Public Schools of the First School District of the State of Pennsylvania, 1821, p. 4.

[9] A Report on the State of Education in Pennsylvania, accompanied with two bills, for the establishment of a general system of public instruction, etc., adopted by a town meeting of workingmen, July 11, 1830.

[10] Governor James Turner. November 21, 1804.

[11] Governor William Hawkins. November 20, 1811.

[12] These reports will be found in The Common Schools of South Carolina, Stephen B. Week. Report of the Commissioner of Education, 1896–'97, chap. xxix. Mr. Week's monograph is a model of its kind.

[13] Governor William Miller, November 20, 1816.

[14] History of Tennessee, James Phelan, p. 233.

James Ford Rhodes (1848–1927) and Slavery as the Cause of the Civil War

By the opening of the twentieth century, although historians were becoming professionals and academicians were dominating historiography, there remained distinguished, free-lance historians such as James Ford Rhodes, who won national prestige. Rhodes was born in Cleveland the son of a wealthy Vermont industrialist who had pioneered in the coal and iron business. He attended the public schools and took many courses, outside of degree requirements, when he went to college. Fascinated by literature, journalism, and history and stimulated by historical and technological lectures both here and abroad, he remained in his father's firm only long enough to retire early on an income sufficient to support him as a historian. His brother-in-law Marcus Alonzo Hanna, who became a United States Senator and a Republican Party boss, entered the Rhodes company and did much to make it flourish despite James's withdrawal in 1885.

In Boston and Cambridge, Rhodes enthusiastically took up his historical researches, basked as the lion of a large literary and social circle, won a national and even international reputation, and declined a Harvard appointment. Harper and Brothers published his major work, *History of the United States from the Compromise of 1850* (7 vols., 1893–1906). This work was later extended to the time of McKinley and Roosevelt. Innumerable readers thought his books engrossing, and scholars for many years regarded them as authoritative for the Civil War and Reconstruction, though not very sound on the period after 1877. He had explored numerous contemporary sources, including much newspaper material, and had showed acuteness in analyzing politics and military history.

But later scholars decided that Rhodes had oversimplified the causes of the Civil War by reducing them to the single issue of slavery. For many years, however, the standard textbook affirmed Rhodes' interpretation of the breakdown of the Compromise of 1850, which made Stephen Douglas the villain, as the selection given here suggests. Douglas, he insisted, and his Kansas-Nebraska Act had precipitated the war by repealing the Missouri Compromise of 1820 which had excluded slavery in the Louisiana Purchase north of 36 degrees, 30 minutes. Douglas's motive, Rhodes thought, was to win Southern Democratic support for his own presidential ambitions. It has been pointed out that if such were the case Douglas certainly miscalculated surprisingly for an experienced politician, and that other factors such as the transcontinental railroad issue and Douglas's desire to unite his divided party seem more likely. This issue is still far from settled. Although Rhodes was a firm antislavery man he was obviously influenced in his interpretation of Reconstruction and, to some extent, of the ante-bellum era by a basic belief in the inherent inferiority of the Negro. Therefore he pictured Reconstruction as an irresponsible experiment by the North to impose Africanization on the South.

History of the United States
from the Compromise of 1850

[Stephen] Douglas professed to have discovered a way by which the slavery question might be put to rest. But everybody North and South, as well as Douglas himself, knew that this report would certainly open up again the agitation. The country was at peace. Business was good; evidences of smiling prosperity were everywhere to be seen. The spirit of enterprise was rampant; great works were in progress, others were projected. Political repose was a marked feature of the

Volume 1, pages 428–35, 491–6 (Macmillan, 1893).

situation. The slavery question seemed settled, and the dream of the
great compromisers of 1850 seemed to be realized. Every foot of land
in the States or in the territories seemed to have, so far as slavery
was concerned, a fixed and settled character. The obnoxious part of
the compromise to the North, the Fugitive Slave law, was no longer
resisted. Another era of good feeling appeared to have set in. The
earnest hope of Clay, that the work in which he had so large a share
would give the country rest from slavery agitation for a generation,
did not seem vain. There has been restored, said the President in his
message, "a sense of repose and security to the public mind throughout the confederacy." This quiet was ruthlessly disturbed by Douglas's
report, which, though professing in one part not to repeal the
Missouri Compromise, closed with a proposition which certainly set
it aside. The Missouri Compromise forever prohibited slavery in what
was now the territory of Nebraska. Douglas proposed to leave to the
inhabitants of Nebraska the decision as to whether or not they would
have slavery. From the circumstances under which the Missouri Compromise was enacted, from the fact that it received the seal of constitutionality from an impartial President and a thoroughly representative cabinet, it had been looked upon as having the moral force of an
article of the Constitution itself. For what purpose was the repose
of the country disturbed by throwing a doubt on the constitutionality
and application of an act which had been acquiesced in and observed
by both parties to the compact for thirty-four years?

The motives which actuate men who alter the current of their time
are ever an interesting study; and in this case no confidential letters
or conversations need be unearthed to arrived at a satisfactory explanation. We may use the expression of the Independent Democrats in
Congress and say that the dearest interests of the people were made
"the mere hazards of a presidential game"; or we may employ the
words of John Van Buren, as astute politician who was in the secrets
of the party, and ask, "Could anything but a desire to buy the South
at the presidential shambles dictate such an outrage?" [1] And this
true statement and the inference from this trenchant question explain
the motives prompting Douglas to this action. Even those who were

very friendly to the measure did not scruple openly to express this opinion. One wrote that Douglas had betrayed "an indiscreet and hasty ambition"; [2] another granted that the object of Douglas "was to get the inside track in the South." [3] The defences made by Douglas and his friends at the time and in the succeeding years, when his political prospects depended upon the justification of his course, are shuffling and delusive. None are satisfactory, and it may with confidence be affirmed that the action of the Illinois senator was a bid for Southern support in the next Democratic convention. In truth, Douglas might have used the words of Frederick the Great when he began the unjust war against Austria for the conquest of Silesia: "Ambition, interest, the desire of making people talk about me, carried the day, and I decided" to renew the agitation of slavery.

Douglas could veil his own ambition under the wish to promote the interest of the Democratic party and, historians appreciating this, have readily believed that he said, that his party, in the election of Pierce, had consumed all its powder, and therefore, without a deep-reaching agitation, it would have no more ammunition for its artillery.[4] Yet it was patent to every one—and none knew it better than Douglas, for he was the ablest politician of the party—that the Democrats needed to make no fresh issue; that to let things drift along and not turn them into new channels was the safest course, and that appeals to past history were the best of arguments. An economical administration, a reduction of the tariff, a vigorous and just foreign policy, were certain to keep the Democrats in power as long as man could foresee. There was, it is true, one element of uncertainty. The factious quarrel in New York had led to defeat at the last State election; but the party was so strong that even without the Empire State it could retain its ascendency in the nation, and there was, moreover, good reason to hope that this trouble would be patched up before another presidential election.

To become the acknowledged and dominating leader of so strong a party seemed to an ardent partisan an object worthy of any exertion and any sacrifice. It was the ambition of Douglas to hold the same position among the Democrats that Clay had held among the Whigs.

Clay attained that position by being the originator of important legislative measures and by carrying them to a successful issue. The ability of Douglas lay in this direction, and he, like Clay, was a natural leader of men. Indeed, they were men of similar parts, strong natures whose private vices were hardly hidden. But Clay had profound moral convictions which, although sometimes set at naught in the heat of partisan conflict, were of powerful influence in his political career; in the view of Douglas, moral ideas had no place in politics.

Douglas prepared the bill without consultation with any Southern men. It was submitted first to two Western senators, and, after their approval was given, was shown to their Southern friends.[5] It became the object of some of those opposed to the Nebraska bill to show that the project was dictated by the South. Much credence was given to a boast of senator Atchison, made under the inspiration of the invisible spirit of wine, that he had forced Douglas to bring in such a bill.[6] It was also charged that Toombs and Stephens had been the potent influence which had brought about the action. The Illinois senator, in April, 1856, denied both of these imputations,[7] and all the circumstances support the truth of this denial.[8] Douglas was a man of too much independence to suffer the dictation of Atchison, Toombs, or Stephens. He always wanted to lead, and was never content to follow.

Immediately on the publication of the report the antislavery people of the North took alarm. The newspapers which were devoted to freedom saw the point at once and made clear the scheme which was in progress. One journal said it was a "proposition to turn the Missouri Compromise into a juggle and a cheat"; it was "presented in so bold and barefaced shape that it is quite as much an insult as it is a fraud." [9] Another called it an overt attempt to override the Missouri Compromise.[10] Another termed the project low trickery, which deluded the South with the idea that it would legalize slavery in Nebraska, and at the same time cheated the North "with a thin pretence of not repealing the existing prohibition." [11] The anti-slavery press responded more quickly than the people whose sentiment they both represented and led. The people of the South were as much surprised at the report as those of the North. Not counting upon

Douglas as one of their adherents through thick and thin, they at first viewed the proposition with distrust, and some even regarded it as "a snare set for the South." [12] But the senators and representatives from the slave-holding States understood the matter better than the people and the press, and knew that Douglas had taken a long stride in their direction. As he could not retrace his steps, he could therefore be easily influenced to alter his bill in a manner that should make it conform pretty nearly to their cherished wish.

On Monday, the 16th of January, Dixon, a Whig senator from Kentucky, who was filling the unexpired term of Henry Clay, offered an amendment to the Nebraska act, which provided in set terms for the repeal of the slavery-restriction feature of the Missouri Compromise. The Senate was astonished and Douglas was startled. He went at once to Dixon's seat and remonstrated courteously against the amendment. He said that in his bill he had used almost the same words which were employed in the Utah and New Mexico acts; and as they were a part of the compromise measures of 1850, he hoped that Dixon, who had been a zealous friend of that adjustment, would do nothing to interfere with it or weaken it before the country. Dixon replied that it was precisely because he was a zealous friend of the compromise of 1850 that he had introduced the amendment; in his view, the Missouri Compromise, unless expressly repealed, would continue to operate in the Territory of Nebraska; and while the bill of Douglas affirmed the principle of non-intervention, this amendment was necessary to carry it legitimately into effect. That being the well-considered opinion of Dixon, he was determined to insist upon his amendment.[13]

On the 17th of January, Sumner offered an amendment to the Nebraska act which expressly affirmed the slavery restriction of the Missouri Compromise.

A few days after Dixon had surprised the Senate, Douglas called to see him and invited him to take a drive. The conversation turned upon the subject which was uppermost in their minds, and, to the great delight of Dixon, the Illinois senator proposed to take charge of his amendment and incorporate it in the Nebraska bill. As Dixon reports the familiar talk, Douglas in substance said: "I have become perfectly satisfied that it is my duty, as a fair-minded national statesman, to co-operate with you as proposed in securing the repeal of the Missouri Compromise restriction. It is due to the South; it is due to the Constitution, heretofore palpably infracted; it is due to that character for *consistency* which I have heretofore labored to maintain. The repeal, if we can effect it, will produce much stir and commotion in the free States of the Union for a season. I shall be assailed by demagogues and fanatics there, without stint or moderation. Every opprobrious epithet will be applied to me. I shall probably be hung in effigy in many places. It is more than probable that I may become permanently odious among those whose friendship and esteem I have heretofore possessed. This proceeding may end my political career. But, acting under the sense of duty which animates me, I am prepared to make the sacrifice; I will do it." Dixon relates that Douglas spoke in an earnest and touching manner; the Kentucky senator was deeply affected and showed emotion in the reply that he made. "Sir," he said, "I once recognized you as a demagogue, a mere party manager, selfish, and intriguing. I now find you a warm-hearted and sterling patriot. Go forward in the pathway of duty as you propose, and though all the world desert you, *I never will.*" [14]

It was a pretty comedy. The words of Douglas are those of a self-denying patriot, and not those of a man who was sacrificing the peace of his country, and, as it turned out, the success of his party, to his own personal ambition. Between the Monday on which the amendment repealing the Missouri Compromise was introduced, and the day of the drive with Dixon, Douglas resolved to take a further step in the path on which he had entered. Of course, all sorts of influences were brought to bear upon him by Southern men, and there was one powerful argument from the Democratic point of view. While the difference between Democrats and Whigs at the South was no longer essential, the party organizations remained intact, and each endeavored to win an advantage over the other by taking more pronounced ground in the interest of slavery. It would not do, therefore, to have a measure of so obvious advantage to the South fathered by a Whig, even by one who truly felt, as he afterwards stated in the Senate: "Upon the question of slavery, I know no Whiggery and I know no Democracy." This argument and others undoubtedly had their influence on Douglas; but, in truth, he had laid out his course when he made the report of the 4th of January. He had then crossed the Rubicon; he was now preparing to burn his bridges behind him.

Unquestionably Douglas would have preferred to stand on the proposition as at first introduced. It is the testimony of two personal and political friends that he was reluctant to incorporate in his bill a clause virtually repealing the Missouri Compromise.[15] The ambiguous character of the first project was not without design, and suited his purpose exactly. At the South it could be paraded as a measure in her interest, while at the North there might be honest differences of opinion whether or not the slavery restriction was set aside; and in the inception of this movement it is probable that Douglas thought that, no matter what legislation was had, none but free States would be formed out of this territory. . . .

It may be asserted with confidence that no man in the country except Douglas could have carried this measure through the necessary stages of becoming a law. Five years later, in familiar talk with his Boswell, he said: "I passed the Kansas-Nebraska act myself. I had the authority and power of a dictator throughout the whole controversy in both houses. The speeches were nothing. It was the marshalling and directing of men, and guarding from attacks, and a ceaseless vigilance preventing surprise," [16] that led to the success of the measure. It is certain that in after-years Douglas came to believe that his doctrine of popular sovereignty was a great political principle; and it is probable that even now he half believed that there was some occult virtue in it as a rule of action. Persistent advocacy often convinces the advocate. Yet, laying aside entirely the moral question, the action of Douglas as a statesman, as a politician and leader of a party, was characterized by a lamentable lack of foresight and the utter absence of the careful reflection which far-reaching measures of legislation demand. Douglas had asserted in 1849 that all the evidences of public opinion seemed to indicate that the Missouri Compromise "had become canonized in the hearts of the American people, as a sacred thing which no ruthless hand would ever be reckless enough to disturb."[17] Having once had that conviction, therefore, he owed it to his country, and to his party as well, not to broach this measure until he had given it deep study and prolonged consideration. For Douglas loved his country; his party was his religion, the Constitution was his creed; and in following the leading of an inordinate ambition he did not imagine that he was sacrificing his party and injuring his country. He made up his mind quickly; confiding, like all spoiled children of fortune who have been endowed with rich natural gifts, in his intuitive judgment, he thought that he had no need of close application and methodical reasoning. "His library was never clear from dust," said a friend and follower;[18] and Greeley, who in these days denounced him without stint,[19] wrote truly after his death that, if Douglas had been a hard student, "it would have been difficult to set limits to his power."[20] He, like his greater Illinois rival, was a good mathematician,[21] but he did not, like Lincoln, wrestle in manhood with the problems of Euclid for mental discipline.[22] He hardly knew any history but that of his own country; he cared not to learn of the development of the world, except when Alexander, Cæsar, and Napoleon were on the stage of action, and of them he could not read too much.[23]

Of all the descriptions of Douglas at this time, none seem to seize the essential characteristics of the man so well as that of a journalist whose soul was wrapped up in the antislavery cause. The writer was impressed with his "pluck, persistency, and muscular self-assurance and self-assertion." To see and hear him was to "comprehend the aptness of that title of 'Little Giant.' " Never was a characteristic name better applied. The historian must sympathize with the regret expressed by this journalist that one who championed bad measures with such indomitable ability was not upon the right side; and one cannot but reflect "of what infinite value this remarkable man might have been to the cause of liberty if the fortune of politics had made him a leader of it."[24]

Douglas had the quality of attaching men to him; he was especially fond of young men, and they repaid his complaisance by devotion. No American statesman but Clay ever had such a personal following. He now became the leader of the Democratic party; he retained the leadership of the Northern Democrats to the last; and since Andrew Jackson, no man has possessed the influence, received the confidence, or had the support that it was the lot of Douglas to enjoy from the Democrats in the northern half of the Union. From 1854 to 1858, he was the centre of the political history of the country; from 1858 to 1860, he was the best-known man in the United States; but after the contest with Lincoln in 1858, it became apparent that the "Little Giant" had met his match in that other son of Illinois.

Douglas was generous and faithful to his friends. He had large ideas in business; he made money easily and spent it lavishly. It was stated during this controversy that he was furthering the interests of slavery because he was himself a slave-holder, but the allegation was untrue. Douglas had, indeed, been offered a plantation with a large number of slaves by his father-in-law, but he had declined the gift because he was unwilling to accept such a responsibility. He answered this charge in the Senate with dignity.[25] Indeed, those who sought a mercenary motive as a key to the course of Douglas strangely misapprehended his character.[26]

In comprehensive views he was a true representative of the West. No public man has ever had more of the spirit of the boundless prairie or has been such a faithful type of the resistless energy that characterizes the city of Chicago. He understood the West, but it is plain that he had not thought out the results of the repeal of the Missouri Compromise, for he seemed to have little apprehension of the political revolution that was destined to take place in his beloved section of country.[27] On January 1st, 1854, Indiana, Illinois, Michigan, Wisconsin, and Iowa were Democratic States;[28] all their senators were Democrats; of twenty-nine representatives only five were Whigs. None but Indiana remained reliably Democratic. Michigan, Wisconsin, and Iowa at once became Republican, and Illinois would have immediately ranged herself at their side had it not been for the strong personal influence of Douglas.

Some writers and many men who were contemporary with the event have maintained that the civil war would not have taken place had it not been for the abrogation of the Missouri Compromise. This will probably not be the mature verdict of history. The more the subject is studied, the more profound will appear the prophetic saying of John Quincy Adams: "I am satisfied slavery will not go down until it goes down in blood." [29] Yet it must be adjudged that Douglas hastened the struggle; he precipitated the civil war.

The North was now in a ferment. At the Connecticut State election in April the Democrats had failed to elect the legislature or governor. While both Whig and Democratic conventions had protested against the repeal of the Missouri Compromise,[30] the result of the election was obviously a rebuke to the dominant party for their support of the Kansas-Nebraska bill. The newly elected legislature passed resolutions averse to the proposed measure; these were presented to the House the day on which the concluding vote was taken, and to the Senate before its final action on the bill. The Whig convention of Pennsylvania resolved against the disturbance of the legislation of 1820, while the Democratic convention of that State was silent.[31]

One phase of the public sentiment has been barely alluded to. The foreign immigration had become a factor in politics of which heed must be taken. The Germans and Irish, for the most part, had joined the Democratic party; but the Germans, from the first, were opposed to the repeal of the Missouri Compromise, for they were against the extension of slavery.[32] Of eighty-eight German newspapers, eight were in favor of the Kansas-Nebraska bill, while eighty were decidedly opposed to it.[33] This change was of enough consequence to determine the political character of Wisconsin and Iowa, and was a great element of anti-slavery strength in Ohio.

The cannon roared in Washington when the Senate enacted the measure, but gloom overspread the minds of Northern men. Pierce and Douglas, said Greeley, have made more abolitionists in three months than Garrison and Phillips could have made in half a century.[34] Crowds of people who had heretofore severely criticised Garrison, Phillips, Parker, and their methods, now flocked to hear them, and were glad to listen to the arguments of these earnest men.[35] It was at once urged by the press and from the platform that an effort should be made to have Kansas enter the Union as a free State, and a systematic movement was begun with this end in view.

The author of the bill was regarded with execration; his middle name was Arnold, and this suggested a comparison to Benedict Arnold. The term which is used in every Christian land as a synonym of traitor was likewise applied to him, and one hundred and three ladies of an Ohio village sent him thirty pieces of silver.[36] He could travel, as he afterwards said, "from Boston to Chicago by the light of his own effigies." Horace Bushnell, a noted preacher in Hartford, applied to Douglas the bitter prophecy of the Hebrew prophet: "Tidings out of the east and out of the north shall trouble him; therefore he shall go forth with great fury to destroy and utterly to make away many, yet he shall come to his end, and none shall help him." A journal which had opposed the Kansas-Nebraska measure with pertinacity asked, in derision, "Who names Douglas for the next President now?"[37] Not a response came from the North.

"Never was an act of Congress so generally and so unanimously hailed with delight at the South" as was the Kansas-Nebraska act, wrote Alexander Stephens six years after its passage.[38] This may be accepted as a fact, although there were some exceptions to the almost universal acclaim. . . .

NOTES

[1] Private letter of John Van Buren to ex-Senator Clemens, Feb. 3d, 1854, published in the New York *Evening Post,* Feb. 11th, 1854.

[2] Washington correspondence Richmond *Enquirer,* quoted by Richmond *Whig,* Jan. 31st, 1854. I am indebted to the New York Historical Society for permission to examine their file of the Richmond *Whig.*

[3] New York *Herald,* Feb. 21st. I am indebted to the Society Library of New York for permission to examine their file of the New York *Herald* and the New York *Courier and Enquirer.* These expressions were used after the formal repeal of the Missouri Compromise had been incorporated into the Kansas-Nebraska bill.

[4] Kapp, Geschichte der Sklaverei, quoted by Von Holst, vol. iv. p. 313. This was in the fall of 1855.

[5] This was the statement of Douglas in the Senate in 1856, *Congressional Globe,* vol. xxxiii. p. 393. I have never seen any well-attested evidence which contradicts this statement. Butler, of South Carolina, said in the Senate during the debate: "I have had very little to do with this bill, and I believe the South has had very little to do with the provisions of the bill." At the time of the greatest unpopularity of this legislation, Douglas said in the Senate (Feb. 23d, 1855): "The Nebraska bill was not concocted in any conclave, night or day. It was written by myself, at my own house, with no man present. Whatever odium there is attached to it, I assume it. Whatever of credit there may be, let the public award it where they think it belongs." The earliest premonition of the report which I have found is in the New York *Herald* of Jan. 2d, 1854: "It is understood that the territory of Nebraska is to be admitted into the confederacy upon such terms as will leave it at the option of her people to make it either a slave or free territory."

[6] This speech was made at Atchison, Kan., Sept. 26th, 1854, reported in the Parkville *Luminary,* Sept. 26th, copied in the New York *Tribune* Oct. 10th; see also the New York *Tribune,* June 4th, 1855, and see Wilson's remarks in the Senate, April 14th, 1856.

[7] *Congressional Globe,* vol. xxxiii. p. 393.

[8] In 1886, Jefferson Davis, in a letter to a friend, said: "So far as I know and believe, Douglas and Atchison never were in such relation to each other as would have caused Douglas to ask Atchison's help in preparing the bill, and I think the whole discussion shows that Douglas originated the bill, and for a year or two vaunted himself on its paternity."—Memoir of Jefferson Davis, by his wife, vol. i. p. 671.

[9] New York *Evening Post,* Jan. 7th, 1854.

[10] New York *Tribune,* Jan. 11th, 1854.

[11] New York *Independent,* Jan. 7th. The *Herald,* which approved of the report of Douglas, said: "Senator Douglas's report has created a great sensation among the abolitionists and their aiders and abettors in this city. Already the *Post* and *Tribune*—and the *Times* will soon follow with the other abolitionist organs—are out in full swoop against the report."

[12] Richmond *Whig,* Jan. 20th; also see Cullom's speech, *Congressional Globe,* vol. xxix. p. 54.

[13] Letter of Dixon to Henry S. Foote, Sept. 30th, 1858, Spring's Kansas, p. 3; Life of Douglas, by a Member of the Western Bar, New York, 1860. Dixon's letter is referred to by Nicolay and Hay, in History of Lincoln, as having been published in the Louisville *Democrat,* Oct. 3d, 1858.

[14] Letter of Dixon, Life of Douglas, p. 172.

[15] Cox, Three Decades of Federal Legislation, p. 49; Foote, Casket of Reminiscences, p. 93.

[16] Constitutional and Party Questions, Cutts, p. 122.

[17] Quoted by Cullom, Appendix, *Congressional Globe,* vol. xxix. p. 539.

[18] S. S. Cox, Eulogy, July, 1861.

[19] "We presume that three more tricky and managing politicians don't. live than Pierce, Cushing, and Soulé. If we were to add a fourth, we should of course name S. A. Douglas."—New York *Tribune,* May 13th, 1854; evidently written by Greeley.

[20] Recollections of a Busy Life, p. 358.

[21] See *Atlantic Monthly,* vol. viii. p. 206.

[22] Herndon's Life of Lincoln, p. 308.

[23] *Atlantic Monthly,* vol. viii: p. 206; Forney's Anecdotes of Public Men.

[24] Reminiscences of a Journalist, C. T. Congdon, p. 286.

[25] Life of Douglas, Sheahan, p. 437.

[26] My authorities for the view of Douglas are, besides those I have named, the two biographies of him by Sheahan and Flint; Constitutional and Party Questions, J. M. Cutts; Representative Men, Savage; Forney's Anecdotes of Public Men; Blaine's Eulogy on Garfield. I have received valuable hints concerning him from Senator John Sherman, General Logan, and my friend Mr. George H. Stone; but for his personal characteristics more than to any other source I am indebted to my father and mother, who were intimately acquainted with him and very often saw him familiarly. Having seen him frequently when a child, my own recollection of his personal appearance and manner of speaking from the stump is vivid.

[27] See his speech, May 25th, 1854.

[28] Minnesota was not a State. "What gain had freedom in the admission of Iowa into the Union? Are Alabama and Mississippi more devoted to the despotic ideas of American panslavism than are Indiana and Illinois?"—New York *Tribune,* March 29th, 1854.

[29] Life of Seward, vol. i. p. 672. This remark was made in 1843.

[30] *National Intelligencer,* March 2d.

[31] *Ibid.,* March 18th.

[32] See New York *Evening Post,* Feb. 4th and 7th; the *Liberator,* April 21st; *National Intelligencer,* April 15th.

[33] List made by Cincinnati *Gazette,* cited by Von Holst, vol. iv. p. 429. See Von Holst's remarks on this subject in his history; also his criticism of Bryce's American Commonwealth. See *The Nation,* April 24th, 1890, which refers to an article in the *Historische Zeitschrift,* neue Folge, vol. xxviii. pp. 1–50.

[34] New York *Tribune,* May 17th.

[35] Life of Garrison, vol. iii. pp. 407, 408; New York *Tribune.* See Bell's speech in the Senate, *Congressional Globe,* Appendix, vol. xxix, p. 943.

[36] The *Liberator,* vol. xxiv. p. 43.

[37] New York *Times,* May 23d.

[38] Life of Alex. H. Stephens, Johnston and Browne, p. 360, letter of May 9th, 1860.

Edward Channing (1856–1931) and His Social History

Edward Channing, whose training and professorial career centered at Harvard, was among the twentieth-century "scientific historians," for he symbolizes to many of his craft the qualities of objectivity and industrious archival research. His ancestors came from England in 1720 and his father was the transcendentalist poet William Ellery Channing. His birthplace was Dorchester, Massachusetts. As a historian, he was influenced by the evolutionary ideas of his Harvard teacher, Henry Adams, and like Adams he turned to the study of American history after first specializing in English history. Students admired his vigorous personality, shrewd judgments, and dry humor.

Despite the label of "scientific historian" there was no effort to conceal definite moral judgments, but he made notable concessions to the new tendency to broaden political history by excursions into economic and social facts. He looked upon the American Revolution partly as a product of the desire of the English governing classes to exploit the colonists for their own pocketbooks. As a New Englander, he minimized Western history and tended to reflect this sectional view as well as the current Anglo-Saxon ethnocentrism.

Still he expressed impatience with extreme filiopietism, criticized Puritan exclusiveness, and tried to be "fair" to the South by suggesting that although slavery was wrong, slaves were often happier than their masters and did not mind bondage unduly; besides, he thought, abolitionism was extreme radicalism. The unifying principle of American history, he said, was the victory of the centralizing forces of the Union over those of decentralization.

He devoted more attention to social themes than his critics admit and dealt more analytically with such themes as education, penology, prohibition, and literature than McMaster did. The selection given here on education shows an effective grasp of the relationship of local government and education and the English antecedents. Perhaps he should be credited with the leadership of the Harvard historians (and their colleagues in related departments) who, in discarding the older view of Puritan and Calvinist fanaticism, emphasized the intellectual and cultural tradition of the first generation of American Puritans. The reader will also note that he is much more traditional in educational theory than the then rising Dewey-Thorndike school, for he assumed that ancient languages had the virtue of strengthening the faculties through mental discipline; thus he argued that they promoted success in the pursuit of any business or profession. He expressed doubt whether the new school system could develop such talents as those of an Emerson, a Poe, or a Washington Irving.

This selection is taken from his chief work, *A History of the United States* (6 vols., 1905–25).

A History of the United States . . .

[LOCAL GOVERNMENT AND EDUCATION IN ENGLAND AND NEW ENGLAND]
In the older time, before the Reformation, indigent and impotent persons were cared for by the church authorities, or by private charity, or were licensed to beg. With the dissolution of the monasteries and the confiscation of church funds, many of these sources of relief dried up, and at about the same time beggars and vagabonds began to be dealt with more strictly. The government sought to place the burden of caring for the poor upon the local administrative units, but did not hand over to the parishes and towns those portions of the ecclesiastical funds which had been used to alleviate suffering. At first no general

Volume I, pages 423–36 (Macmillan, 1905).

compulsory law was passed, but an effort was made to raise the necessary money by means of more or less voluntary contributions; but those who were backward in giving were to be reasoned with by the various church authorities from the parson and churchwardens of the parish to the bishop of the diocese. If one remained obstinate, the justices of the peace or the mayor of the city should charitably and gently move the "said obstinate person to extend his charity toward the relief of the poor of the parish where he dwelleth," and if he still remained obstinate, he should pay such sum as the magistrates thought reasonable or go to jail. This means of supply proved precarious, probably because the obstinate persons who had money and the magistrates whose business it was to coerce them belonged to the same class of society. After many experiments, in 1598 Parliament placed the responsibility of the care of the poor upon the parishes or towns, and in case they failed to raise such sums as seemed reasonable to the county court, the justices could themselves rate the parishioners or, at their discretion, join a poor parish with a rich one, or a parish which had been overcome by some calamity with a parish which had been more fortunate, thereby equalizing the burden. The result of this poor law, which was made permanent in 1601, was to make the town and parish organization vastly more important than it had been before. Furthermore, it compelled the towns and parishes to guard themselves jealously against incoming strangers, so that members of the laboring classes became practically tied to the locality where they happened to come into the world.

The parishes discharged their obligations by a separate tax levy, which was known as the poor rate. In some places, however, gifts of money or of land were held in trust for the relief of the poor, sometimes being invested in a flock of sheep. Persistent attempts were also made to compel the poor to become self-supporting, by spinning flax or working up other raw material, which was provided at public charge; in Boston in 1595, twenty boys and maidens were so employed. At Northampton another course was taken. There the poor children were turned over to Roger Williams, pin maker, who paid the parish twelvepence per week for each child, and in return was permitted to work them from seven in the morning until six or eight in the evening. Whatever plan was tried, some other scheme was certain to seem preferable in no long time. The burden was unquestionably heavy. Strangers were carefully looked after. In Boston, for instance, it was provided that an inquiry should be made every fortnight as to all newcomers, and those who were likely to become chargeable be removed from the town; and no householder was permitted to let a dwelling to any "foreigner" unless he first obtained a license.[1] The communal spirit rapidly strengthened, and we find that at Ipswich no one could sell a house to a stranger without permission of the authorities, and at one time, indeed, no inhabitant of Northampton was permitted to sell corn to any outsider. Moreover, in years of threatened scarcity, the towns sometimes purchased food stuffs in quantity, and doled them out at cost price to the inhabitants of the town.

In each parish there was one ecclesiastical edifice which was taken care of at the expense of the parishioners, and in which every man, woman, and child in the town was obliged to attend divine service, or incur certain penalties ascertained by law. This requirement applied to all persons, whether they were Conformists, Nonconformists, Independents, or Roman Catholics. Every one was expected to attend the religious service provided by the State. The affairs of the parish were managed by the church-wardens and vestrymen, aided and guided by the parson. The tendency was to increase the amount of hierarchical control, but at the time of the settlement of Massachusetts the secular element was still powerful. It is especially worthy of note in this connection that in the management of local affairs in New England the parson had no official recognition, as he had in England, and exercised only such power in town affairs as his personal influence gave him. It was natural that it should be so because the Puritan movement was largely a revolt of the landed gentry against clerical control; Winthrop, Saltonstall, and Bellingham, were not likely to establish in America that influence which they left England to avoid.

The Massachusetts colonists brought with them to their new homes the ideas with which they had been familiar from their childhood.

We may suppose that William Coddington and Richard Bellingham in the Massachusetts town meeting argued for the restrictions with which they had been familiar in the older Boston. So too did those who came from Ipswich and Dorchester, England, to Ipswich and Dorchester, Massachusetts. Sometimes a whole parish, parson and all, removed to Massachusetts, thereby upsetting all the social and ecclesiastical arrangements of that part of the country.

The religious edifice of the New England town was known locally as the meetinghouse. As in England, it was the center of local life in Church and State. In it were held the town meetings, as the parish meetings were held in the parish churches of England, and to it on the Lord's day came every dweller in the village unless prevented by some serious illness. It also served as a convenient place in which to store the town's stock of powder and extra military equipment; but, owing to the exigencies of frontier life, every able-bodied man in the early New England towns was obliged to have his weapons near at hand, instead of hanging them on the walls of the meetinghouses. As was the case in England, the town took care of the construction and repair of the religious edifices, and, there being no tithes, supported the minister directly by taxation, to which every one was obliged to contribute.[2] In the earlier time, the lack of tithes had been made up by voluntary contribution; but by 1660, throughout New England, except, of course, in Rhode Island, the support of the clergy formed a part of the regular business of the town.

There were few, if any, indigent and impotent poor for the towns to take care of in earliest New England; but the obligation to do so was plainly recognized from an early time. The towns, in the beginning, besides being local administrative units like the English parishes, were quasi corporations[3] endowed by the Massachusetts Bay Company with large tracts of land; in later times, bodies of proprietors exercised this function. At first, however, a very important part of each town's business was the allotment of lands among the heads of families in the town. Over this problem, as might be expected, fierce contests were often waged. In Boston, for example, the more farseeing and, possibly, the richer men felt that it was desirable to reserve a portion of the town's domain for later comers. The other townsmen wished to divide the whole land grant among those on the spot. There was something to be said on both sides of the question, because the territory of Boston was necessarily limited in geographical extent; and yet, on the other hand, to men like Winthrop, it might seem to be important to reproduce in the capital of New England some of the social and political conditions which gave London a part of its place in English institutions and history. Similar considerations did not obtain in other towns; but in all, in the years 1640–50, the feeling spread among the townsmen that they and their descendants should alone be considered in future allotments of land,[4] so that from about 1650 the towns generally ceased to exercise this function. Then, however, the question of providing for the support of the poor became one of importance. In New England, as in the mother country, the communal spirit was strong and was strengthened by the position which the religious organization occupied in the social fabric. For these four reasons: (1) the peculiarities of the land system, (2) the care of the poor, (3) the prevalent communal ideas, and (4) the peculiar religious institutions of the place, it became necessary carefully to scrutinize the qualification of each newcomer before he or she was permitted to acquire legal rights.[5] It is for these reasons that all the New England colonists made stringent regulations for the exclusion of undesirable persons; and when as in the case of Providence, for example, admission to the rights of inhabitancy carried with it the right to a share in the undivided land, the taking in of a newcomer might well be regarded as an act of disinterestedness deserving of praise. The American nation in the nineteenth century, however, was so liberal in its policy of giving land to every immigrant that it has come to be a habit of historical writers to look at this matter from the other point of view and to stigmatize these early regulations of the New England colonies for preserving their corporate rights as alien and sedition acts on the supposition, probably, that they bore some resemblance to the famous laws of the end of the eighteenth century.

The meetinghouse, besides serving for religious uses and for the secular needs of the inhabitants, was sometimes occupied during the week by the town school. The settlers of New England were well educated, for in the time of the early Stuarts elementary education in England was widely diffused. It is, indeed, astonishing to turn over in one's mind the names of persons of learning in those days. Shakespeare and Hooker, William Bradford and John Winthrop, Captain John Smith and George Sandys, six men of different attainments and scenes of activity, probably received their first intellectual impulses in the local schools of their boyhoods' homes. Another way of showing how rapidly education was spreading in the first colonizing period is to note the increasing number of convicted felons who escaped the gallows by the process known as "benefit of clergy." Complete statistics on this point of course are unavailable; but the Middlesex County Records contain statistics which may fairly be regarded as typical. These show that in the reign of Edward VI only eight and one-half per cent of convicted felons "read like a clerk"; in Mary's reign the percentage rose slightly; in Elizabeth's time no less than thirty-one out of every hundred successfully called for the "Book"; and in James's reign thirty-nine per cent escaped the felon's doom by reading the "neck verse."

This education was confined to men, although the reigning monarch was a woman, and at about this time a woman acted as churchwarden of Tavistock, England. As a rule the girls grew up in ignorance of learning, with the result that their letters are very instructive as examples of phonetic spelling, and as showing us how English was pronounced in the days of Spenser and Milton. For instance, Lady Sussex exhibited an ingenuity which was credible enough in a woman who outlived three husbands including in the number that Puritan nobleman, Robert Rich, Earl of Warwicke, who is so often mentioned in this volume. Yorkshire, this good lady turned into "Oyskessher," while Lincoln's-Inn-Fields becomes "Lingeslindsfilds," and "a maisismee" stands in her interesting letters for "amazes me."

By the end of James's reign there were at least five hundred endowed schools in England besides many more which were supported entirely by public contributions. These schools were scattered broadcast over the land: in Lancashire there were forty, in Yorkshire sixty, in Lincolnshire twenty, in Devonshire ten, and in Dorsetshire ten. Many of these were based on old foundations which had come down from pre-Reformation days or were reëndowments which had been made to satisfy the conscience of some religiously minded person; but the vitality of the system in early Stuart time was the outcome of the Renaissance and the Reformation. The local records contain many entries of money payments for educational purposes. At Ipswich, for instance, Mr. Eaton was employed as grammar schoolmaster at an annual salary of thirty pounds, and in 1608, Mr. George Downing was engaged to teach the children to cipher, to cast accounts, and to recite the elements of grammar. In what would now be called the primary grades the instruction was largely by catechizing, which consisted in an oral give and take between teacher and pupil. The early schoolbooks contain a medley of A B C D'isms, religious instructions, and moral precepts; for example, in the A B C of 1538, the first page of which is reproduced in Mr. Littlefield's *Early Schools and School Books,* is given the alphabet in "black letter," and the opening lines of the Lord's Prayer in Latin and in English.

The English local records of that time contain many entries of the payment of money for school purposes; but, usually, the schools were supported partly and often wholly by endowments. At Tavistock the parish provided a "new schoolhouse" in 1576,—which phrase shows that there had been an older schoolhouse in that parish. The new edifice must have been a building of some pretensions as it had glass windows which were still uncommon. The small boy of that time and place, however, resembled the small boy of all times and places, and in 1588 the churchwardens found it advisable to protect the glass windows with wire netting. Within the building there was, at least, one dictionary which was chained to the desk.

The New England settlers numbered among them a good proportion of university men; their religion demanded a knowledge of the Bible; and the form of their local government shows that they assumed that the voters could read and write. The men of Massachusetts had scarcely settled themselves in the New World before they began the establishment of a school system on practically the English model.[6] Many of the early schools were supported in part by the income of lands which were devoted to that purpose by the town or by the General Court, or were given by some private individual. In almost every case, however, these gifts proved insufficient and the deficit was made good, either by public subscription or by vote of the town. These schools were public only in the sense that they were open to the children of all the inhabitants of a town, but it was generally expected that those who could afford it would pay something for their children's tuition, but neither poverty nor lack of social rank in the parents excluded a boy from the benefit of primary education.

The school system having been evolved by custom, as was so frequently the case, was recognized by the colonial government and made the basis of a general educational system by the passage of the well-known law of 1649, as soon as the increasing number of remote settlements made it likely that some of the newer immigrants would neglect this part of their duty to the Commonwealth. The preamble of this act is worth reprinting as showing the combined religious and æsthetic motives which actuated the founders:—

It being one chief project of Sathan to keep men from the knowledge of the Scripture, as in the former times, keeping them in unknown Tongues, so in these latter times, by perswading from the use of Tongues, that so at least the true sense and meaning of the Original might be clouded and corrupted with false glosses of Deceivers; to the end that Learning may not be buried in the Graves of our fore Fathers, in Church and Commonwealth, the Lord assisting our endeavours.

According to this act every township of fifty householders or more should appoint one to teach "all such children as shall resort to him to read and write." Furthermore, when any town should increase to the number of one hundred families, they should set up a grammar school wherein youths "may be fitted for the University." It is interesting to note in this connection that the smaller towns were only obliged to have "writing schools," but they might combine with neighboring towns so that their brighter boys could receive secondary education. This general educational system of Massachusetts was adopted by Connecticut and New Haven and, at a considerably later period, by Plymouth. At the time of the Revolution, Rhode Island, alone of the New England colonies, lacked a public school system, although one of the earliest public schools had been opened at Newport in 1640.

Six years after the beginning of the Great Emigration, the General Court of Massachusetts appropriated a large proportion of the public revenue for the beginning of an institution of learning at Newtowne, which name was later changed to Cambridge to commemorate the Alma Mater of three college men out of every four in the colony. Two years later, a young clergyman, dying at Charlestown, left half of his property and all of his books to the new institution, which was appropriately named Harvard College in grateful recognition of John Harvard, its first private benefactor. Its first class graduated four years later in 1642. From this beginning its reputation for piety and learning rapidly spread.[7] Other New England colonies contributed to its support, and to it came students from other parts of New England, from New Netherland and even from old England. Its curriculum would seem appalling to a modern college student, and its discipline savored of the English public school where the belief still prevailed that sparing the rod spoiled the child.[8] In the day when most learned men were clergymen and when the thought of the time centered in religion, it was natural that the principal interest of the new establishment should be ecclesiastical. As early as 1647, however, Giles Firmin lectured upon anatomy; and in the same year, possibly to encourage this earliest English medical lecturer in America, the General Court voted that it conceived it to be very necessary that such as study physic or chirurgery should have liberty to anatomize once in four years some malefactor, in case there be such. It is to be hoped that this instruction in physic and chirurgery proved to be possible since those were the days when pharmaceutical knowledge relied for its efficacy largely on the terror which the name of a medicine inspired. In 1643, for example, Governor Winthrop received a paper from his friend, Dr. Stafford of England, containing a list of what were then regarded as valuable prescriptions. One of these consisted of the ashes of toads cremated in the month of March. This medicine was to be taken internally and might well have frightened one into health or the grave. In concluding his list, Dr. Stafford declared that "no man can with a good conscience take a fee or reward before the party receive benefit apparent: and then he is not to demand anything, but what God shall put into the heart of the party to give him." [9] This learned gentleman would have received the sympathy of the Maryland magistrate who put a chirurgeon of that colony under bonds to prosecute to its fulfillment a cure for which he had received compensation before there was any "benefit apparent."

The first generation of New England Puritans resembled closely in their modes of thought and in their personal habits the Puritans of the older England which they had left behind. We find the elder Winthrop taking his family and friends down Boston harbor for a day's outing, and the birds and flowers of the New World interested him and the other first comers. The more learned among them were careful students of one of the greatest of modern books, John Calvin's *Institutes of the Christian Religion* and, no doubt, agreed with that great man that the enjoyment of the gifts of God is not wrongful since he has created them for our benefit. "In herbs, trees, and fruits, beside their various uses, his design has been to gratify us by graceful forms and pleasant odors." "Shall the Lord," asks Calvin, "have endued flowers with such beauty, to present itself to our eyes, with such sweetness of smell, to impress our sense of smelling; and shall it be unlawful for our eyes to be affected with the beautiful sight, or our olfactory nerves with the agreeable order?" [10] So, too, the Creator in providing clothing has had in view not merely man's necessity, but propriety and decency as well. Nevertheless, he asks, "Where is gratitude towards God for clothing, if, on account of our sumptuous apparel, we admire ourselves and despise others?" John Calvin was one of the greatest of men and recognized that one form of religion would not be adapted to all ages and therefore declared that one church should not despise another on account of a variety of discipline. "The Lord gave not that law by the hand of Moses to be promulgated among all nations, and to be universally binding; . . . he had a special regard to their [the Jews] peculiar circumstances." [11] The difficulty of keeping body and soul together in early New England, however, brought out the sterner and severer qualities of the early New Englanders, so that by the time the second generation of native born appeared in public life the race had lost much of the geniality which has usually marked the users of the English speech; but this was due to a variety of causes, among which their religion should be reckoned as only one. The Puritan creed only slowly assumed the sternness of aspect which made intellectual excitation save for religious purposes an impossibility.[12]

NOTES

[1] See also *Pittington Records,* 1622, and *Houghton Records,* 1658.

[2] There is an excellent article on the "Support of Religion in Plymouth and Massachusetts," by Samuel S. Green, in American Antiquarian Society's *Proceedings* for 1886, p. 86.

[3] On the legal position of the towns, see an article by Andrew McF. Davis on "Corporations in the Days of the Colony" in Colonial Society of Massachusetts *Publications,* i, and Gray's decision in the case of Hill *vs.* City of Boston, *Massachusetts Reports,* cxxii, 129.

[4] See, for example, *Boston Records,* i, 88; ii, 68.

[5] For examples of the working of these forces, see *Boston Records,* i, 37, 90, 103, 135; ii, 7, 11, 16, 44, 49, 148; other entries may be found in the index under Strangers; and the Massachusetts Colony Law of 1651, Whitmore's *Laws of 1672,* p. 143, and index under Strangers. The form used for warning an undesirable person out of town may be seen in *Early Records of Lancaster* (Massachusetts), 89.

[6] The early Virginia settlers, who were drawn from the same social strata as the New Englanders, were equally solicitous about education. The *Virginia Magazine of History,* the *William and Mary Quarterly,* Hening's *Statutes,* and the records of the Virginia Company contain numerous entries of gifts and bequests for educational purposes; but trifling results, if any, flowed from these benefactions before 1660. In his famous report to the Privy Council, Governor Sir William Berkeley states (Hening's *Statutes,* ii, 517) that "the same course" is taken as "in England out of towns, every man according to his ability instructing his children." In other words the lack of communal life made a duplication of the English town school system an impossibility in the Old Dominion.

[7] December 27, 1645, Thomas Shepard of Cambridge in New England wrote to Hugh Peters, suggesting, among other things, that he should send some of Laud's books to Harvard College. Whether anything came of the proposal is not known; it certainly would have been an interesting sight to see a fledgling Massachusetts minister perusing the Archbishop's books. See *American Historical Review*, iv, 105.

[8] See Quincy's *Harvard University*. Interesting old college laws are printed in Massachusetts Historical Society's *Proceedings* for 1875, p. 207, and *ibid.*, Second Series, xi, 200.

[9] See an interesting article on "Medicine in Early Massachusetts," by Dr. Oliver Wendell Holmes in Massachusetts Historical Society's *Proceedings*, v, 379. See also *ibid.*, Second Series, i, 46; Johnson's *Wonder-working Providence*, 165. The vote of the General Court noted above was passed on October 27, 1647.

[10] *Institutes*, bk iii, ch. x, §§ 2 and 3. It was not until the first half of the seventeenth century that much attention was given to the cultivation of flowers (*Verney Memoirs*, i, 9).

[11] *Institutes*, bk. iv, ch. xx, § 16.

[12] See an interesting paper by Barrett Wendell on the "Characteristics of the Puritans" in American Historical Association's *Reports* for 1891, p. 245.

Frederick Jackson Turner (1861–1932) and the Frontier Theories

Perhaps no one has influenced the writing and teaching of American history as much as has Frederick Jackson Turner, for he turned professional emphasis from European determinants to the influence of the frontier. His birth and rearing in the frontier community of Portage, Wisconsin, and his first two degrees earned at the frontier-minded University of Wisconsin fostered his early scholarly interest in the Wisconsin fur trade and the Indians. He developed these interests as a doctoral student under Herbert Baxter Adams of the Johns Hopkins University, but resisted the tendency of his mentor to explain the growth of American local institutions as offshoots of ancient Teutonic influences. Though he did not reject the germ theory which located democratic roots in the customs of these German tribesmen, he felt that this cultural diffusionist approach had been grossly overemphasized at the expense of indigenous factors. This view is expressed in the famous essay reprinted here: "The Significance of the Frontier in American History."

Turner's professorial career included both the University of Wisconsin and Harvard University, where he gained many disciples and wrote interpretive articles and books on the West. Among these were *The Rise of the New West* (1906), *The Significance of Sections in American History* (1932), and *The United States, 1830–1850* (1933); all are commentary upon the seminal ideas of his 1893 essay—written unfortunately without literary skill. He taught historians to seek out frontier determinants upon specific American developments in politics, economics, and culture, to study land policies as an index of individual opportunities, and to see cheap lands as a safety valve for the dissatisfaction caused by Eastern industrialism. Some drew pessimistic inferences from the idea that the frontier had gone at the time of the 1890 census, but Turner himself suggests the idea in later essays that an era of social planning and city development would provide the dynamics hitherto afforded by cheap lands and unlimited resources.

Turner's disciples discovered fertile themes in sectionalism, farm revolts, conservation, land speculation, Indian influences, transportation, the influence of barbed wire upon the Great Plains, the impact of the frontier upon diplomacy, etc. During the Great Depression, when economic interpretations were especially popular, the frontier approach captured many history classrooms. By 1940, however, younger historians challenged this Turner hypothesis as narrow and even harmful in its emphasis upon what was unique in American life at the expense of cosmopolitan non-American influences. Among the critics' questions were: Did his idea of "sections" confuse the role of classes as social factors? Did he think that the frontier really produced new political institutions? (Actually he denied this.) How could he argue that the frontier acted as a safety valve for eastern labor when it was obviously the experienced eastern farmers who hastened to seek western homesteads? A careful reading of the 1893 essay shows that Turner qualified many of his controversial positions.

It is surprising to note that only two years before Turner published the famous essay, he took quite a different position in another essay given here, "The Significance of History." This invoked Herbert B. Adams's teaching that "our history is only to be understood as a growth from European history under the new conditions of the new world." A contrasting philosophy of history is apparent in the two essays. Like Adams, he stresses here the evolutionary germ theory that society is an ever-growing organism. Especially interesting is his partial anticipation of James Harvey Robinson's *New History* (1911), for he asserts, "History is the biography of society in all of its departments." It is concerned with the "masses" whose welfare it promotes and it comprises what came into the present from the past which each generation sees through its own lenses. But he does not go as far as Robinson in enumerating the new social science tools for the historian, although he shares his interest in an economic interpretation of history. Certain of these ideas in the *New History,* particularly the broadening of political history to include social, economic, and geographic factors, reappear in the frontier essay of 1893.

The Significance of History

The conceptions of history have been almost as numerous as the men who have written history. To Augustine Birrel [1] history is a pageant; it is for the purpose of satisfying our curiosity. Under the touch of a literary artist the past is to become living again. Like another Prospero the historian waves his wand, and the deserted streets of Palmyra sound of the tread of artisan and officer, warrior gives battle to warrior, ruined towers rise by magic, and the whole busy life of generations that have long ago gone down to dust comes to life again in the pages of a book. The artistic prose narration of past events— this is the ideal of those who view history as literature. To this class belong romantic literary artists who strive to give to history the coloring and dramatic action of fiction, who do not hesitate to paint a character blacker or whiter than he really was, in order that the interest of the page may be increased, who force dull facts into vivacity, who create impressive situations, who, in short, strive to realize as an ideal the success of Walter Scott. It is of the historian Froude that Freeman says: "The most winning style, the choicest metaphors, the neatest phrases from foreign tongues would all be thrown away if they were devoted to proving that any two sides of a triangle are not always greater than the third side. When they are devoted to prove that a man cut off his wife's head one day and married her maid the next morning out of sheer love for his country, they win believers for

Wisconsin Journal of Education XXI (1891), 230–34, 253–6.

the paradox." It is of the reader of this kind of history that Seeley writes: "To him by some magic parliamentary debates shall always be lively, officials always men of strongly marked interesting character. There shall be nothing to remind him of the blue-book or the law book, nothing common or prosaic but he shall sit as in a theater and gaze at splendid scenery and costume. He shall never be called upon to study or to judge, but only to imagine and enjoy. His reflections as he reads shall be precisely those of the novel reader; he shall ask: Is this character well drawn? is it really amusing? is the interest of the story well sustained? and does it rise properly toward the close?"

But after all these criticisms we may gladly admit that in itself an interesting style, even a picturesque manner of presentation, is not to be condemned, provided that truthfulness of substance rather than vivacity of style be the end sought. But granting that a man may be the possessor of a good style which he does not allow to run away with him, either in the interest of the artistic impulse or the cause of party, still there remain differences as to the aim and method of history. To a whole school of writers among whom we find some of the great historians of our time, history is the study of politics, that is, politics in the high signification given the word by Aristotle, as meaning all that concerns the activity of the state itself. "History is past politics and politics present history," says the great author of the Norman Conquest. Maurenbrecher, of Leipsic, speaks in no less uncertain tones; "The bloom of historical studies is the history of politics"; and Lorenz, of Jena, asserts: "The proper field of historical investigation, in the closer sense of the word, is politics." Says Seeley: "The modern historian works at the same task as Aristotle in his politics." "To study history is to study not merely a narrative but at the same time certain theoretical studies." "To study history is to study problems." And thus a great circle of profound investigators, with true scientific method, have expounded the evolution of political institutions, studying their growth as the biologist might study seed, bud, blossom and fruit. The results of these labors may be seen in such monumental works as those of Waitz on German institutions, Stubbs on English Constitutional History and Maine on Early Institutions.

There is another and an increasing class of historians to whom history is the study of the economic growth of the people, who aim to show that property, the distribution of wealth, the social condition of the people, are the underlying and determining factors to be studied. This school, whose advance-guard was led by Roscher, having already transformed orthodox political economy by its historical method, is now going on to rewrite history from the economic point of view. Perhaps the best English expression of the ideas of the school is to be found in Thorold Rogers' "Economic Interpretation of History." He truly asserts that "very often the cause of great political events and great social movements is economical and has hitherto been undetected." So important does the fundamental principle of this school appear to me, that I desire to quote from Mr. Rogers a specific illustration of this new historical method.

"In the twelfth and thirteenth centuries," he says, "there were numerous and well frequented routes from the markets of Hindostan to the Western world, and for the conveyance of that Eastern produce which was so greatly desired as a seasoning to the coarse and often unwholesome diet of our forefathers. The principal ports to which this produce was conveyed were Seleucia (latterly called Licia) in the Levant, to Trebizond, on the Black Sea, and to Alexandria. From these ports this Eastern produce was collected mainly by the Venetian and Genoese traders, and conveyed over the passes of the Alps to the upper Danube and the Rhine. Here it was a source of great wealth to the cities which were planted on these water-ways from Ratisbon and Nuremberg, to Bruges and Antwerp. The stream of commerce was not deep or broad, but it was singularly fertilizing, and every one who has any knowledge of the only history worth knowing, knows how important these cities were in the later Middle Ages.

"In the course of time, all but one of these routes had been blocked by the savages who desolated Central Asia, and still desolate it. It was, therefore, the object of the most enterprising of the Western nations to get, if possible, in the rear of these destructive brigands, by discovering a long sea passage to Hindostan. All Eastern trade depended on the Egyptian road being kept open, and this remaining road was already threatened. The beginning of this discovery was the work of a Portuguese prince. The expedition of Columbus was an attempt to discover a passage to India over the Western sea. By a curious coincidence the Cape passage was doubled, and the new world discovered almost simultaneously.

"The discoveries were made none too soon. Selim I (1512–20) the sultan of Turkey conquered Mesopotamia and the holy towns of Arabia, and annexed Egypt during his brief reign. This conquest blocked the only remaining road which the Old World knew. The thriving manufactures of Alexandria were at once destroyed. Egypt ceased to be the highway from Hindostan. I discovered that some cause must be at work which had hitherto been unsuspected in the sudden and enormous rise of prices in all Eastern products, at the close of the first quarter of the sixteenth century, and found that it must have come from the conquest of Egypt. The river of commerce was speedily dried up. The cities which had thriven on it were gradually ruined, at least in so far as this source of their wealth was concerned, and the trade of the Danube and Rhine ceased. The Italian cities fell into rapid decay. The German nobles, who had got themselves incorporated among the burghers of the free cities, were impoverished, and betook themselves to the obvious expedient of reimbursing their losses by the pillage of their tenants. Then came the Peasants' war, its ferocious incidents, its cruel suppression, and the development of those wild sects which disfigured and arrested the German Reformation. The battle of the Pyramids, in which Selim gained the Sultanate of Egypt for the Osmanli Turks, brought loss and misery into thousands of homes where the event had never been heard of. It is such facts as these which the economic interpretation of history illustrates and expounds."

Viewed from this position, the past is filled with new meaning. The focal point of modern interest is the fourth estate, the great mass of the people. History has been a romance and a tragedy. In it we read the brilliant annals of the few. The intrigues of courts, knightly valor, palaces and pyramids, the loves of ladies, the songs of minstrels, and the chants from cathedrals, pass like a pageant, or linger like a strain of music as we turn the pages. But history has its tragedy as well, which tells of the degraded tillers of the soil, toiling that others might dream, the slavery that rendered possible the "glory that was Greece," the serfdom into which decayed the "grandeur that was Rome"— these as well demand their annals. Far oftener than has yet been shown have these underlying economic facts affecting the bread-winners of the nation, been the secret of the nation's rise or fall, by the side of which much that has passed as history is the merest frippery.

But I must not attempt to exhaust the list of the conceptions of history. To a large class of writers represented by Hume, the field of historical writing is an arena whereon are to be fought out present partisan debates. Whig is to struggle against Tory, and the party of the writer's choice is to be victorious at whatever cost to the truth. We do not lack these partisan historians in America. To Carlyle, the hero-worshipper, history is the stage on which a few great men play their parts. To Max Müller, history is the exposition of the growth of religious ideas. To the moralist, history is the text whereby to teach a lesson. To the metaphysician history is the fulfillment of a few primary laws.

Plainly we may make choice out of many ideals. If, now, we strive to reduce them to some kind of order, we find that in each *age* a different ideal of history has prevailed. To the savage history is the painted scalp, with its symbolic representations of the victims of his valor; or it is the legend of the gods and heroes of his race—attempts to explain the origin of things. Hence the vast body of mythologies, folk-lore and legends, in which science, history, fiction, are all blended together, judgment and imagination inextricably confused. As time passes the artistic instinct comes in and historical writing takes the form of Iliad, or Niebelungen Lied. Still we have in these writings the reflection of the imaginative, credulous age that believed in the divinity of its heroes and wrote down what it believed. Artistic and critical faculty find expression in Herodotus, father of Greek history, and in Thucydides, the ideal Greek historian. Both write from the standpoint of an advanced civilization and strive to present a real picture of the events and an explanation of the causes of the events.

But Thucydides is a Greek; literature is to him an art, and history a part of literature; and so it seems to him no violation of historical truth to make his generals pronounce long orations that were composed for them by the historian. Moreover early men and Greeks alike believed their own tribe or state to be the favored of the gods: the rest of humanity was for the most part outside the range of history.

To the medieval historian history was the annals of the monastery, or the chronicle of court and camp.

In the nineteenth century a new ideal and method of history arose. Philosophy prepared the way for it. Schelling taught the doctrine "that the state is not in reality governed by laws of man's devising, but is a part of the moral order of the universe, ruled by cosmic forces from above." Herder proclaimed the doctrine of growth in human institutions. He saw in history the development of given germs; religions were to be studied by comparison and by tracing their origins from superstitions up toward rational conceptions of God. Language, too, was no sudden creation, but a growth and to be studied as such; and so with political institutions. Thus he paved the way for the study of comparative philology, of mythology, and of political evolution. Wolfe, applying Herder's suggestions to the Iliad, found no single Homer as its author, but many. This led to the critical study of the texts. Niebuhr applied this mode of study to the Roman historians and proved their incorrectness. Livy's history of early Rome became legend. Then Niebuhr tried to find the real facts. He believed that, although the Romans had forgotten their own history, still it was possible by starting with institutions of known reality to construct their predecessors, as the botanist may infer bud from flower. He would trace causes from effects. In other words, so strongly did he believe in the growth of an institution according to fixed laws that he believed he could reconstruct the past, reaching the real facts even by means of the incorrect accounts of the Roman writers. Although he carried his method too far, still it was the foundation of the modern historical school. He strove to reconstruct old Rome as it really was out of the original authorities that remained. By critical analysis and interpretation he attempted so to use these texts that the buried truth should come to light. To skill as an antiquary he added great political insight—for Niebuhr was a practical statesman. It was his aim to unite critical study of the materials with the interpretative skill of the political expert and this has been the aim of the new school of historians. Leopold von Ranke applied this critical method to the study of modern history. To him a document surviving from the past itself was of far greater value than any amount of tradition regarding the past. To him the contemporary account, rightly used, was of far higher authority than the second-hand relation. And so he diligently sought in the musty archives of European courts, and the results of his labors and those of his scholars have been the rewriting of modern diplomatic and political history. Charters, correspondence, contemporary chronicles, inscriptions—these are the materials on which he and his disciples worked. To "tell things as they really were" was Ranke's ideal. But to him also, history was primarily past politics.

Superficial and hasty as this review has been, I think you see that the historical study of the first half of the nineteenth century reflected the thought of that age. It was an age of political agitation and inquiry, as our own age still so largely is. It was an age of science. That inductive study of phenomena which has worked a revolution in our knowledge of the external world was applied to history. In a word the study of history became scientific and political.

To-day the questions that are uppermost, and that will become increasingly important, are not so much political as economic questions. The age of machinery, of the factory system, is also the age of socialistic inquiry.

It is not strange that the predominant historical study is coming to be the study of past social conditions, inquiry as to land-holding, distribution of wealth and the economic basis of society in general. Our conclusion, therefore is, that there is much truth in all these conceptions of history: history is past literature, it is past politics, it is past religion, it is past economics.

Each age tries to form its own conception of the past. *Each age writes the history of the past anew with reference to the conditions uppermost in its own time.* Historians have accepted the doctrine of

Herder. Society grows. They have accepted the doctrine of Comte. Society is an organism. History is the biography of society in all of its departments. There is objective history and subjective history. Objective history applies to the events themselves; subjective history is man's conception of these events. "The whole mode and manner of looking at things alters with every age," but this does not mean that the real events of a given age change: it means that our comprehension of these facts changes.

History, both objective and subjective, is ever *becoming*—never completed. The centuries unfold to us more and more the meaning of past times. To-day we understand Roman history better than did Livy or Tacitus; not only because we know how to use sources·better, but also because the significance of events develops with time; because to-day is so much a product of yesterday that yesterday can only be understood as explained by to-day. The aim of history, then, is to know the elements of the present by understanding what came into the present from the past. For the present is simply the developing past, the past the undeveloped present. As well try to understand the egg without a knowledge of its developed form, the chick, as to try to understand the past without bringing to it the explanation of the present; and equally as well try to understand an animal without study of its embryology as to try to understand one time without the study of events that went before. The antiquarian strives to bring back the past for the sake of the past; the historian strives to show the present to itself by revealing its origin from the past. The goal of the antiquarian is the dead past: the goal of the historian is the living present. Droysen has put this true conception into the statement: "History is the 'Know Thyself' of humanity"—"the self consciousness of mankind."

If now, you accept with me the statement of this great master of historical science, the rest of our way is clear. If history be, in truth, the self consciousness of humanity, the "self consciousness of the living age, acquired by understanding its development from the past," all the rest follows.

First we recognize why all the spheres of man's activity must be considered. Not only is this the only way in which we can get a complete view of the society, but no one department of social life can be understood in isolation from the others. The economic life and the political life touch, modify and condition one another. Even the religious life needs to be studied in conjunction with the political and economic life, and *vice versa*. Therefore all kinds of history are essential—history as politics, history as art, history as economics, history as religion—all are truly parts of society's endeavor to understand itself by understanding its past.

Next, we see that history is not shut up in a book—not in many books. The first lesson the student of history has to learn is to discard his conception that there are standard ultimate histories. In the nature of the case this is impossible. *History is all the remains that have come down to us from the past, studied with all the critical and interpretative power that the present can bring to the task.* From time to time great masters bring their investigations to fruit in books. To us these serve as the latest words, the best results of the most recent efforts of society to understand itself—but they are not the final words. To the historian the materials for his work are found in all that remains from the ages gone by—in papers, roads, mounds, customs, languages; in monuments, coins, medals, names, titles, inscriptions, charters; in contemporary annals and chronicles, and finally in the secondary sources or histories in the common acceptance of the term. Wherever there remains a chipped flint, a spear-head, a piece of pottery, a pyramid, a picture, a poem, a colosseum, or a coin, there is history. Says Taine:

"What is your first remark on turning over the great stiff leaves of a folio, the yellow sheets of a manuscript, a poem, a code of laws, a declaration of faith? This you say was not created alone. It is but a mould, like a fossil shell, an imprint like one of those shapes embossed in stone by an animal which lived and perished. Under the shell there was an animal, and behind the document there was a man. Why do you study the shell except to represent to yourself the animal? So do you study the document only in order to know the man. The shell and the document are lifeless wrecks, valuable only as a clue to the

entire and living existence. We must reach back to this existence,
endeavor to re-create it."

But observe that when a man writes a narration of the past, he
writes with all his limitations as regards ability to test the real value
of his sources, and as able rightly to interpret them. Does he make use
of a chronicle? first he must determine whether it is genuine; then
whether it was contemporary, or at what period written; then what
opportunities its author had to know the truth; then what were his
personal traits; was he likely to see clearly, to relate impartially? If
not, what was his bias, what his limitations? Next comes the harder
task—to interpret the significance of events; causes must be understood, results seen. Local affairs must be described in relation to
affairs of the world—all must be told with just selection, emphasis,
perspective; with that historical imagination and sympathy that does
not judge the past by the canons of the present, nor read into it the
ideas of the present. Above all the historian must have a passion for
truth above that for any party or idea. Such are some of the difficulties that lie in the way of our science. When, moreover, we consider
that each man is conditioned by the age in which he lives and must
perforce write with limitations and prepossessions, I think we shall
all agree that no historian can say the ultimate word.

Another thought that follows as a corollary from our definition is,
that in history there is a unity and a continuity. Strictly speaking
there is no gap between ancient, medieval and modern history. Strictly
speaking there are no such divisions. Baron Bunsen dates modern
history from the migration of Abraham. Bluntschli makes it begin
with Frederick the Great. The truth is, as Freeman has shown, that
the age of Pericles, or the age of Augustus has more in common
with modern times than has the age of Alfred or of Charlemagne.
There is another test than that of chronology; namely, stages of
growth. In the past of the European world peoples have grown from
families into states, from peasantry into the complexity of great city
life, from animism into monotheism, from mythology into philosophy;
and have yielded place again to primitive peoples who in turn have
passed through stages like these and yielded to new nations. Each

nation has bequeathed something to its successor; no age has suffered
the highest content of the past entirely to be lost. By unconscious
inheritance, and by conscious striving after the past as part of the
present, history has acquired continuity. Freeman's statement that
into Rome flowed all the ancient world and out of Rome came the
modern world is as true as it is impressive. In a strict sense imperial
Rome never died. You may find the eternal city still living in the
Kaizer and the Czar, in the language of the Romance peoples, in the
codes of European states, in the eagles of their coats of arms, in every
college where the classics are read—in a thousand political institutions. Even here in young America old Rome still lives. When the
inaugural procession passes toward the senate chamber, and the president's address outlines the policy he proposes to pursue—there is
Rome! You may find her in the code of Louisiana, in the French and
Spanish portions of our history, in the idea of checks and balances
in our constitution. Clearest of all, Rome may be seen in the titles,
government, and ceremonials of the Roman Catholic church; for
when the Cæsar passed away, his scepter fell to that new Pontifex
Maximus, the Pope, and to that new Augustus, the Holy Roman Emperor of the Middle Ages, an empire which in name, at least, continued till those heroic times when a new Imperator recalled the
days of the great Julius, and sent the eagles of France to proclaim that
Napoleon was king over kings. So it is true in fact, as we should
presume, *a priori,* that to history there are only artificial divisions.
Society is an organism, ever growing. History is the self-consciousness of this organism. "The roots of the present lie deep in the past."
There is no break. But not only is it true that no country can be
understood without taking account of all the past; it is also true that
we cannot select a stretch of land and say we will limit our study to
this land; for local history can only be understood in the light of the
history of the world. There is unity as well as continuity. To know
the history of contemporary Italy, we must know the history of
contemporary France, of contemporary Germany. Each acts on each.
Ideas, commodities even, refuse the bounds of a nation. All are inextricably connected, so that each is needed to explain the others. This

is true especially of our modern world with its complex commerce and means of intellectual connection. In history, then, there is unity and continuity. Each age must be studied in the light of all the past; local history must be viewed in the light of world-history.

Now, I think, we are in a position to consider the utility of historical studies. I will not dwell on the dignity of history considered as the self-consciousness of humanity; nor on the mental growth that comes from such a discipline; nor on the vastness of the field— all these occur to you, and their importance will impress you increasingly as you consider history from this point of view. To enable us to behold our own time and place as a part of the stupendous progress of the ages—to see primitive man; to recognize in our midst the undying ideas of Greece; to find Rome's majesty and power alive in present law and institution, still living in our superstitions and our folk-lore; to enable us to realize the richness of our inheritance, the possibility of our lives, the grandeur of the present—these are some of the priceless services of history.

But I must conclude my remarks with a few words upon the utility of history as affording a training for good citizenship. Doubtless good citizenship is the end for which the public schools exist. Were it otherwise there might be difficulty in justifying the support of them at public expense. The direct and important utility of the study of history in the achievement of this end hardly needs argument.

In the union of public service and historical study, Germany has been pre-eminent. For certain governmental positions in that country, a university training in historical studies is essential. Ex-President Andrew D. White affirms that a main cause of the efficiency of German administration is the training that officials get from the university study of history and politics. In Paris there is the famous School of Political Sciences which fits men for the public service of France. In the decade closing with 1887 competitive examinations showed the advantages of this training. Of 60 candidates appointed to the council of state, 40 were graduates of this school. Of 42 appointed to the inspection of finance, 39 were from the school; 16 of the 17 appointees to the court of claims; and 20 of 26 appointees to the department of foreign affairs held diplomas from the School of Political Sciences. In these European countries not merely are the departmental officers required to possess historical training; the list of leading statesmen reveals many names eminent in historical science. I need hardly recall to you the great names of Niebuhr, the councilor, whose history of Rome gave the impetus to our new science; of Stein, the reconstructor of Germany, and the projector of the Monumenta Germanicae, that priceless collection of original sources of medieval history. Read the roll of Germany's great public servants and you will find among them such eminent men as Gneist, the authority on English constitutional history; Bluntschli, the able historian of politics; von Holst, the historian of our own political development; Knies, Roscher and Wagner, the economists, and many more. I have given you Droysen's conception of history, but Droysen was not simply a historian, he belonged with the famous historians, Treitschke, Mommsen, von Sybel, to what Lord Acton calls "that central band of writers and statesmen and soldiers, who turned the tide that had run for six hundred years, and conquered the centrifugal forces that had reigned in Germany longer than the commons have sat at Westminster."

Nor does England fail to recognize the value of the union of history and politics as exemplified by such men as Macaulay, Dilke, Morley and Bryce, all of whom have been eminent members of parliament, as well as distinguished historical writers. From France and Italy such illustrations could easily be multiplied.

When we turn to America and ask what marriages have occurred between history and statesmanship, we are filled with astonishment at the contrast. It is true that our country has tried to reward literary men: Motley, Irving, Bancroft, Lowell held official positions, but these positions were in the diplomatic service. The "literary fellow" was good enough for Europe. The state gave these men aid rather than called their services to its aid. To this statement I know of but one important exception—George Bancroft. In America statesmanship has been considered something of spontaneous generation, a miraculous birth from our republican institutions. To demand of the statesmen who debate such topics as the tariff, European and South American relations, emigration, the labor and the railroad problems, a scientific acquaintance with historical politics or economics, would be to expose one's self to ridicule in the eyes of the public. I have said that the tribal stage of society demands tribal history and tribal politics. When a society is isolated it looks with contempt upon the history and institutions of the rest of the world. We shall not be altogether wrong if we say that such tribal ideas concerning our institutions and society have prevailed for many years in this country. Lately historians have turned to the comparative and historical study of our political institutions. The actual working of our constitution as contrasted with the literary theory of it has engaged the attention of able young men. Foreigners like von Holst and Bryce have shown us a mirror of our political life in the light of the political life of other peoples. Little of this influence has yet attracted the attention of our public men. Count the roll in Senate and House, Cabinet and diplomatic service—to say nothing of the state governments—and where are the names famous in history and politics? It is shallow to express satisfaction with this condition, and sneer at "literary fellows." To me it seems that we are approaching a pivotal point in our country's history.

In an earlier part of my remarks I quoted from Thorold Rogers showing how the Turkish conquest of far off Egypt brought ruin to homes in Antwerp and Bruges. If this was true in that early day, when commercial threads were infinitely less complex than they are now, how profoundly is our present life interlocked with the events of all the world. Heretofore America had measurably remained aloof from the Old World affairs. Under the influence of a wise policy, she has avoided political relations with other powers. But it is one of the profoundest lessons that history has to teach, that political relations, in a highly developed civilization, are inextricably connected with economic relations. Already there are signs of a relaxation of our policy of commercial isolation. Reciprocity is a word that meets with increasing favor from all parties. But, once fully afloat on the sea of world-wide economic interests, we shall soon develop political interests. Our fishery disputes furnish one example; our Samoan interests another; our Congo relations a third. But, perhaps, most important

are our present and future relations with South America, coupled
with our Monroe doctrine. It is a settled maxim of International
law that the government of a foreign state whose subjects have lent
money to another state may interfere to protect the rights of the bondholders, if they are endangered by the borrowing state. As Prof.
H. B. Adams has pointed out, South American states have close
financial relations with many European money-lenders; they are also
prone to revolutions. Suppose, now, that England, finding the interests of her bondholders in jeopardy, should step in to manage the
affairs of some South American country as she has those of Egypt for
the same reason. Would the United States abandon its popular interpretation of the Monroe doctrine, or would she give up her policy of
non-interference in political affairs of the outer world? Or suppose
our own bondholders in New York, say, to be in danger of loss by
revolution in South America—and our increasing tendency to close
connection with South American affairs makes this a supposable case
—would our government stand idly by while her citizens' interests
were sacrificed? Take another case, the protectorate of the proposed
inter-oceanic canal. England will not be content to allow the control
of this to rest solely in our hands. Will the United States form an
alliance with England for the purpose of this protection? Such questions as these indicate that we are drifting out into European political
relations; and that a new statesmanship is demanded; a statesmanship
that shall clearly understand European history and present relations
which depend on history. Again, consider the problems of socialism
brought to our shores by European immigrants. We shall never deal
rightly with such problems until we understand the historical conditions under which they grew. Thus we not only meet Europe outside
our borders, but in our very midst. The problem of immigration
furnishes many examples of the need of historical study. Consider
how our vast western domain has been settled. Louis XIV devastates
the Palatinate, and soon hundreds of its inhabitants are hewing down
the forests of Pennsylvania. The bishop of Salsburg persecutes his
Protestant subjects, and the woods of Georgia sound to the crack of
Teutonic rifles. Presbyterians are oppressed in Ireland, and soon in

Tennessee and Kentucky the fires of pioneers gleam. These were but advance-guards of the mighty army that has poured into our midst ever since. Every economic change, every political change, every military conscription, every socialistic agitation in Europe has sent us groups of colonists who have passed out on to our prairies to form new self-governing communities, or who have entered the life of our great cities. These men have come to us historical products, they have brought to us, not merely so much bone and sinew, not merely so much money, not merely so much manual skill—they have brought with them deep-inrooted customs and ideas. They are important factors in the political and economic life of the nation. Our destiny is interwoven with theirs; how shall we understand American history, without understanding European history? The story of the peopling of America has not yet been written. We do not understand ourselves.

One of the most fruitful fields of study in our country has been the process of growth of our own institutions, local and national. The town and the county, the germs of our political institutions, have been traced back to old Teutonic roots. Gladstone's remark that "The American Constitution is the most wonderful work ever struck off at a given time by the brain and purpose of man," has been shown to be misleading, for the Constitution was, with all the constructive powers of the fathers, still a growth; and our history is only to be understood as a growth from European history under the new conditions of the new world. Says Dr. H. B. Adams:

"American local history should be studied as a contribution to national history. This country will yet be viewed and reviewed as an organism of historic growth, developing from minute germs, from the very protoplasm of state-life. And some day this country will be studied in its international relations, as an organic part of a larger organism now vaguely called the World-State, but as surely developing through the operation of economic, legal, social and scientific forces as the American Union, the German and British Empires are evolving into higher forms." * * * "The local consciousness must be expanded into a fuller sense of its historic worth and dignity. We must understand the cosmopolitan relations of modern local life, and its own wholesome conservative power in these days of growing centralization."

If any added argument were needed to show that good citizenship demands the careful study of history, it is in the examples and lessons that the history of other peoples has for us. It is profoundly true that each people makes its own history in accordance with its past. It is true that a purely artificial piece of legislation, unrelated to present and past conditions, is the most short-lived of things. Yet it is to be remembered that it was history that taught us this truth, and that there is, within the limits of the constructive action possible to a state, large scope for the use of this experience of foreign peoples.

I have aimed to offer, then, these considerations: History, I have said, is to be taken in no narrow sense. It is more than past literature, more than past politics, more than past economics. It is the self-consciousness of humanity—humanity's effort to understand itself through the study of its past. Therefore it is not confined to books— the *subject* is to be studied, not books simply. History has a unity and a continuity: the present needs the past to explain it; and local history must be read as a part of world history. The study has a utility as a mental discipline, and as expanding our ideas regarding the dignity of the present. But perhaps its most practical utility to us, as *public school teachers,* is its service in fostering good citizenship.

The ideals presented may at first be discouraging. Even to him who devotes his life to the study of history the ideal conception is impossible of attainment. He must select some field and till that thoroughly —be absolute master of it; for the rest he must seek the aid of others whose lives have been given in the true scientific spirit of the study of special fields. The public school teacher must do the best with the libraries at his disposal. We teachers must use all the resources we can obtain and not pin our faith to a single book; we must make history living instead of allowing it to seem mere literature, a mere narration of events that might have occurred in the moon. We must teach the history of a few countries thoroughly, rather than that of many countries superficially. The popularizing of scientific knowledge is one of the best achievements of this age of book-making. It is typical of that social impulse which has led university men to bring the fruits of their study home to the people. In England the social impulse has led to what is known as the university extension movement. University men have left their traditional cloister, and gone to live among the working classes, in order to bring to them a new intellectual life. Chautauqua, in our own country, has begun to pass beyond the period of superficial work to real union of the scientific and the popular. In their summer school they offer courses in American history. Our own State university carries on extensive work in various lines. I believe that this movement in the direction of popularizing historical and scientific knowledge will work a real revolution in our towns and villages as well as in our great cities. The school teacher is called to do a work above and beyond the instruction in his school. He is called upon to be the apostle of the higher culture to the community in which he is placed. Given a good school or town library—such an one is now within the reach of every hamlet that is properly stimulated to the acquisition of one—and given an energetic, devoted teacher to direct and foster the study of history and politics and economics, and we would have an intellectual regeneration of the state. Historical study has for its end to let the community see itself in the light of the past—to give it new thoughts and feelings, new aspirations and energies. Thoughts and feelings flow into deeds. Here is the motive-power that lies behind institutions. This is therefore one of the ways to create good politics; here we can touch the very "age and body of the time, its form and pressure." Have you a thought of better things, a reform to accomplish? "Put it in the air," says the great teacher. Ideas have ruled, will rule. We must make university-extension into state life felt in this country as did Germany. Of one thing beware. Avoid as the very unpardonable sin, any one-sidedness, any partisan, any partial treatment of history. Do not misinterpret the past for the sake of the present. The man who enters the temple of history must devoutly respond to that invocation of the church *"Sursum corda"*—lift up your heart. No looking at history as an idle tale, a compend of anecdotes; no servile devotion to a text book, no carelessness of truth about the dead that can no longer speak, must be permitted in its sanctuary. "History," says Droysen, "is not the truth and the light; but a striving for it, a sermon on it, a consecration to it."

NOTES

¹ NOTE. In the preparation of this lecture free use has been made of the following sources: Notes on the lectures of Prof. H. B. Adams, of Johns Hopkins University; Morrison, in Encyclopedia Britanica, "History": Birrell, in Contemporary Review, June, 1885; Freeman, Lectures on the Methods of Historical Study; *Ibid.,* How the Study of History is Let and Hindered; *Ibid.,* The Office of the Historical Professor; Seeley, in Macmillan's Magazine, vol. 40, pp. 289, 369, 499 vol. 47, p. 67; Adams, Manual of Historical Literature, preface; Andrews, Institutes of General History, ch. I; Lord Acton, in English Historical Review, vol. I No. 1; Bernheim, Lehrbuch der Historischen Methode; *Ibid.,* Geschichtsforschung, etc.; Maurenbrecher, Ueber Methode und Aufgabe der Historischen Forschung; *Ibid.,* Geschichte und Politik; Lorenz, Die Geschichtswissenschaft; Rocholl, Philosophie der Geschichte; Droysen, Grundriss der Historik.

The Significance of the Frontier in American History

In a recent bulletin of the Superintendent of the Census for 1890 appear these significant words: "Up to and including 1880 the country had a frontier of settlement, but at present the unsettled area has been so broken into by isolated bodies of settlement that there can hardly be said to be a frontier line. In the discussion of its extent, its westward movement, etc., it can not, therefore, any longer have a place in the census reports." This brief official statement marks the closing of

Annual Report of the American Historical Association for 1893 (Washington, 1894), 199–227.

a great historic movement. Up to our own day American history has been in a large degree the history of the colonization of the Great West. The existence of an area of free land, its continuous recession, and the advance of American settlement westward, explain American development.

Behind institutions, behind constitutional forms and modifications, lie the vital forces that call these organs into life and shape them to meet changing conditions. The peculiarity of American institutions is, the fact that they have been compelled to adapt themselves to the changes of an expanding people—to the changes involved in crossing a continent, in winning a wilderness, and in developing at each area of this progress out of the primitive economic and political conditions of the frontier into the complexity of city life. Said Calhoun in 1817, "We are great, and rapidly—I was about to say fearfully—growing!" [1] So saying, he touched the distinguishing feature of American life. All peoples show development; the germ theory of politics has been sufficiently emphasized. In the case of most nations, however, the development has occurred in a limited area; and if the nation has expanded, it has met other growing peoples whom it has conquered. But in the case of the United States we have a different phenomenon. Limiting our attention to the Atlantic coast, we have the familiar phenomenon of the evolution of institutions in a limited area, such as the rise of representative government; the differentiation of simple colonial governments into complex organs; the progress from primitive industrial society, without division of labor, up to manufacturing civilization. But we have in addition to this a recurrence of the process of evolution in each western area reached in the process of expansion. Thus American development has exhibited not merely advance along a single line, but a return to primitive conditions on a continually advancing frontier line, and a new development for that area. American social development has been continually beginning over again on the frontier. This perennial rebirth, this fluidity of American life, this expansion westward with its new opportunities, its continuous touch with the simplicity of primitive society, furnish the forces dominating American character. The true point of view in the history of this nation is not the Atlantic coast, it is the great West. Even the slavery struggle, which is made so exclusive an object of attention by writers like Prof. von Holst, occupies its important place in American history because of its relation to westward expansion.

In this advance, the frontier is the outer edge of the wave—the meeting point between savagery and civilization. Much has been written about the frontier from the point of view of border warfare and the chase, but as a field for the serious study of the economist and the historian it has been neglected.

The American frontier is sharply distinguished from the European frontier—a fortified boundary line running through dense populations. The most significant thing about the American frontier is, that it lies at the hither edge of free land. In the census reports it is treated as the margin of that settlement which has a density of two or more to the square mile. The term is an elastic one, and for our purposes does not need sharp definition. We shall consider the whole frontier belt, including the Indian country and the outer margin of the "settled area" of the census reports. This paper will make no attempt to treat the subject exhaustively; its aim is simply to call attention to the frontier as a fertile field for investigation, and to suggest some of the problems which arise in connection with it.

In the settlement of America we have to observe how European life entered the continent, and how America modified and developed that life and reacted on Europe. Our early history is the study of European germs developing in an American environment. Too exclusive attention has been paid by institutional students to the Germanic origins, too little to the American factors. The frontier is the line of most rapid and effective Americanization. The wilderness masters the colonist. It finds him a European in dress, industries, tools, modes of travel, and thought. It takes him from the railroad car and puts him in the birch canoe. It strips off the garments of civilization and arrays him in the hunting shirt and the moccasin. It puts him in the log cabin of the Cherokee and Iroquois and runs an Indian palisade around him. Before long he has gone to planting Indian corn and plowing with a sharp stick; he shouts the war cry and takes the scalp in orthodox Indian fashion. In short, at the frontier the environment is at first too strong for the man. He must accept the conditions which it furnishes, or perish, and so he fits himself into the Indian clearings and follows the Indian trails. Little by little he transforms the wilderness, but the outcome is not the old Europe, not simply the development of Germanic germs, any more than the first phenomenon was a case of reversion to the Germanic mark. The fact is, that here is a new product that is American. At first, the frontier was the Atlantic coast. It was the frontier of Europe in a very real sense. Moving westward, the frontier became more and more American. As successive terminal moraines result from successive glaciations, so each frontier leaves its traces behind it, and when it becomes a settled area the region still partakes of the frontier characteristics. Thus the advance of the frontier has meant a steady movement away from the influence of Europe, a steady growth of independence on American lines. And to study this advance, the men who grew up under these conditions, and the political, economic, and social results of it, is to study the really American part of our history.

STAGES OF FRONTIER ADVANCE

In the course of the seventeenth century the frontier was advanced up the Atlantic river courses, just beyond the "fall line," and the tidewater region became the settled area. In the first half of the eighteenth century another advance occurred. Traders followed the Delaware and Shawnese Indians to the Ohio as early as the end of the first quarter of the century.[2] Gov. Spotswood, of Virginia, made an expedition in 1714 across the Blue Ridge. The end of the first quarter of the century saw the advance of the Scotch-Irish and the Palatine Germans up the Shenandoah Valley into the western part of Virginia, and along the Piedmont region of the Carolinas.[3] The Germans in New York pushed the frontier of settlement up the Mohawk to German Flats.[4] In Pennsylvania the town of Bedford indicates the line of settlement. Settlements had begun on New River, a branch of the Kanawha, and on the sources of the Yadkin and French Broad.[5] The King attempted to arrest the advance by his proclamation of 1763,[6] forbidding settlements beyond the sources of the rivers flowing into the Atlantic; but in vain. In the period of the Revolution the frontier crossed the Alleghanies into Kentucky and Tennessee, and the upper waters of the Ohio were settled.[7] When the first census was taken in 1790, the continuous settled area was bounded by a line which ran near the coast of Maine, and included New England except a portion of Vermont and New Hampshire, New York along the Hudson and up the Mohawk about Schenectady, eastern and southern Pennsylvania, Virginia well across the Shenandoah Valley, and the Carolinas and eastern Georgia.[8] Beyond this region of continuous settlement were the small settled areas of Kentucky and Tennessee, and the Ohio, with the mountains intervening between them and the Atlantic area, thus giving a new and important character to the frontier. The isolation of the region increased its peculiarly American tendencies, and the need of transportation facilities to connect it with the East called out important schemes of internal improvement, which will be noted farther on. The "West," as a self-conscious section, began to evolve.

From decade to decade distinct advances of the frontier occurred. By the census of 1820 [9] the settled area included Ohio, southern Indiana and Illinois, southeastern Missouri, and about one-half of Louisiana. This settled area had surrounded Indian areas, and the management of these tribes became an object of political concern. The frontier region of the time lay along the Great Lakes, where Astor's American Fur Company operated in the Indian trade,[10] and beyond the Mississippi, where Indian traders extended their activity even to the Rocky Mountains; Florida also furnished frontier conditions. The Mississippi River region was the scene of typical frontier settlements.[11]

The rising steam navigation [12] on western waters, the opening of the Erie Canal, and the westward extension of cotton [13] culture added five frontier states to the Union in this period. Grund, writing in 1836, declares: "It appears then that the universal disposition of Americans to emigrate to the western wilderness, in order to enlarge their dominion over inanimate nature, is the actual result of an expansive power which is inherent in them, and which by continually agitating all classes of society is constantly throwing a large portion of the whole population on the extreme confines of the State, in order to gain space for its development. Hardly is a new State or Territory formed before the same principle manifests itself again and gives rise to a further emigration; and so is it destined to go on until a physical barrier must finally obstruct its progress." [14]

In the middle of this century the line indicated by the present eastern boundary of Indian Territory, Nebraska, and Kansas marked the frontier of the Indian country.[15] Minnesota and Wisconsin still exhibited frontier conditions,[16] but the distinctive frontier of the period is found in California, where the gold discoveries had sent a sudden tide of adventurous miners, and in Oregon, and the settlements in Utah.[17] As the frontier had leaped over the Alleghanies, so now it skipped the Great Plains and the Rocky Mountains; and in the same way that the advance of the frontiersmen beyond the Alleghanies had caused the rise of important questions of transportation and internal improvement, so now the settlers beyond the Rocky Mountains needed means of communication with the East, and in the furnishing of these arose the settlement of the Great Plains and the development of still another kind of frontier life. Railroads, fostered by land grants, sent an increasing tide of immigrants into the far West. The United States Army fought a series of Indian wars in Minnesota, Dakota, and the Indian Territory.

By 1880 the settled area had been pushed into northern Michigan, Wisconsin, and Minnesota, along Dakota rivers, and in the Black Hills region, and was ascending the rivers of Kansas and Nebraska. The development of mines in Colorado had drawn isolated frontier settlements into that region, and Montana and Idaho were receiving settlers. The frontier was found in these mining camps and the ranches of the Great Plains. The superintendent of the census for 1890 reports, as previously stated, that the settlements of the West lie so scattered over the region that there can no longer be said to be a frontier line.

In these successive frontiers we find natural boundary lines which have served to mark and to affect the characteristics of the frontiers, namely: The "fall line"; the Alleghany Mountains; the Mississippi; the Missouri, where its direction approximates north and south; the line of the arid lands, approximately the ninety-ninth meridian; and the Rocky Mountains. The fall line marked the frontier of the seventeenth century; the Alleghanies that of the eighteenth; the Mississippi that of the first quarter of the nineteenth; the Missouri that of the middle of this century (omitting the California movement); and the belt of the Rocky Mountains and the arid tract, the present frontier. Each was won by a series of Indian wars.

THE FRONTIER FURNISHES A FIELD FOR COMPARATIVE STUDY OF SOCIAL DEVELOPMENT

At the Atlantic frontier one can study the germs of processes repeated at each successive frontier. We have the complex European life sharply precipitated by the wilderness into the simplicity of primitive conditions. The first frontier had to meet its Indian question, its question of the disposition of the public domain, of the means of intercourse with older settlements, of the extension of political organization, of religious and educational activity. And the settlement of these and similar questions for one frontier served as a guide for the next. The American student needs not to go to the "prim little townships of Sleswick" for illustrations of the law of continuity and development. For example, he may study the origin of our land policies in the colonial land policy: he may see how the system grew by adapting the statutes to the customs of the successive frontiers.[18] He may see how the mining experience in the lead regions of Wisconsin, Illinois, and Iowa was applied to the mining laws of the Rockies,[19] and how our Indian policy has been a series of experimentations on successive frontiers. Each tier of new States has found in the older ones material for its constitutions.[20] Each frontier has made similar contributions to American character, as will be discussed farther on.

But with all these similarities there are essential differences, due to the place element and the time element. It is evident that the farming frontier of the Mississippi Valley presents different conditions from the mining frontier of the Rocky Mountains. The frontier reached by the Pacific Railroad, surveyed into rectangles, guarded by the United States Army, and recruited by the daily immigrant ship, moves forward at a swifter pace and in a different way than the frontier reached by the birch canoe or the pack horse. The geologist traces patiently the shores of ancient seas, maps their areas, and compares the older and the newer. It would be a work worth the historian's labors to mark these various frontiers and in detail compare one with another. Not only would there result a more adequate conception of American development and characteristics, but invaluable additions would be made to the history of society.

Loria,[21] the Italian economist, has urged the study of colonial life as an aid in understanding the stages of European development, affirming that colonial settlement is for economic science what the mountain is for geology, bringing to light primitive stratifications. "America," he says, "has the key to the historical enigma which Europe has sought for centuries in vain, and the land which has no history reveals luminously the course of universal history." There is much truth in this. The United States lies like a huge page in the history of society. Line by line as we read this continental page from west to east we find the record of social evolution. It begins with the Indian and the hunter; it goes on to tell of the disintegration of savagery by the entrance of the trader, the pathfinder of civilization; we read the annals of the pastoral stage in ranch life; the exploitation of the soil by the raising of unrotated crops of corn and wheat in sparsely settled farming communities; the intensive culture of the denser farm settlement; and finally the manufacturing organization with city and factory system.[22] This page is familiar to the student of census statistics, but how little of it has been used by our historians. Particularly in eastern States this page is a palimpsest. What is now a manufacturing State was in an earlier decade an area of intensive farming. Earlier yet it had been a wheat area, and still earlier the "range" had attracted the cattle-herder. Thus Wisconsin, now developing manufacture, is a State with varied agricultural interests. But earlier it was given over to almost exclusive grain-raising, like North Dakota at the present time.

Each of these areas has had an influence in our economic and political history; the evolution of each into a higher stage has worked political transformations. But what constitutional historian has made any adequate attempt to interpret political facts by the light of these social areas and changes? [23]

The Atlantic frontier was compounded of fisherman, fur-trader, miner, cattle-raiser, and farmer. Excepting the fisherman, each type of industry was on the march toward the West, impelled by an irresistible attraction. Each passed in successive waves across the continent. Stand at Cumberland Gap and watch the procession of civilization, marching single file—the buffalo following the trail to the salt springs, the Indian, the fur-trader and hunter, the cattle-raiser, the pioneer farmer—and the frontier has passed by. Stand at South Pass in the Rockies a century later and see the same procession with wider intervals between. The unequal rate of advance compels us to distinguish the frontier into the trader's frontier, the rancher's frontier, or the miner's frontier, and the farmer's frontier. When the mines and the cow pens were still near the fall line the traders' pack trains were tinkling across the Alleghanies, and the French on the Great Lakes were fortifying their posts, alarmed by the British trader's birch canoe. When the trappers scaled the Rockies, the farmer was still near the mouth of the Missouri.

THE INDIAN TRADER'S FRONTIER

Why was it that the Indian trader passed so rapidly across the continent? What effects followed from the trader's frontier? The trade was coeval with American discovery. The Norsemen, Vespuccius, Verrazani, Hudson, John Smith, all trafficked for furs. The Plymouth pilgrims settled in Indian cornfields, and their first return cargo was of beaver and lumber. The records of the various New England colonies show how steadily exploration was carried into the wilderness by this trade. What is true for New England is, as would be expected, even plainer for the rest of the colonies. All along the coast from Maine to Georgia the Indian trade opened up the river courses. Steadily the trader passed westward, utilizing the older lines of

French trade. The Ohio, the Great Lakes, the Mississippi, the Missouri, and the Platte, the lines of western advance, were ascended by traders. They found the passes in the Rocky Mountains and guided Lewis and Clarke,[24] Fremont, and Bidwell. The explanation of the rapidity of this advance is connected with the effects of the trader on the Indian. The trading post left the unarmed tribes at the mercy of those that had purchased fire-arms—a truth which the Iroquois Indians wrote in blood, and so the remote and unvisited tribes gave eager welcome to the trader. "The savages," wrote La Salle, "take better care of us French than of their own children; from us only can they get guns and goods." This accounts for the trader's power and the rapidity of his advance. Thus the disintegrating forces of civilization entered the wilderness. Every river valley and Indian trail became a fissure in Indian society, and so that society became honeycombed. Long before the pioneer farmer appeared on the scene, primitive Indian life had passed away. The farmers met Indians armed with guns. The trading frontier, while steadily undermining Indian power by making the tribes ultimately dependent on the whites, yet, through its sale of guns, gave to the Indians increased power of resistance to the farming frontier. French colonization was dominated by its trading frontier; English colonization by its farming frontier. There was an antagonism between the two frontiers as between the two nations. Said Duquesne to the Iroquois, "Are you ignorant of the difference between the king of England and the king of France? Go see the forts that our king has established and you will see that you can still hunt under their very walls. They have been placed for your advantage in places which you frequent. The English, on the contrary, are no sooner in possession of a place than the game is driven away. The forest falls before them as they advance, and the soil is laid bare so that you can scarce find the wherewithal to erect a shelter for the night."

And yet, in spite of this opposition of the interests of the trader and the farmer, the Indian trade pioneered the way for civilization. The buffalo trail became the Indian trail, and this because the trader's "trace"; the trails widened into roads, and the roads into turnpikes, and these in turn were transformed into railroads. The same origin can be shown for the railroads of the South, the far West, and the Dominion of Canada.[25] The trading posts reached by these trails were on the sites of Indian villages which had been placed in positions suggested by nature; and these trading posts, situated so as to command the water systems of the country, have grown into such cities as Albany, Pittsburgh, Detroit, Chicago, St. Louis, Council Bluffs, and Kansas City. Thus civilization in America has followed the arteries made by geology, pouring an ever richer tide through them, until at last the slender paths of aboriginal intercourse have been broadened and interwoven into the complex mazes of modern commercial lines; the wilderness has been interpenetrated by lines of civilization growing ever more numerous. It is like the steady growth of a complex nervous system for the originally simple, inert continent. If one would understand why we are to-day one nation, rather than a collecting of isolated states, he must study this economic and social consolidation of the country. In this progress from savage conditions lie topics for the evolutionist.[26]

The effect of the Indian frontier as a consolidating agent in our history is important. From the close of the seventeenth century various intercolonial congresses have been called to treat with Indians and establish common measures of defense. Particularism was strongest in colonies with no Indian frontier. This frontier stretched along the western border like a cord of union. The Indian was a common danger, demanding united action. Most celebrated of these conferences was the Albany congress of 1754, called to treat with the Six Nations, and to consider plans of union. Even a cursory reading of the plan proposed by the congress reveals the importance of the frontier. The powers of the general council and the officers were, chiefly, the determination of peace and war with the Indians, the regulation of Indian trade, the purchase of Indian lands, and the creation and government of new settlements as a security against the Indians. It is evident that the unifying tendencies of the Revolutionary period were facilitated by the previous cooperation in the regulation of the frontier. In this connection may be mentioned the importance of the frontier, from that day to this, as a military training school, keeping alive the power of resistance to aggression, and developing the stalwart and rugged qualities of the frontiersman.

THE RANCHER'S FRONTIER

It would not be possible in the limits of this paper to trace the other frontiers across the continent. Travelers of the eighteenth century found the "cowpens" among the canebrakes and peavine pastures of the South, and the "cow drivers" took their droves to Charleston, Philadelphia, and New York.[27] Travelers at the close of the War of 1812 met droves of more than a thousand cattle and swine from the interior of Ohio going to Pennsylvania to fatten for the Philadelphia market.[28] The ranges of the Great Plains, with ranch and cowboy and nomadic life, are things of yesterday and of to-day. The experience of the Carolina cowpens guided the ranchers of Texas. One element favoring the rapid extension of the rancher's frontier is the fact that in a remote country lacking transportation facilities the product must be in small bulk, or must be able to transport itself, and the cattle raiser could easily drive his product to market. The effect of these great ranches on the subsequent agrarian history of the localities in which they existed should be studied.

THE FARMER'S FRONTIER

The maps of the census reports show an uneven advance of the farmer's frontier, with tongues of settlement pushed forward and with indentations of wilderness. In part this is due to Indian resistance, in part to the location of river valleys and passes, in part to the unequal force of the centers of frontier attraction. Among the important centers of attraction may be mentioned the following: fertile and favorably situated soils, salt springs, mines, and army posts.

ARMY POSTS

The frontier army post, serving to protect the settlers from the Indians, has also acted as a wedge to open the Indian country, and has been a nucleus for settlement.[29] In this connection mention should also be made of the Government military and exploring expeditions in determining the lines of settlement. But all the more important expeditions were greatly indebted to the earliest pathmakers, the Indian guides, the traders and trappers, and the French voyageurs, who were inevitable parts of governmental expeditions from the days of Lewis and Clarke.[30] Each expedition was an epitome of the previous factors in western advance.

SALT SPRINGS

In an interesting monograph, Victor Hehn [31] has traced the effect of salt upon early European development, and has pointed out how it affected the lines of settlement and the form of administration. A similar study might be made for the salt springs of the United States. The early settlers were tied to the coast by the need of salt, without which they could not preserve their meats or live in comfort. Writing in 1752, Bishop Spangenburg says of a colony for which he was seeking lands in North Carolina, "They will require salt & other necessaries which they can neither manufacture nor raise. Either they must go to Charleston, which is 300 miles distant * * * Or else they must go to Boling's Point in V^a on a branch of the James & is also 300 miles from here * * * Or else they must go down the Roanoke—I know not how many miles—where salt is brought up from the Cape Fear." [32] This may serve as a typical illustration. An annual pilgrimage to the coast for salt thus became essential. Taking flocks or furs and ginseng root, the early settlers sent their pack trains after seeding time each year to the coast.[33] This proved to be an important educational influence, since it was almost the only way in which the pioneer learned what was going on in the East. But when discovery was made of the salt springs of the Kanawha, and the Holston, and Kentucky, and central New York, the West began to be freed from dependence on the coast. It was in part the effect of finding these salt springs that enabled settlement to cross the mountains.

From the time the mountains rose between the pioneer and the seaboard, a new order of Americanism arose. The West and the East

began to get out of touch of each other. The settlements from the sea
to the mountains kept connection with the rear and had a certain
solidarity. But the over-mountain men grew more and more independent. The East took a narrow view of American advance, and
nearly lost these men. Kentucky and Tennessee history bears abundant witness to the truth of this statement. The East began to try to
hedge and limit westward expansion. Though Webster could declare
that there were no Alleghanies in his politics, yet in politics in
general they were a very solid factor.

LAND

The exploitation of the beasts took hunter and trader to the west, the
exploitation of the grasses took the rancher west, and the exploitation
of the virgin soil of the river valleys and prairies attracted the farmer.
Good soils have been the most continuous attraction to the farmer's
frontier. The land hunger of the Virginians drew them down the
rivers into Carolina, in early colonial days; the search for soils took
the Massachusetts men to Pennsylvania and to New York. As the
eastern lands were taken up migration flowed across them to the west.
Daniel Boone, the great backwoodsman, who combined the occupations of hunter, trader, cattle-raiser, farmer, and surveyor—learning,
probably from the traders, of the fertility of the lands on the upper
Yadkin, where the traders were wont to rest as they took their way to
the Indians, left his Pennsylvania home with his father, and passed
down the Great Valley road to that stream. Learning from a trader
whose posts were on the Red River in Kentucky of its game and
rich pastures, he pioneered the way for the farmers to that region.
Thence he passed to the frontier of Missouri, where his settlement
was long a landmark on the frontier. Here again he helped to open
the way for civilization, finding salt licks, and trails, and land. His
son was among the earliest trappers in the passes of the Rocky Mountains, and his party are said to have been the first to camp on the
present site of Denver. His grandson, Col. A. J. Boone, of Colorado,
was a power among the Indians of the Rocky Mountains, and was

appointed an agent by the Government. Kit Carson's mother was a Boone.[34] Thus this family epitomizes the backwoodsman's advance across the continent.

The farmer's advance came in a distinct series of waves. In Peck's New Guide to the West, published in Boston in 1837, occurs this suggestive passage:

Generally, in all the western settlements, three classes, like the waves of the ocean, have rolled one after the other. First comes the pioneer, who depends for the subsistence of his family chiefly upon the natural growth of vegetation, called the "range," and the proceeds of hunting. His implements of agriculture are rude, chiefly of his own make, and his efforts directed mainly to a crop of corn and a "truck patch." The last is a rude garden for growing cabbage, beans, corn for roasting ears, cucumbers, and potatoes. A log cabin, and, occasionally, a stable and corn-crib, and a field of a dozen acres, the timber girdled or "deadened," and fenced, are enough for his occupancy. It is quite immaterial whether he ever becomes the owner of the soil. He is the occupant for the time being, pays no rent, and feels as independent as the "lord of the manor." With a horse, cow, and one or two breeders of swine, he strikes into the woods with his family, and becomes the founder of a new county, or perhaps state. He builds his cabin, gathers around him a few other families of similar tastes and habits, and occupies till the range is somewhat subdued, and hunting a little precarious, or, which is more frequently the case, till the neighbors crowd around, roads, bridges, and fields annoy him, and he lacks elbow room. The preemption law enables him to dispose of his cabin and corn-field to the next class of emigrants; and, to employ his own figures, he "breaks for the high timber," "clears out for the New Purchase," or migrates to Arkansas or Texas, to work the same process over.

The next class of emigrants purchase the lands, add field to field, clear out the roads, throw rough bridges over the streams, put up hewn log houses with glass windows and brick or stone chimneys, occasionally plant orchards, build mills, schoolhouses, court-houses, etc., and exhibit the picture and forms of plain, frugal, civilized life.

Another wave rolls on. The men of capital and enterprise come. The settler is ready to sell out and take the advantage of the rise in property, push farther into the interior and become, himself, a man of capital and enterprise in turn. The small village rises to a spacious town or city; substantial edifices of brick, extensive fields, orchards, gardens, colleges, and churches are seen. Broadcloths, silks, leghorns, crapes, and all the refinements, luxuries, elegancies, frivolities, and fashions are in vogue. Thus wave after wave is rolling westward; the real Eldorado is still farther on.

A portion of the two first classes remain stationary amidst the general movement, improve their habits and condition, and rise in the scale of society.

The writer has traveled much amongst the first class, the real pioneers. He has lived many years in connection with the second grade; and now the third wave is sweeping over large districts of Indiana, Illinois, and Missouri. Migration has become almost a habit in the West. Hundreds of men can be found, not over 50 years of age, who have settled for the fourth, fifth, or sixth time on a new spot. To sell out and remove only a few hundred miles makes up a portion of the variety of backwoods life and manners.[35]

Omitting those of the pioneer farmers who move from the love of adventure, the advance of the more steady farmer is easy to understand. Obviously the immigrant was attracted by the cheap lands of the frontier, and even the native farmer felt their influence strongly. Year by year the farmers who lived on soil whose returns were diminished by unrotated crops were offered the virgin soil of the frontier at nominal prices. Their growing families demanded more lands, and these were dear. The competition of the unexhausted, cheap, and easily tilled prairie lands compelled the farmer either to go west and continue the exhaustion of the soil on a new frontier, or to adopt intensive culture. Thus the census of 1890 shows, in the Northwest, many counties in which there is an absolute or a relative decrease of population. These States have been sending farmers to advance the frontier on the plains, and have themselves begun to turn to intensive farming and to manufacture. A decade before this, Ohio had shown the same transition stage. Thus the demand for land and the love of wilderness freedom drew the frontier ever onward.

Having now roughly outlined the various kinds of frontiers, and their modes of advance, chiefly from the point of view of the frontier itself, we may next inquire what were the influences on the East and on the Old World. A rapid enumeration of some of the more noteworthy effects is all that I have time for.

COMPOSITE NATIONALITY

First, we note that the frontier promoted the formation of a composite nationality for the American people. The coast was preponderantly English, but the later tides of continental immigration flowed across to the free lands. This was the case from the early colonial days. The Scotch Irish and the Palatine Germans, or "Pennsylvania Dutch," furnished the dominant element in the stock of the colonial frontier. With these peoples were also the freed indented servants, or redemptioners, who at the expiration of their time of service passed to the frontier. Governor Spotswood of Virginia writes in 1717, "The inhabitants of our frontiers are composed generally of such as have been transported hither as servants, and, being out of their time, settle themselves where land is to be taken up and that will produce the necessarys of life with little labour." [36] Very generally these redemptioners were of non-English stock. In the crucible of the frontier the immigrants were Americanized, liberated, and fused into a mixed race, English in neither nationality nor characteristics. The process has gone on from the early days to our own. Burke and other writers in the middle of the eighteenth century believed that Pennsylvania [37] was "threatened with the danger of being wholly foreign in language, manners, and perhaps even inclinations." The German and Scotch-Irish elements in the frontier of the South were only less great. In the middle of the present century the German element in Wisconsin was already so considerable that leading publicists looked to the creation of a German state out of the commonwealth by concentrating their colonization.[38] Such examples teach us to beware of misinterpreting the fact that there is a common English speech in America into a belief that the stock is also English.

INDUSTRIAL INDEPENDENCE

In another way the advance of the frontier decreased our dependence on England. The coast, particularly of the South, lacked diversified industries, and was dependent on England for the bulk of its supplies. In the South there was even a dependence on the Northern colonies for articles of food. Governor Glenn, of South Carolina, writes in the middle of the eighteenth century: "Our trade with New York and Philadelphia was of this sort, draining us of all the little money and bills we could gather from other places for their bread, flour, beer, hams, bacon, and other things of their produce, all which, except beer, our new townships begin to supply us with, which are settled with very industrious and thriving Germans. This no doubt diminishes the number of shipping and the appearance of our trade, but it is far from being a detriment to us." [39] Before long the frontier created a demand for merchants. As it retreated from the coast it became less and less possible for England to bring her supplies directly to the consumer's wharfs, and carry away staple crops, and staple crops began to give way to diversified agriculture for a time. The effect of this phase of the frontier action upon the northern section is perceived when we realize how the advance of the frontier aroused seaboard cities like Boston, New York, and Baltimore, to engage in rivalry for what Washington called "the extensive and valuable trade of a rising empire."

EFFECTS ON NATIONAL LEGISLATION

The legislation which most developed the powers of the National Government, and played the largest part in its activity, was conditioned on the frontier. Writers have discussed the subjects of tariff, land, and internal improvement, as subsidiary to the slavery question. But when American history comes to be rightly viewed it will be seen that the slavery question is an incident. In the period from the end of the first half of the present century to the close of the civil war slavery rose to primary, but far from exclusive, importance. But this does not justify Dr. von Holst (to take an example) in treating our constitutional history in its formative period down to 1828 in a single volume, giving six volumes chiefly to the history of slavery from 1828 to 1861, under the title "Constitutional History of the United States." The growth of nationalism and the evolution of American political institutions were dependent on the advance of the frontier. Even so recent a writer as Rhodes, in his "History of the United States Since the Compromise of 1850," has treated the legislation called out by the western advance as incidental to the slavery struggle.

This is a wrong perspective. The pioneer needed the goods of the coast, and so the grand series of internal improvement and railroad legislation began, with potent nationalizing effects. Over internal improvements occurred great debates, in which grave constitutional questions were discussed. Sectional groupings appear in the votes, profoundly significant for the historian. Loose construction increased as the nation marched westward.[40] But the West was not content with bringing the farm to the factory. Under the lead of Clay—"Harry of the West"—protective tariffs were passed, with the cry of bringing the factory to the farm. The disposition of the public lands was a third important subject of national legislation influenced by the frontier.

THE PUBLIC DOMAIN

The public domain has been a force of profound importance in the nationalization and development of the Government. The effects of the struggle of the landed and the landless States, and of the ordinance of 1787, need no discussion.[41] Administratively the frontier called out some of the highest and most vitalizing activities of the General Government. The purchase of Louisiana was perhaps the constitutional turning point in the history of the Republic, inasmuch as it afforded both a new area for national legislation and the occasion of the downfall of the policy of strict construction. But the purchase of Louisiana was called out by frontier needs and demands. As frontier States accrued to the Union the national power grew. In a speech on the dedication of the Calhoun monument Mr. Lamar explained: "In 1789 the States were the creators of the Federal Government; in 1861 the Federal Government was the creator of a large majority of the States."

When we consider the public domain from the point of view of the sale and disposal of the public lands we are again brought face to face with the frontier. The policy of the United States in dealing with its lands is in sharp contrast with the European system of scientific administration. Efforts to make this domain a source of revenue, and to withhold it from emigrants in order that settlement might be compact, were in vain. The jealousy and the fears of the East were power-less in the face of the demands of the frontiersmen. John Quincy Adams was obliged to confess: "My own system of administration, which was to make the national domain the inexhaustible fund for progressive and unceasing internal improvement, has failed." The reason is obvious; a system of administration was not what the West demanded; it wanted land. Adams states the situation as follows: "The slaveholders of the South have bought the cooperation of the western country by the bribe of the western lands, abandoning to the new Western States their own proportion of the public property and aiding them in the design of grasping all the lands into their own hands. Thomas H. Benton was the author of this system, which he brought forward as a substitute for the American system of Mr. Clay, and to supplant him as the leading statesman of the West. Mr. Clay, by his tariff compromise with Mr. Calhoun, abandoned his own American system. At the same time he brought forward a plan for distributing among all the States of the Union the proceeds of the sales of the public lands. His bill for that purpose passed both Houses of Congress, but was vetoed by President Jackson, who, in his annual message of December, 1832, formally recommended that all public lands should be gratuitously given away to individual adventurers and to the States in which the lands are situated.[42]

"No subject," said Henry Clay, "which has presented itself to the present, or perhaps any preceding, Congress, is of greater magnitude than that of the public lands." When we consider the far-reaching effects of the Government's land policy upon political, economic, and social aspects of American life, we are disposed to agree with him. But this legislation was framed under frontier influences, and under the lead of Western statesmen like Benton and Jackson. Said Senator Scott of Indiana in 1841: "I consider the preemption law merely declaratory of the custom or common law of the settlers."

NATIONAL TENDENCIES OF THE FRONTIER

It is safe to say that the legislation with regard to land, tariff, and internal improvements—the American system of the nationalizing

Whig party—was conditioned on frontier ideas and needs. But it was not merely in legislative action that the frontier worked against the sectionalism of the coast. The economic and social characteristics of the frontier worked against sectionalism. The men of the frontier had closer resemblances to the Middle region than to either of the other sections. Pennsylvania had been the seed-plot of frontier emigration, and, although she passed on her settlers along the Great Valley into the west of Virginia and the Carolinas, yet the industrial society of these Southern frontiersmen was always more like that of the Middle region than like that of the tide-water portion of the South, which later came to spread its industrial type throughout the South.

The Middle region, entered by New York harbor, was an open door to all Europe. The tide-water part of the South represented typical Englishmen, modified by a warm climate and servile labor, and living in baronial fashion on great plantations; New England stood for a special English movement—Puritanism. The Middle region was less English than the other sections. It had a wide mixture of nationalities, a varied society, the mixed town and county system of local government, a varied economic life, many religious sects. In short, it was a region mediating between New England and the South, and the East and the West. It represented that composite nationality which the contemporary United States exhibits, that juxtaposition of non-English groups, occupying a valley or a little settlement, and presenting reflections of the map of Europe in their variety. It was democratic and nonsectional, if not national; "easy, tolerant, and contented"; rooted strongly in material prosperity. It was typical of the modern United States. It was least sectional, not only because it lay between North and South, but also because with no barriers to shut out its frontiers from its settled region, and with a system of connecting waterways, the Middle region mediated between East and West as well as between North and South. Thus it became the typically American region. Even the New Englander, who was shut out from the frontier by the Middle region, tarrying in New York or Pennsylvania on his westward march, lost the acuteness of his sectionalism on the way.[43]

The spread of cotton culture into the interior of the South finally broke down the contrast between the "tide-water" region and the rest of the State, and based Southern interests on slavery. Before this process revealed its results the western portion of the South, which was akin to Pennsylvania in stock, society, and industry, showed tendencies to fall away from the faith of the fathers into internal improvement legislation and nationalism. In the Virginia convention of 1829-'30, called to revise the constitution, Mr. Leigh, of Chesterfield, one of the tide-water counties, declared:

One of the main causes of discontent which led to this convention, that which had the strongest influence in overcoming our veneration for the work of our fathers, which taught us to contemn the sentiments of Henry and Mason and Pendleton, which weaned us from our reverence for the constituted authorities of the State, was an overweening passion for internal improvement. I say this with perfect knowledge, for it has been avowed to me by gentlemen from the West over and over again. And let me tell the gentleman from Albemarle (Mr. Gordon) that it has been another principal object of those who set this ball of revolution in motion, to overturn the doctrine of State rights, of which Virginia has been the very pillar, and to remove the barrier she has interposed to the interference of the Federal Government in that same work of internal improvement, by so reorganizing the legislature that Virginia, too, may be hitched to the Federal car.

It was this nationalizing tendency of the West that transformed the democracy of Jefferson into the national republicanism of Monroe and the democracy of Andrew Jackson. The West of the war of 1812, the West of Clay, and Benton, and Harrison, and Andrew Jackson, shut off by the Middle States and the mountains from the coast sections, had a solidarity of its own with national tendencies.[44] On the tide of the Father of Waters, North and South met and mingled into a nation. Interstate migration went steadily on—a process of cross-fertilization of ideas and institutions. The fierce struggle of the sections over slavery on the western frontier does not diminish the truth of this statement; it proves the truth of it. Slavery was a sectional trait that would not down, but in the West it could not remain sectional. It was the greatest of frontiersmen who declared: "I believe this

Government can not endure permanently half slave and half free. It will become all of one thing or all of the other." Nothing works for nationalism like intercourse within the nation. Mobility of population is death to localism, and the western frontier worked irresistibly in unsettling population. The effects reached back from the frontier and affected profoundly the Atlantic coast and even the Old World.

GROWTH OF DEMOCRACY

But the most important effect of the frontier has been in the promotion of democracy here and in Europe. As has been indicated, the frontier is productive of individualism. Complex society is precipitated by the wilderness into a kind of primitive organization based on the family. The tendency is anti-social. It produces antipathy to control, and particularly to any direct control. The tax-gatherer is viewed as a representative of oppression. Prof. Osgood, in an able article,[45] has pointed out that the frontier conditions prevalent in the colonies are important factors in the explanation of the American Revolution, where individual liberty was sometimes confused with absence of all effective government. The same conditions aid in explaining the difficulty of instituting a strong government in the period of the confederacy. The frontier individualism has from the beginning promoted democracy.

The frontier States that came into the Union in the first quarter of a century of its existence came in with democratic suffrage provisions, and had reactive effects of the highest importance upon the older States whose peoples were being attracted there. An extension of the franchise became essential. It was *western* New York that forced an extension of suffrage in the constitutional convention of that State in 1821; and it was *western* Virginia that compelled the tide-water region to put a more liberal suffrage provision in the constitution framed in 1830, and to give to the frontier region a more nearly proportionate representation with the tide-water aristocracy. The rise of democracy as an effective force in the nation came in with western preponderance under Jackson and William Henry Harrison, and it meant the triumph of the frontier—with all of its good and with all of its evil elements.[46] An interesting illustration of the tone of frontier democracy in 1830 comes from the same debates in the Virginia convention already referred to. A representative from western Virginia declared:

But, sir, it is not the increase of population in the West which this gentleman ought to fear. It is the energy which the mountain breeze and western habits impart to those emigrants. They are regenerated, politically I mean, sir. They soon become *working politicians;* and the difference, sir, between a *talking* and a *working* politician is immense. The Old Dominion has long been celebrated for producing great orators; the ablest metaphysicians in policy; men that can split hairs in all abstruse questions of political economy. But at home, or when they return from Congress, they have negroes to fan them asleep. But a Pennsylvania, a New York, an Ohio, and a western Virginia statesman, though far inferior in logic, metaphysics, and rhetoric to an old Virginia statesman, has this advantage, that when he returns home he takes off his coat and takes hold of the plow. This gives him bone and muscle, sir, and preserves his republican principles pure and uncontaminated.

So long as free land exists, the opportunity for a competency exists, and economic power secures political power. But the democracy born of free land, strong in selfishness and individualism, intolerant of administrative experience and education, and pressing individual liberty beyond its proper bounds, has its dangers as well as its benefits. Individualism in America has allowed a laxity in regard to governmental affairs which has rendered possible the spoils system and all the manifest evils that follow from the lack of a highly developed civic spirit. In this connection may be noted also the influence of frontier conditions in permitting lax business honor, inflated paper currency and wild-cat banking. The colonial and revolutionary frontier was the region whence emanated many of the worst forms of an evil currency.[47] The West in the war of 1812 repeated the phenomenon on the frontier of that day, while the speculation and wild-cat banking of the period of the crisis of 1837 occurred on the new frontier belt of the next tier of States. Thus each one of the periods of lax financial integrity coincides with periods when a new set of frontier communities had arisen, and coincides in area with these successive frontiers, for the most part. The recent Populist agitation is a case in point. Many a State that now declines any connection with the tenets of the Populists, itself adhered to such ideas in an earlier stage of the development of the State. A primitive society can hardly be expected to show the intelligent appreciation of the complexity of business interests in a developed society. The continual recurrence of these areas of paper-money agitation is another evidence that the frontier can be isolated and studied as a factor in American history of the highest importance.[48]

ATTEMPTS TO CHECK AND REGULATE THE FRONTIER

The East has always feared the result of an unregulated advance of the frontier, and has tried to check and guide it. The English authorities would have checked settlement at the headwaters of the Atlantic tributaries and allowed the "savages to enjoy their deserts in quiet lest the peltry trade should decrease." This called out Burke's splendid protest:

If you stopped your grants, what would be the consequence? The people would occupy without grants. They have already so occupied in many places. You can not station garrisons in every part of these deserts. If you drive the people from one place, they will carry on their annual tillage and remove with their flocks and herds to another. Many of the people in the back settlements are already little attached to particular situations. Already they have topped the Appalachian mountains. From thence they behold before them an immense plain, one vast, rich, level meadow; a square of five hundred miles. Over this they would wander without a possibility of restraint; they would change their manners with their habits of life; would soon forget a government by which they were disowned; would become hordes of English Tartars; and, pouring down upon your unfortified frontiers a fierce and irresistible cavalry, become masters of your governors, and your counselors, your collectors and comptrollers, and of all the slaves that adhered to them. Such would, and in no long time must, be the effect of attempting to forbid as a crime and to suppress as an evil the command and blessing of Providence, "Increase and multiply." Such would be the happy result of an endeavor to keep as a lair of wild beasts that earth which God, by an express charter, has given to the children of men.

But the English Government was not alone in its desire to limit the advance of the frontier and guide its destinies. Tide-water Virginia [49] and South Carolina [50] gerrymandered those colonies to insure the dominance of the coast in their legislatures. Washington desired to settle a State at a time in the Northwest; Jefferson would reserve from settlement the territory of his Louisiana purchase north of the thirty-second parallel, in order to offer it to the Indians in exchange for their settlements east of the Mississippi. "When we shall be full on this side," he writes, "we may lay off a range of States on the western bank from the head to the mouth, and so range after range, advancing compactly as we multiply." Madison went so far as to argue to the French minister that the United States had no interest in seeing population extend itself on the right bank of the Mississippi, but should rather fear it. When the Oregon question was under debate, in 1824, Smyth, of Virginia, would draw an unchangeable line for the limits of the United States at the outer limit of two tiers of States beyond the Mississippi, complaining that the seaboard States were being drained of the flower of their population by the bringing of too much land into market. Even Thomas Benton, the man of widest views of the destiny of the West, at this stage of his career declared that along the ridge of the Rocky mountains "the western limits of the Republic should be drawn, and the statue of the fabled god Terminus should be raised upon its highest peak, never to be thrown down." [51] But the attempts to limit the boundaries, to restrict land sales and settlement, and to deprive the West of its share of political power were all in vain. Steadily the frontier of settlement advanced and carried with it individualism, democracy, and nationalism, and powerfully affected the East and the Old World.

MISSIONARY ACTIVITY

The most effective efforts of the East to regulate the frontier came through its educational and religious activity, exerted by interstate migration and by organized societies. Speaking in 1835, Dr. Lyman Beecher declared: "It is equally plain that the religious and political destiny of our nation is to be decided in the West," and he pointed out that the population of the West "is assembled from all the States of the Union and from all the nations of Europe, and is rushing in like the waters of the flood, demanding for its moral preservation the immediate and universal action of those institutions which discipline the mind and arm the conscience and the heart. And so various are the opinions and habits, and so recent and imperfect is the acquaintance, and so sparse are the settlements of the West, that no homogeneous public sentiment can be formed to legislate immediately into being the requisite institutions. And yet they are all needed immediately in their utmost perfection and power. A nation is being 'born in a day.' * * * But what will become of the West if her prosperity rushes up to such a majesty of power, while those great institutions linger which are necessary to form the mind and the conscience and the heart of that vast world. It must not be permitted. * * * Let no man at the East quiet himself and dream of liberty, whatever may become of the West. * * * Her destiny is our destiny." [52]

With the appeal to the conscience of New England, he adds appeals to her fears lest other religious sects anticipate her own. The New England preacher and school-teacher left their mark on the West. The dread of Western emancipation from New England's political and economic control was paralleled by her fears lest the West cut loose from her religion. Commenting in 1850 on reports that settlement was rapidly extending northward in Wisconsin, the editor of the Home Missionary writes: "We scarcely know whether to rejoice or mourn over this extension of our settlements. While we sympathize in whatever tends to increase the physical resources and prosperity of our country, we can not forget that with all these dispersions into remote and still remoter corners of the land the supply of the means of grace is becoming relatively less and less." Acting in accordance with such ideas, home missions were established and Western colleges were erected. As seaboard cities like Philadelphia, New York, and Baltimore strove for the mastery of Western trade, so the various denominations strove for the possession of the West. Thus an intellectual stream from New England sources fertilized the West. Other sections sent their missionaries; but the real struggle was between sects. The contest for power and the expansive tendency furnished to the various sects by the existence of a moving frontier must have had important results on the character of religious organization in the United States. The multiplication of rival churches in the little frontier towns had deep and lasting social effects. The religious aspects of the frontier make a chapter in our history which needs study.

INTELLECTUAL TRAITS

From the conditions of frontier life came intellectual traits of profound importance. The works of travelers along each frontier from colonial days onward describe certain common traits, and these traits have, while softening down, still persisted as survivals in the place of their origin, even when a higher social organization succeeded. The result is that to the frontier the American intellect owes its striking characteristics. That coarseness and strength combined with acuteness and inquisitiveness; that practical, inventive turn of mind, quick to find expedients; that masterful grasp of material things, lacking in the artistic but powerful to effect great ends; that restless, nervous energy;[53] that dominant individualism, working for good and for evil, and withal that buoyancy and exuberance which comes with freedom—these are traits of the frontier, or traits called out elsewhere because of the existence of the frontier. Since the days when the fleet of Columbus sailed into the waters of the New World, America has been another name for opportunity, and the people of the United States have taken their tone from the incessant expansion which has not only been open but has even been forced upon them. He would be a rash prophet who should assert that the expansive character of American life has now entirely ceased. Movement has been its dominant fact, and, unless this training has no effect upon a people, the American energy will continually demand a wider field for its exercise. But never again will such gifts of free land offer themselves. For a moment, at the frontier, the bonds of custom are broken and unrestraint is triumphant. There is not *tabula rasa*. The stubborn American environment is there with its imperious summons to accept its conditions; the inherited ways of doing things are also there; and yet, in spite of environment, and in spite of custom, each frontier did indeed furnish a new field of opportunity, a gate of escape from the bondage of the past; and freshness, and confidence, and scorn of older society, impatience of its restraints and its ideas, and indifference to its lessons, have accompanied the frontier. What the Mediterranean Sea was to the Greeks, breaking the bond of custom, offering new experiences, calling out new institutions and activities, that, and more, the ever retreating frontier has been to the United States directly, and to the nations of Europe more remotely. And now, four centuries from the discovery of America, at the end of a hundred years of life under the Constitution, the frontier has gone, and with its going has closed the first period of American history.

NOTES

[1] Abridgment of Debates of Congress, v., p. 706.

[2] Bancroft (1860 ed.), iii, pp. 344, 345, citing Logan MSS.; [Mitchell] Contest in America, etc. (1752), p. 237.

[3] Kercheval, History of the Valley; Bernheim, German Settlements in the Carolinas; Winsor, Narrative and Critical History of America, v, p. 304; Colonial Records of North Carolina, iv, p. xx; Weston, Documents Connected with the History of South Carolina, p. 82; Ellis and Evans, History of Lancaster County, Pa., chs. iii, xxvi.

[4] Parkman, Pontiac, ii; Griffis, Sir William Johnson, p. 6; Simms's Frontiersmen of New York.

[5] Monette, Mississippi Valley, i, p. 311.

[6] Wis. Hist. Cols., xi, p. 50; Hinsdale, Old Northwest, p. 121; Burke, "Oration on Conciliation," Works (1872 ed.), i, p. 473.

[7] Roosevelt, Winning of the West, and citations there given; Cutler's Life of Cutler.

[8] Scribner's Statistical Atlas, xxxviii, pl. 13; MacMaster, Hist. of People of U. S., i, pp. 4, 60, 61; Imlay and Filson, Western Territory of America (London, 1793); Rochefoucault-Liancourt, Travels Through the United States of North America (London, 1799); Michaux's "Journal," in Proceedings American Philosophical Society, xxvi, No. 129; Forman, Narrative

of a Journey Down the Ohio and Mississippi in 1780–'90 (Cincinnati, 1888); Bartram, Travels Through North Carolina, etc. (London, 1792); Pope, Tour Through the Southern and Western Territories, etc. (Richmond, 1792); Weld, Travels Through the States of North America (London, 1799); Baily, Journal of a Tour in the Unsettled States of North America, 1796–'97 (London, 1856); Pennsylvania Magazine of History, July, 1886; Winsor, Narrative and Critical History of America, VII, pp. 491, 492, citations.

[9] Scribner's Statistical Atlas, xxxix.

[10] Turner, Character and Influence of the Indian Trade in Wisconsin (Johns Hopkins University Studies, Series IX), pp. 61 ff.

[11] Monette, History of the Mississippi Valley, II; Flint, Travels and Residence in Mississippi; Flint, Geography and History of the Western States; Abridgment of Debates of Congress, VII, pp. 397, 398, 404; Holmes, Account of the U. S.; Kingdom, America and the British Colonies (London, 1820); Grund, Americans, II, chs. i, iii, vi (although writing in 1836, he treats of conditions that grew out of western advance from the era of 1820 to that time); Peck, Guide for Emigrants (Boston, 1831); Darby, Emigrants' Guide to Western and Southwestern States and Territories; Dana, Geographical Sketches in the Western Country; Kinzie, Waubun; Keating, Narrative of Long's Expedition; Schoolcraft, Discovery of the Sources of the Mississippi River, Travels in the Central Portions of the Mississippi Valley, and Lead Mines of the Missouri; Andreas, History of Illinois, I, 86–99; Hurlbut, Chicago Antiquities; McKenney, Tour to the Lakes; Thomas, Travels through the Western Country, etc. (Auburn, N. Y., 1819).

[12] Darby, Emigrants' Guide, pp. 272 ff.; Benton, Abridgment of Debates, VII, p. 397.

[13] De Bow's Review, IV, p. 254; XVII, p. 428.

[14] Grund, Americans, II, p. 8.

[15] Peck, New Guide to the West (Cincinnati, 1848), ch. IV; Parkman, Oregon Trail; Hall, The West (Cincinnati, 1848); Pierce, Incidents of Western Travel; Murray, Travels in North America; Lloyd, Steamboat Directory (Cincinnati, 1856); "Forty Days in a Western Hotel" (Chicago), in Putnam's Magazine, December, 1894; Mackay, The Western World, II, ch. II, III; Meeker, Life in the West; Bogen, German in America (Boston, 1851); Olmstead, Texas Journey; Greeley, Recollections of a Busy Life; Schouler, History of the United States, V, 261–267; Peyton, Over the Alleghanies and Across the Prairies (London, 1870); Loughborough, The Pacific Telegraph and Railway (St. Louis, 1849); Whitney, Project for a Railroad to the Pacific (New York, 1849); Peyton, Suggestions on Rail-

road Communication with the Pacific, and the Trade of China and the Indian Islands; Benton, Highway to the Pacific (a speech delivered in the U. S. Senate, December 16, 1850).

[16] A writer in The Home Missionary (1850), p. 239, reporting Wisconsin conditions, exclaims: "Think of this, people of the enlightened East. What an example, to come from the very frontiers of civilization!" But one of the missionaries writes: "In a few years Wisconsin will no longer be considered as the West, or as an outpost of civilization, any more than western New York, or the Western Reserve."

[17] Bancroft (H. H.), History of California, History of Oregon, and Popular Tribunals; Shinn, Mining Camps.

[18] See the suggestive paper by Prof. Jesse Macy. The Institutional Beginnings of a Western State.

[19] Shinn, Mining Camps.

[20] Compare Thorpe, in Annals American Academy of Political and Social Science, September, 1891; Bryce, American Commonwealth (1888), II, p. 689.

[21] Loria, Analisi della Proprieta Capitalista, II., p. 15.

[22] Compare Observations on the North American Land Company, London, 1796, pp. xv, 144; Logan, History of Upper South Carolina, I, pp. 149–151; Turner, Character and Influence of Indian Trade in Wisconsin, p. 18; Peck, New Guide for Emigrants (Boston, 1837), ch. iv; Compendium Eleventh Census, I, p. xl.

[23] See pages 220, 221, 223, post, for illustrations of the political accompaniments of changed industrial conditions.

[24] But Lewis and Clarke were the first to explore the route from the Missouri to the Columbia.

[25] Narrative and Critical History of America, VIII, p. 10; Sparks' Washington Works, IX, pp. 303, 327; Logan, History of Upper South Carolina, I; McDonald, Life of Kenton, p. 72; Cong. Record, XXIII, p. 57.

[26] On the effect of the fur trade in opening the routes of migration, see the author's Character and Influence of the Indian Trade in Wisconsin.

[27] Lodge, English Colonies, p. 152 and citations; Logan, Hist. of Upper South Carolina, I, p. 151.

[28] Flint, Recollections, p. 9.

[29] See Monette, Mississippi Valley, I, p. 344.

[30] Coues', Lewis and Clarke's Expedition, I, pp. 2, 253–259; Benton, in Cong. Record, XXIII, p. 57.

[31] Hohn, Das Salz (Berlin, 1873).

[32] Col. Records of N. C., V, p. 3.

[33] Findley, History of the Insurrection in the Four Western Counties of

Pennsylvania in the Year 1794 (Philadelphia, 1796), p. 35.

[34] Hale, Daniel Boone (pamphlet).

[35] Compare Baily, Tour in the Unsettled Parts of North America (London, 1856), pp. 217–219, where a similar analysis is made for 1796. See also Collot, Journey in North America (Paris, 1826), p. 109; Observations on the North American Land Company (London, 1796), pp. xv, 144; Logan, History of Upper South Carolina.

[36] "Spotswood Papers," in Collections of Virginia Historical Society, I, II.

[37] [Burke], European Settlements, etc. (1765 ed.), II, p. 200.

[38] Everest, in Wisconsin Historical Collections, XII, pp. 7 ff.

[39] Weston, Documents connected with History of South Carolina, p. 61.

[40] See, for example, the speech of Clay, in the House of Representatives, January 30, 1824.

[41] See the admirable monograph by Prof. H. B. Adams, Maryland's Influence on the Land Cessions; and also President Welling, in Papers American Historical Association, III, p. 411.

[42] Adams Memoirs, IX, pp. 247, 248.

[43] Author's article in The Ægis (Madison, Wis.), November 4, 1892.

[44] Compare Roosevelt, Thomas Benton, ch. i.

[45] Political Science Quarterly, II, p. 457. Compare Sumner, Alexander Hamilton, Chs. ii–vii.

[46] Compare Wilson, Division and Reunion, pp. 15, 24.

[47] On the relation of frontier conditions to Revolutionary taxation, see Sumner, Alexander Hamilton, Ch. iii.

[48] I have refrained from dwelling on the lawless characteristics of the frontier, because they are sufficiently well known. The gambler and desperado, the regulators of the Carolinas and the vigilantes of California, are types of that line of scum that the waves of advancing civilization bore before them, and of the growth of spontaneous organs of authority where legal authority was absent. Compare Barrows, United States of Yesterday and To-morrow; Shinn, Mining Camps; and Bancroft, Popular Tribunals. The humor, bravery, and rude strength, as well as the vices of the frontier in its worst aspect, have left traces on American character, language, and literature, not soon to be effaced.

[49] Debates in the Constitutional Convention, 1829–1830.

[50] [McCrady] Eminent and Representative Men of the Carolinas, I, p. 43; Calhoun's Works, I, pp. 401–406.

[51] Speech in the Senate, March 1, 1825; Register of Debates, I, 721.

[52] Plea for the West (Cincinnati, 1835), pp. 11 ff.

[53] Colonial travelers agree in remarking on the phlegmatic characteristics of the colonists. It has frequently been asked how such a people could have

developed that strained nervous energy now characteristic of them. Compare Sumner, Alexander Hamilton, p. 98, and Adams's History of the United States, I, p. 60; IX, pp. 240, 241. The transition appears to become marked at the close of the war of 1812, a period when interest centered upon the development of the West, and the West was noted for restless energy. Grund, Americans, II, ch. i.

Ulrich B. Phillips (1877–1934)
and the Old South

Interest in the history of the South grew rapidly after the Civil War, especially in Southern history written by Southerners. In the twentieth century, the industrious historian Ulrich Bonnell Phillips, born in La Grange, Georgia, had stimulated researches both North and South in the ante-bellum world of the planter and the slave. He had known the cotton fields as a youth and had acquired his neighbors' racial interpretation of the Civil War and Reconstruction. It was commonly held in the Deep South that Secession and the War had grown out of the need to protect white supremacy against radical abolitionist interference, and that Reconstruction was a Northern experiment to impose social equality and Africanization upon a defeated people.

Phillips took his first two degrees at the University of Georgia, specializing as a graduate student in ante-bellum Georgia. He took his Ph.D. at Columbia under Dunning and Burgess, both of whom shared the idea that slavery was a modus vivendi of preserving white supremacy, although they were antislavery men. Once a summer school student of Frederick Jackson Turner, Phillips became a close associate of this noted frontier historian as a professor at the University of Wisconsin. He tried to develop a theory of the evolving plantation just as Turner did for the evolving frontier. Later he taught at Tulane University, the University of Michigan, and Yale, training many able doctoral students and rewriting plantation history with an emphasis on economic and racial determinants. He went far beyond the ordinary historical sources to examine the surviving records of the large plantations and published many of these documents. Unfortunately, this emphasis on the large plantations meant the neglect of the small slaveholder and the overwhelming number of nonslaveholders—the "plain people" of the Old South. The big planter, as he clearly made apparent, was the hero of the plantation world.

His early biography, *The Life of Robert Toombs* (1913), dealt with one of the largest slaveholders of the South and reflected a sophisticated, though sectional, viewpoint. Subsequently, *American Negro Slavery* (1918) appeared and was regarded by professional reviewers as a most factual and analytical book on the subject. This book, like his other works, assumed that race was the central factor in Southern history, minimized the role of the nonslaveholder, and also assumed that the free Negro was an unassimilable economic unit in plantation life. These ideas are not far from the surface, but are better qualified in *Life and Labor in the Old South* (1929), which is still widely read in colleges. Posthumously, certain of his significant essays, from which the following selection is taken, were collected and published as *The Course of the South to Secession* (1939). Many of Phillips's social ideas, which put slavery in a context of white supremacy, have been taken up by other historians, including those who have rejected the ideal of white supremacy. His explanations often have seemed preferable to those of revisionists like James Randall of Illinois, who stressed emotional factors as causes of the Civil War.

The Central Theme of Southern History

An Ohio River ferryman has a stock remark when approaching the right bank: "We are nearing the American shore." A thousand times has he said it with a gratifying repercussion from among his passengers; for its implications are a little startling. The northern shore is American without question; the southern is American with a difference. Kentucky had by slender pretense a star in the Confederate flag; for a time she was officially neutral; for all time her citizens have been self-consciously Kentuckians, a distinctive people. They are Southerners in main sentiment, and so are Marylanders and Missourians.

Southernism did not arise from any selectiveness of migration, for the sort of people who went to Virginia, Maryland, or Carolina, were not as a group different from those who went to Pennsylvania or the West Indies. It does not lie in religion or language. It was not created by one-crop tillage, nor did agriculture in the large tend to produce a Southern scheme of life and thought. The Mohawk valley was for decades as rural as that of the Roanoke; wheat is as dominant in Dakota as cotton has ever been in Alabama; tobacco is as much a staple along the Ontario shore of Lake Erie as in the Kentucky pennyroyal; and the growing of rice and cotton in California has not prevented Los Angeles from being in a sense the capital of Iowa. On the other hand the rise of mill towns in the Carolina piedmont and the growth of manufacturing at Richmond and Birmingham have not made these Northern. It may be admitted, however, that Miami, Palm Beach, and Coral Gables are Southern only in latitude. They were vacant wastes until Flagler, Fifth Avenue, and the realtors discovered and subdivided them.

The South has never had a focus. New York has plied as much of its trade as Baltimore or New Orleans; and White Sulphur Springs did not quite eclipse all other mountain and coast resorts for vaca-

American Historical Review 34 (1928–29), 30–43. Reprinted by permission of the American Historical Association.

tion patronage. The lack of a metropolis was lamented in 1857 by an advocate of Southern independence,[1] as an essential for shaping and radiating a coherent philosophy to fit the prevailing conditions of life. But without a consolidating press or pulpit or other definite apparatus the South has maintained a considerable solidarity through thick and thin, through peace and war and peace again. What is its essence? Not state rights—Calhoun himself was for years a nationalist, and some advocates of independence hoped for a complete merging of the several states into a unitary Southern republic; not free trade—sugar and hemp growers have ever been protectionists; not slavery—in the eighteenth century this was of continental legality, and in the twentieth it is legal nowhere; not Democracy—there were many Federalists in Washington's day and many Whigs in Clay's; not party predominance by any name, for Virginia, Georgia, and Mississippi were "doubtful states" from Jackson's time to Buchanan's. It is not the land of cotton alone or of plantations alone; and it has not always been the land of "Dixie," for before its ecstatic adoption in 1861 that spine-tingling tune was a mere "walk around" of Christie's minstrels. Yet it is a land with a unity despite its diversity, with a people having common joys and common sorrows, and, above all, as to the white folk a people with a common resolve indomitably maintained—that it shall be and remain a white man's country. The consciousness of a function in these premises, whether expressed with the frenzy of a demagogue or maintained with a patrician's quietude, is the cardinal test of a Southerner and the central theme of Southern history.

It arose as soon as the negroes became numerous enough to create a problem of race control in the interest of orderly government and the maintenance of Caucasian civilization. Slavery was instituted not merely to provide control of labor but also as a system of racial adjustment and social order. And when in the course of time slavery was attacked, it was defended not only as a vested interest, but with vigor and vehemence as a guarantee of white supremacy and civilization. Its defenders did not always take pains to say that this was what they chiefly meant, but it may nearly always be read between their lines, and their hearers and readers understood it without overt expression.[2]

Otherwise it would be impossible to account for the fervid secession-
ism of many non-slaveholders and the eager service of thousands in
the Confederate army.

The non-slaveholders of course were diverse in their conditions and
sentiments. Those in the mountains and the deep pine woods were
insulated to such degree that public opinion hardly existed, and they
chose between alternatives only when issues created in other quarters
were forced upon them. Those in the black belts, on the other hand,
had their lives conditioned by the presence of the negroes; and they
had apparatus of court days, militia musters, and political barbecues
as well as neighborhood conversation to keep them abreast of affairs.
A mechanic of Iuka, Mississippi, wrote in the summer of 1861: "I am
a Georgian Raised I am Forty years Old A tinner By Trade I
Raised the First Confederate Flag that I Ever Heard Of that was in
1851 in the Town of Macon Miss. Notwithstanding the Many Radi-
cules I Encounter'd I Told the Citizens that they would All Be Glad
to Rally under Such a Flag Some Day which is at present true." [3]
This personal tale was told to prove his title to a voice in Confederate
policy. His main theme was a demand that the permanent Confederate constitution exclude negroes from all employment except
agricultural labor and domestic service in order that the handicrafts
be reserved for white artisans like himself.

The overseer of a sugar estate forty miles below New Orleans
inscribed a prayer on the plantation journal:

Thursday 13 June 1861
This Day is set a part By presedent Jefferson Davis for fasting and
praying owing to the Deplorable condition ower southern country is In
My Prayer Sincerely to God is that every Black Republican in the Hole
combined whorl either man woman o chile that is opposed to negro
slavery as it existed in the Southern confederacy shal be trubled with
pestilents and calamitys of all Kinds and Drag out the Balance of there
existance in Misray and Degradation with scarsely food and rayment
enughf to keep sole and Body to gather and o God I pray the to Direct
a bullet or a bayonet to pirce The Hart of every northern soldier that
invades southern soile and after the Body has rendered up its traterish
sole gave it a trators reward a Birth In the Lake of Fires and Brim-

stone my honest convicksion is that every man wome and chile that has gave aide to the abolishionist are fit subjects for Hell I all so ask the to aide the southern Confederacy in maintaining ower rites and establishing the confederate Government Believing this case the prares from the wicked will prevaileth much Amen [4]

This overseer's pencilled prayer is the most rampant fire-eating expression which I have encountered in any quarter. He and the tinner had an economic interest in the maintenance of slavery, the one to assure the presence of laborers for him to boss, the other to restrain competition in his trade. But both of them, and a million of their non-slaveholding like, had a still stronger social prompting: the white men's ways must prevail; the negroes must be kept innocuous.

In the 'forties when most of the planters were Whig some of the Democratic politicians thought it strange that their own party should be the more energetic in defense of slavery; and in 1860 they were perhaps puzzled again that the Bell and Everett Constitutional Union ticket drew its main support from among the slaveholders. The reason for this apparent anomaly lay doubtless in the two facts, that men of wealth had more to lose in any cataclysm, and that masters had less antipathy to negroes than non-slaveholders did. In daily contact with blacks from birth, and often on a friendly basis of patron and retainer, the planters were in a sort of partnership with their slaves, reckoning upon their good-will or at least possessing a sense of security as a fruit of long habituation to fairly serene conditions. But the white toilers lived outside this partnership and suffered somewhat from its competition. H. R. Helper in his *Impending Crisis* (1857) urged them to wreck the system by destroying slavery; and when this had been accomplished without their aid he vented in his fantastic *Nojoque* (1867) a spleen against the negroes, advocating their expulsion from the United States as a preliminary to their universal extermination. Thus he called for class war upon a double front, to humble the "lords of the lash" and then to destroy the "black and bi-colored caitiffs" who cumbered the white man's world. By his alliterative rhetoric and shrewdly selected statistics Helper captured some Northern propagandists and the historians whom they begat, but if he made any converts among Southern yeomen they are not of record. His notions had come to him during residence in California and the North; they were therefore to be taken skeptically. His programmes repudiated humane tradition, disregarded vital actualities, and evoked Northern aid to make over the South in its own image. These things, and perhaps the last especially, were not to be sanctioned. In fact, for reasons common in the world at large, the Southern whites were not to be divided into sharply antagonistic classes. Robert J. Walker said quite soundly in 1856:

In all the slave States there is a large majority of voters who are non-slaveholders; but they are devoted to the institutions of the South—they would defend them with their lives—and on this question the South are [*sic*] a united people. The class, composed of many small farmers, of merchants, professional men, mechanics, overseers, and other industrial classes, constitute mainly the patrol of the South, and cheerfully unite in carrying out those laws essential to preserve the institution. Against a powerful minority and constant agitation slavery could not exist in any State.[5]

He wrote this to explain the poor prospect of slavery in Kansas; he might have used the same phrasing to explain its persistence in Delaware or Missouri. Habitat grouping, it is clear, had a cementing force great enough to overcome the cleaving tendency of economic stratification. So strong was it, indeed, that sundry free negroes gave warm endorsement to the project of Southern independence.[6]

It is perhaps less fruitful to seek the social classes at large which were warm and those which were cool toward independence than to inquire why the citizens of certain areas were prevailingly ardent while those in another zone were indifferent or opposed, why for example the whole tier from South Carolina to Texas seceded spontaneously but no other states joined them until after Lincoln's call for troops. The reason lay in preceding history as well as in current conditions. The economic factor of the cotton belt's interest in free trade and its recurrent chagrin at protective tariff enactments is by no means negligible. The rancor produced by nullification and the "force bill" had been revived in South Carolina by the repeal of the compromise tariff in 1842, and it did not then die. The quarrels of Georgia with the federal authorities over Indian lands, with Alabama and Mississippi looking on in interested sympathy, were contributing episodes to make the lower South alert; and the heavy negro proportions in their black belts, together with immaturity in the social order, made their people more sensitive than those of Virginia to the menace of disturbance from outside.

Slavery questions, which had never been quite negligible since the framing of the Constitution, gained a febrile activity from the abolition agitation; and the study of Congressional mathematics focussed the main attention upon the rivalry of the sections in territorial enlargement. The North had control of the lower house, as recurrent votes on the Wilmot Proviso showed; and California's admission upset the sectional equilibrium in the Senate. For Yancey, Rhett, and Quitman and for the pamphleteers Longstreet, Bryan, and Trescot, this was enough. The North now had the strength of a giant; the South should strike for independence before that strength should grow yet greater and be consolidated for crushing purposes. But the gestures of Cass, Webster, and Fillmore gave ground for hope that the giant would not use his power against Southern home rule, and the crisis was deferred. Southern friends and foes of the Compromise of 1850 were alert thenceforward for tokens of Northern will. Events through the ensuing decade, somewhat assisted by the fire-eaters and culminating in a Republican's election to the Presidency, converted a new multitude to the Shibboleth: "The alternative: a separate nationality or the Africanization of the South." [7]

Walter Lippmann has analyzed political process in general as if he had our present study specifically in mind:

Since the general opinions of large numbers of persons are almost certain to be a vague and confusing medley, action cannot be taken until those opinions have been factored down, canalized, compressed and made uniform. The making of one general will out of a multitude of general wishes . . . consists essentially in the use of symbols which assemble emotions after they have been detached from their ideas. . . . The process, therefore, by which general opinions are brought to co-operation consists in an intensification of feeling and a degradation of significance.[8]

The tension of 1850 had brought much achievement in this direction. "Southern rights" had come to mean racial security, self-determination by the whites whether in or out of the Union, and all things ancillary to the assured possession of these. Furthermore a programme had been framed to utilize state sovereignty whether to safeguard the South as a minority within the Union or to legitimate its exit into national independence.

The resurgence of these notions and emotions after their abeyance in 1851 need not be traced in detail. Suffice it to say that legal sanction for the spread of slaveholding, regardless of geographical potentialities, became the touchstone of Southern rights; and the rapid rise of the Republican party which denied this sanction, equally regardless of geographical potentialities, tipped the balance in lower Southern policy. Many were primed in 1856 for a stroke in case Frémont should be elected that year; and though he fell short of an electoral majority, the strength shown by his ticket increased the zeal of South-savers through the next quadrennium. The so-called Southern commercial conventions became a forum and *DeBow's Review* an organ for the airing of projects, mad or sane, for annexing Cuba, promoting direct trade with Europe, boycotting Northern manufactures and Northern colleges, procuring Southern text-books for Southern schools, reopening the African slave trade—anything and everything which might agitate and perhaps consolidate the South in a sense of bafflement within the Union and a feeling of separate destiny. Many clergymen gave their aid, particularly by praising slavery as a biblical and benevolent institution.

Pierre Soulé tried in 1857, as Calhoun had done eight years before, to create a Southern party separate from the Democrats;[9] and next year Yancey launched his League of United Southerners. Ere long a rural editor blurted what many must have been thinking:

That the North sectionalized will acquire possession of this Government at no distant day we look upon as no longer a matter of doubt. . . . It is inevitable. The South—the whole South even—cannot avert it. We may determine to fight the battle with our foes within the Union, . . . but we will fight only to be defeated. The Union of the South is indeed of great moment—not however for successful resistance in this Union, but for going out of it under circumstances the most favorable to the speedy formation of a separate and independent government.[10]

Various expressions in Northern papers, debates in Congress, and events in Kansas and elsewhere had fanned these flames when the stroke of John Brown fell upon Harper's Ferry. This event was taken as a demonstration that abolitionists had lied in saying they were concerned with moral suasion only, and it stimulated suspicion that Republicans were abolitionists in disguise. In December the South Carolina legislature when expressing sympathy with Virginia intimated that she was ripe for secession and invited all Southern states to meet in convention at once to concert measures for united action. In February the Alabama legislature asserted that under no circumstances would the commonwealth submit to "the foul domination of a sectional Northern party," and it instructed the governor in the event of a Republican's election to the Presidency to order the election of delegates to a convention of the state to consider and do whatever in its judgment her rights, interests, and honor might require.

There was little to do in the interim but discuss principles and portents and to jockey the situation slightly to prepare for the crisis or try to prevent it according to what individuals might think best. In an editorial of January 9, 1860, on "The true position of the South: Not aggrandisement but safety," the New Orleans *Crescent,* which was long an advocate of moderation, said:

The South does not claim the right of controlling the North in the choice of a President; she admits fully and explicitly that the Northern people possess the prerogative of voting as they please. But at the same time the South asserts that while the North holds the legal right of casting her voice as to her may seem best, she has no *moral* right to so cast it as to effect the ruin of the South; and if she does so cast it, in full view of its injurious effects upon us, . . . she, in effect, commits an act of covert hostility upon us that will render it impossible for us to live longer in intimate relations.

On April 15, the *Delta,* replying to a recent lecture at New Orleans by George D. Prentice of Louisville, denied that Clay and Webster, "those demiurgic heroes of his political faith," could have sufficed for the present occasion:

The period of mere political formation is past, and the period for the solution of great social and industrial problems is at hand. Mere constitutional lore here can do nothing; mere skill in adjusting balances of political power can do nothing. Is it just to hold the negro in bondage? Is negro slavery inimical to the rights of white men? Is it best for both the white and black man—best for the interests of agriculture, best for the needs of commerce and useful arts, and best for social stability and civilization? These and kindred questions imperiously demand to be answered, and they are precisely the questions which the old school of statesmen strenuously refused to look in the face. . . . The truth is, we are in the midst of facts having a philosophy of their own which we must master for ourselves, leaving dead men to take care of the dead past. The Sphinx which is now propounding its riddles to us the dead knew nothing about; consequently no voice from the grave can tell us how to get rid of the monster.

After the nominating conventions had put four tickets in the field the newspapers began a running debate upon the relative merits of Douglas, Breckinridge, and Bell for Southern purposes and the degree of menace in the Lincoln candidacy. The Natchez *Free Trader,* which until June 27 mastheaded the names of Albert G. Brown and Fernando Wood, accepted next day the Richmond nominations:

We hoist today the flag of the Union-saving National Democratic nominees, Breckinridge and Lane, *sans peur et sans reproche.* With records so fair that none can attack them, they will win the hearts of all the people of the land, be elected by a vote so flattering as to cause the hearts of the noblest and best to beat with honest exaltation and pride, and so administer the Government as to have the blessings of the people showered on them and elicit the unrestrained admiration of an enlightened world.

Such bombast as this might survive the summer; but when the October elections brought a virtual certainty of Lincoln's election the discussion took another phase. The friends of each minor ticket demanded that the other two be withdrawn or forsaken. Douglas and Bell men agreed at least that Breckinridge ought to be abandoned. The Nashville *Union and American,* in reply on October 16 to such a demand from the Nashville *Patriot,* said that Breckinridge might still be elected by Southern concentration upon him, "in as much as it will prove to the North that we are determined to have our rights." And as a last appeal, November 6, the New Orleans *Delta* said, urging votes for Breckinridge as against Bell or Douglas:

Is this the time to indorse the representatives of a half-way, compromising, submissive policy? When the whole North is sectional shall the South be national, when nationality can mean nothing but an acquiescence in the employment of national means to accomplish sectional purposes? Never before in the history of any free and brave people was so bold a challenge as that which the North now throws at us received in any other way than the stern and proud defiance of a united and determined community.

Among the Bell organs the New Orleans *Bee* gave a remarkably sound analysis in an editorial of July 27: "The restlessness of the South touching the agitation of the slavery question arises rather from the apprehension of what the aggressive policy of the North may hereafter effect, than from what it has already accomplished. For . . . we may safely affirm that thus far no practical injury has resulted." The Southern failure in colonizing Kansas, it continued, was not a grievance, for: "prudent and far-seeing men predicted the utter impracticability of carrying the design into execution. . . . Slavery will go where it will pay. No slaveholder for the sake of an abstraction will amuse himself by earning five per cent in Kansas on the labor of his chattels, when with absolutely less toil it will give him fifteen per cent in the cotton or sugar fields of Louisiana." On its own score the *Bee* concluded: "We apprehend that the Black Republicans are dogs whose bark is more dangerous than their bite. The South is too precious to the North to be driven out of the Union." Its colleague the *Crescent* expressed a belief as late as October 20 that, if the Republican party should win the contest, its "unnatural and feverish vitality" would reach exhaustion within a year or two.

In the United States thus far, the *Crescent* argued, parties had arisen and fallen in rapid succession.

But all of these parties were national. The principles they advocated were of common application to the whole country, and their members and adherents were found in every quarter and every State of the Union. If these parties were temporary and short-lived in their character and constitution, still more so must the Black Republican party be, sectional as it is in its organization and principles, and obnoxious to a deeper hatred and more bitter opposition than any other organization that has yet made its appearance in the political arena. It is impossible that such a party can long exist.

Just before election day George Fitzhugh of Virginia wrote to the Charleston *Mercury* a long letter concluding: "In the Union there is no hope for us. Let us gather courage from despair, and quit the Union." The editor when printing this, November 9, remarked: "Mr. Fitzhugh is a little excitable. We intend to 'quit the Union,' but without any 'despair' whatever. We'll quit it with a round hip! hip! hurrah!!"

But now that the partizans of Breckinridge, Bell, and Douglas had met a common defeat, their lines were broken with regard to the Southern recourse. Some of the Breckinridge men opposed secession unless and until the Lincoln government should commit an "overt act" of injury, but many supporters of Bell and Douglas turned to the policy of prompt strokes.[11] The New Orleans *Crescent* and *Bee* are again clear exponents. On November 8 the *Crescent* said: "We read the result in the face of every citizen upon the street. There is an universal feeling that an insult has been deliberately tendered our people, which is responded to not by noisy threats or passionate objurgations, but a settled determination that the South shall never be oppressed under Mr. Lincoln's administration." But it cherished a shadowy hope that electors chosen on the Republican ticket might yet refrain from putting "a sectional President in the chair of Washington!." On December 17 the *Bee* admitted that it had yielded to the prodigious tide of public sentiment, and said in explanation: "It was evident indeed, that amid all the lip service professed for the Union there had dwelt in the hearts of Southerners a tacit determination to regard the election of Lincoln as proof of a settled and immutable policy of aggression by the North toward the South, and to refuse further political affiliation with those who by that act should declare themselves our enemies." On the following January 3 the *Crescent* said:

It is by secession alone that we [Louisiana] can be placed in close affinity with all of our sisters of the Gulf and South Atlantic seaboard, who have given guarantees . . . that they will be out of the Union long in advance of our action and ready to receive us in the Government that shall have been established.[12] South Carolina, Georgia, Mississippi, Florida, Alabama, Louisiana and Texas are knit by God and their own hearts indissolubly together. . . .

Believe not that any State has the right to expect another to await her action in an emergency like this. *We have as much right to complain of the tardiness of the border States as they have of our haste.* . . . A people who wait for others to aid them in vindicating their rights are already enslaved, for now, as in every other period of history—

"In native swords and native ranks
The only hope of freedom dwells."

The upper South had votaries of independence no less outspoken than those of the cotton belt, but they were too few to carry their states prior to a Northern "overt act." Arguments and eloquence by visiting commissioners might sway the minds and thrill the hearts of delegates, but none of these conventions took a decisive step until Lincoln's call for troops. Indeed there was a project of organizing the border states for a course of their own, even to the extreme of a central confederacy separate alike from the "Black Republican" North and the "hotspur" South. When this was pinched out, the sequel showed that the boundary of predominant Southern loyalty was not Mason and Dixon's line but a curving zone seldom touching that landmark.

Many Virginians, perhaps most of them, sanctioned the change of allegiance reluctantly; and some, chiefly in the Wheeling panhandle, revolted sharply against it. On the other hand the course of the Federal government during the war and after its close alienated so many borderers that in a sense Kentucky joined the Confederacy after the war was over.

While the war dragged its disheartening length and the hopes of independence faded, queries were raised in some Southern quarters as to whether yielding might not be the wiser course. Lincoln in his plan of reconstruction had shown unexpected magnanimity; the Republican party, discarding that obnoxious name, had officially styled itself merely Unionist; and the Northern Democrats, although outvoted, were still a friendly force to be reckoned upon. Die-hard statesmen and loyal soldiers carried on till the collapse. The governors in the "late so-called Confederate States" were now ready with soft speeches, but the Federal soldiery clapped them into prison until Andrew Jackson relaxed from his brief punitive phase.

With Johnson then on Lincoln's path "back to normalcy," Southern hearts were lightened only to sink again when radicals in Congress, calling themselves Republicans once more, overslaughed the Presidential programme and set events in train which seemed to make "the Africanization of the South" inescapable. To most of the whites, doubtless, the prospect showed no gleam of hope.

But Edward A. Pollard, a Virginian critic of Davis, chronicler of the war and bewailer of the "lost cause," took courage in 1868 to write his most significant book, *The Lost Cause Regained*. The folly of politicians, he said, had made the South defend slavery seemingly "as a property tenure, or as a peculiar institution of labour; when the true ground of defence was as a barrier against a contention and war of races": [13] The pro-slavery claims on the basis of constitutional right he denounced in retrospect as flimsily technical and utterly futile in the face of a steadily encroaching moral sentiment; and the stroke for independence in the name of liberty he thought as fallacious as the later expectation of generosity which had brought the Confederate collapse.[14]

It has been curiously reserved for the South to obtain *after* the war the actual experience of oppression, and of that measure of despotism which would have amply justified the commencement of hostilities. If it fought, in 1860, for principles too abstract, it has superabundant causes for rebellion now, which although they may not, and need not produce another war, yet have the effect to justify, in a remarkable way, the first appeal to arms.[15]

In elaboration of this: "The black thread of the Negro has been spun throughout the scheme of Reconstruction. A design is betrayed to give to him the political control of the South, not so much as a benefit to him, . . . as to secure power to the Republican party."[16]

But in the defeats of proposals for negro suffrage in seven states from Connecticut to Colorado, and particularly in the ovation with which the Philadelphia convention of 1866 had received a resolution urging the Southern whites not to submit to negro rule, he saw promise of effective support and eventual success in undoing Reconstruction.[17] Therefore:

Let us come back to the true hope of the South. It is to enter bravely with new allies and new auspices the contest for the supremacy of the white man, and with it the preservation of the dearest political traditions of the country. "WHITE" is the winning word, says a North Carolina paper, and let us never be done repeating it. . . . It is the irresistible sympathy of races, which will not, cannot fail. . . . It is this instinct which the South will at last summon to her aid, when her extremity demands it.[18]

Before the farther bank of the slough of despond was fully attained, the question was raised as to the path beyond. In a remarkable address in 1875 Wiley P. Harris of Mississippi lamented the political exploitation of the negroes: "The mass of them don't vote, but are literally voted. They are ridden and driven by a little nest of men who are alien to the state in feeling. . . . The result is a government at once imperious and contemptible, a tyranny at once loathesome and deadly." He bade the carpet-baggers farewell in advance of their going: "I assure these men that their last card has been played, and it has not won. This trumpery no longer deceives anybody, and it matters not which party prevails in 1876, no national administration will again incur the odium of propping them up." But with merely restoring white local domination he would not be content. Appealing specifically for a renewed and permanent union of Democrats with liberal Republicans throughout the country, he said:

To reconcile and nationalize the South, to lead it out of the cul de sac of sectionalism into the broad stream of national life, . . . to restore peace, good will and confidence between the members of this great family of States, will lay the solid and durable foundation of a party which will surely win and long retain the hearts of the American people. . . . For one, I long to see a government at Washington, and a government here, toward which I can feel a genuine sentiment of reverence and respect. It is a dreary life we lead here, with a national government ever suspicious and ever frowning, and a home government feeble, furtive, false and fraudulent. Under such influences the feeling of patriotism must die out amongst us, and this will accomplish the ruin of a noble population. . . . We are in a new world. We are moving on a new plane. It is better that we hang a millstone about our necks than cling to these old issues. To cling to them is to perpetuate sectional seclusion.[19]

Lamar's eulogy of Sumner and the speeches and editorials of Grady were much to the same effect, and likewise were the efforts of other broad-minded men. But a certain sense of bafflement and of defensive self-containment persists to our own day, because the negro population remains as at least a symbolic potentiality. Virtually all respectable whites had entered the Democratic ranks in the later 'sixties to combat à outrance the Republican programme of negro incitement. A dozen years sufficed to restore white control, whereupon they began to differ among themselves upon various issues. Many joined the People's party; and in some quarters a fusion was arranged of Populists and Republicans to carry elections. In the stress of campaigning this threatened to bring from within the South a stimulus to negroes as political auxiliaries.

But by Southern hypothesis, exalted into a creed, negroes in the mass were incompetent for any good political purpose and by reason of their inexperience and racial unwisdom were likely to prove subversive. To remove the temptation to white politicians to lead negroes to the polls again, "white primaries" were instituted to control nominations, educational requirements for the suffrage were inserted in the state constitutions, and the Bryanizing of the Democratic party was accepted as a means of healing a white rift. Even these devices did not wholly lay the spectre of "negro domination"; for the fifteenth amendment stood in the Constitution and the calendar of Congress was not yet free of "force bills." For every Lodge and Foraker there arose a Tillman and a Vardaman, with a Watson and a Blease to spare.

The sentiments and symbols have not been wholly divorced from reason. When California whites made extravagant demands in fear that her three per cent. of Japanese might increase to four and capture the business of "The Coast," Congress responded as if it were an appendage of the state legislature. But white Southerners when facing problems real or fancied concerning the ten million negroes in their midst can look to the federal authorities for no more at best than a tacit acquiescence in what their state governments may do. Acquiescence does not evoke enthusiasm; and until an issue shall arise predominant over the lingering one of race, political solidarity at the price of provincial status is maintained to keep assurance doubly, trebly sure that the South shall remain "a white man's country."

NOTES

[1] *Russell's Magazine* (Charleston), I. 106.

[2] Many expressions were explicit, for example, the remarks of Mr. Standard at Richmond in 1829: "The property we seek to protect . . . is not mere brute matter . . . but it consists of intelligent, sentient, responsible beings, that have passions to be inflamed, hearts to feel, understandings to be enlightened, and who are capable of catching the flame of enthusiasm from the eloquent effusions of agitators . . . ; and who may not only be lost to their masters as property, but may change conditions and become masters themselves, so far at least as the ravages of a servile war shall have [error for leave] any subject to be ruled over." *Proceedings and Debates of the Virginia State Convention of 1829–30* (Richmond, 1830), p. 306.

[3] Manuscript letter in private possession.

[4] When I made this transcript twenty years ago the manuscript journal was on Magnolia plantation in Plaquemines Parish, Louisiana. The item is in the handwriting of J. A. Randall, overseer.

[5] *DeBow's Review*, XXI. 591–592.

[6] U. B. Phillips, *American Negro Slavery*, p. 436; R. H. Williams, *With the Border Ruffians* (London, 1908), p. 441.

[7] The title of a pamphlet by William H. Holcombe, M.D. (New Orleans, 1860).

[8] *The Phantom Public* (New York, 1925), p. 47.

[9] New Orleans *Crescent*, June 17, 1857.

[10] The *Southron* (Orangeburg, S. C.), quoted in the *Southern Guardian* (Columbia, S. C.), May 20, 1859.

[11] Unionism among many of the Bell supporters had been conditioned from the first, almost explicitly, upon constitutionalism as interpreted in favor of Southern rights. For example the convention in Georgia which responded to the call for organizing the party and sent delegates to Baltimore adopted a platform asserting that slavery was established in the Constitution, that the territories were the property of the states jointly, that Congress and the territorial legislatures were alike incapable of impairing the right of slave property, and that it was the duty of Congress to protect the rights of slaveholders in the territories. *Southern Recorder* (Milledgeville, Ga.), May 8, 1860.

[12] These pledges had been conveyed by commissioners appointed by the governors of sundry commonwealths to convey to the governors, legislatures, and conventions of other states assurances of secession as soon as the procedure could be completed and invitations for union in a new nation or confederacy. A study of these commissioners as agents of coördination has been made by Mr. Dwight L. Dumond of the University of Michigan, but has not yet been published.

[13] E. A. Pollard, *The Lost Cause Regained* (New York, 1868), p. 13.

[14] *Ibid.*, pp. 20, 50, 116.

[15] *Ibid.*, pp. 51–52.

[16] *Ibid.*, p. 129.

[17] *Ibid.*, pp. 133, 162.

[18] *Ibid.*, p. 165.

[19] Speech of W. P. Harris at a Democratic campaign meeting, Jackson, Miss., Aug. 23, 1875. Lowry and McCardle, *History of Mississippi*, pp. 396–400.

Charles Beard (1874–1948) and the Economic Interpretation of History

Perhaps the most stimulating scholar in American historiography has been Charles Austin Beard. He was born near Knightstown, Indiana, the son of a successful banker, newspaper owner, and farm owner, who sent him to De Pauw College, a Methodist institution. Despite his parents' conservative Republican and Methodist background, Beard became converted to a secular, welfare-state philosophy as a result of his education in Europe, his contacts with Bismarck's social program in Germany, the Settlement movement at Oxford, and his work for the British Labour party. He returned to earn his doctorate in politics and history at Columbia in 1904 and apparently picked up the ideas of the New History from James Harvey Robinson and others. This approach called for a broad cultural background, the use of the newer social sciences as tools, an emphasis upon modern history as the clue to present-day problems, and a generally reformist outlook.

From 1907 to 1917, Beard taught at Columbia until he quarreled with the Board of Trustees over what he felt was an arbitrary dismissal of several colleagues. Thereafter, until 1922, he was a director of New York's Training School for Public Service. He became an adviser to Japan's Institute of Municipal Research and, after the disastrous Tokyo earthquake of 1923, an adviser to that country's Minister of Home Affairs; he later published a book on his observations. His publications in political science and history won him a reputation in both fields and the presidencies of the American Political Science Association (1926) and the American Historical Association (1933). His college textbooks, also in both fields, contained original analytical theories and had an unusual popularity and influence.

Most significant and controversial was his *An Economic Interpretation of the Constitution* (1913), which in those Bull Moose days was assumed to be a muckraking volume intended to debunk the motives of the framers of the Constitution. Actually, as the following selection shows, the central argument is that the permanence of this document rests upon the fact that the founding fathers were economic realists who believed that self-interest was a far stronger motive in history than sentimental idealism. There is a similar assumption in *Economic Origins of Jeffersonian Democracy* (1915).

He and his wife Mary, also a gifted historian, wrote *The Rise of American Civilization* (2 vols., 1927), which exemplified the cultural approach of the New History, although its economic philosophy was tempered by the current conservative trend. Much more critical of the social order and of the economic pressure groups of the Depression era was *America in Midpassage* (1939), which reflected sympathies for New Deal domestic reforms but suspicions of its foreign policies.

Beard became emphatically isolationist, although he preferred the label "continentalist," suspected that New Deal internationalism meant war, and wrote economic interpretations of foreign policy as a product of material interests. In 1947 he angered many scholars and laymen as well by publishing *President Roosevelt and the Coming of the War, 1941,* a book attacking the Roosevelt policies for allegedly promoting American intervention in World War II.

He greatly stimulated interest in historiography through his presidential address, "Written History as an Act of Faith," and again in "That Noble Dream," a challenging paper on objectivity and relativism written for the American Historical Association journal in 1935, which is reproduced here in full. Note his attack on what seemed to him the naïve assumptions of the self-styled objective historians who ignored the overwhelming element of subjective conditioning of class, race, culture, heredity, etc., upon human beings. He denied that his emphasis upon economic tools as an objective approach meant that he was a Marxist. For these articles, he was called an extreme relativist. The reader can make up his mind whether or not the arguments given here indicate that Beard had foresworn historical objectivity and believed that all knowledge was relative to the nature of the mind and hence without independent reality.

An Economic Interpretation of the Constitution
of the United States

In fact, the inquiry which follows is based upon the political science of James Madison, the father of the Constitution and later President of the Union he had done so much to create. This political science runs through all of his really serious writings and is formulated in its most precise fashion in *The Federalist* as follows: "The diversity in the faculties of men, from which the rights of property originate, is not less an insuperable obstacle to a uniformity of interests. The protection of these faculties is the first object of government. From the protection of different and unequal faculties of acquiring property, the possession of different degrees and kinds of property immediately results; and from the influence of these on the sentiments and views of the respective proprietors, ensues a division of society into different interests and parties. . . . The most common and durable source of factions has been the various and unequal distribution of property. Those who hold and those who are without property have ever formed distinct interests in society. Those who are creditors, and those who are debtors, fall under a like discrimination. A landed interest, a manufacturing interest, a mercantile interest, a moneyed interest, with many lesser interests, grow up of necessity in civilized nations and divide them into different classes, actuated by different sentiments and views. The regulation of these various and interfering interests forms the principal task of modern legislation, and involves the spirit of party and faction in the necessary and ordinary operations of the government."

Here we have a masterly statement of the theory of economic determinism in politics.[1] Different degrees and kinds of property inevitably exist in modern society; party doctrines and "principles" originate in

Pages 14–18, 324–5 (Macmillan, 1913). Reprinted by permission of the publishers.

the sentiments and views which the possession of various kinds of property creates in the minds of the possessors; class and group divisions based on property lie at the basis of modern government; and politics and constitutional law are inevitably a reflex of these contending interests. Those who are inclined to repudiate the hypothesis of economic determinism as a European importation must, therefore, revise their views, on learning that one of the earliest, and certainly one of the clearest, statements of it came from a profound student of politics who sat in the Convention that framed our fundamental law.

The requirements for an economic interpretation of the formation and adoption of the Constitution may be stated in a hypothetical proposition which, although it cannot be verified absolutely from ascertainable data, will at once illustrate the problem and furnish a guide to research and generalization.

It will be admitted without controversy that the Constitution was the creation of a certain number of men, and it was opposed by a certain number of men. Now, if it were possible to have an economic biography of all those connected with its framing and adoption,— perhaps about 160,000 men altogether,—the materials for scientific analysis and classification would be available. Such an economic biography would include a list of the real and personal property owned by all of these men and their families: lands and houses, with incumbrances, money at interest, slaves, capital invested in shipping and manufacturing, and in state and continental securities.

Suppose it could be shown from the classification of the men who supported and opposed the Constitution that there was no line of property division at all; that is, that men owning substantially the same amounts of the same kinds of property were equally divided on the matter of adoption or rejection—it would then become apparent that the Constitution had no ascertainable relation to economic groups or classes, but was the product of some abstract causes remote from the chief business of life—gaining a livelihood.

Suppose, on the other hand, that substantially all of the merchants, money lenders, security holders, manufacturers, shippers, capitalists, and financiers and their professional associates are to be found on one side in support of the Constitution and that substantially all or the major portion of the opposition came from the non-slaveholding farmers and the debtors—would it not be pretty conclusively demonstrated that our fundamental law was not the product of an abstraction known as "the whole people," but of a group of economic interests which must have expected beneficial results from its adoption? Obviously all the facts here desired cannot be discovered, but the data presented in the following chapters bear out the latter hypothesis, and thus a reasonable presumption in favor of the theory is created.

Of course, it may be shown (and perhaps can be shown) that the farmers and debtors who opposed the Constitution were, in fact, benefited by the general improvement which resulted from its adoption. It may likewise be shown, to take an extreme case, that the English nation derived immense advantages from the Norman Conquest and the orderly administrative processes which were introduced, as it undoubtedly did; nevertheless, it does not follow that the vague thing known as "the advancement of general welfare" or some abstraction known as "justice" was the immediate, guiding purpose of the leaders in either of these great historic changes. The point is, that the direct, impelling motive in both cases was the economic advantages which the beneficiaries expected would accrue to themselves first, from their action. Further than this, economic interpretation cannot go. It may be that some larger world process is working through each series of historical events; but ultimate causes lie beyond our horizon. . . .

CONCLUSIONS

The movement for the Constitution of the United States was originated and carried through principally by four groups of personalty interests which had been adversely affected under the Articles of Confederation: money, public securities, manufactures, and trade and shipping.

The first firm steps toward the formation of the Constitution were taken by a small and active group of men immediately interested through their personal possessions in the outcome of their labors.

No popular vote was taken directly or indirectly on the proposition to call the Convention which drafted the Constitution.

A large propertyless mass was, under the prevailing suffrage qualifications, excluded at the outset from participation (through representatives) in the work of framing the Constitution.

The members of the Philadelphia Convention which drafted the Constitution were, with a few exceptions, immediately, directly, and personally interested in, and derived economic advantages from, the establishment of the new system.

The Constitution was essentially an economic document based upon the concept that the fundamental private rights of property are anterior to government and morally beyond the reach of popular majorities.

The major portion of the members of the Convention are on record as recognizing the claim of property to a special and defensive position in the Constitution.

In the ratification of the Constitution, about three-fourths of the adult males failed to vote on the question, having abstained from the elections at which delegates to the state conventions were chosen, either on account of their indifference or their disfranchisement by property qualifications.

The Constitution was ratified by a vote of probably not more than one-sixth of the adult males.

It is questionable whether a majority of the voters participating in the elections for the state conventions in New York, Massachusetts, New Hampshire, Virginia, and South Carolina, actually approved the ratification of the Constitution.

The leaders who supported the Constitution in the ratifying conventions represented the same economic groups as the members of the Philadelphia Convention; and in a large number of instances they were also directly and personally interested in the outcome of their efforts.

In the ratification, it became manifest that the line of cleavage for

and against the Constitution was between substantial personalty interests on the one hand and the small farming and debtor interests
on the other.

The Constitution was not creàted by "the whole people" as the
jurists have said; neither was it created by "the states" as Southern
nullifiers long contended; but it was the work of a consolidated group
whose interests knew no state boundaries and were truly national in
their scope.

NOTES

[1] The theory of the economic interpretation of history as stated by Professor Seligman seems as nearly axiomatic as any proposition in social science
can be: "The existence of man depends upon his ability to sustain himself;
the economic life is therefore the fundamental condition of all life. Since
human life, however, is the life of man in society, individual existence
moves within the framework of the social structure and is modified by it.
What the conditions of maintenance are to the individual, the similar
relations of production and consumption are to the community. To economic causes, therefore, must be traced in the last instance those transformations in the structure of society which themselves condition the relations
of social classes and the various manifestations of social life." *The Economic Interpretation of History*, p. 3.

That Noble Dream

In a thought-provoking paper read at the last meeting of the American Historical Association Mr. Theodore Clarke Smith laid his colleagues under a deep obligation.[1] His essay is not only significant for its intrinsic merits; it indicates an interest in problems of historiography that have been long neglected. If it had been merely expository, it might well be accepted without further analysis as opening the way for an extension of thought along the same lines. But it is in spirit and declaration challenging as well as descriptive, monitory as well as narrative. Mr. Smith makes a division between scholars affiliated with the Association. He insists that they must be, broadly speaking, grouped under two banners and that there is a gulf between them which cannot be bridged. One group, with which he ranges himself, had "a noble dream," and produced sound, creditable, and in many cases masterly works on American history. Although he does not say that the opposition is ignoble, unsound, discreditable, and weak, that implication lurks in the dichotomy which he makes.

The issues presented by Mr. Smith transcend personalities and call for the most thoughtful consideration that the intelligence of the Association can bring to bear upon them. Is there in fact a deep-seated division in the Association? Has a battle line been drawn in such a fashion that members must align themselves on the one side or the other? Is it impossible to find a synthesis that will reconcile apparent contradictions or suggest a suspension of judgment, at least for the time being? Are the facts employed by Mr. Smith to illustrate his thesis so precisely accurate in every case as to be beyond amendment in a quest for "objective truth"? Surely these questions are of more than passing importance. They concern the young members of the Association and the fate of the society. They invite us to stop for a moment to review the assumptions on which historical work is to be

American Historical Review 41 (1935–36), 74–87. Reprinted by permission of the American Historical Association.

done in the future; and perhaps answers to them may reveal some overarching hypothesis or suggest a healing diffidence, at least.

The division which Mr. Smith makes in the Association seems to be positive and sharp. On the one side are the scholars who have made "the impressive output of sound, creditable, and in many cases masterly, works on American history during the period under review" [1884–1934]. The works of this class of scholars "are dominated, from monograph to many-volumed work, by one clear-cut ideal—that presented to the world first in Germany and later accepted everywhere, the ideal of the effort for objective truth." Theirs was "a noble dream," now threatened with extinction, and the hope is expressed that members of this school may go down, if necessary, "with our flags flying." "In that case, it will be time for the American Historical Association to disband, for the intellectual assumptions on which it is founded will have been taken away from beneath it." Here then is a clear-cut ideal, a noble dream, and the American Historical Association was "founded" on it. And who are the men who threaten this ideal, dream, and Association? They are writers who do not "consider it necessary to be impartial or even fair." They are partial and doctrinaire. Especially doctrinaire are those who resort to an economic interpretation of history. Among the menaces to the old and true faith, mentioned by Mr. Smith, is James Harvey Robinson who once flatly declared that what is called "objective history" is simply history without an object, and proposed that historical knowledge be used to throw light on "the quandaries of our life today"—to facilitate "readjustment and reform." Here are the contending parties of light and darkness.

The dichotomy so presented seems to involve ideal, method, and belief in the possibility of achievement. Scholars of the Old Guard desired above all things to search for "objective truth." Were the men whom Mr. Smith puts on the other side of the fence opposed to the ideal of the search for truth? Is the scholar who seeks knowledge useful to contemporaries wrestling with "the quandaries of our life today" unconcerned about the truth of that knowledge? His end may be different but surely he does not seek falsehood or believe that false history can be serviceable to the cause posited. Nor can it be said that the student who tries to penetrate the pageant of politics to the economic interests behind the scenes is necessarily hostile to the ideal of the search for truth. Conceivably he might be as much interested in truth as the scholar who ignores or neglects the economic aspects of history. As far as method goes, those scholars who are placed in opposition to the noble dream may be as patient in their inquiries and as rigorous in their criticism and use of documentation as the old masters of light and leading. In intentions and methods, therefore, no necessary antagonism appears to arise.

Now we come to achievement—to the possibility of finding and stating the objective truth of history. Here we encounter something more difficult to fathom than intentions or methods. We encounter questions which run deeply into the nature of the human mind, the substance of history as actuality, and the power of scholarship to grasp history objectively. Beyond doubt, scholars of competence can agree on many particular truths and on large bodies of established facts. But is it possible for men to divest themselves of all race, sex, class, political, social, and regional predilections and tell the truth of history as it actually was? Can Mr. Smith's noble dream, his splendid hope, be realized in fact? That is the fundamental issue at stake.

This theory that history as it actually was can be disclosed by critical study, can be known as objective truth, and can be stated as such, contains certain elements and assumptions. The first is that history (general or of any period) has existed as an object or series of objects outside the mind of the historian (a *Gegenüber* separated from him and changing in time). The second is that the historian can face and know this object or series of objects and can describe it as it objectively existed.[2] The third is that the historian can, at least for the purposes of research and writings, divest himself of all taint of religious, political, philosophical, social, sex, economic, moral, and aesthetic interests, and view this *Gegenüber* with strict impartiality, somewhat as the mirror reflects any object to which it is held up. The fourth is that the multitudinous events of history as actuality had some structural organization through inner (perhaps causal) relations, which the impartial historian can grasp by inquiry and observation and accurately reproduce or describe in written history. The fifth is that the substances of this history can be grasped in themselves by purely rational or intellectual efforts, and that they are not permeated by or accompanied by anything transcendent—God, spirit, or materialism. To be sure the theory of objective history is not often so fully stated, but such are the nature and implications of it.[3]

This theory of history and of human powers is one of the most sweeping dogmas in the recorded history of theories. It condemns philosophy and throws it out of doors. As practiced, it ignores problems of mind with which philosophers and theologians have wrestled for centuries and have not yet settled to everybody's satisfaction. As developed into Historicism (it may be well to Anglicize *Historismus*), it takes on all the implications of empiricism, positivism, and, if not materialism, at least that rationalism which limits history to its purely experiential aspects. If sound and appealing, it is nonetheless an all-embracing philosophy of historiography, even though it denies philosophy.

Although Ranke contributed powerfully to the growth of this historical theory, and claimed to be writing history as it actually had been, he did not in fact follow the logic of his procedure to its empirical conclusion. He opposed the philosophic method of Hegel—that powerful thinker who boldly attempted to grasp the scheme entire—and at the same time Ranke conceived history as, in some strange manner, "a revelation of God." But he did not openly employ this belief in selecting and arranging "objectively" the facts of history as it actually had been. He did not think that man could know God as history, but he imagined that man could see "God's finger" in human affairs and dimly grasp God's handiwork in history. In history, as Ranke conceived it, God stood there, "wie eine heilige Hieroglyphe, an seinem Äussersten aufgefasst und bewahrt." [4] History was "der Gang Gottes in der Welt." In the true spirit of Lutheran piety, Ranke flung himself down before the impenetrable mystery of things: "Allgewaltiger, Einer und Dreifaltiger, du hast mich aus dem Nichts gerufen. Hier liege ich vor deines Thrones Stufen." Yet he fain would write history, so enclosed in mystery, as it actually had been, impartially, from the critical study of written documents. He rejected philosophy, proclaimed positive history, and still was controlled by a kind of *Pantheismus.*

Ranke could write history, certainly, with a majestic air of impartiality and say that he had written as it actually had been. For example, he could write of popes in a manner pleasing to both Catholics and Protestants of the upper classes. He doubtless believed that he was telling this history of the popes as it actually had been. Did he realize his claim? There is stark validity in the Jesuit objection that Ranke avoided the chief actuality of the story: Was the papacy actually what it affirmed itself to be, "an institution of the Son of God made man," or was it a combination of false claims, craft, and man-made power? [5] How could Ranke avoid that question and yet even claim to be writing history as it actually was?

I make no pretensions to knowing Ranke as he actually was or his motives in writing the kind of history he chose to write. But records are available to establish the fact that he did not abstain entirely from those hot political controversies which are supposed to warp the pure thought of the empirical historian. In directing the *Historisch-Politische Zeitschrift* he chose a way between French constitutionalism and that extreme Prussian conservatism which would yield not a point to democratic aspirations. After the July Revolution Ranke favored a confederate law against the political press and political literature— a proposition that must have pleased Metternich and Gentz, who opened their archives to him.[6] After the March upheaval of 1848 Ranke came vigorously to the support of Frederick William IV in resistance to popular demands for a constitution based on democratic principles. On this occasion the "impartial" historian proved to be a bulwark for Prussian authoritarianism—against which so many "impartial" historians in the United States wrote vigorously in 1917–1918. Ranke also rejoiced in the events of 1870–1871 "as the victory of conservative Europe over the Revolution," showing that he could not completely separate his political from his historical conceptions. Persistently neglecting social and economic interests in history, successfully avoiding any historical writing that offended the most conservative interests in the Europe of his own time, Ranke may be correctly characterized as one of the most "partial" historians produced by the nineteenth century.

Whether Ranke was fully conscious of what he was doing himself, he was able to see that other historians were writing from some angle of vision. He once said to George Bancroft: "I tell my hearers, that your history is the best book ever written from the democratic point of view. You are thoroughly consistent; adhere strictly to your method, carry it out in many directions but in all with fidelity, and are always true to it." In making this statement, Ranke expressed the hope that it would not make Bancroft angry.[7] Bancroft was not certain that this was "high praise." Shortly afterward he declared: "I deny the charge; if there is democracy in history it is not subjective, but objective as they say here, and so has necessarily its place in history and gives its colour as it should. . . ." Is it possible that Ranke, who was quick to discover subjective ideas in Bancroft's writings, was totally unaware of the fact that he might be writing from the point of view of the conservative reaction in Europe? If he never applied the criterion to himself, then he was doubly "partial" and utterly devoid of any sense for reality and humor.

If, as Mr. Smith says, the "objective" method of Ranke and his school was "accepted everywhere," it is due to history as it was to record that the conception was subjected all along to a running fire of criticism by German historians, even by those "von Fach." Leaving aside the penetrating skepticism of Schopenhauer (who certainly was no mean thinker) and the critique of Eugen Dühring, we find searching examinations of the theory and logic of Historicism by German scholars in the early issues of the *Historische Zeitschrift,* and in the writings of Droysen, Ottokar Lorenz, Bernheim, and Lamprecht, for instance.[8] There were not wanting at that time historians "die in naiver, selbstgewisser Technik ihre Historie trieben, ohne zu ahnen, an welchen theoretischen Abgründen sie sich bewegten"; but many German scholars early went behind Ranke's formula and challenged its validity. They did this long before a host of critical thinkers fell upon it during the opening years of the twentieth century.

And if the Ranke formula or theory of history was accepted in the United States by members of the American Historical Association, as Mr. Smith states, it is not quite in line with the facts in the case to say that it was "everywhere" accepted. Was it in reality adopted as the official creed of the Association in the good old days before ignoble, doctrinaire, and partial students appeared upon the scene? Surely the creed was never drawn up and signed by all faithful members. Whether the majority were acquainted with the philosophical discussion that had long raged around it and threw themselves positively on the Ranke side seems to be a statistical problem not yet solved. Hence judgment should be suspended.

Pending the determination of this historical fact by research, one item in the story may be cited—the presidential address delivered at the opening session of the American Historical Association in 1884 by Andrew D. White. Ranke was yet living. Did Mr. White commit himself or the Association to Historicism or the Ranke formula? Emphatically, he did not, as any member can discover by reading again that noteworthy address. In fact Mr. White, with mature wisdom, recognized both sides of the problem of historiography: the special, the detailed, the verified, the documented—and the philosophical. He said categorically: "While acknowledging the great value of special investigations . . . to historical knowledge in individual nations, it is not too much to say that the highest effort and the noblest result toward which these special historical investigations lead is the philosophical synthesis of all special results in a large, truth-loving, justice-loving spirit."

"Bearing on this point, Buckle, in a passage well worthy of meditation, has placed *observation* at the foot of the ladder, *discovery* next above it, and *philosophical method* at the summit." In this spirit Mr. White declared that at the annual meetings of the Association there ought to be a session or sessions dealing with special studies, and also a session or sessions "devoted to general history, the history of civilization, and the philosophy of history." He recognized the dangers of the latter—"looseness and vagueness"—but thought that the consideration of both aspects of history would contribute to a sounder development of each. "These difficulties," Mr. White warned us, "the Association must meet as they arise." [9]

Nor did the first President, Andrew D. White, see in the use of history as an instrument of "social control" the perils to scholarship lamented by Mr. Smith. On the contrary, Mr. White closed with an exordium in line with the thought later expressed by James Harvey Robinson, whose ideal Mr. Smith puts on the other side of the fence from "a noble dream." Mr. White proposed no neutral, value-free history. "Certainly," he said near the close of his address, "a confederation like this—of historical scholars . . . ought to elicit most valuable work in both fields [special and philosophical], and to contribute powerfully to the healthful development on the one hand of man as man, and on the other to the opening up of a better political and social future for the nation at large." This is asking historians to do what James Harvey Robinson suggested: bring historical knowledge to bear "on the quandaries of our life today."

Henry Adams was also once President of the American Historical Association. He cannot be placed among those who have recently invaded the circle of the pure faith and threatened to destroy the Association by "the final extinction of a noble dream," driving Mr. Smith and his adherents to consider the frightful alternative of going down "with our flags flying." Did Henry Adams limit the function and thought of the historian to Historicism, the Ranke formula, or neutrality in the face of life's exigent forces? Members who care to know before they take sides in a discussion of the theory of history must read the letter which Henry Adams, as President of the Association, wrote to his colleagues as long ago as 1894.[10] There he invited the members to consider what a science of history would look like and the devastating challenge which it would make to the church, the state, property, or labor. Mr. Adams, with amazing foresight, predicted a crisis in Western economy and thought, and warned his colleagues that they "may at any time in the next fifty years be compelled to find an answer, 'Yes' or 'No,' under the pressure of the most powerful organizations the world has ever known for the suppression of influences hostile to its safety."

One more colleague may be mentioned. Mr. Smith has referred to H. L. Osgood as holding to the "high ideals" of the school which now seems to be threatened by doctrinaire writers. Mr. Osgood was, as Mr. Smith says, expository, analytical, and for the most part impersonal. Did Mr. Osgood imagine himself to be writing history as it actually was? His ambition was more limited. He sought to tell the truth, as best he could, about certain aspects of history. Did he imagine himself to stand outside the *Zeitgeist?* Not for a moment. Mr. Osgood had been one of my masters, and shortly after I presented him with a copy of my *Economic Interpretation of the Constitution* I asked him whether it offended him or appeared to be *ultra vires?* His response was positive. He said in effect: "Men of my generation grew up in the midst of great constitutional and institutional debates and our interest turned to institutional history. Profound economic questions have now arisen and students of the younger generation, true to their age, will occupy themselves with economic aspects of history." Far from deeming this interest reprehensible, Mr. Osgood regarded it as "natural" and proper. Near the end of his life he spoke to me of the heavy hand of time that lies upon all our work, dating us, revealing our limitations.

How many other members of the older generation did in fact think their way through the assumptions and convictions enclosed in Mr. Smith's "noble dream" and accept it wholeheartedly? The data for answering that question are not at hand. How many watched carefully the development of the critical attitude toward Historicism in Europe at the turn of the century, and especially after 1914? Materials for answering that query are not available either. Judging by the files of the *American Historical Review* and the programs of annual meetings such philosophical issues have received scant consideration, little exploration and examination. Judging by the writings of American historians slight attention has been given to the intellectual problems involved in the choice of subjects, the selection of facts, and the construction of monographs and many-volumed works. If there has been any real searching of historical minds and hearts in the United States, any fearless and wide-reaching inquiry into preliminary assumptions, tacit or deliberate, any procedure save on the level of ingenuous convictions, historical literature bears only a few evidences of its fruits. If engines of skepticism and verification have been mercilessly applied to what passes for constructive thought, as distinguished from eclecticism and documentation, news of the fact has not spread far and wide enough in the American Historical Association to make a profound impression upon its proceedings. Some countervailing evidence may be cited, no doubt, but the exceptions would seem merely to prove the rule. It may be that the major portion of American scholars in the good old days imagined that they could discover and know the objective truth of history as it actually was, but there is good reason for thinking that a large number of them did not labor under that impression respecting their activities and powers.

Having indicated some grounds for holding that Historicism is not and never has been "accepted everywhere" as the official creed of the American Historical Association, it is now appropriate to inquire whether the Ranke formula is valid in itself. Can the human mind discover and state the "objective truth" of history as it actually was? Space does not admit even a brief summation of the voluminous literature dealing with this conception and demonstrating, if not its delusive character, its rejection by scholars and thinkers of high competence in Europe. Those American students who care to examine the history and nature of the European revolt against Historicism may find guidance in Croce, *History: Its Theory and Practice,* in Heussi, *Die Krisis des Historismus,* and in the numerous works cited by Heussi as supporting evidence. In these volumes is presented the development of historical thought which culminated in the rejection of the Ranke theory and its formulation as Historicism.

At this point only a bare outline of the argument is possible, but it may be given, very inadequately, in the following propositions:

1. The idea that history took place in the past as actuality outside

the mind of the contemporary historian is accepted as the common-sense view.

2. The historian is not an observer of the past that lies beyond his own time. He cannot see it *objectively* as the chemist sees his test tubes and compounds. The historian must "see" the actuality of history through the medium of documentation. That is his sole recourse.

3. The documentation (including monuments and other relics) with which the historian must work covers only a part of the events and personalities that make up the actuality of history. In other words multitudinous events and personalities escape the recording of documentation. To realize the significance of this, as Heussi says, it is only necessary to consider an effort to describe the battle of Leipzig alone, to say nothing of the Napoleonic wars or the history of the Roman Empire.

4. Not only is the documentation partial. In very few cases can the historian be reasonably sure that he has assembled all the documents of a given period, region, or segment. In most cases he makes a partial selection or a partial reading of the partial record of the multitudinous events and personalities involved in the actuality with which he is dealing.

5. Since the history of any period embraces all the actualities involved, and since both documentation and research are partial, it follows that the total actuality is not factually knowable to any historian, however laborious, judicial, or faithful he may be in his procedures. History as it actually was, as distinguished, of course from particular facts of history, is not known or knowable, no matter how zealously is pursued "the ideal of the effort for objective truth."

6. The idea that there was a complete and actual structurization of events in the past, to be discovered through a partial examination of the partial documentation, is pure hypothesis, as Th. Lessing shows in his *Geschichte als Sinngebung des Sinnlosen*.

7. The events and personalities of history in their very nature involve ethical and aesthetic considerations. They are not mere events in physics and chemistry inviting neutrality on the part of the "observer."

8. Any overarching hypothesis or conception employed to give coherence and structure to past events in written history is an interpretation of some kind, something transcendent. And as Croce says, "transcendency is always transcendency, whether it be thought of as that of a God or of reason, of nature, or of matter."

9. The historian seeking to know the past, or about it, does not bring to the partial documentation with which he works a perfect and polished neutral mind in which the past streaming through the medium of documentation is mirrored as it actually was. Whatever acts of purification the historian may perform he yet remains human, a creature of time, place, circumstance, interests, predilections, culture. No amount of renunciation could have made Andrew D. White into a Frederick Jackson Turner or either of them into a neutral mirror.

10. Into the selection of topics, the choice and arrangement of materials, the specific historian's "me" will enter. It may enter with a conscious clarification of philosophy and purpose or, as Croce says, surreptitiously, without confession or acknowledgment.

11. The validity of the Ranke formula and its elaboration as Historicism is destroyed by internal contradictions and rejected by contemporary thought. The historian's powers are limited. He may search for, but he cannot find, the "objective truth" of history, or write it, "as it actually was."

Now we come to the validity of an antithesis of the Ranke formula —the economic interpretation of history. Is it partial, in the sense that it does not cover all the events of history? It certainly is. Surely none will contend that it could be otherwise than partial in its scope. Is it "the correct" interpretation of history? If the word interpretation is taken to mean "explanation," then neither it nor any other historical hypothesis can be regarded as valid and final, on the ground that in the nature of things—documentation and the human mind—the past as it actually was cannot be known. If the word be taken, however, in a manner equally admissible under linguistic usage, to mean simply the writer's version, construction, or conception of his subject, then an economic interpretation is merely what it professes to be—a version, not the absolute truth, of history.

Seekers after truth in particular and general have less reason to fear it than they have to fear any history that comes under the guise of the Ranke formula or Historicism. It bears its own warning. A book entitled *An Economic Interpretation of the Constitution,* like every other book on history, is a selection and an organization of facts; but it serves advance notice on the reader, telling him what to expect. A book entitled *The Formation of the Constitution* or *The Making of the Constitution* is also a selection and organization of facts, hence an interpretation or conception of some kind, but it does not advise the reader at the outset concerning the upshot to be expected.

Does an economic interpretation, open and avowed, violate the "ideal of the effort for objective truth"? Not necessarily. The historian who searches out and orders economic aspects of life, events, and interests may possibly be as zealous in his search for truth as any other historian searching out and ordering his facts in his way. Is the student who seeks an economic interpretation more partial, in the sense of partisanship, or more doctrinaire than the historian, who assumes that he can know the past as it actually has been? Not necessarily. He may conceivably view the structure of classes, their ideologies, formulas, projects, and conflicts as coldly and impartially as any disciple of Ranke that the American Historical Association has furnished.

Did the economic interpretation of history, as Mr. Smith alleges, have "its origin, of course, in the Marxian theories"? I cannot speak for others, but so far as I am concerned, my conception of the economic interpretation of history rests upon documentation older than Karl Marx—Number X of the *Federalist,* the writings of the Fathers of the Republic, the works of Daniel Webster, the treatises of Locke, Hobbes, and Machiavelli, and the *Politics* of Aristotle—as well as the writings of Marx himself.

Yet I freely pay tribute to the amazing range of Marx's scholarship and the penetrating character of his thought. It may be appropriate to remind those who may be inclined to treat Marx as a mere revolutionary or hot partisan that he was more than that. He was a doctor of philosophy from a German university, possessing the hallmark of the scholar. He was a student of Greek and Latin learning. He read, besides German, his native tongue, Greek, Latin, French, English, Italian, and Russian. He was widely read in contemporary history and economic thought. Hence, however much one may dislike Marx's personal views, one cannot deny to him wide and deep knowledge—and a fearless and sacrificial life. He not only interpreted history, as everyone does who writes any history, but he helped to make history. Possibly he may have known something. At least the contemporary student, trying to look coldly and impartially on thought and thinkers in the field of historiography, may learn a little bit, at least, from Karl Marx.

But that does not mean that any economic interpretation of history must be used for the purposes which Marx set before himself. It may well be used for opposite purposes. It has been. It may be again. Or it may be employed as the basis for impartiality and inaction on the ground that a conflict of mere material interests cannot be a matter of concern to virtue itself. In other words there is nothing in the nature of an economic interpretation of history that compels the interpreter to take any partisan or doctrinaire view of the struggle of interests. In fact such an interpretation of the Constitution is less liable to invite a surge of feeling than Mr. Smith's interpretation that the formation and adoption of the Constitution was "a contest between sections ending in the victory of straight-thinking national-minded men over narrower and more local opponents." An economic interpretation does not inquire whether men were straight-thinking or crooked-thinking. It inquires not into their powers of mind or virtues, but into the nature and effects of their substantial possessions. Nor is it necessarily in conflict with Mr. Smith's conclusions. It pushes the inquiry one step further than he does. It asks how it happened that some men were national-minded and others were local-minded, and perhaps throws some light upon the subject.

What conclusions, then, may be drawn from this excursion, hur-

ried and cursory, into historiography, for members of the American
Historical Association? In my opinion, they are as follows: The
formula of Ranke and its extension as Historicism do not and have
never formed an official creed for the Association. From Andrew D.
White down to the present moment there have been members who
have believed that the wider and deeper philosophic questions involved
in the interpretation of history should be considered as having an
importance equal to, if not greater than, the consideration of documentation, special studies, and writings done on the assumption that
history "wie es eigentlich gewesen ist" can be known and expounded
by historians. The Ranke formula and Historicism are not the official
creed of the Association and ought not to be, for they now lie amid
the ruins of their own defeat. Nor are the other creeds placed in
antithesis to the "noble dream" by Mr. Smith deemed official. They
should not be. No school that makes pretensions to exclusive omnis-
cience or exclusive virtue, that claims to know history as it actually
was can long escape the corroding skepticism that search and thought
bring to it. It is undesirable to invite the Association to split over
two absolutes. It is not necessary for any member, faction, or group,
however large or small, to feel that a war to the hilt is on and that the
one or the other must go down with, or without, "flying colors."

The task before the American Historical Association seems to be
something other than that of deepening a division artificially made.
The collection, preservation, and publication of archives must be
carried on with ever increasing zeal. All the engines of criticism,
authentication, and verification, so vigorously used by the German
school, must be employed with all the powers of intelligence available. Monographic studies must be promoted. But this is not enough.

The philosophic side of historiography, as Andrew D. White
warned the Association, must also receive the consideration required
for all constructive work in historical writing. The effort to grasp at
the totality of history must and will be continued, even though the
dream of bringing it to earth must be abandoned. This means a
widening of the range of search beyond politics to include interests
hitherto neglected—economic, racial, sex, and cultural in the most

general sense of the term. Certainly by this broadening process the scholar will come nearer to the actuality of history as it has been. The distinction between particular facts that may be established by the scientific method and the "objective" truth of history must be maintained, if illusions are to be dispelled.

Still more pressing, because so generally neglected, is the task of exploring the assumptions upon which the selection and organization of historical facts proceed. In the nature of things they proceed upon some assumptions concerning the substance of history as actuality. We do not acquire the colorless, neutral mind by declaring our intention to do so. Rather do we clarify the mind by admitting its cultural interests and patterns—interests and patterns that will control, or intrude upon, the selection and organization of historical materials. Under what formulas is it possible to conceive history? What types of controlling patterns are to be found in the declarations of historical writers, in the diverse opinions of the world at large, and in the works of historians already before us? Instead of waging a war, followed by victory or defeat, we need to provide for the Association's annual meetings a section or sections dealing with the assumptions and procedures of historiography. What do we think we are doing when we are writing history? What kinds of philosophies or interpretations are open to us? Which interpretations are actually chosen and practiced? And why? By what methods or processes can we hope to bring the multitudinous and bewildering facts of history into any coherent and meaningful whole? Through the discussion of such questions the noble dream of the search for truth may be brought nearer to realization, not extinguished; but in the end the members of the American Historical Association will be human beings, not immortal gods.

NOTES

[1] *Am. Hist. Rev.*, XL, 439–449.

[2] If the historian could do this, then so far as he covers the past there would be nothing left for posterity to do. The task of writing the history

of countries and periods could be definitively discharged. To that extent students would have no work before them except that of reading the masters. A new historical treatment of an age would be as unthinkable as a new multiplication table.

³ Karl Heussi, *Die Krisis des Historismus* (Tübingen, 1932), pp. 1–21.

⁴ Friedrich Meinecke, *Die Idee der Staatsräson* (Munich, 3d ed., 1929), pp. 469 ff.

⁵ Benedetto Croce, *History: its Theory and Practice* (New York, 1921), p. 300.

⁶ *Historische Zeitschrift*, XCIII, 78.

⁷ M. A. DeWolfe Howe, *Life and Letters of George Bancroft* (New York, 1908), II, 183.

⁸ Heussi, p. 24. On Ranke's substitution of Universal History for the Philosophy of History, Henri Sée remarks: "Conception, qui, aujourd'hui, nous paraît de pensée assez pauvre, depuis que l'horizon de l'historien s'est singulièrement élargi." *Science et philosophie de l'histoire* (2nd ed., Paris, 1933), pp. 20–21; citing Ernst Troeltsch, *Der Historismus und seine Probleme* (Vol. III, *Gesammelte Schriften*, Tübingen, 1922).

⁹ American Historical Association, *Papers*, I, 49–72.

¹⁰ *Ibid., Annual Report*, 1894, pp. 17–23. Reprinted in *The Degradation of the Democratic Dogma* (New York, 1920), pp. 125 ff.

Samuel E. Morison (1887–) and the Attack on Relativism

Like Allan Nevins, Professor Samuel E. Morison of Harvard has stressed literary style in history writing and as a proud (but not uncritical) New Englander has pioneered in the upward assessment of Puritan culture. He was born in Boston, educated in private preparatory schools, and earned his A.B. (1908) and Ph.D. (1912) at Harvard. Interested in Anglo-American cultural rapprochement, he took an M.A. (1922) at Oxford and later held the distinguished Harmsworth professorship in American History at that institution. In 1927 he published the attractively written *Oxford History of the United States*.

Among his most important books on New England, written from a scholarly and appreciative viewpoint, are *Builders of the Bay Colony* (1930), the *History of Harvard University*—under various titles (3 vols., 1930–36), and *Puritan Pronaos* (1936), dealing with cultural history. His Harvard colleagues, Kenneth Murdock, Perry Miller, and Ralph Barton Perry, continued this process of rescuing the Puritan tradition from the blue-nose caricature popularized by H. L. Mencken. To these men, the Puritans were not sectarian bigots, but courageous, creative, and imaginative people who shaped the early American tradition in education (e.g. the tax-supported school system), literature, religion, and democratic institutions.

Always interested in the sea, Morison acted as commodore for Harvard's Columbus Expedition (1939–40), wrote two Pulitzer Prize biographies, of Columbus, *Admiral of the Ocean Sea* (1942), and *John Paul Jones* (1960). As a naval historian he produced the monumental *History of the United States Naval Operations During World War II* (14 vols., 1947–60). His oft-reprinted book, *The Mari-*

time History of Massachusetts, 1783–1860 (Houghton Mifflin, 1921) tells the fascinating tale of the China trade.

Morison's presidential address to the American Historical Association, "Faith of a Historian," contains a clear statement of his principles of teaching and writing which would probably be accepted by most practicing historians. Particularly significant is his discussion of the meaning of objectivity and his criticisms of Charles Beard's venture into relativism. Morison defends the traditional common-sense idea of objectivity against the relativist notion of a subjective "frame of reference" with an ever changing image of truth. He assails Beard and like-minded relativists for confusing youth with disillusionment and imbuing them with a pacifism that left a generation spiritually unprepared to stop Hitler. These historians had minimized military history. But his attack on the New History of Robinson and Beard still leaves room for New Deal historians like himself and he shares their enthusiasm for social, cultural, and intellectual history-writing, providing that it is done with literary skill as well as accuracy.

Faith of a Historian

To you, fellow members, who have honored me by election to your presidency this year, I feel that I owe a sort of *apologia pro vita mea,* a statement of the beliefs and principles that have guided my teaching and writing during the thirty-eight years since my first article was published in the *American Historical Review.* I have nothing revolu-

Presidential address read at the annual dinner of the American Historical Association in Chicago on December 29, 1950. *American Historical Review* 56 (1951), 261–75. Reprinted by permission of the American Historical Association and Samuel E. Morison.

tionary or even novel to offer. Very early in my professional career I observed a certain frustration in a historian whom I greatly admired, Henry Adams, who had spent much time and thought searching for a "law of history." So I have cultivated the vast garden of human experience which is history, without troubling myself over-much about laws, essential first causes, or how it is all coming out. My creed or confession is probably no different from that of the great majority of practicing historians in the Western world.

The late Charles A. Beard, certainly one of the most beloved and by all odds the most provocative of my predecessors, described all writing of history as "an act of faith." With that I agree, although after reading some of his books I suspect that Beard's "act of faith" was a literal translation of the Spanish auto-da-fe. Every historian with professional standards speaks or writes what he believes to be true. But he must also have faith in the receptiveness of his audience. If a lecturer, he wishes to be heard; if a writer, to be read. He always hopes for a public beyond that of the long-suffering wife.

This legitimate desire of the historian to interest, to instruct, and to please, is at once a leading motive for his labors, a challenge to present his work in artistic form, and a danger to his professional integrity. It tempts him to deviate from the truth in order to satisfy school committees on whom he depends for "adoptions"; or the prejudices of reviewers and the emotions of the public to whom he looks for circulation. Historians of repute have sold their skill for a mess of royalties; and I hope we do not envy them. Most writers of pseudo-history, however, are gifted amateurs seeking to bolster some pet theory with carefully screened facts, or people trained in journalism or some similar calling in which the story's the thing. If it accords with the facts, fine; if not, so much the worse for the facts.

No person without an inherent loyalty to truth, a high degree of intellectual honesty, and a sense of balance, can be a great or even a good historian. Truth about the past is the essence of history and historical biography, the thing that distinguishes them from every other branch of literature. Everyone agrees to that; but when we come to define truth, dissension starts.

For my part, I stand firm on the oft-quoted sentence of Leopold von Ranke, which we American historians remember when we have forgotten all the rest of our German. "The present investigation," said Ranke in the preface to his first volume, published in 1824, "will simply explain the event exactly as it happened." [1] Ranke was far from being the first to say that. He picked up the phrase, I imagine, from Wilhelm von Humboldt, who, in an address to the Prussian Academy three years earlier, declared the proper function of history to be "the exposition of what has happened." [2] Some 2200 years earlier, Thucydides wrote, "The absence of romance in my history will, I fear, detract somewhat from its interest. But if he who desires to have before his eyes a true picture of the events which have happened, and of the like events which may be expected to happen hereafter . . . shall pronounce what I have written to be useful, then I shall be satisfied." [3]

One might add quotation to quotation, merely to show that for almost 2500 years, in the Hebraic-Hellenic-Christian civilization that we inherit, truth has been recognized as the essence of history. In other words, the historian must be intellectually honest. Sublimating his own views of what ought to have been or should be, he must apply himself to ascertaining what really happened. Of course his own sense of values will enter into his selection and arrangement of facts. It goes without saying that complete, "scientific" objectivity is unattainable by the historian. His "choice of facts to be recorded, his distribution of emphasis among them, his sense of their significance and relative proportion, must be governed by his philosophy of life." [4] No historian of my generation has ever pretended otherwise. Certain mid-nineteenth century historians fancied that they could be as objectively scientific about the multitudinous, unrefractory materials of human history as a physiologist should be (but seldom is) in describing muscular reactions. But none of these, from Ranke down, if pressed, would have denied that their philosophy of life influenced, if it did not dictate, their selection, emphasis, and arrangement.

So much has been written in recent years about these limitations on "scientific" objectivity as to obscure the plain, outstanding principle that the historian's basic task is one of presenting a corpus of ascertained fact. That is the hardest thing to get across to students today, especially to those who have been to the so-called progressive schools. Somewhere along the assembly-line of their education, these students have had inserted in them a bolt called "points of view," secured with a nut called "trends," and they imagine that the historian's problem is simply to compare points of view and describe trends. It is not. The fundamental question is, "What actually happened, and why?" [5]

It matters little what "method" the young historian follows, if he acquires the necessary tools of research, a sense of balance, and an overriding urge to get at the truth. Courses on historical methodology are not worth the time that they take up. I shall never give one myself, and I have observed that many of my colleagues who do give such courses refrain from exemplifying their methods by writing anything. It is much more fun to pick to pieces the works of their contemporaries who do write. Historical methodology, as I see it, is a product of common sense applied to circumstances. If the period be one of which few *monumenta* have survived, the historian must use his imagination to bring the disjointed fragments into some logical pattern, as paleontologists reconstruct a prehistoric monster out of a bone or two. If the era be a recent one for which there are mountains of facts, the historian may sink a few experimental tunnels and examine what they bring up; or he may laboriously try to pan out the "color" from the dirt, or he may employ a corps of miners to do the preliminary sifting for him. In any case, his judgment and set of values, acting alone or through his assistants, determine not only what is gold and what is dross but the design of the history which he creates out of the metal. The historian decides what is significant, and what is not.

Significant for what, you ask? Significant for understanding that stretch or segment of the past which he is examining. The historian's professional duty is primarily to illuminate the past for his hearers or readers; only secondarily and derivatively should he be concerned with influencing the future. He must frankly look backward, with frequent glances over his shoulder at the world in which he lives, and perhaps a prayer for the future world in which he hopes his descendants may live out their lives in peace. But, you will ask, whence cometh the light with which he illuminates the past? The Light of the World, as reflected by the Church? The red light of dialectical materialism? Or merely the klieg lights of modern publicity? And will not the light vary from age to age? Surely, Governor William Bradford's bayberry candle cast a different light from Governor Thomas Hutchinson's whale-oil lamp; Prescott's student lamp and Parkman's gaslight differ from the 1950 model fluorescent bulbs under which most of us work. No historian can be free, or indeed ought to be free, of the best light that his own day and age affords, because he is writing *of* the past but not *for* the past; he is writing for the public of today and tomorrow, and his contemporaries ask very different questions of historians from those that his grandfather's generation asked.[6]

Intellectual honesty is the quality that the public in free countries always has expected of historians; much more than that it does not expect, nor often get. Any child knows that history can only be a reduced representation of reality, but it must be a true one, not distorted by queer lenses. Commodore Richard W. Bates and another officer at the Naval War College, with part-time assistance of a third, spent two years on an intensive, blow-by-blow study of the battle of Savo Island, which lasted exactly 42 minutes in the graveyard watch on August 9, 1942, and they have just produced a 400-page monograph on it. They have honestly tried to find out exactly what happened and why, sparing nobody, praising few, although shocked to the core at the faulty tactics that their search revealed. Skilled, honest, and laborious though he was, Commodore Bates, for want of records sunk or lost, for lack of knowledge of what individual sailors, Japanese and American, out of the some ten thousand engaged, thought, felt, and did, could produce only an approximation of what happened on that tragic night. Like the best professional historians he took no short cuts, tested all *a priori* generalizations by ascertainable facts, and hesitated not to scrap his charts and shape a new course whenever new soundings revealed uncharted reefs. His Savo Island

monograph is a fine example of intellectual honesty, because it was
motivated by an earnest desire to "explain the event exactly as it happened." Gustaaf J. Renier rightly observes that "intellectual honesty
is even more important for the historian than for the scientist, for,
unlike the scientist, the historian cannot submit his conclusions to the
test of experiment. He knows that his work may go unchecked for
generations, and that he is therefore put on his honor." [7]

As one aspect of intellectual honesty, the historian should feel a
sense of responsibility to his public. The same contingencies of time
and space that force a statesman or soldier to make decisions, impel
the historian, though with less urgency, to make up his mind. His
decisions will not, as the statesman's may, throw his country into a
bloody war or a shameful capitulation; they will not, like the soldier's,
win or lose a campaign; but they may well enter into the stream of
history and vitally affect the future. Would the American Union have
been preserved if Bancroft had not so vividly portrayed the struggle
to achieve union? Would Napoleon III have made the fatal cast of
dice in 1870 if French historians had not glorified Napoleon I?
Would the English people have clung to their liberties through good
and evil fortune if Hume, Lingard, and Mommsen had gained their
ear, instead of Green, Macaulay, and Trevelyan? A mad or obstinate
people may not hear the voice of a historian. The Greeks did not
listen to Isocrates, who warned them with even greater authority than
the Delphic Sybil, that, if they went on as they had gone on, their
civilization would be torn asunder and they would be subjected to
an alien domination. But the historian who knows, or thinks he
knows, an unmistakable lesson of the past, has the right and the duty
to point it out, even though it counteract his own beliefs or social
theories.

Now some of you are doubtless thinking, Morison is skating on
thin ice; if he doesn't look out, he will crash through into the bottom-
less pit where the spirits of James Harvey Robinson and Charles A.
Beard are ready to embrace him as one of theirs! So, without further
ado, I shall pay my disrespects to what Robinson called "The New

History," and what Beard called "Written History as an Act of Faith." [8]

Beard, in his confession of faith, sets up a straw Ranke who pretended to reproduce past "actuality" in toto, and in a syllogism that makes one gasp for breath, goes on to assert that, since no historian can escape his personal limitations or transcend those of space and time, he must so select and arrange the facts of history as to influence the present or future in the direction that *he* considers socially desirable. The historian's value in the long run will "depend upon the length and correctness of his forecast." [9] Beard's personal guess was that American history was moving forward to a collectivist democracy, which he defined as "a worker's republic" without poverty or luxury, "a beautiful country . . . labor requited and carried on in conditions conducive to virtue." [10] In other words, the Fabian dream that his English friends shared at the turn of the century.

While Beard's end was constant, his means, and so his "frame of reference" changed with the times. His first famous book, *An Economic Interpretation of the Constitution* (1913), was written apparently to break down that excessive respect for the Federal Constitution which he believed to be the main legal block to social justice. The book had an immense success, promptly becoming the Progressives' Bible. Through it, Beard probably contributed more than any other writer, except Henry L. Mencken, to the scornful attitude of intellectuals toward American institutions, that followed World War I. But in course of time Beard came to believe that he had made a mistake; that if the millennial "worker's republic" was to be attained, the isolationists must come in first, like Kerensky before Lenin. This is evident in his *Basic History of the United States* (1944) and transparently clear in *The Enduring Federalist* (1948). In that, his penultimate work, the *Federalist* papers, which, with few exceptions, he had formerly dismissed as rationalizations of the money-grabbers, become one of the greatest political treatises of all time, expressing deep political and moral truths.[11] Thus Beard came full circle. His 1913 book was received with greatest acclaim in the camp of Eugene Debs; his 1948 book evoked the wild enthusiasm of the Hearst press and the Chicago *Tribune*.

Throughout this evolution from left to right, Beard always detested war. Hence his writings were slanted to show that the military side of history was insignificant of a mere reflection of economic forces. In his *Rise of American Civilization* (1927) he led a procession of historians who, caught in the disillusion that followed World War I, ignored wars, belittled wars, taught that no war was necessary and no war did any good, even to the victor. All these antiwar historians were sincere, and few of them were doctrinaire pacifists, as their actions in the last few years prove; nevertheless, their zeal against war did nothing to preserve peace. It only rendered the generation of youth which came to maturity around 1940 spiritually unprepared for the war they had to fight. One may share Beard's detestation for war—most Americans do—but one must admit that few of the things Americans value most, such as independence, liberty, union, or westward expansion, could have been won or secured unless men had been willing to fight for them. Nor may the social historian ignore the part that war and violence have played in American society. Think of the colonial train bands, the expeditions to Cartagena and Louisburg, Indian wars and western desperadoes, crack militia companies doing fancy drills in gaudy uniforms, soldiers' land bounties and veterans' assaults on the United States Treasury, the curious American craving for military titles, and the romantic militarism of Richard Harding Davis. Even Beard's fixed belief that war retarded the worker's millennium was a mere hypothesis; future historians may well find that the two world wars that Beard hated, and the Roosevelt administrations that he despised, did more for collective bargaining and for the worker's well-being and security than any previous half-century of peace.

Of course we historians were not altogether to blame for American spiritual unpreparedness for World War II. Pacifism, disillusion, and a disregard for settled values were rampant in literature, on murals and the screen, and over the air. But historians bear the greater blame, for they are the ones who should have pointed out that war does accomplish something, that war is better than servitude, that war has been an inescapable aspect of the human story. Any American historian could subscribe to the sentiment that Isocrates expressed for his native Athens: "To our forefathers let honor be rendered no less for their hazardous enterprises than for their other good deeds; for not slight, nor few, nor obscure, but many, great and terrible were the battles that they sustained, some for their own land, some for the freedom of others." [12]

I wish that every young historian might read Beard's final book, *President Roosevelt and the Coming of the War* (1948), as an example of what happens when a historian consciously writes to shape the future instead of to illuminate the past; of a man becoming the victim or the prisoner of his "frame of reference." Without misstating many facts or garbling quotations, as the vulgar distorters of history do, Beard by ingenious arrangement and selection, ruthless rejection of attendant circumstances, and a liberal use of innuendo, compiled a powerful brief for the thesis that Franklin D. Roosevelt was the aggressor against Germany and Japan; that he wanted American entry into the war for his own purposes, planned and plotted for it and maneuvered Japan into striking Pearl Harbor in order to gain these sordid ends.[13] If this be the New History, give me the old! But there is nothing new about it; to go back no farther, we can find the same sort of thing, not so well done to be sure, in *Mr. Madison's War* (1812) by John Lowell, and *A View of the Conduct of the Executive in the Foreign Affairs of the United States* (1797) by James Monroe. Beard used the facts of history—"actualities" he calls them—as Romain Rolland said politicians always use them: "History furnishes to politics all the arguments that it needs, for the chosen cause." [14] I submit that this sort of thing is not history in the accepted, traditional sense of the word; but, at best, a sort of imprecatory preaching.

So, contrary to Beard who urges you to adopt a conscious "frame of reference" or form of Utopia as a basis for the selection and arrangement of facts, I say that every historian should be wary of his preconceptions, and be just as critical of them, skeptical of them, as of the writings of his predecessors.

Skepticism is an important historical tool. It is the starting point of all revision of hitherto accepted history. As Alfred Sidgwick says, "Our skepticism . . . consists of a recognition of the defects of knowledge only in the hope of helping knowledge forward. Among its leading principles are these:—that doubt is always lawful but not always expedient; that human fallibility is only worth remembering for the sake of discovering and correcting actual errors; and that beliefs may be unquestioned without being unquestionable. So far from using the notion that man is fallible as an excuse for despair, or for tendering the advice that nothing should ever be believed, we use it as a justification of the effort to improve our knowledge little by little for ever." [15]

Skepticism is properly a two-edged sword in the hands of the historian; and if one edge of the two is keener than the other, it should be turned against oneself. Every honest historian has, time and again, rejected the theory or "frame" with which he started his research, and has built another to suit the facts that he plows up.

"Frame of reference" history [16] is of course the only kind that historians are allowed to write under a dictatorship, but they are not allowed to construct the frame. George Orwell's *Nineteen Eighty-Four* gives us a glance into the future. In that totalitarian England of his imagination—so horribly like certain regimes of today that it makes one shudder—the government keeps a corps of writers constantly at work writing new histories to replace the old, at every new turn of its policy. National figures associated with liberalism or democracy are either smeared, or, like Trotsky under the present Red regime, ignored as though they had never been.

Enough of what I do not believe. The positive task for the honest historian, I do believe, is to illuminate the past. He will inevitably try to answer some of the questions that contemporary society asks of the past, such as the causes of and prevention of war, the working of democracy under different sets of conditions and by various peoples, and the part that personality, climate, and environment play in determining events. But these considerations should be secondary in the historian's mind. After his main object of describing events "simply as they happened," his principal task is to *understand* the motives and objects of individuals and groups, even those that he personally dislikes, and to point out mistakes as well as achievements by persons and movements, even by those that he loves. In a word, he must preserve *balance*.

This principle of balance or proportion—what the French mean by *mesure*—is, I believe, the most valuable quality for a historian, after intellectual honesty. *Mesure* means, for instance, that you should not relate diplomatic history in a vacuum, confining your narrative to the exchange of notes, but try to discover the forces of economics, public opinion, and the like behind the foreign offices. *Mesure* means that in describing the humanitarian movement in the United States a century ago, you must at least refer to similar movements in other countries, which influenced ours. *Mesure* means that you can no longer write political history without considering social forces, or social history without describing political acts and conditions that translate aspirations into deeds, or naval history without touching on concomitant efforts of the ground and air forces. *Mesure* means that you should not write the history of an industry from the management point of view without considering labor; or a history of a labor union without considering the capitalist side. There is no royal road for a young historian to acquire a sense of balance, although a becoming humility toward his fellow workers, and skepticism directed toward himself as toward them, will be of assistance. It may be that a sense of balance and proportion is innate rather than acquired; possibly it may be patiently inculcated by a teacher who has it. That I do not pretend to know. But I do predict that no unbalanced history can live long; that in due time it will be a mere curiosity like those nasty antipapist and anti-Protestant tracts of the seventeenth century, which serve only to illustrate the partisan passions of the times.

Those partisan passions may not be ignored. Since the life of man, at least in his great moments, is emotional, prejudiced, and passionate, the historian should try to express some of the emotion, the prejudice, and the passion in his prose; and he must, through his imagination, enter to some extent into those feelings in order to portray them with

sympathetic warmth or appropriate indignation. He will have no difficulty in doing this if he approach his subject with verve and enthusiasm. Unless it be the dull pedantry of the average doctoral
dissertation in history, there is no quality more repugnant to readers
than a chilly impartiality.[17] Yet enthusiasm is no excuse for the historian going off balance. He should remind the reader that outcomes
were neither inevitable nor foreordained, but subject to a thousand
changes and chances. And if he records the passions of past times, he
must appease them as well by showing how the "pointers with pride"
were too complacent, and the "viewers with alarm" were too nervous;
how every winning cause had elements of evil, and every losing cause
had some kernel of good. He should be wary of numbers and statistics
and not fall into the common fallacy that "mostest" is more important
than "fustest," that the big battalions or the big production figures
inevitably make the decisions.

A historian owes respect to tradition and to folk memory; for "History is corrected and purified tradition, enlarged and analyzed
memory." Rosenstock-Huessy, in an address before this Association
in 1934 from which this dictum is quoted,[18] warned our profession
that we were losing our hold on the public through wanton and
unnecessary flouting of tradition. He meant not only the "debunkers"
but the historians who embraced dialectical materialism as an easy
explanation of past reality—which saved them a great deal of painful
thought. One result was the mass murder of historical characters.
Personality ceased to be important if statesmen were puppets of
economic and social forces; hence in many works written in the 1920's
and 1930's, there are no great men or leading characters, only
automata whose speeches, ideas, or aspirations are mentioned merely
to give the historian an opportunity to sneer or smear. Dialectical
materialism will admit no highmindedness, no virtue, no nobility
of character—unless on the part of a revolutionist. It made a great
appeal to young scholars, as perhaps was natural during those two
woeful decades, 1920–1940; yet none the less unfortunate. For the
"debunkers" and dialectical materialists, by robbing the people of
their heroes, by insulting their folk-memory of great figures whom

they admired, repelled men of good will from written history and turned other men, including many not of good will, to communism.

Dialectical materialists who did not go communist are now rather lonely. The age of "debunking" has passed; even Woodward, who coined the term, is dead; a new generation both here and in Europe is sounding and elucidating national and sectional traditions. But much harm was done, and little good. So, although it is less cogent today than fifteen years ago, I wish to repeat Rosenstock-Huessy's warning—historians, deal gently with your people's traditions! If you feel the urge to pull something apart, try your hand on a myth rather than a tradition. Some historical myths, like the Magna Carta one, were very useful in their day. Others, like Jamestown log cabins, Marcus Whitman's journey, or the exclusively Celtic composition of the Notre Dame football team, are harmless. But still others, like the Cavalier myth of Virginia, the forged letters of Washington and Franklin, the myth that the Pilgrim Fathers invented democracy and free enterprise, and the old "perfidious Albion" myth which still has currency, cater to regional *hubris* or racial prejudice, and need deflation.

Too rigid specialization is almost as bad for a historian's mind, and for his ultimate reputation, as too early an indulgence in broad generalization and synthesis. Everyone should, I believe, study something general or national in scope and something special or local; should do research on a remote period and on a contemporary period, and work on more than one type of history. The national field teaches you what to look for in local history; whilst intensive cultivation of grass-roots—or, as in my case, coral reefs and mudflats—teaches you things that you cannot see in the broad national view. Local history as a sideline also serves to integrate a historian with his community, to make him a valued and respected member of it, instead of "just another professor."

Contemporary history offers many pitfalls, and poses more and different problems than eras long past; as I know very well, after jumping from 1492 to 1942. There is an advantage in writing about admirals like Columbus who cannot answer back! Yet, my recent venture into contemporary naval history has been rich in experience and has taught me much. For one thing, I no longer have the reverence for documents that I once had, or the distrust for oral sources that I was once taught. Military documents vary in value as their writers know the truth and try honestly to tell what really happened; one could not get along without them, but one must check them, not only against the enemy's documents but by the oral testimony of participants, provided always it be fresh; for "the strongest memory is weaker than the palest ink." [19]

Participation in naval actions has taught me a greater tolerance of the mistakes of naval commanders than I could have entertained if I had fought the war in Washington. One has to experience the noise and confusion of battle to appreciate how difficult it is for the responsible commander to estimate a fluid situation correctly, and to make the right decision under pressure. And, although Tolstoy exaggerated the role of chance and denied the role of intellect in warfare, both are present. A sailor's opportunity for fame, or even for survival, often depends on a fortunate shot, or on a decision that was wrong in view of what he did know, yet right in view of the factors that he could not grasp. The planner of operations, in modern war, is just as important as the men who execute the plans; military planning calls for intellectual qualities of the highest order.

Fashions in history are constantly changing. Back in the 1930's few publishers would take a source book on American history. Since 1945 a spate of "liberty documents" and the like are competing for adoptions, and for the tedium of required readers. There is now a seller's market in early Americana—colonial history, folklore, early westerns, and the like—and I wish that more of our members would take advantage of it instead of letting journalists and novelists rake in the cash. There is a decided change of attitude toward our past, a friendly, almost affectionate attitude, as contrasted with the cynical, almost hateful one of young intellectuals twenty-five years ago. At that time Kenneth Murdock and I were voices crying in the wilderness against the common notion of the grim Puritan painted by

J. Truslow Adams and other popular historians of the day: the steeple-hatted, long-faced Puritan living in a log cabin and planning a witch-hunt or a battue of Quakers as a holiday·diversion. That picture has given way to one of the jolly Puritan sitting in a little frame house furnished with early American furniture, silverware and pewter, one arm around a pretty Priscilla and the other reaching for a jug of hard cider. Twenty years ago it was difficult to get any hearing for our denial that English colonists in general and Puritans in particular were hostile to the arts; now we have to discourage students from comparing a tavern-sign portrait of George II to a Romney, or going into ecstasies over the beautiful "functionalism" of a seventeenth century Connecticut hog-yoke.

Fifty years ago, it was difficult to find any general history of the United States that did not present the Federalist-Whig-Republican point of view, or express a very dim view of all Democratic leaders except Cleveland. This fashion has completely changed; it would be equally difficult today to find a good general history of the United States that did not follow the Jefferson-Jackson-F. D. Roosevelt line. That, I confess, is my own approach. I was converted to it, forty years ago, by doing my first piece of intensive research on New England Federalism, and discovering that the "wise and good and rich," whom Fisher Ames thought should rule the nation, were stupid, narrow-minded, and local in their outlook compared with the Republicans. I still believe that the Jeffersonian "line" is the one that the main stream of United States "actuality" has followed, just as British "actuality" is best explained by historians who write in the Whig-Liberal-Labour tradition. But I also believe that there has been alto-gether too much of it, and that the present situation is unbalanced and unhealthy, tending to create a sort of neoliberal stereotype.[20] We need a United States history written from a sanely conservative point of view, like Keith Feiling's recent *History of England*. But we do not want nostalgic histories that merely invoke an impossible return to the policies and conditions of some past era. For, as every classicist knows, the Stoic doctrine of recurrence impelled the political scientists and statesmen of Rome "to seek solutions for the ever more complex problems of Roman civilization by abortive effort to rejuvenate the virtues, and to reenact the policies, of the past."[21] Frustration and failure will attend any American historian who tries to do that; but fame and success await one who will make a fresh distillation of our entire history, with the conservative tradition acting as the leaven.

Social history exhibits a similar uninventiveness, for it seems very difficult for social historians to describe anything but improvements, as they move on from decade to decade. But the main ill of American social historians is indigestion. You cannot include everything from wonder-working providences to badly working plumbing; better leave the one to Edward Johnson and the other to the Quennells. Social history puts a greater strain on literary expression and on the sense of balance than any other kind. Hitherto the novelists have been very much better at writing it than the historians. We need to improve our human perception as well as our literary style if we expect to be the teachers of social history that, for instance, Marcel Proust was and Conrad Richter is. Historians notably lack the talent at description which novelists have developed to a high degree; Prescott had it, of course, and Parkman; but you can count on the fingers of one hand the American historians now writing who can describe a scene, an event, or a natural setting in such a way that the reader can see it. (The reason is largely that the writer cannot see it himself; he sits in a library and writes instead of going about by whatever means of transportation is available, and finding out for himself what historic sites look like today.) Then, too, some social historians forget that history is a *story* that moves; they divorce their subject altogether from the main stream of political history, giving it no context and no time. In the Western countries, political and constitutional history must always be the skeleton on which any other kind of history is hung; and if you are concerned over the decay of liberty, you should be also concerned lest political and constitutional history fall into desuetude. The American historian of architecture, education, labor, medicine, or any other social subject, should have a sense of chronology and not apply to 1850 the standards of 1950, or ignore the context and attendant circumstances of ideas, principles, and events that he may consider abominable.

Although the present conception of history as the sum total of all aspects of human activity has vastly complicated and increased the burdens of the general historian, he must accept the challenge. He should welcome, and must do his best to read and grasp, the flood of monographs that the presses are issuing on social-history subjects. He must do his best to apply to history the principles that the sociologists are painfully (and usually in horrible English) working out in human relations. He must admit that there is a vast amount to do in the social history of any Western country, with the whole of Asia opening up new fields to Western historians.

Although the magnitude of work before you younger historians, and the conditions under which you may have to perform it, are appalling, you are nevertheless to be envied. For the world has revolved to one of those "seasons, in human affairs," in the words of William Ellery Channing 120 years ago, "of inward and outward revolution, when new depths seem to be broken up in the soul, when new wants are unfolded in multitudes, and a new and undefined good is thirsted for." [22] The times are your challenge; what will be your response? The historical profession will have little use for timid pedants, whose ambition goes no farther than to get a firm footing on one of the lower steps of the academic escalator, proceeding painlessly from one professorial grade to another until overtaken by death and oblivion. It wants men and women of courage as well as of honesty and balance. A historical career can be a great adventure, and not in ideas alone; witness the lives of Bolton and Trevelyan, men who write history that sings to the heart while it informs the understanding. A historian's life may be filled with conflict, not only the relatively clean fighting of armed forces but the dirty fighting of political campaigns and congressional investigations. We want more bold and positive characters to enter the profession.

Finally, a bit of advice nineteen centuries old, which St. Paul offered to all the faithful of Ephesus, but which seems particularly applicable to historians: "Henceforth walk not as other Gentiles walk, in the vanity of their mind, having the understanding darkened, being alienated from the life of God through the ignorance that is in them, because of the blindness of their heart." Seek guidance from the Author of all lights, of all history, "and be renewed in the spirit of your mind." [23] Or, as St. Thomas Aquinas put it, in his noble prayer for a scholar, "Grant me sharpness in understanding, sagacity in interpretation, facility in learning, and abundant grace in expression."

With honesty of purpose, balance, a respect for tradition, courage, and, above all, a philosophy of life, any young person who embraces the historical profession will find it rich in rewards and durable in satisfaction.

Such is the substance of my faith; and if I were to sum up my credo in a single word, it would be that proud motto of Fustel de Coulanges, *Quaero*—I seek to learn.

NOTES

[1] Preface to 1st ed. (1824) of *Geschichte der Romanischen und Germanischen Völker* (3rd ed., Leipzig, 1885), p. vii. The whole sentence in which this appears, is: *"Man hat der Historie das Amt, die Vergangenheit zu richten, die Mitwelt zum Nutzen zukünftiger Jahre zu belehren, beigemessen: so hoher Aemter unterwindet sich gegenwärtiger Versuch nicht: er will blos zeigen, wie es eigentlich gewesen."* "People have given History the function of judging the past, to serve the world for the instruction of years to come; but nothing beyond the present investigation will be attempted here—it will simply explain the event exactly as it happened."

[2] Quoted in Benedetto Croce, *History as the Story of Liberty* (Sprigge trans., New York 1941), p. 89.

[3] *Peloponnesian War* i.22; in part Crawley's translation, in part Jowett's.

[4] F. M. Cornford, writing of Thucydides, in *The Unwritten Philosophy and Other Essays* (1950), p. 1.

[5] Laurence L. Howe, "Historical Method and Legal Education," American Assoc. Univ. Professors *Bulletin*, XXVII (1950), 353.

[6] Benedetto Croce has often been quoted as writing, "All history is contemporary history." What he did write is: "The practical requirements which underlie every historical judgment give to all history the character of 'contemporary history' because, however remote in time events there

recounted may seem to be, the history in reality refers to present needs and present situations wherein those events vibrate." *History as the Story of Liberty*, p. 19.

[7] *History: Its Purposes and Method* (1949), p. 154.

[8] His presidential address at Urbana, 1933; printed in *American Historical Review*, XXXIX (January, 1934), 219.

[9] *Ibid.*, p. 226.

[10] "The World as I Want It," *Forum*, June, 1934, p. 333.

[11] Richard Hofstadter, "Beard and the Constitution: The History of an Idea," *American Quarterly*, II (Fall, 1950).

[12] *Panegyricus*, 51–52.

[13] My own review of this book is in *Atlantic Monthly*, CLXXXII (August, 1948), 91; see also Herbert Feis, *The Road to Pearl Harbor: The Coming of the War between the United States and Japan* (Princeton, 1950); Basil Rauch, *Roosevelt: From Munich to Pearl Harbor* (New York, 1950).

[14] *Jean Christophe*, VII (*Dans la maison*, 26th ed.), 236.

[15] *The Use of Words in Reasoning* (London, 1901), p. 233.

[16] Renier, p. 219, calls it "A Priorism," and has a good succinct statement of its dangers.

[17] George M. Trevelyan, "Bias in History," *An Autobiography and Other Essays* (London and New York, 1949), p. 78.

[18] "The Predicament of History," *Journal of Philosophy*, XXXII (Feb. 14, 1935), 3.

[19] Title of an article by Capt. Ralph C. Parker USN in *U. S. Naval Institute Proceedings*, LXXVI (January, 1950), 59.

[20] Peter Viereck, "Babbitt Revisited," *Harvard Alumni Bulletin*, June 24, 1950.

[21] Reinhold Niebuhr, *Faith and History* (New York, 1949), p. 21.

[22] "Essay on the Union [1829]," in *Works* (1886 ed.), p. 641.

[23] Ephesians iv: 17–18, 23.

ALLAN NEVINS (1890–) AND THE ART OF BIOGRAPHY

The professionalization of history-writing meant a domination by academicians who were too often unskilled in literary craftsmanship. Allan Nevins is a delightful exception. He began life on a farm in central Illinois, took two degrees at the University of Illinois (but never bothered about a Ph.D.), taught English, and then turned to journalism. He wrote a history of his alma mater in 1917 and served as an editorial writer for the *New York Evening Post,* publishing in 1922 an outstanding history of that paper, in which he used extensive manuscript as well as newspaper sources. In 1927 he was invited to contribute a volume in the *History of American Life* series, entitled *The Emergence of Modern America, 1865–78,* a successful effort in social history. In 1931, after years of free-lance writing and part-time teaching, he became a professor of American history at Columbia University.

Nevins regards biography as a most revealing phase of history and literature, of life itself, but his forte is of the life and times tradition in which character, morals, and personality rather than psychological analysis predominate. He wrote two biographies of Frémont (1928, 1939), an authorized biography of Henry White (1930), and a solid biography of Grover Cleveland (1932) dealing with the great issues of his day. In 1940 he embarked upon an intensive and fascinating biography of Rockefeller and later issued two volumes (partly in collaboration) on Henry Ford. He has gone far beyond the earlier business biographers in the use of archival sources and personal correspondence. Many critics consider him an economic conservative. Yet he has certainly never been anti-labor, even though he does like to dwell upon the technological contributions of the great tycoons.

Especially significant are his extraordinarily successful efforts to parallel the multi-volume series of James Ford Rhodes, using fresh sources and the most recent authorities. These volumes, which are far better written than those of Rhodes, include *Ordeal of the Union,* *Emergence of Lincoln,* and *The War for the Union,* each in two volumes. He explained the Civil War as a consequence of not only slavery but of the race issue, unlike Rhodes who stressed slavery alone, or the "revisionists" who thought that emotional conflicts were primary factors. Going beyond Rhodes in one major aspect, he gave considerable attention to social and cultural history, integrating this story with the general theme.

The Gateway to History

BIOGRAPHY AND HISTORY *

The biographer appeared on the stage of letters hand in hand with the historian; hand in hand they walk there still. Biography may be termed a form of history—a form applied not to nations or groups of people, but to the single man or woman; history is certainly from one point of view a compound of innumerable biographies. All study of the past, whether for pleasure, instruction, or moral growth, must be based upon a reading of both history and biography, and it is a poor literary prescription which demands one at the expense of the other. While some men have a preference for life in general, and some for *the* life of the individual, each so illustrates the other that neither can be put aside. The commemorative instinct of mankind found expression in biography as early as in history, and very nearly as vigorously. In the Bible, the story of Noah, the story of Abraham,

Pages 318–41 (D. C. Heath, 1938). Reprinted by permission of D. C. Heath of Boston.

the story of Isaac, and above all the story of Joseph (its length considered, almost a model biography), belong to the category of lives rather than history. Xenophon's *Memoirs of Socrates* is not in strict form a biography, being a defence of the philosopher against his defamers, but in its effect it is a brief biographical masterpiece. During the first century of the Christian era Plutarch produced a book which has ever since been "a pasturage of great minds," his parallel lives of forty-six Greek and Roman heroes; and in the second century Suetonius wrote his untrustworthy but unforgettable *Lives of the Twelve Caesars*. Since the birth of modern memoir-writing in France and Britain, since Rohan and De Retz, Walton's *Lives* and Fuller's *Worthies,* biography has been an even more fecund mother of books than history, and has yielded as many masterpieces.

Like history, biography has its overtones and undertones. It is more than a literary recreation, more than a portrait-gallery of striking faces, more than a study which makes the past vivid with personalities. As H. H. Asquith said: "It brings comfort, it enlarges sympathy, it expels selfishness, it quickens aspiration." But the principal reason for its fascination to many readers may be stated in a sentence: It humanizes the past, while at the same time it enriches the present by showing us life with a vividness and completeness that few men experience in life itself. Particularly in recent decades the biographical approach to history has become the principal highroad in that field. For every man who reads a history of the Civil War, there are probably ten who read lives of Lincoln, Jefferson Davis, Grant, or Lee; for every man who reads a history of the Tudors, there are probably ten who read lives of Queen Elizabeth or Henry VIII. In English and American literature the greatest publishing successes of the first third of the twentieth century, apart from fiction, lay in biography and autobiography. Now and then a volume of history, such as H. G. Wells's *Outline,* rose to a mass-circulation, but far more frequently the vogue lay with a work like Strachey's *Queen Victoria,* Beveridge's life of John Marshall, Emil Ludwig's *Napoleon,* the autobiography of Henry Adams, the memoirs of Lloyd George. Many of the historical works which did attain a wide circulation had been cast in a form closely akin to biography, one or two personalities dominating such books as Maurois's *The Edwardian Era* and Claude G. Bowers's *Jefferson and Hamilton*. To men who lack imagination, history is difficult to visualize, while biography brings them the past in concrete, real, and vivid terms. To men who have known little of life or dwelt in narrow environments, history is often a meaningless confusion, while the reading of a series of biographies holds out all the richness that human existence can present.

Because biography humanizes the past and enriches personal experience of the present in a way that history can seldom do, its continued popularity is certain. It is perfectly valid to argue that the personal element in the past is less important than the communal element; that the cultural tendencies of any period, its great economic forces, its governmental forms and traditions, its social fabric, are in general more potent than the actions of any single man or coterie. The ordinary reader will readily admit this. But he will assert that what he most readily understands, and what interests him most strongly, is the play of personality in history; that he likes to view the past as a swift drama, with the principal figures of the dramatis personae strongly lighted up. Those economic forces, those governmental institutions, those cultural traditions and ideas, he will say, are interesting to me chiefly as elements against which the figures of the drama contend or which they use to achieve their victories. I prefer to select some eminent person as protagonist, and observe how he wrestles with these elements; to learn whether his talents and energy are more than a match for them, or whether he allows himself to be conquered by rival men and adverse social forces. Having said this, the lay reader (not, we hope, the student) respectfully lays aside the history of England in the nineteenth century, and opens Morley's life of Gladstone.

It is a defensible position for the general reader; and, in answering the chief objections to it, three arguments may be offered for biography as an approach to history. It may be objected that biography tends to oversimplify the past; that it invites us to scrutinize the Reformation, the Napoleonic era, or the American Civil War with reference to the ideas and acts of a single man. But the lay student of history will reply that, since the full history of the Reformation, the Napoleonic era, or the Civil War is too vast and complex to be comprehended without great effort—since it overloads the memory and fatigues the attention—a certain amount of simplification is a virtue. It is better to take a well-laid road through a rough and diversified country than to explore every square mile. Again, it may be objected that the biographical approach to history is always subjective and frequently biassed; that instead of trying to view events impartially, the biographer of necessity presents them as colored by the ideas, emotions, and interests of his hero. But the reader may reply that biography at its best is hardly more biassed than history at its best; that he can make allowance for any natural sympathy with the subject of the biography; and that he is more than compensated for any bias by the increased vividness of the personal view. Impersonal history, he will declare, is too often history robbed of all color and immediacy. When I read a general description of Waterloo I am not particularly thrilled. But when, approaching the climax of Philip Guedalla's *Wellington,* I sit with the Duke on his hill while the tall bearskins of the Guard follow Ney to break against the British squares, my heart is sick with suspense, and I rise from watching the pursuit roll away with a new sense of the reality of history. When I read Pepys's account of the great fire in London—how he lay in a boat on the Thames, shedding tears as he watched the deep red flames destroy the wealth and pride of the city—I feel that spectacle far more keenly than any general record. I would rather have less impartiality and more personal emotion.

The third objection to the biographical approach to history is that it offers no understanding of mass action or social law. The objection is of course irrefutable, and presents a firm basis for our contention that history should always be combined with biography. But, assuming such a combination, defenders of biography can point out that it supplies its unique element no less than history. It furnishes a knowledge of individual psychology just as history furnishes a knowledge of social motives and actions. As history invites us to study the race or mass, biography invites us to explore the mind and heart of man; it, and still more autobiography, lays bare the will and emotions in relation to events and environment. "Personality was Plutarch's quarry"—and has since been the goal of every good biographer. How can we understand the past without understanding in detail the psychology of its principal agents? What is the Reformation without Luther, Calvin, and Knox? How can we comprehend these three without listening to their table talk, reading their letters, hearing the anecdotes which illustrate their character? It would be going too far to take the advice of Disraeli, who made the father of Contarini Fleming counsel his son: "Read the memoirs of Cardinal de Retz, the life of Richelieu, everything about Napoleon; read works of that kind. Read no history, nothing but biography, for that is life without theory." But, says the general reader, good biography, recreating the individual, does give us one set of psychological truths for which history has not the time or space. The two are complementary; each is essential.

Even the sociologist, who deprecates emphasis on the individual and calls for ever-greater attention to social and economic elements, must admit the force of these arguments. Herbert Spencer presents a balanced view in his *Principles of Ethics*. After registering his objections to the great-man theory of history, "tacitly held by the ignorant in all ages," and declaring that the impersonal elements of the past should chiefly occupy our attention, he goes on to say that some study should be given to personal elements. "While no information concerning kings and popes, and ministers and generals, even when joined to exhaustive acquaintance with intrigues and treaties, battles and sieges, gives any insight into the laws of social evolution—while the single fact that division of labor has been progressing in all advancing nations regardless of the wills of lawmakers, and unobserved by them, suffices to show that the forces which mould society work out their results apart from, and often in spite of, the aims of leading men; yet a certain moderate number of leading men and their actions may properly be contemplated. The past stages in human progress, which everyone should know something about, would be conceived in too shadowy a form if wholly divested of ideas of the persons and events associated with them. Moreover, some amount of such knowledge is requisite to enlarge adequately the conception of human nature in general—to show the extreme, occasionally good but mostly bad, which it is capable of reaching." If this statement can be questioned, it is only because it is too grudging and allows too little to biography.

For Spencer does not state adequately the historical values of biography—quite apart from its literary and moral values. Biography is useful, as we have said, as a means of breaking down the complexity of wide movements and crowded periods into parts sufficiently simple to be readily grasped and long retained. It is useful as a means of gaining a vivid insight into past conditions of life; still more useful in drenching past events with some poignancy of personal emotion. It is valuable as a gallery of portraits, a presentation of character in history. It is generally agreed that biography in the English tongue is richer and has reached greater heights than in other languages; that Boswell's *Johnson*, Lockhart's *Scott*, Froude's *Carlyle*, Morley's *Gladstone*, Albert Bigelow Paine's *Mark Twain*, and Beveridge's *John Marshall* have hardly been equalled by French and German biographers. The reason beyond question lies in the deep-rooted individualism of the English-speaking peoples, a race especially rich in character. Biography is valuable, again, as a means of understanding the psychology of past generations of men. Its best examples lay bare the man's inner soul and explain the motives back of human actions with a finesse that the pen of history, drawing bolder, cruder strokes, cannot match. Particularly instructive in this respect are those great autobiographies which give us authentic human documents, divested of all self-consciousness; books like Cellini's, Rousseau's, Benjamin Franklin's, Aksakov's, John Stuart Mill's, and Anthony Trollope's. Finally, biography is valuable as a study of one important form of historical force—for we cannot question the fact that some historic personages have been sufficiently powerful to constitute each a great force in himself. Caesar was a force; Mohammed was a force; Luther was a force; Napoleon was a force. Mussolini, remarking that "I am not a man but an event," would have us believe that he is a force. Still other men, by no means so powerful, have at least been typical of an age and worth studying because they embody so many of its characteristics. Cobden was not in himself a great force, but was admirably representative of the force called Manchester Liberalism. Mazzini, though not a great force, was typical of one entire side of European nationalism.

II

But if biography is well worth studying, only the best biography deserves any sustained attention; and what is the best? Boswell remarked: "Biography occasions a degree of trouble far beyond that of any other species of literary composition"—and it is true that a world of pains must go to the making of any really excellent life of a man. Biography in the modern sense did not appear in the English language until Izaak Walton, beginning in 1640, produced that collection of works known as *The Lives of Dr. John Donne, Sir Henry Wotton, Mr. Richard Hooker, Mr. George Herbert, and Dr. Robert Sanderson.* Even this was not strictly modern biography; he wished to edify a little, to amuse a little, above all to collect and present enough of the acts and virtues of departed friends to save them from oblivion, and he was more eulogist than biographer. Nevertheless, he showed simplicity, genuineness, and vividness, while his use of letters and anecdotes (as in the tale of Donne and the apparition of his wife and dead child) to illustrate character was admirable. Fuller's *Worthies* and John Aubrey's *Minutes of Lives* also evinced an understanding of the personal element essential to good biography. The same element is likewise prominent in Mrs. Lucy Hutchinson's *Memoirs of the Life of Colonel Hutchinson,* written about 1670; a book interesting to historians for its light on the Roundhead side of the English Civil War, but more interesting to general readers for the vividness of its courtship scenes, the pungency of its dialogue, and the pathos of its detailed description of the colonel's imprisonment and death. We all know how highly Charles Lamb thought of the Duchess of Newcastle's intimate biography of her husband—"No casket is rich enough . . . to honour . . . such a jewel."

But as the first great archetypes of modern history appeared in the eighteenth century, so did those of modernized biography. It is customary, after due obeisance to Dr. Johnson's *Life of Richard Savage,* to point to William Mason's *Life and Letters of Thomas Gray* (1774) as breaking the old moulds and bringing in a freer, fuller, more truthful form. Mason had the happy idea, never before really used by any writer, of telling the story of Gray's life by means of his letters, with a ribbon of editorial narrative. Unfortunately, he used but a small part of the letters and papers he collected, while he grossly tampered with the correspondence, altering, transposing, omitting, and redating at his own sweet will. Boswell enormously improved upon Mason's example when he published his life of Dr. Samuel Johnson in 1791. With justice he boasted that he had shown Johnson as no man had ever been shown in a book before, and had "Johnsonized the land." This prince of all biographers was, if not a great man, at least a natural artist, with a quick and sure instinct for obtaining the best materials and making the best use of them. To live, talk, and breathe with his subject, "to become strongly impregnated with the Johnsonian aether," to treasure every detail which added to the completeness and truth of the portrait, in the conviction that "every little spark adds something to the general blaze"—this was his method. For the first time the world found in a biography a photographic—nay, a cinematic—delineation of an arresting personality by a minute observer who used dialogue, letters, anecdotes, and a thousand trifles as well as great acts and events to fill out his portrait. After Boswell, the recipe was open to all. Southey's lives of Nelson and Wesley struck the true note again; Lockhart's magnificent life of Scott (1837-38) came near equalling the performance of Bozzy; Stanhope's four-volume life of Pitt brought in the long series of distinguished political biographies.

The chief requirement of a really good biography is that it recreate an individual, convincing the reader that he lived, moved, spoke, and enjoyed a certain set of human attributes. We must not merely be shown what he did, but what he was, and why he was that kind of man. In other words, his inner soùl, or at least his personality, must be revealed. The task is obviously more difficult with well-balanced, self-contained, and reticent personalities than with those which present deeply-stamped traits and picturesque eccentricities. Irving, who in his life of George Washington produced the first great American biography, faced a far more baffling undertaking than Boswell; the first President was notable for the harmony of his traits, the iron restraint of his will, and the smooth dignity of his private and public appearances. Nevertheless, some of Irving's successors, notably Paul Leicester Ford in *The True George Washington,* succeeded in penetrating to the inner springs of Washington's personality. In general, the portraiture of personality is easier in dealing with literary men than with political, military, or business leaders, because the former usually have richer minds, and almost always have been more articulate, more self-expressive; they have written more letters and more autobiographical passages, have figured in more anecdotes. It is no accident that the best English biographies are of writers: Boswell's *Johnson,* Lockhart's *Scott,* Froude's *Carlyle,* Trevelyan's *Macaulay,* Forster's *Dickens.* It is no accident that the richest American biography is Albert Bigelow Paine's *Mark Twain.* But even when a character has lineaments as strongly marked as those of Walter Savage Landor, Andrew Jackson, or Bismarck, even when a wealth of personalia exists, to seize upon the main elements of character is a task demanding the highest talents—a task that can be executed with perfection only by something like genius.

For personality is an elusive matter, and the best indications of character are often so subtle that they escape all but the keenest observers. What is a man's soul? How can his motives be disentangled? How can his acts be generalized? Perhaps personality, whether developing, static, or deliquescent, is primarily the sum of a man's habits. A kindly man has the habit of doing kindly acts, an avaricious man the habit of avaricious acts, an arrogant man the habit of arrogant acts. But the biographer must realize that cruel men may

occasionally do benevolent deeds, a kindly man may once or twice
commit a cruel action; that the rogue may meet some compelling
crisis with an honest act, like Sidney Carton walking to the guillo-
tine, while the honest man may wreck himself, as Lord Jim did, by
a single base deed. An American who gave long years to searching
men's hearts, Gamaliel Bradford, has written: "The most minute
study, the widest experience in the investigation of human actions and
their motives, only make us feel more and more the shifting, terrible
uncertainty of the ground under our feet." The keenest perception
must be allied with the most rigorous honesty in using the scalpel.
Not merely must no significant detail be overlooked, in the spirit of
Plutarch's remark that "an act of small note, a short saying, a jest,
will distinguish the real character better than the greatest sieges and
most decisive battles." Insight must be applied to these details. It was
Bradford who observed how much the taciturn Robert E. Lee had
revealed of his character in his pregnant remark at Fredericksburg:
"It is well that war is so terrible, or else we should grow too fond
of it."

Yet biography must do a great deal more than recreate a personality. Essayists, like Sainte-Beuve in his *Monday Chats*, Gamaliel
Bradford in his psychographs, and Lord Bryce in *Studies in Contemporary Biography*, can sometimes vividly evoke a character. They
can limn a rapid, arresting portrait which reveals essential traits like
a miniature by Isabey. But this is far from sufficient. Dr. Johnson wisely
remarked that "a character is not a life"; that "a character furnishes
so little detail, that scarcely anything is distinctly known, but all is
shown confused and enlarged through a mist."

A good biography must also present as complete, accurate, and
unbiassed an account of the deeds and experiences of its subject as
can be executed; provided, of course, that the completeness does not
extend to impertinent and tiresome detail. Most great biographies
have been planned on full, copious lines. In Lockhart's *Scott*, Froude's
Carlyle, Morley's *Gladstone*, Monypenny and Buckle's *Disraeli*, Nicolay and Hay's *Lincoln*, Beveridge's *Marshall*, and Baker's *Woodrow
Wilson*, exhaustive research was applied to establish and record every

useful fact. Douglas Freeman gave twenty years to his *Robert E. Lee* to make every part of the four volumes as nearly definitive as possible. Men of lesser stature than the heroes just named can of course be dismissed more briefly; four volumes on Martin Van Buren or Calvin Coolidge would be ridiculous, as would even two volumes on a career so devoid of external incident as Edward Fitzgerald's or Emily Dickinson's. But in steering the middle course between meagreness and redundancy, the biographer has most to fear from the former. The lives of important men are often so eventful and rich that justice cannot be done them in narrow compass; details are essential to *vitality;* and traits must be illustrated again and again before their force can be grasped. The hurried or indolent reader may think an outline life of Walter Scott or John Marshall—such as John Buchan and E. S. Corwin have ably provided—quite adequate; but the impression made by such brief volumes rapidly fades, while that left by immersion in the full stream of narrative, anecdote, letters, utterances, and comment provided by Lockhart and Beveridge is permanent. A great biography is a creation on the symphonic or operatic order, not a lyric.

To make a biography factually accurate is materially easier, especially in dealing with recent figures, than to make it unbiassed. Voltaire was quite just in saying, "We owe consideration to the living; to the dead we owe truth alone." But in addition to all the forms of bias which may injure history, biographical work is subject to some cankerworms peculiarly its own. The most frequent and striking is the family bias. The papers of great men are usually held after death by widows, children, or other close relatives. Not a few important biographies have been written by sons (Alfred Tennyson, Nathaniel Hawthorne); by widows (Charles Kingsley); by widowers (George Eliot); by daughters (Julia Ward Howe); by sons-in-law (Scott, William Cullen Bryant); by daughters-in-law (Joel Chandler Harris); by brothers (Longfellow); by nephews (Washington Irving); and by assorted relatives (William Lloyd Garrison). It is unnecessary to say that all the figures just named were presented as faultless—some as archangels. Pierre M. Irving, to draw a portrait of his uncle as faithful to the memory of Matilda Hoffman until death, suppressed the evidence of his courtship of other women. Of course it is more frequent for the family to consign its papers to some literary man for the preparation of a life, but this is too often done with express or implied conditions. Mr. Burton J. Hendrick's *Carnegie* barely hints that the ironmaster had one small fault, vanity; many "authorized" biographies are of necessity equally eulogistic. The obstacles which widows in particular throw before honest biography sometimes inspire a wish for the revival of *suttee*. One of the last acts of Robert Louis Stevenson's widow was to suppress a book which revealed certain facts about the novelist which a few years later were far more frankly related by others.

Closely allied with this impediment is the bias of official or social decorum. The "authorized" biographer of a man of high station is frequently moved by a false sense of propriety to suppress or color his evidence. He shows his figure in the most dignified light; he omits matter which would reflect on living men. A more sensible attitude was taken by Carlyle when Froude, preparing Mrs. Carlyle's letters for publication, asked whether he had not better exclude some sharp criticisms of a public man still living. Carlyle rejoined that it "would do the public personage no harm to know what a sensible woman thought of him." But some Americans would think it highly improper to publish an incident, however authentic, which reflected discredit on George Washington; many Southerners would think it treason to print anything which derogated from Robert E. Lee's merit. Still another distortion common in biography is what Sir Leslie Stephen called the ethical or edificatory bias—the desire to use a life as an improving example. Nearly all ecclesiastical biographies fall under this disability. When Archdeacon Hare wrote the life of his onetime curate, John Sterling, he treated it as a tragedy of spiritual torment, a spectacle of the misery caused by religious doubt. Carlyle, who knew that Sterling's life was not tragic and who honored his honest skepticism, retorted by a biography which has become classic. The biographer's business is to tell the truth about Lincoln and Poe, not to use them respectively to illustrate the glories of patriotism and the woes of intemperance.

Finally, one indispensable requirement of a good biography is that it carefully relate the man it treats to history—that it define his position and significance in the broad stream of events. Obviously this is a requirement which historians will most of all emphasize. They know full well that much of their material first reaches them through biographical and autobiographical channels. American history from 1910 to 1920, for example, could not be written with any approach to completeness until the papers of Taft, Theodore Roosevelt, Woodrow Wilson, Bryan, Lansing, Baker, and numerous others had become available. In no instance were these papers released to general historians until biographic use had been made of them, while in several instances they were withheld even after the biographies appeared. It was therefore important to history that the biographies be full; but it was also important to biography. Critics who take a purely literary view sometimes deplore the tendency to write books which treat the "lives and times" of eminent men; the times, they declare, should be omitted, the writer confining himself to the depiction of personality and the recital of acts and thoughts. But to this the historian could never consent, and the biographer never should. Every life is to a great extent a reflection of—a response to, or a reaction against—the conditions of its time, whether political, economic, literary, or artistic. And no biography succeeds unless it brings out the import of every life to its own generation and those which follow. A memoir of Howells, Meredith, or Anatole France must relate him accurately and expertly to American, English, or French literature—and to the social life of his own land; a biography of Cleveland, Peel, or Gambetta must relate him to every contemporaneous turn of national politics. This cannot be done by a few brief allusions.

The demand for spare and stripped lives would deprive us of the great panoramic biographies like Morley's *Gladstone*, Monypenny and Buckle's *Disraeli*, J. L. Garvin's *Chamberlain*, Gardiner's *Harcourt*, Spender's *Campbell-Bannerman*, Ronaldshay's *Curzon;* of the

six volumes of David Alec Wilson's *Carlyle,* the three of W. L.
Cross's *Fielding;* of Freeman's *Lee,* Nicolay and Hay's *Lincoln,* and
Baker's *Woodrow Wilson.* Some of these neither biography nor history could well spare. It may be true that a certain amount of repetition is involved in long biographies; that readers of the lives of Gladstone, Disraeli, Harcourt, and Chamberlain get the Home Rule quarrel four times over, and readers of biographies of Cleveland, Blaine,
McKinley, and Aldrich four treatments of the tariff. But the repetition in good biography is slight. What is a common denominator of
knowledge can be very briefly summarized; for the rest, the reader
studies Home Rule or the tariff under four lights, from four points of
view, each with its own novelty. None of the multitude of intelligent
users of Morley's *Gladstone* and Buckle's *Disraeli* has ever complained of irksome duplication; rather, they have been surprised to
find how unlike the same issues appear when seen from opposed
sides. To be sure, in treating the "times" of a hero all that is irrelevant
to his career should be omitted. This Nicolay and Hay's old-fashioned
biography, essentially a history of the Civil War, does not do; but the
younger biographers named above commit no such error. The day
that the "life and times" expires and all biographies are reduced to
one volume, that day the full-bodied, vigorous, convincing presentation of distinguished men, so depicted that we can walk all around
them and see them in their natural surroundings, will be dealt a fatal
blow.

III

The mistaken demand for briefer, sketchier lives is connected with
the emergence of a so-called New Biography, which André Maurois
tells us first originated about 1910. From one point of view, there was
less novelty in the short biography fixing its attention upon character
alone and presenting personality by a few sharp strokes than its prac-
titioners supposed. Gamaliel Bradford had been anticipated in general fashion by Plutarch, and much more directly by Sainte-Beuve,
who was great less as a literary critic than as an exquisitely finished
painter of the chief intellectual figures of France. In England a "new

biography" had been born soon after 1850, when the scientific spirit was gaining ground fast and Darwin, Huxley, and Spencer had affected all thought. Realism was coming into fiction; sculptors, ceasing to drape their statesmen in togas, were putting them into honest trousers. In biography the result of the new spirit was seen in such books as John Morley's *Voltaire,* his *Burke,* his *Rousseau,* and his *Cobden,* works of a type not previously known in English. He abandoned chronological outlines, fixed his attention upon the inner man, and adopted oblique methods of portraiture. A rigidly critical attitude, avoiding all attempt at panegyric, permitted a keener insight. Froude in several brief biographies, notably his *Erasmus* and *Caesar,* used a similarly incisive approach and drew a sharply-outlined portrait with great economy. These works were realistic without being irreverent or iconoclastic.

Yet a still newer biography was unquestionably born from the travail of the World War years, and was closely connected with changes in the spirit of the age.* The principal agent in introducing it to the world was Lytton Strachey, who scored so brilliant a success in 1918 with *Eminent Victorians.* The date was significant. In that quietly caustic work he registered his protest against the idealization of the past, against the hero-worship which still characterized so much biography and history. His attack on the Victorian era was the voice of a great disillusion, and fell upon the world in the bitterest year of disillusion in modern history. Mr. Strachey directed his readers' gaze at four heroic pieces of statuary—General Gordon, Arnold of Rugby, Florence Nightingale, Cardinal Manning—and by a deft twirl of the pedestal showed the seamed and pitted brass, the hollow artificiality of the image. With artistic skill he demonstrated that much of seeming greatness is after all mere pomposity; that the Carlylean heroes who pretended to compel the clouds and direct the lightning were after all mere puppets jerked by the great social and economic forces, by fate, or by their own passions. He was happy in his moment. A world looking at Clemenceau, Lloyd George, and

---

* Be it noted that Georg Brandes's incisive works on Goethe, Nietzsche, Voltaire, Caesar, Michelangelo, and Heine all followed 1910.

Sonnino was quite willing to admit the hollowness of the great. A world helpless under the bludgeonings of circumstance was quite aware that events are greater than men. Even had Strachey's irony been less deft, witty, and entertaining than it was, it would have struck the mood of the age, and have found many imitators.

But Strachey's method no less than his message had a compelling novelty. He carried a long step further the art of Sainte-Beuve in his brief portraits, of Morley in his *Voltaire* and *Rousseau,* of Frederic Harrison's *Cromwell,* of Rosebery's *Pitt* and *Lord Randolph Churchill.* Abandoning chronology, substituting a dexterous, keen-sighted, and highly allusive exposition for narrative, using high-lights and shadows as effectively as Velasquez, wringing a world of meaning from a single incident or quotation, and employing a mordant satire where older writers would have sacrificed truth to sympathy, he obtained striking effects by the most delightful means. He was, in fact, a consummate literary artist. Behind the rapid brushwork was a memory packed with learning, and a brain of very exceptional acuteness and power. Unfortunately, just as his ironic attitude could be imitated by anybody, so the superficial quality of his brushwork could be—and was—copied by a host of men who had none of his erudition or insight.

The result was that the newer biography which followed the World War in a veritable spate of books did much to lower the standards of this branch of literature, and brought in a larger and more unabashed body of charlatans than were produced in the same years by the New Poetry, New Novel, and New History (which also flourished) all combined. Honest, painstaking craftsmanship was for a time shouldered rudely aside; an inexperienced writer would gather a half-dozen books about some great figure of the past, reshuffle the facts, add a strong dash of contempt, lard with epigrams, and turn out a new portrait. Critics appeared who sneered at the dull men who went to the trouble to investigate sources and write thorough, well-documented lives. It is not difficult to understand why, although the New Biography of Froude and Morley in 1870 had produced a restricted and creditable list of imitators, the Newer Biography of Strachey in 1918 loosed such a huge and in part disreputable stream of works. Morley and Froude had offered no easy formula. Their scientific, thoughtful, and learned method obviously required high gifts, prolonged study, and intense intellectual exertion. Strachey, on the contrary, offered a formula which *appeared* easy of imitation. A passable copy, indeed, such as Maurois's *Ariel: The Life of Shelley,* could be achieved by merely superficial study of the subject and by substituting cleverness for profundity. This statement does not imply that Strachey was a lesser writer than Morley; Rembrandt and Raphael are possibly of equal stature, but Rembrandt defies easy imitation, while Raphael offered a formula which gave birth to a large school. Readers of *Eminent Victorians* saw what effects Strachey had achieved by his ironic detachment—by turning the hero into an unheroic mediocrity—and many writers rushed to choose subjects, and treat them with condescending disrespect. Moreover, Strachey had with enviable skill suppressed all evidence of the more wearisome labors of the historian and biographer. The labor had really been expended, but by delightful anecdote, amusing epigram, unerring selection of facts, and expert interpretation, he concealed it. His imitators leaped at the conclusion that because the labor had been suppressed it was unnecessary; that they could just dispense with it. Biography was becoming a form which cost neither the writer nor the reader any real effort.

To realize just what harm this facile doctrine did we must recur to our definition of the three principal objects of biography. A good biography must vividly recreate a character; it must present a full, careful, and unbiassed record of his acts and experiences; and it must indicate the place of the hero in history. Strachey himself, in the light of these tests, was rather an essayist and interpreter than biographer; and his more reckless followers achieved something like a perversion of biography. Theirs has well been called "plastic biography."

In presenting a personality, the ironic approach has its advantages —especially in depicting a villain or imposter, as Fielding long ago showed in *Jonathan Wild*. But in general, it is much easier for the writer to succeed with his presentation if he happens to be in sympathy with his subject. Boswell was rather unblushingly in sympathy with Dr. Johnson, Lockhart with Walter Scott, Morley with Gladstone, Dr. Harvey Cushing with William Osler—and all the resulting books we count major successes. Indeed, of the principal biographies in English, it would be hard to mention a successful depiction of personality which is malicious rather than sympathetic. Even Lytton Strachey, when he came to Queen Victoria, hauled down his flag, surrendered to the Victorian glamour, and closed in a burst of commemorative eloquence; he had been ironic in spots, but the final effect was of admiration. Even Philip Guedalla, after doing his worst with Napoleon III, made a true hero out of Wellington. It is impossible to present a personality merely by showering it with brickbats, while the attempt to make Longfellow and Washington more real by patting them affably on the back and calling them "Henry" and "George" on every page (as Mr. Herbert Gorman and Mr. W. E. Woodward did) is indescribably feeble. Satire and irony are not biography, and their uses in biography are after all singularly limited. We all know nowadays that Wordsworth had an illegitimate daughter and that Washington fell in love with a neighbor's wife, but these facts tell us more about personality when stated with dignity and sympathy than when offered with a sly jeer. Even Ben Butler and Warren G. Harding can be better understood if approached with an effort to comprehend them than if gibbetted for ridicule.

But the failure in inexpert hands of this part of the Stracheyan formula—the ironic or satiric detachment—was nothing compared with the failure of another supposed part: the rule that the biographer must be entertaining at all hazards, and that the less labor he gives himself or the reader the better. This rule (to which Strachey himself would have been the last to subscribe) made it impossible to meet the second and third tests of good biography. A distinguished biography, which traces fully a man's career and defines expertly his historical station, is never all entertainment. It demands not merely enormous toil from the author, but a wholesome mental exertion from the reader. It cannot compete with the detective story, the current film, or other forms of intellectual anaesthesia. The books of M. Maurois, assuredly among the ablest of Strachey's successors, are delightful. They give us for a time the virtuous feeling that we are combining instruction and pleasure without baser alloy; but in the end they are hardly more nourishing than ginger ale, for they hopelessly over-simplify their subjects. We are offered a stream of anecdote about Shelley, Byron, and Disraeli, an engrossing adventure-story based upon their careers, and some amusing thumbnail portraits of collateral figures. But we do not attain any particular understanding of the complexities and depths of character, we get a sadly incomplete record of the subject's acts and ideas—many of the most important being omitted—and we miss a thorough appraisal of the hero's position in history. We are told nothing about Byron's standing and influence as a poet, about Shelley's special rôle in the romantic movement, or about Disraeli's final achievements and failures as a statesman. A Southern professor of philosophy, when his class raised some particularly intricate question, was wont to say, "That is a bit difficult just now; we'll come to it later on." M. Maurois never comes to it, and at length, much as we admire his artistry, the fact breeds in us a certain suspicion. From his *Disraeli* we turn back, with a not unhappy sigh, to the six volumes of Monypenny and Buckle, sure of finding there the real man in his complete setting.

Some of the defects of another post-Stracheyan author, Emil Ludwig, may be due to a slight tendency toward overproduction. Philip Guedalla once caustically referred to the German school of biography, "the day shift of which compiles the life of Napoleon while the night shift is pumping the life out of Lincoln." But the deeper and more vital defects would remain if Ludwig had written no more volumes than Morley. His volume on Napoleon had every ingredient for a popular success. With all the blood and fire, all the charges and retreats, all the amours, all the backstairs gossip, all the horrors of the Moscow debacle, told in a style that now reminded the reader of a George Arliss movie and now of a Bernard Shaw lecture, it was precisely suited to those who had never before opened a book on Napoleon. As history, it was excellent melodrama. Perhaps no deeper meaning inheres in Napoleon's career than such a Sunday-supplement chronicle of his life would indicate, but those who believe that it does would never send amateurs to Emil Ludwig. When Francis Hackett's life of Henry VIII appeared, it was observed that the enthusiasm of the critics was in inverse proportion to their knowledge of Tudor England. When the book was finally reviewed by Wallace Notestein of Yale University, though due tribute was paid to its fine literary qualities, the general verdict upon it was cool. The idea that exact and patient scholarship, the scholarship matured through years of study, can be dispensed with in biography is analogous to the belief that an architect or engineer can raise magnificent structures without long years of training and apprenticeship.

The radical leaders in the newer biography might be regarded with more tolerance had not some of them added critical insults to the injury that was done by meretricious books. Mr. Lewis Mumford in 1932 reviewed a sheaf of biographies in the *Atlantic*. Two kinds of biography existed, he remarked: the good, which was post-Stracheyan in character, and the bad, which was pre-Stracheyan. Pointing to Van Wyck Brooks's *Emerson* as an admirable example of the former, he condemned with an indignant gesture Burton J. Hendrick's *Carnegie* and Claude G. Bowers's *Beveridge* as deplorable illustrations of the latter—stuffy, pedantic, uncritical, excessively long. It seems not to have occurred to the critic that he was regarding two wholly different types of work. Mr. Brooks's *Emerson,* though possessing numerous excellences, is for whole chapters a close paraphrase of Emerson's journals, letters, and the works of previous biographers. Parts of it are founded so largely upon these previous works that they raise a rather nice question of literary method. It has hardly more originality, so far as its factual content goes, than Mr. Mumford's own *Herman Melville,* whose reliable materials (for a great deal of unreliable guessing at psychology was added) were nearly all borrowed from Raymond Weaver's scholarly biography. Mr. Hendrick's *Carnegie* and Mr. Bowers's *Beveridge,* on the contrary, were primary works. Each author, writing the life of his subject for the first time, had to be reasonably exhaustive, thoroughly attentive to scholarship, and ready to take the prosaic along with the dramatic. Each was unfortunate, from one point of view, that he could not sack some previous biographer, appropriate his materials, and write a book which played up all the succulent, sparkling parts of the story. Had he done this, with a curt, contemptuous acknowledgment of his debts in the preface, Mr. Mumford would have praised him. Each was fortunate, from another and better point of view, that he could write a book which is likely to remain standard while ephemeral snapshots of the subject appear and fade away.

The fact is, of course, that a distinction must be drawn between three literary types: the source biography, the popular biography, and the critical interpretation of a life. Nothing should be allowed to diminish the respect paid to the original biographer who spends toilsome years in poring over old letterbooks and manuscripts, hunting through crackling newspaper files, interviewing ancient survivors—by myriad labors slowly bringing to light the essential facts of a great man's life; particularly if he shows literary art in shaping his results. Every such biographer is a true servant of history. Even greater respect may sometimes be due to the learned and profound interpreter, who takes the salient facts gathered by another and pours a flood of new light through them. But such an interpreter must have both a great mind and a solid foundation of knowledge; he must be a Sainte-Beuve or John Morley. Commanding interpretive studies like W. C. Brownell's volume on six *Victorian Prose Masters,* like Goldwin Smith's *Three English Statesmen,* no more come from hasty amateurs than figs from thistles. The popularizer deserves the least respect, and if he is slipshod and dishonest, the very opposite of respect. He often tends to bring the whole art of biography into disrepute, and to convince lay readers that it and history are without standards or enduring values. It is important to keep in the foreground the trustworthy source biography, and the trustworthy interpretation; important, since neither can be dispensed with, to avoid invidious comparisons between them. Van Wyck Brooks's *Mark Twain* is a stimulating interpretation, though Mr. Bernard De Voto tells us in *Mark Twain's America* that it is ill-informed and ridden by an erroneous interpretation. Critics like Mr. Mumford would doubtless assert that it is shapelier, more artistic, and more acute than the work on which it so largely draws, Albert Bigelow Paine's solid volumes on Mark Twain; but they would go too far when they would contemptuously brush Paine from the earth. No Albert Bigelow Paine, no Van Wyck Brooks!

The ideal in biography is the patient investigator who can write lives which combine scholarship, interpretive power, and literary charm; which are thorough, expert, and yet full of popular interest. In the past this ideal has repeatedly been attained. It better than anything else puts the charlatans to shame and deprives the biographical popularizers of their chief excuse for being. Dogmatism as to form and content in this field is as dangerous as in history. A great biography may be as long as Lockhart's ten volumes on *Scott,* or as short as Edmund Gosse's *Father and Son,* J. E. Neale's *Queen Elizabeth,* or Arthur Bryant's *Pepys;* it may be as acidly critical as Froude's *Carlyle* or as sympathetic as Lord David Cecil's *The Stricken Deer* (William Cowper); it may be as full of interpretation as Lounsbury's admirable life of Fenimore Cooper, or as devoid of it as Thomas Beer's highly objective life of Stephen Crane. But it is seldom difficult to discriminate between pure gold and base metal. And when found, the distinguished life is always an indispensable ally and supporter of history. Not seldom is biography the best means of gaining an introduction to a historical period; almost invariably it is the best means of filling out the *human* meaning of any era.

Arthur M. Schlesinger, Jr. (1917–), and the Moral Issue in History

Arthur M. Schlesinger, Jr., is the son of the noted social historian, and both father and son have been history professors at Harvard. Young Arthur was born in Columbus, Ohio, where his father taught history at Ohio State University. In 1938 he attained his A.B. summa cum laude at Harvard but did not go on for the Ph.D. Something of a child prodigy, he completed an excellent biography of Orestes Brownson (1939) as a youth. In 1945, his thoughtful *The Age of Jackson* attracted enthusiastic reviews and earned a Pulitzer Prize. Since then his books have won the Francis Parkman and Bancroft prizes in history. The Jackson book challenged the older view that Jackson and Jacksonian democracy swept to power on a wave of Western debtor support, inflationist in nature. He argued that a major source of strength was the "hard-money" Eastern workingman. Readers saw a sympathetic analogy between Jacksonian democracy and the New Deal.

This historian's open avowal of his liberal social viewpoints became increasingly apparent in subsequent writings. Thus in his multivolume history of the Franklin D. Roosevelt era, three volumes of which have been published, *The Crisis of the Old Order* (1957), *The Coming of the New Deal* (1959), and *The Politics of Upheaval* (1960), there is never any doubt of where he stands in the great New Deal controversies. The reception, especially from sympathetic New Dealers, has been enthusiastic. In 1961, he was chosen as an adviser to President John Kennedy. For historiography, he strengthened the New History by synthesizing politics with social and intellectual changes.

The following essay, "The Causes of the Civil War," not only reveals Schlesinger's basic social assumptions regarding the central role of moral judgments in history, but marks an outspoken reaction to the alleged objectivity of "revisionists" like James Randall and Avery Craven, who blamed emotionalism on both sides and a "blundering generation" for making a "repressible conflict" like the Civil War "irrepressible." For decades many American historians had held up Leopold von Ranke as their ideal of "scientific history"—a neutral, value-free kind of history. They tended to condemn the emphatic moral judgments of Von Holst and Rhodes and their exclusive emphasis upon slavery as a cause of the Civil War. Some historians had almost eliminated the slavery factor by stressing the conflict between planters and industrialists. Schlesinger criticizes the tendency to ignore the essential fact that slavery was indeed evil and he focuses upon the maneuvers of powerful politicians like Stephen A. Douglas in order to prove that rational compromise could have prevented this war.

The Causes of the Civil War:
A Note on Historical Sentimentalism

The Civil War was our great national trauma. A savage fraternal conflict, it released deep sentiments of guilt and remorse—sentiments which have reverberated through our history and our literature ever since. Literature in the end came to terms with these sentiments by yielding to the South in fantasy the victory it had been denied in fact; this tendency culminated on the popular level in *Gone with the Wind* and on the highbrow level in the Nashville cult of agrarianism. But history, a less malleable medium, was constricted by the intractable fact that the war had taken place, and by the related assumption

In *The Partisan Review*, XVI (1949), 969–981. Reprinted by permission of the *Partisan Review* and Arthur M. Schlesinger, Jr.

that it was, in William H. Seward's phrase, an "irrepressible conflict," and hence a justified one.

As short a time ago as 1937, for example, even Professor James G. Randall could describe himself as "unprepared to go to the point of denying that the great American tragedy could have been avoided." Yet in a few years the writing of history would succumb to the psychological imperatives which had produced *I'll Take my Stand* and *Gone with the Wind;* and Professor Randall would emerge as the leader of a triumphant new school of self-styled "revisionists." The publication of two vigorous books by Professor Avery Craven— *The Repressible Conflict* (1939) and *The Coming of the Civil War* (1942)—and the appearance of Professor Randall's own notable volumes on Lincoln—*Lincoln the President: Springfield to Gettysburg* (1945), *Lincoln and the South* (1946), and *Lincoln the Liberal Statesman* (1947)—brought about a profound reversal of the professional historian's attitude toward the Civil War. Scholars now denied the traditional assumption of the inevitability of the war and boldly advanced the thesis that a "blundering generation" had transformed a "repressible conflict" into a "needless war."

The swift triumph of revisionism came about with very little resistance or even expressed reservations on the part of the profession. Indeed, the only adequate evaluation of the revisionist thesis that I know was made, not by an academic historian at all, but by that illustrious semi-pro, Mr. Bernard De Voto; and Mr. De Voto's two brilliant articles in *Harper's* in 1945 unfortunately had little influence within the guild. By 1947 Professor Allan Nevins, summing up the most recent scholarship in *Ordeal of the Union,* his able general history of the eighteen-fifties, could define the basic problem of the period in terms which indicated a measured but entire acceptance of revisionism. "The primary task of statesmanship in this era," Nevins wrote, "was to furnish a workable adjustment between the two sections, while offering strong inducements to the southern people to regard their labor system not as static but evolutionary, and equal persuasions to the northern people to assume a helpful rather than scolding attitude."

This new interpretation surely deserves at least as meticulous an examination as Professor Randall is prepared to give, for example, to such a question as whether or not Lincoln was playing fives when he received the news of his nomination in 1860. The following notes are presented in the interests of stimulating such an examination.

The revisionist case, as expounded by Professors Randall and Craven, has three main premises. First:

1) that the Civil War was caused by the irresponsible emotionalization of politics far out of proportion to the real problems involved. The war, as Randall put it, was certainly not caused by cultural variations nor by economic rivalries nor by sectional differences; these all existed, but it was "stupid," as he declared, to think that they required war as a solution. "One of the most colossal of misconceptions" was the "theory" that "fundamental motives produce war. The glaring and obvious fact is the artificiality of war-making agitation." After all, Randall pointed out, agrarian and industrial interests had been in conflict under Coolidge and Hoover; yet no war resulted. "In Illinois," he added, "major controversies (not mere transient differences) between downstate and metropolis have stopped short of war."

Nor was slavery the cause. The issues arising over slavery were in Randall's judgment "highly artificial, almost fabricated ones. They produced quarrels out of things that would have settled themselves were it not for political agitation." Slavery, Craven observed, was in any case a much overrated problem. It is "perfectly clear," he wrote, "that slavery played a rather minor part in the life of the South and of the Negro."

What then was the cause of war? "If one word or phrase were selected to account for the war," wrote Randall, ". . . it would have to be such a word as fanaticism (on both sides), misunderstanding, misrepresentation, or perhaps politics." Phrases like "whipped-up crisis" and "psychopathic case" adorned Randall's explanation. Craven similarly described the growing sense of sectional differences as "an artificial creation of inflamed minds." The "molders of public opinion steadily created the fiction of two distinct peoples." As a result, "distortion led a people into bloody war."

If uncontrolled emotionalism and fanaticism caused the war, how did they get out of hand? Who whipped up the "whipped-up crisis"? Thus the second revisionist thesis:

2) that sectional friction was permitted to develop into needless war by the inexcusable failure of political leadership in the fifties. "It is difficult to achieve a full realization of how Lincoln's generation stumbled into a ghastly war," wrote Randall. ". . . If one questions the term 'blundering generation,' let him inquire how many measures of the time he would wish copied or repeated if the period were to be approached with a clean slate and to be lived again."

It was the politicians, charged Craven, who systematically sacrificed peace to their pursuit of power. Calhoun and Adams, "seeking political advantage," mixed up slavery and expansion; Wilmot introduced his "trouble-making Proviso as part of the political game"; the repeal clause in the Kansas-Nebraska Act was "the afterthought of a mere handful of politicians"; Chase's Appeal to the Independent Democrats was "false in its assertions and unfair in its purposes, but it was politically effective"; the "damaging" section in the Dred Scott decision was forced "by the political ambitions of dissenting judges." "These uncalled-for moves and this irresponsible leadership," concluded Craven, blew up a "crack-pot" crusade into a national conflict.

It is hard to tell which was under attack here—the performance of a particular generation or democratic politics in general. But, if the indictment "blundering generation" meant no more than a general complaint that democratic politics placed a premium on emotionalism, then the Civil War would have been no more nor less "needless" than any event in our blundering history. The phrase "blundering generation" must consequently imply that the generation in power in the fifties was *below* the human or historical or democratic average in its blundering. Hence the third revisionist thesis:

3) that the slavery problem could have been solved without war. For, even if slavery were as unimportant as the revisionists have insisted, they would presumably admit that it constituted the real

sticking-point in the relations between the sections. They must show therefore that there were policies with which a non-blundering generation could have resolved the slavery crisis and averted war; and that these policies were so obvious that the failure to adopt them indicated blundering and stupidity of a peculiarly irresponsible nature. If no such policies could be produced even by hindsight, then it would seem excessive to condemn the politicians of the fifties for failing to discover them at the time.

The revisionists have shown only a most vague and sporadic awareness of this problem. "Any kind of sane policy in Washington in 1860 might have saved the day for nationalism," remarked Craven; but he did not vouchsafe the details of these sane policies; we would be satisfied to know about one.* Similarly Randall declared that there were few policies of the fifties he would wish repeated if the period were to be lived over again; but he was not communicative about the policies he would wish pursued. Nevins likewise blamed the war on the "collapse of American statesmanship," but restrained himself from suggesting how a non-collapsible statesmanship would have solved the hard problems of the fifties.

In view of this reticence on a point so crucial to the revisionist argument, it is necessary to reconstruct the possibilities that might lie in the back of revisionism. Clearly there could be only two "solutions" to the slavery problem: the preservation of slavery, or its abolition.

Presumably the revisionists would not regard the preservation of slavery as a possible solution. Craven, it is true, has argued that "most of the incentives to honest and sustained effort, to a contented, well-rounded life, might be found under slavery. . . . What owning and being owned added to the normal relationship of employer and employee is very hard to say." In describing incidents in which slaves beat up masters, he has even noted that "happenings and reactions like these were the rule [sic], not the exception." But Craven would

---

* It is fair to say that Professor Craven seems in recent years to have modified his earlier extreme position; see his article "The Civil War and the Democratic Process," *Abraham Lincoln Quarterly,* June 1947.

doubtless admit that, however jolly this system might have been, its perpetuation would have been, to say the least, impracticable.

If, then, revisionism has rested on the assumption that the non-violent abolition of slavery was possible, such abolition could conceivably have come about through internal reform in the South; through economic exhaustion of the slavery system in the South; or through some government project for gradual and compensated emancipation. Let us examine these possibilities.

1) *The internal reform argument.* The South, the revisionists have suggested, might have ended the slavery system if left to its own devices; only the abolitionists spoiled everything by letting loose a hysteria which caused the southern ranks to close in self-defense.

This revisionist argument would have been more convincing if the decades of alleged anti-slavery feeling in the South had produced any concrete results. As one judicious southern historian, Professor Charles S. Sydnor, recently put it, "Although the abolition movement was followed by a decline of antislavery sentiment in the South, it must be remembered that in all the long years before that movement began no part of the South had made substantial progress toward ending slavery. . . . Southern liberalism had not ended slavery in any state."

In any case, it is difficult for historians seriously to suppose that northerners could have denied themselves feelings of disapproval over slavery. To say that there "should" have been no abolitionists in America before the Civil War is about as sensible as to say that there "should" have been no anti-Nazis in the nineteen-thirties or that there "should" be no anti-Communists today. People who indulge in criticism of remote evils may not be so pure of heart as they imagine; but that fact does not affect their inevitability as part of the historic situation.

Any theory, in short, which expects people to repress such spontaneous aversions is profoundly unhistorical. If revisionism has based itself on the conviction that things would have been different if only there had been no abolitionists, it has forgotten that abolitionism was as definite and irrevocable a factor in the historic situation as was slavery itself. And, just as abolitionism was inevitable, so too was the southern reaction against it—a reaction which, as Professor Clement Eaton has ably shown, steadily drove the free discussion of slavery out of the South. The extinction of free discussion meant, of course, the absolute extinction of any hope of abolition through internal reform.

2) *The economic exhaustion argument.* Slavery, it has been pointed out, was on the skids economically. It was overcapitalized and inefficient; it immobilized both capital and labor; its one-crop system was draining the soil of fertility; it stood in the way of industrialization. As the South came to realize these facts, a revisionist might argue, it would have moved to abolish slavery for its own economic good. As Craven put it, slavery "may have been almost ready to break down of its own weight."

This argument assumed, of course, that southerners would have recognized the causes of their economic predicament and taken the appropriate measures. Yet such an assumption would be plainly contrary to history and to experience. From the beginning the South has always blamed its economic shortcomings, not on its own economic ruling class and its own inefficient use of resources, but on northern exploitation. Hard times in the eighteen-fifties produced in the South, not a reconsideration of the slavery system, but blasts against the North for the high prices of manufactured goods. The overcapitalization of slavery led, not to criticisms of the system, but to increasingly insistent demands for the reopening of the slave trade. Advanced southern writers like George Fitzhugh and James D. B. DeBow were even arguing that slavery was adapted to industrialism. When Hinton R. Helper did advance before the Civil War an early version of Craven's argument, asserting that emancipation was necessary to save the southern economy, the South burned his book. Nothing in the historical record suggests that the southern ruling class was preparing to deviate from its traditional pattern of self-exculpation long enough to take such a drastic step as the abolition of slavery.

3) *Compensated emancipation.* Abraham Lincoln made repeated proposals of compensated emancipation. In his annual message to Congress of December 1, 1862, he set forth a detailed plan by which

States, on an agreement to abolish slavery by 1900, would receive government bonds in proportion to the number of slaves emancipated. Yet, even though Lincoln's proposals represented a solution of the problem conceivably gratifying to the slaveholder's purse as well as to his pride, they got nowhere. Two-thirds of the border representatives rejected the scheme, even when personally presented to them by Lincoln himself. And, of course, only the pressure of war brought compensated emancipation its limited hearing of 1862.

Still, granted these difficulties, does it not remain true that other countries abolished slavery without internal convulsion? If emotionalism had not aggravated the situation beyond hope, Craven has written, then slavery "might have been faced as a national question and dealt with as successfully as the South American countries dealt with the same problem." If Brazil could free its slaves and Russia its serfs in the middle of the nineteenth century without civil war, why could not the United States have done as well?

The analogies are appealing but not, I think, really persuasive. There are essential differences between the slavery question in the United States and the problems in Brazil or in Russia. In the first place, Brazil and Russia were able to face servitude "as a national question" because it was, in fact, a national question. Neither country had the American problem of the identification of compact sectional interests with the survival of the slavery system. In the second place, there was no race problem at all in Russia; and, though there was a race problem in Brazil, the more civilized folkways of that country relieved racial differences of the extreme tension which they breed in the South of the United States. In the third place, neither in Russia nor in Brazil did the abolition of servitude involve constitutional issues; and the existence of these issues played a great part in determining the form of the American struggle.

It is hard to draw much comfort, therefore, from the fact that other nations abolished servitude peaceably. The problem in America was peculiarly recalcitrant. The schemes for gradual emancipation got nowhere. Neither internal reform nor economic exhaustion contained much promise for a peaceful solution. The hard fact, indeed, is that the revisionists have not tried seriously to describe the policies by which the slavery problem could have been peacefully resolved. They have resorted instead to broad affirmations of faith: if only the conflict could have been staved off long enough, then somehow, somewhere, we could have worked something out. It is legitimate, I think, to ask how? where? what?—at least, if these affirmations of faith are to be used as the premise for castigating the unhappy men who had the practical responsibility for finding solutions and failed.

Where have the revisionists gone astray? In part, the popularity of revisionism obviously parallels that of *Gone with the Wind*—the victors paying for victory by pretending literary defeat. But the essential problem is why history should be so vulnerable to this literary fashion; and this problem, I believe, raises basic questions about the whole modern view of history. It is perhaps stating the issue in too portentous terms. Yet I cannot escape the feeling that the vogue of revisionism is connected with the modern tendency to seek in optimistic sentimentalism an escape from the severe demands of moral decision; that it is the offspring of our modern sentimentality which at once evades the essential moral problems in the name of a superficial objectivity and asserts their unimportance in the name of an invincible progress.

The revisionists first glided over the implications of the fact that the slavery system was producing a closed society in the South. Yet that society increasingly had justified itself by a political and philosophical repudiation of free society; southern thinkers swiftly developed the anti-libertarian potentialities in a social system whose cornerstone, in Alexander H. Stephens's proud phrase, was human bondage. In theory and in practice, the South organized itself with mounting rigor against ideas of human dignity and freedom, because such ideas inevitably threatened the basis of their own system. Professor Frank L. Owsley, the southern agrarian, has described inadvertently but accurately the direction in which the slave South was moving. "The abolitionists and their political allies were threatening the existence of the South as seriously as the Nazis threaten the

existence of England," wrote Owsley in 1940; ". . . Under such circumstances the surprising thing is that so little was done by the South
to defend its existence."

There can be no question that many southerners in the fifties had
similar sentiments; that they regarded their system of control as
ridiculously inadequate; and that, with the book-burning, the censor-
ship of the mails, the gradual illegalization of dissent, the South
was in process of creating a real machinery of repression in order
more effectively "to defend its existence." No society, I suppose,
encourages criticism of its basic institutions. Yet, when a democratic
society acts in self-defense, it does so at least in the name of human
dignity and freedom. When a society based on bond slavery acts to
eliminate criticism of its peculiar institution, it outlaws what a believer in democracy can only regard as the abiding values of man.
When the basic institutions are evil, in other words, the effect of
attempts to defend their existence can only be the moral and intellectual stultification of the society.

A society closed in the defense of evil institutions thus creates
moral differences far too profound to be solved by compromise. Such
a society forces upon every one, both those living at the time and
those writing about it later, the necessity for a moral judgment; and
the moral judgment in such cases becomes an indispensable factor in
the historical understanding.

The revisionists were commendably anxious to avoid the vulgar
errors of the post-Civil War historians who pronounced smug individual judgments on the persons involuntarily involved in the tragedy
of the slave system. Consequently they tried hard to pronounce no
moral judgments at all on slavery. Slavery became important, in
Craven's phrase, "only as a very ancient labor system, probably at
this time rather near the end of its existence"; the attempt to charge
this labor system with moral meanings was "a creation of inflamed
imaginations." Randall, talking of the Kansas-Nebraska Act, could
describe it as "a law intended to subordinate the slavery question
and hold it in *proper* proportion" (my italics). I have quoted Randall's even more astonishing argument that, because major con-

troversies between downstate and metropolis in Illinois stopped short of war, there was reason to believe that the Civil War could have been avoided. Are we to take it that the revisionists seriously believe that the downstate-metropolis fight in Illinois—or the agrarian-industrial fight in the Coolidge and Hoover administrations—were in any useful sense comparable to the difference between the North and South in 1861?

Because the revisionists felt no moral urgency themselves, they deplored as fanatics those who did feel it, or brushed aside their feelings as the artificial product of emotion and propaganda. The revisionist hero was Stephen A. Douglas, who always thought that the great moral problems could be solved by sleight-of-hand. The phrase "northern man of southern sentiments," Randall remarked, was "said opprobriously . . . as if it were a base thing for a northern man to work with his southern fellows."

By denying themselves insight into the moral dimension of the slavery crisis, in other words, the revisionists denied themselves a historical understanding of the intensities that caused the crisis. It was the moral issue of slavery, for example, that gave the struggles over slavery in the territories or over the enforcement of the fugitive slave laws their significance. These issues, as the revisionists have shown with cogency, were not in themselves basic. But they were the available issues; they were almost the only points within the existing constitutional framework where the moral conflict could be faced; as a consequence, they became charged with the moral and political dynamism of the central issue. To say that the Civil War was fought over the "unreal" issue of slavery in the territories is like saying that the Second World War was fought over the "unreal" issue of the invasion of Poland. The democracies could not challenge fascism inside Germany any more than opponents of slavery could challenge slavery inside the South; but the extension of slavery, like the extension of fascism, was an act of aggression which made a moral choice inescapable.

Let us be clear what the relationship of moral judgment to history is. Every historian, as we all know in an argument that surely does not have to be repeated in 1949, imports his own set of moral judgments into the writing of history by the very process of interpretation; and the phrase "every historian" includes the category "revisionist." Mr. De Voto in his paraphrases of the revisionist position has put admirably the contradictions on this point: as for "moral questions, God forbid. History will not put itself in the position of saying that any thesis may have been wrong, any cause evil. . . . History will not deal with moral values, though of course the Republican radicals were, well, culpable." The whole revisionist attitude toward abolitionists and radicals, repeatedly characterized by Randall as "unctuous" and "intolerant," overflows with the moral feeling which is so virtuously excluded from discussions of slavery.

An acceptance of the fact of moral responsibility does not license the historian to roam through the past ladling out individual praise and blame: such an attitude would ignore the fact that all individuals, including historians, are trapped in a web of circumstance which curtails their moral possibilities. But it does mean that there are certain essential issues on which it is necessary for the historian to have a position if he is to understand the great conflicts of history. These great conflicts are relatively few because there are few enough historical phenomena which we can confidently identify as evil. The essential issues appear, moreover, not in pure and absolute form, but incomplete and imperfect, compromised by the deep complexity of history. Their proponents may often be neurotics and fanatics, like the abolitionists. They may attain a social importance only when a configuration of non-moral factors—economic, political, social, military—permit them to do so.

Yet neither the nature of the context nor the pretensions of the proponents alter the character of the issue. And human slavery is certainly one of the few issues of whose evil we can be sure. It is not just "a very ancient labor system"; it is also a betrayal of the basic values of our Christian and democratic tradition. No historian can understand the circumstances which led to its abolition until he writes about it in its fundamental moral context. "History is supposed to understand the difference between a decaying economy and an expanding one," as Mr. De Voto well said, "between solvency and bankruptcy, between a dying social idea and one coming to world acceptance. . . . It is even supposed to understand implications of the difference between a man who is legally a slave and one who is legally free."

"Revisionism in general has no position," De Voto continues, "but only a vague sentiment." Professor Randall well suggested the uncritical optimism of that sentiment when he remarked, "To suppose that the Union could not have been continued or slavery outmoded without the war and without the corrupt concomitants of war is hardly an enlightened assumption." We have here a touching afterglow of the admirable nineteenth-century faith in the full rationality and perfectibility of man; the faith that the errors of the world would all in time be "outmoded" (Professor Randall's use of this word is suggestive) by progress. Yet the experience of the twentieth century has made it clear that we gravely overrated man's capacity to solve the problems of existence within the terms of history.

This conclusion about man may disturb our complacencies about human nature. Yet it is certainly more in accord with history than Professor Randall's "enlightened" assumption that man can solve peaceably all the problems which overwhelm him. The unhappy fact is that man occasionally works himself into a log-jam; and that the log-jam must be burst by violence. We know that well enough from the experience of the last decade. Are we to suppose that some future historian will echo Professor Nevins' version of the "failure" of the eighteen-fifties and write: "The primary task of statesmanship in the nineteen-thirties was to furnish a workable adjustment between the United States and Germany, while offering strong inducements to the German people to abandon the police state and equal persuasions to the Americans to help the Nazis rather than scold them"? Will some future historian adapt Professor Randall's formula and write that the word "appeaser" was used "opprobriously" as if it were a "base" thing for an American to work with his Nazi fellow? Obviously this revisionism of the future (already foreshadowed in the work of Charles A. Beard) would represent, as we now see it, a fantastic evasion of the hard and unpleasant problems of the thirties. I doubt whether our present revisionism would make much more sense to the men of the eighteen-fifties.

The problem of the inevitability of the Civil War, of course, is in its essence a problem devoid of meaning. The revisionist attempt to argue that the war could have been avoided by "any kind of sane policy" is of interest less in its own right than as an expression of a characteristically sentimental conception of man and of history. And the great vogue of revisionism in the historical profession suggests, in my judgment, ominous weaknesses in the contemporary attitude toward history.

We delude ourselves when we think that history teaches us that evil will be "outmoded" by progress and that politics consequently does not impose on us the necessity for decision and for struggle. If historians are to understand the fullness of the social dilemma they seek to reconstruct, they must understand that sometimes there is no escape from the implacabilities of moral decision. When social conflicts embody great moral issues, these conflicts cannot be assigned for solution to the invincible march of progress; nor can they be by-passed with "objective" neutrality. Not many problems perhaps force this decision upon the historian. But, if any problem does in our history, it is the Civil War.

To reject the moral actuality of the Civil War is to foreclose the possibility of an adequate account of its causes. More than that, it is to misconceive and grotesquely to sentimentalize the nature of history. For history is not a redeemer, promising to solve all human problems in time; nor is man capable of transcending the limitations of his being. Man generally is entangled in insoluble problems; history is consequently a tragedy in which we are all involved, whose keynote is anxiety and frustration, not progress and fulfillment. Nothing exists in history to assure us that the great moral dilemmas can be resolved without pain; we cannot therefore be relieved from the duty of moral judgment on issues so appalling and inescapable as those involved in human slavery; nor can we be consoled by sentimental theories about the needlessness of the Civil War into regarding our own struggles against evil as equally needless.

One must emphasize, however, that this duty of judgment applies to issues. Because we are all implicated in the same tragedy, we must judge the men of the past with the same forbearance and charity which we hope the future will apply toward us.

Selected Bibliography

EUROPEAN HISTORIOGRAPHY AND GENERAL THEORY

Berlin, Isaiah, *Karl Marx: Life and Environment* (Oxford Galaxy paperback, 1959).

Bury, J. B., *The Ancient Greek Historians* (Dover paperback, 1958).

Butterfield, Herbert M., *Man on His Past* (Cambridge Univ., 1955).

Collingwood, R. G., *The Idea of History* (Oxford Galaxy paperback, 1956).

Encyclopedia of the Social Sciences (especially for articles on "Progress," "History and Historiography").

Feuer, Lewis S. (ed.), *Marx and Engels: Basic Writings on Politics and Philosophy* (Anchor paperback, 1959).

Gardiner, Patrick (ed.), *Theories of History* (Free Press, 1959).

Geyl, Pieter, *Debates with Historians* (Meridian paperback, 1958), has analytical essays on Ranke, Macaulay, Carlyle, Toynbee, the Civil War, and historical inevitability.

Gooch, G. P., *History and Historians of the Nineteenth Century* (Longmans, 1952). Also in paperback.

Halperin, S. W. (ed.), *Some 20th Century Historians* (Univ. of Chicago, 1961), includes Pirenne, Trevelyan, Butterfield, Lefebvre, and others.

Lee, D. E., and R. N. Beck, "The Meaning of Historicism," *American Historical Review* 59 (1954), 568–77.

Mannheim, Karl, *Ideology and Utopia* (Harvest paperback, 1936), valuable for the problems of philosophical, historical, and social objectivity.

Meyerhoff, Hans (ed.), *The Philosophy of History in Our Time* (Anchor paperback, 1959), includes Carl Becker, "What Are Historical Facts?" C. A. Beard, "Written History as an Act of Faith"; Herbert Butterfield, "Moral Judgments in History"; Isaiah Berlin, "Historical Inevitability"; and Karl Popper, "Has History Any Meaning?"

Muller, Herbert J., *The Uses of the Past* (Oxford, 1952).

Teggart, Frederick J., *Theory and Processes of History* (Univ. of California paperback, 1960).

Thompson, James W., *A History of Historical Writing* (2 vols., Macmillan, 1942).

AMERICAN HISTORIOGRAPHY

Adams, Charles F., *An Autobiography* (Houghton Mifflin, 1916).

Adams, Herbert B., *Historical Scholarship in the United States, 1876–1901: As Revealed in Correspondence* (Johns Hopkins, 1938).

Ausubel, Herman, *Historians and Their Craft* (Columbia, 1950), critical study of presidential addresses of AHA.

Ausubel, Herman, et al., *Some Modern Historians of Britain* (Dryden, 1951), includes George L. Beer.

Bassett, J. S., *The Middle Group of American Historians* (Macmillan, 1917), includes Belknap, Bancroft, Sparks, and others.

Beale, Howard K., "What Historians Have Said about the Causes of the Civil War," in *Theory and Practice in Historical Study* (Social Science Research Council Bulletin 54, New York, 1946), 55–102.

Beale, Howard K (ed.), *Charles A. Beard* (University of Kentucky, 1954).

Becker, Carl, *Every Man His Own Historian* (Crofts, 1935).

Becker, Carl, "What Is Historiography?" in *American Historical Review* 44 (1938), 20–28.

Bellot, H. Hale, *American History and American Historians* (Univ. of Oklahoma, 1952), strong on frontier theories.

Benson, Lee, *Turner and Beard* (Free Press of Glencoe, 1960).

Berman, Milton, *John Fiske* (Harvard, 1961).

Billington, Ray A., *The American Frontier* (AHA Service Center Pamphlet, Washington, D.C.).

Bridges, Hal, *Civil War and Reconstruction* (AHA Service Center Pamphlet, Washington, D. C.).

Burgess, John W., *Reminiscences of an American Scholar* (Columbia, 1934).

Cadden, J. P., *The Historiography of the American Catholic Church, 1785–1943* (Catholic Univ., 1944).

Cartwright, W. H., and Watson, R. L. Jr., *Interpreting and Teaching American History* (31st Yearbook, National Council for the Social Studies, NEA, 1961).

Cater, Harold D. (ed.), *Henry Adams and His Friends* (Houghton Mifflin, 1947), correspondence.

Caughey, John, *Hubert Howe Bancroft: Historian of the West* (Univ. of Cal., 1946).

Cockroft, G. A., *The Public Life of George Chalmers* (Columbia, 1939).

Cole, C. W., "Jeremy Belknap, Pioneer Nationalist," *New England Quarterly* 10 (1937), 743–51.

Craven, Avery O., "The 'Turner Theories' and the South,' *Journal of Southern History* 5 (1937), 291–314.

Cruden, Robert, *James Ford Rhodes* (Western Reserve, 1961).

De Conde, Alexander, *New Interpretations in American Foreign Policy* (AHA Service Center Pamphlet, Washington, D.C.).

Destler, Chester McA., "Some Observations on Contemporary Historical Theory," *American Historical Review* 55 (1950), 503–29.

Dictionary of American Biography (especially "William Smith," "Cadwallader Colden," "John G. Palfrey," "Herman E. von Holst").

Donovan, Timothy P., *Henry Adams and Brooks Adams* (Univ. of Oklahoma, 1961), an analysis of ideas.

Eaton, Clement, "Recent Trends in the Writing of Southern History," *Louisiana Hist. Quar.* 38 (1955), 26–42.

Eisenstadt, A. S., *Charles McLean Andrews* (Columbia, 1956).

Emerson, Donald E., *Richard Hildreth* (Johns Hopkins, 1946).

Foran, William, "John Marshall as a Historian." *American Hist. Rev.* 43 (1937–38), 51–64.

Gipson, L. H., "Charles M. Andrews and the Reorientation of the Study of American History," *Pennsylvania Magazine of History and Biography* LIX (1935), 209–22.

Glaser, William A., "Algie M. Simons and Marxism in America," *Miss. Vall. Hist. Rev.* 41 (1954–55), 419–34.

Goldman, Eric, *John Bach McMaster* (Univ. of Penn., 1943).

Goldman, Eric F. (ed.), *Historiography and Urbanization* (Johns Hopkins, 1941).

Greene, Jack P., "The Flight from Determinism: . . . Recent Literature on the . . . American Revolution," *South Atlantic Quarterly* LXI (1962), 235–59.

Hesseltine, W. B., *Pioneer's Mission; The Story of Lyman C. Draper* (State Historical Society of Wisconsin, 1954).

Higham, John, "The Rise of American Intellectual History," *Amer. Hist. Rev.* 56 (1951), 453–71.

Hofstadter, Richard, "Parrington and the Jeffersonian Tradition," *Journal of the Hist. of Ideas* 2, (1941), 391–400.

Hutchinson, William T. (ed.), *The Marcus W. Jernegan Essays in American Historiography* (Univ. of Chicago, 1937), includes the major historians.

Jordy, William, *Henry Adams, Scientific Historian* (Yale, 1952).

Kraus, Michael, *The Writing of American History* (Univ. of Oklahoma, 1953).

Libby, Orin G., "Ramsay as a Plagiarist," *American Hist. Rev.* 7 (1901).

Lingelbach, W. E. (ed.), *Approaches to American Social History* (D. Appleton-Century, 1937).

Lovejoy, Arthur O., *Essays on the History of Ideas* (Capricorn, 1960), stresses romanticism and the Enlightenment philosophy of history.

McKelvey, Blake, "American Urban History Today," *Amer. Hist. Rev.* LVII (1952), 919–29.

Malin, James, *Essays in Historiography* (Lawrence, Kansas, 1946).

Morgan, Edmund S., *American Revolution* (AHA Service Center Pamphlet, Washington, D.C.).

Morison, S. E., "Edward Channing," *Mass. Hist. Soc. Proc.* 64 (1930–32), 250–84.

Mowry, George E. *The Progressive Movement, 1900–1920* (AHA Service Center Pamphlet #10, Washington, D.C.).

Nettels, Curtis, "Frederick Jackson Turner and the New Deal," *Wisconsin Magazine of History* 17 (1934), 257–65.

Nevins, Allan, *The Gateway to History* (D. C. Heath, 1938).

Nye, Russel B., *George Bancroft* (Knopf, 1945).

Odum, Howard W. (ed.), *American Masters of Social Science* (Holt, 1927).

Pease, O. A., *Parkman's History* (Yale, 1953).

Pingel, Martha M., *An American Utilitarian: Richard Hildreth as a Philosopher* (Columbia, 1948).

Pressly, Thomas J., *Americans Interpret Their Civil War* (Princeton, 1954).

Rhodes, James F., *Historical Essays* (Macmillan, 1909).

Robinson, James Harvey, *The New History* (Macmillan, 1912).

Rozwenc, Edwin C. (ed.), *The Causes of the American Civil War* (Amherst Series, D. C. Heath, 1961), includes essays from Rhodes, Beard, Owsley, Osterweis, Craven, Randall, Ramsdell, Nevins, Pressly, and others.

Rozwenc, Edwin C. (ed.), *Reconstruction in the South* (Amherst Series, D. C. Heath, 1952), includes Shugg, Fleming, DuBois, Simkins, and Coulter.

Salmon, Lucy M., *The Newspaper and the Historian* (Oxford, 1923).

Samuels, Ernest, *The Young Henry Adams* (Harvard, 1948); and *Henry Adams, the Middle Years* (Harvard, 1958).

Saveth, E. N., *American Historians and European Immigrants, 1875–1925* Columbia, 1948).

Saveth, E. N. (ed.), *Understanding the American Past; American History and Its Interpretation* (Little, Brown, 1954).

Schlesinger, Arthur M. Jr., "The Problem of Richard Hildreth," *The New England Quarterly* 13 (1940), 223–45.

Sellers, Charles G. Jr., *Jacksonian Democracy* (AHA Service Center Pamphlet #9, Washington, D.C.).

Sheehan, Donald H. (ed.), *Essays in American Historiography* (Columbia 1960), includes scientific history, Radical Reconstruction, pragmatism, the muckrakers, and so forth.

Singletary, Otis A., *The South in American History* (AHA Service Center Pamphlet, Washington, D.C.).

Sorenson, Lloyd R., "Charles A. Beard and German Historiographical Thought," *Mississippi Valley Hist. Rev.* 42 (1955–56), 274–87.

Stephenson, Wendell H., *The South Lives in History* (Louisiana State Univ., 1955).

Stern, Fritz (ed.), *Varieties of History* (Meridian paperback, 1956), includes essays by Voltaire, Ranke, Macaulay, Carlyle, Buckle, Engels, Bury, Turner, Beard, Robinson, and others.

Stevens, Harry R., *The Middle West* (AHA Service Center Pamphlet, Washington, D.C.).

Stevenson, Elizabeth, *Henry Adams* (Macmillan, 1955).

Strout, Cushing, *The Pragmatic Revolt in American History: Carl Becker and Charles Beard* (Yale, 1958).

Taylor, A. A., "Historians of the Reconstruction," *Journal of Negro History* (Jan. 1938).

Taylor, G. R. (ed.), *Turner Thesis . . .* Amherst Series, (D. C. Heath, 1949).

Taylor, G. R. (ed.), *Jackson versus Biddle* (Amherst Series, D. C. Heath, 1949).

Van Tassell, David, *Recording America's Past, An Interpretation of the Development of Historical Studies in America, 1607–1884* (Univ. of Chicago, 1960).

Wade, Mason, *Francis Parkman, Heroic Historian* (Viking, 1942).

Wade, Mason (ed.), *The Journals of Francis Parkman* (2 vols., Harper 1947).

Wahlke, John C. (ed.), *The Causes of the American Revolution* (Amherst Series, D. C. Heath, 1962), includes selections from Hacker, Andrews, Dickerson, Gipson, Jensen, Becker, and others.

Waller, George M. (ed.), *Puritanism in Early America* (Amherst Series, D. C. Heath, 1950), includes essays by Beard, Perry, Miller, Wertenbaker, Parrington, C. F. Adams, Morison, and others.

Weisberger, Bernard A., "The Dark and Bloody Ground of Reconstruction Historiography" *Journal of Southern History* 25 (1959), 427–47.

White, Morton, *Social Thought in America* (Beacon, 1947; paperback, 1957), includes *The New History*.

Wilkins, Burleigh T., *Carl Becker* (Harvard, 1961).

Williams, S. T., *The Life of Washington Irving* (2 vols., Oxford, 1935).

Wish, Harvey, *The American Historian* (Oxford, 1960), emphasis on social conditioning. Includes chief historians.

Wright, Louis B., *New Interpretations of American Colonial History* (AHA Service Center Pamphlet #16, Washington, D.C.).